Sustainable Web Development with Ruby on Rails

Practical Tips for Building Web Applications that Last

David Bryant Copeland

This book is copyright ©2023 by David Bryant Copeland, All Rights Reserved. All text, code, images, and diagrams were produced without any assistance from any generative AI. See http://declare-ai.org/1.0.0/declare.html for details.

For more information about this book, visit https://sustainable-rails.com

Contents

Contents

Acknowledgements   1

Changes from Previous Versions   3
    December, 12, 2020 3
    January, 21, 2021 3
    March 15, 2022 3
    Dec 4, 2023 3

I   Introduction

1   Why This Book Exists   9
    1.1   What is Sustainability? 9
    1.2   Why Care About Sustainability? 10
    1.3   How to Value Sustainability 10
    1.4   Assumptions 12
        1.4.1   The Software Has a Clear Purpose 12
        1.4.2   The Software Needs To Exist For Years 13
        1.4.3   The Software Will Evolve 13
        1.4.4   The Team Will Change 13
        1.4.5   You Value Sustainability, Consistency, and Quality . . 13
    1.5   Opportunity and Carrying Costs 15
    1.6   Why should you trust me? 16

2   The Rails Application Architecture   19
    2.1   Boundaries 20
    2.2   Views 21
    2.3   Models 23
    2.4   Everything Else 23
    2.5   The Pros and Cons of the Rails Application Architecture . . 24

3   Following Along in This Book   27
    3.1   Typographic Conventions 27
    3.2   Software Versions 29
    3.3   Sample Code 30

4   Start Your App Off Right   33

	4.1	Creating a Rails App	34
	4.2	Using The Environment for Runtime Configuration	35
	4.3	Configuring Local Development Environment with dotenv	36
	4.4	Automating Application Setup with `bin/setup`	40
	4.5	Running the Application Locally with `bin/dev`	46
	4.6	Putting Tests and Other Quality Checks in `bin/ci`	49
	4.7	Improving Production Logging with lograge	52

5 Business Logic (Does Not Go in Active Records) — 57

- 5.1 Business Logic Makes Your App Special... and Complex . . . 58
  - 5.1.1 Business Logic is a Magnet for Complexity 58
  - 5.1.2 Business Logic Experiences Churn 58
- 5.2 Bugs in Commonly-Used Classes Have Wide Effects 59
- 5.3 Business Logic in Active Records Puts Churn and Complexity in Critical Classes 61
- 5.4 Active Records Were Never Intended to Hold All the Business Logic 64
- 5.5 Example Design of a Feature 65

II Deep Dive into Rails

6 Routes and URLs — 73

- 6.1 Always Use Canonical Routes that Conform to Rails' Defaults — 74
- 6.2 Never Configure Routes That Aren't Being Used 77
- 6.3 Vanity URLs Should Redirect to a Canonical Route 79
- 6.4 Don't Create Custom Actions, Create More Resources 83
- 6.5 Use Nested Routes Strategically 87
  - 6.5.1 Create Sub-Resources Judiciously 87
  - 6.5.2 Namespacing Might (or Might Not) be an Architecture Smell 89
- 6.6 Nested Routes Can Organize Content Pages 90

7 HTML Templates — 93

- 7.1 Use Semantic HTML 93
  - 7.1.1 Build Views by Applying Meaningful Tags to Content — 94
  - 7.1.2 Use `<div>` and `<span>` for Styling 95
- 7.2 Ideally, Expose One Instance Variable Per Action 100
  - 7.2.1 Name the Instance Variable After the Resource . . . 101
  - 7.2.2 Reference Data, Global Context, and UI State are Exceptions 106
- 7.3 Wrangling Partials for Simple View Re-use 107
  - 7.3.1 Partials Allow Simple Code for Simple Re-use 107
  - 7.3.2 Reference Only Locals in Partials 108
  - 7.3.3 Partials Should Use Strict Locals 109
  - 7.3.4 Use Default Values for Strict Locals to Simplify Partial APIs 110

	7.4	Use the View Component Library for Complex UI Logic	111
		7.4.1 Creating a View Component	112
		7.4.2 Testing Markup from a Unit Test	115
		7.4.3 Deciding Between a Partial or a View Component	117
	7.5	Just Use ERB	117

8 Helpers — 119

- 8.1 Don't Conflate Helpers with Your Domain ... 120
- 8.2 Helpers are Best at Exposing Global UI State and Generating Markup ... 123
  - 8.2.1 Global UI Logic and State ... 123
  - 8.2.2 Small, Inline Components ... 124
- 8.3 Configure Rails based on Your Strategy for Helpers ... 126
  - 8.3.1 Consolidating Helpers in One File ... 126
  - 8.3.2 Configure Helpers to Be Actually Modular ... 127
  - 8.3.3 Use `helper_method` to Share Logic Between Views and Controllers ... 128
- 8.4 Use Rails' APIs to Generate Markup ... 128
- 8.5 Helpers Should Be Tested and Thus Testable ... 130
- 8.6 Tackle Complex View Logic with Better Resource Design or View Components ... 133
  - 8.6.1 Presenters Obscure Reality and Breed Inconsistency ... 133
  - 8.6.2 Custom Resources and Active Model Create More Consistent Code ... 134
  - 8.6.3 View Components can Render Entire Pages When Logic is Complex ... 136

9 CSS — 139

- 9.1 Adopt a Design System ... 140
- 9.2 Adopt a CSS Strategy ... 141
  - 9.2.1 A CSS Framework ... 142
  - 9.2.2 Object-Oriented CSS ... 142
  - 9.2.3 Functional CSS ... 144
- 9.3 Create a Living Style Guide to Document Your Design System and CSS Strategy ... 147

10 Minimize JavaScript — 157

- 10.1 How and Why JavaScript is a Serious Liability ... 157
  - 10.1.1 You Cannot Control The Runtime Environment ... 158
  - 10.1.2 JavaScript's Behavior is Difficult to Observe ... 158
  - 10.1.3 The Ecosystem Values Highly-Decoupled Modules that Favor Progress over Stability ... 160
- 10.2 Embrace Server-Rendered Rails Views ... 161
  - 10.2.1 Architecture of Rails Server-Rendered Views ... 161
  - 10.2.2 Architecture of the JAM Stack ... 163
  - 10.2.3 Server-Rendered Views by Default, JAM Stack Only When Needed ... 165

    10.3 Tweak Turbo to Provide a Slightly Better Experience 166

11 Carefully Manage the JavaScript You Need — 169
    11.1 Embrace Plain JavaScript for Basic Interactions 169
    11.2 Carefully Choose One Framework When You Need It 176
    11.3 Ensure System Tests Fail When JavaScript is Broken 178

12 Testing the View — 181
    12.1 Understand the Value and Cost of Tests 181
    12.2 Use `:rack_test` for non-JavaScript User Flows 182
    12.3 Test Against Default Markup and Content Initially 184
    12.4 Cultivate Explicit Diagnostic Tools to Debug Test Failures . . 186
    12.5 Fake The Back-end To Get System Tests Passing 190
    12.6 Use `data-testid` Attributes to Combat Brittle Tests 193
    12.7 Test JavaScript Interactions with a Real Browser 195
        12.7.1 Setting Up Headless Chrome 196
        12.7.2 Writing a Browser-driven System Test Case 199
        12.7.3 Enhancing `with_clues` to Dump Browser Logs 201

13 Models, Part 1 — 203
    13.1 Active Record is for Database Access 203
        13.1.1 Creating Some Example Active Records 204
        13.1.2 Model the Database With Active Record's DSL 205
        13.1.3 Class Methods Should Be Used to Re-use Common Database Operations 206
        13.1.4 Instance Methods Should Implement Domain Concepts Derivable Directly from the Database 208
    13.2 Active Model is for Resource Modeling 209

14 The Database — 213
    14.1 Logical and Physical Data Models 213
    14.2 Create a Logical Model to Build Consensus 214
    14.3 Planning the Physical Model to Enforce Correctness 216
        14.3.1 The Database Should Be Designed for Correctness . 217
        14.3.2 Use a SQL Schema 218
        14.3.3 Use `TIMESTAMP WITH TIME ZONE` For Timestamps . . 219
        14.3.4 Planning the Physical Model 220
    14.4 Creating Correct Migrations 224
        14.4.1 Creating the Migration File and Helper Scripts 227
        14.4.2 Iteratively Writing Migration Code to Create the Correct Schema 230
    14.5 Writing Tests for Database Constraints 237

15 Business Logic Code is a Seam — 241
    15.1 Business Logic Code Must Reveal Behavior 242
    15.2 Services are Stateless, Explicitly-Named Classes with Explicitly-Named Methods 243

    15.2.1 A `ThingDoer` Class With a `do_thing` Method is Fine . 244
    15.2.2 Methods Receive Context and Data on Which to Operate, *not* Services to Delegate To 245
    15.2.3 Return Rich Result Objects, not Booleans or Active Records 247
15.3 Implementation Patterns You Might Want to Avoid 249
    15.3.1 Creating Class Methods Closes Doors 250
    15.3.2 "Service Objects" Using `call` Solve No Problem and Obscure Behavior 251
    15.3.3 Dependency Injection *also* Obscures Behavior 252

16 Models, Part 2   255
16.1 Validations Don't Provide Data Integrity 255
    16.1.1 Outside Code Naturally Skips Validations 256
    16.1.2 Rails' Public API Allows Bypassing Validations 257
    16.1.3 Some Validations Don't Technically Work 257
16.2 Validations Are Awesome For User Experience 258
16.3 How to (Barely) Use Callbacks 259
16.4 Scopes are Often Business Logic and Belong Elsewhere . . . 261
16.5 Model Testing Strategy 262
    16.5.1 Active Record Tests Should Test Database Constraints 262
    16.5.2 Tests For Complex Validations or Callbacks 262
    16.5.3 Ensure Anyone Can Create Valid Instances of the Model using Factory Bot 262

17 End-to-End Example   271
17.1 Example Requirements 271
17.2 Building the UI First 272
    17.2.1 Setting Up To Build the UI 272
    17.2.2 Create Useful Seed Data for Development 273
    17.2.3 Sketch the UI using Semantic Tags 274
    17.2.4 Provide Basic Polish 276
    17.2.5 Style the Form 277
    17.2.6 Style Error States 279
17.3 Writing a System Test 284
17.4 Sketch Business Logic and Define the Seam 291
17.5 Fully Implement and Test Business Logic 295
17.6 Finished Implementation 304

18 Controllers   313
18.1 Controller Code is Configuration 313
18.2 Don't Over-use Callbacks 314
18.3 Controllers Should Convert Parameters to Richer Types . . . 316
18.4 Don't Over Test 318
    18.4.1 Writing a Controller Test 318
    18.4.2 Implementing a Basic Confidence-checking System . 320
    18.4.3 Avoiding Duplicative Tests 323

19 Jobs   **325**

  19.1 Use Jobs To Defer Execution or Increase Fault-Tolerance . . 325
      19.1.1 Web Workers, Worker Pools, Memory, and Compute Power 326
      19.1.2 Network Calls and Third Parties are Slow 326
      19.1.3 Network Calls and Third Parties are Flaky 328
      19.1.4 Use Background Jobs Only When Needed 328
  19.2 Understand How Your Job Backend Works 329
      19.2.1 Understand Where and How Jobs (and their Arguments) are Queued 329
      19.2.2 Understand What Happens When a Job Fails 330
      19.2.3 Observe the Behavior of Your Job Backend 331
  19.3 Sidekiq is The Best Job Backend for Most Teams 331
  19.4 Queue Jobs Directly, and Have Them Defer to Your Business Logic Code 335
      19.4.1 Do Not Use Active Job - Use the Job Backend Directly 335
      19.4.2 Job Code Should Defer to Your Service Layer 337
  19.5 Job Testing Strategies 339
  19.6 Jobs Will Get Retried and Must Be Idempotent 342

20 Other Boundary Classes   **349**

  20.1 Mailers 349
      20.1.1 Mailers Should Just Format Emails 349
      20.1.2 Mailers are Usually Jobs 350
      20.1.3 Previewing, Styling, and Checking your Mail 351
      20.1.4 Using Mailcatcher to Allow Emails to be Sent in Development 356
  20.2 Rake Tasks 357
      20.2.1 Rake Tasks Are For Automation 357
      20.2.2 One Task Per File, Namespaces Match Directories . . 358
      20.2.3 Rake Tasks Should Not Contain Business Logic . . . 359
      20.2.4 Prefer Ruby Command Line Apps for Developer Automation 362
  20.3 Mailboxes, Cables, and Active Storage 363
      20.3.1 Action Mailbox 363
      20.3.2 Action Cable 363
      20.3.3 Active Storage 364

III Beyond Rails

21 Authentication and Authorization   **367**

  21.1 When in Doubt Use Devise or OmniAuth 367
      21.1.1 Use OmniAuth to Authenticate Using a Third Party . 368
      21.1.2 Building Authentication Into your App with Devise . 369
  21.2 Authorization and Role-based Access Controls 370

      21.2.1 Map Resources and Actions to Job Titles and Departments 371
      21.2.2 Use Cancancan to Implement Role-Based Access . . . 372
      21.2.3 You Don't Have to Use All of Cancancan's Features . 374
  21.3 Test Access Controls In System Tests 374

22 API Endpoints   377
  22.1 Be Clear About What—and Who—Your API is For 377
  22.2 Write APIs the Same Way You Write Other Code 378
  22.3 Use the Simplest Authentication System You Can 381
  22.4 Use the Simplest Content Type You Can 387
  22.5 Just Put The Version in the URL 389
  22.6 Use `.to_json` to Create JSON 392
      22.6.1 How Rails Renders JSON 393
      22.6.2 Customizing JSON Serialization 394
      22.6.3 Customize JSON in the Models Themselves 395
      22.6.4 Always Use a Top Level Key 397
  22.7 Test API Endpoints 398

23 Sustainable Process and Workflows   405
  23.1 Use Continuous Integration To Deploy 405
      23.1.1 What is CI? 406
      23.1.2 CI Configuration Should be Explicit and Managed . . 406
      23.1.3 CI Should be Based on `bin/setup` and `bin/ci` 408
  23.2 Frequent Dependency Updates 411
      23.2.1 Update Dependencies Early and Often 412
      23.2.2 A Versioning Policy 413
      23.2.3 Automate Dependency Updates 414
  23.3 Leverage Generators and Sample Repositories over Documentation 417
      23.3.1 Create and Configure Rails Generators 417
      23.3.2 Use Template Repositories for Ruby Gems and Rails Apps 419
  23.4 RubyGems and Railties Can Distribute Configuration 420

24 Operations   425
  24.1 Why Observability Matters 425
  24.2 Monitor Business Outcomes 427
  24.3 Logging is Powerful 428
      24.3.1 Include a Request ID in All Logs 430
      24.3.2 Log What Something is and Where it Came From . . 433
      24.3.3 Use `Current` to Include User IDs 436
  24.4 Manage Unhandled Exceptions 436
  24.5 Measure Performance 438
  24.6 Managing Secrets, Keys, and Passwords 440

IV Appendices

A Setting Up Docker for Local Development — 445
- A.1 Installing Docker — 445
- A.2 What *is* Docker? — 446
- A.3 Overview of the Environment — 447
- A.4 Creating the Image — 448
- A.5 Starting Up the Environment — 449
- A.6 Executing Commands and Doing Development — 449
- A.7 Customizing the Dev Environment — 450
    - A.7.1 Installing Software — 450
    - A.7.2 Copying Your Dotfiles Into the Image — 451

B Monoliths, Microservices, and Shared Databases — 453
- B.1 Monoliths Get a Bad Rap — 454
- B.2 Microservices Are Not a Panacea. — 455
- B.3 Sharing a Database Is Viable — 456

C Technical Leadership is Critical — 463
- C.1 Leadership Is About Shared Values — 463
- C.2 Leaders Can be Held Accountable — 464
- C.3 Accountability Can be Implicit — 465

Colophon — 467

Acknowledgements

If there were no such thing as Rails, this book would be, well, pretty strange. So I must acknowledge and deeply thank DHH and the Rails core team for building and maintaining such a wonderful framework for all of us to use.

I have to thank my wife, Amy, who gave me the space and encouragement to work on this. During a global pandemic. When both of us were briefly out of work. And we realized our aging parents require more care than we thought. And when we got two kittens named Carlos Rosario and Zoni. And when we bought a freaking car. And when I joined a pre-seed startup. It's been quite a time.

I also want to thank the technical reviewers, Noel Rappin, Chris Gibson, Zach Campbell, Lisa Sheridan, Raul Murciano, Geoff The, and Sean Miller. Also special thanks to Brigham Johnson for identifying an embarrassing number of typos.

Changes from Previous Versions

This book is intended to be somewhat timeless, and able to be used as a reference. Much of what's in here hasn't changed and I wouldn't expect it to. That said, some things have changed, and this section captures them.

December, 12, 2020

- Updated for Rails 6.1 to remove deprecated method of setting errors on Active Records

January, 21, 2021

- No need to disable Ajax form submissions by default, since Rails 6.1 changed the default behavior.
- Use of `add_check_constraint` and `add_index` instead of SQL wrapped in `reversible`.
- Fixed color issues with sidebars on some e-readers

March 15, 2022

- Updated for Rails 7
- Removal of all NodeJS-related stuff, including removal and re-thinking of the value of unit-testing JavaScript.
- Softened language around using React by default given Hotwire's existence.
- Changed guidance around nested routes to account for content-heavy marketing pages.
- Clarified the use of controller instance variables for managing UI state.
- Links to gems extracted from code based on the book.

Dec 4, 2023

This is a more substantial update that previous updates. Chapter numbers refer to the PDF or printed book's numbering. e-book numbering continues to be a byzantine nightmare.

- General Changes
    - Updated for Rails 7.1.
    - Updated for Ruby 3.2
    - Added explicit language in each section about where to find the sample code for that section.
    - New cover
- Chapter 1
    - Update my experience, given the passage of time.
- Chapter 4
    - Remove mention of Spring and Listen, since they aren't included and haven't been in a few versions.
    - Remove mention of having to add the rexml gem, since selenium-webdriver brings it in.
    - Change `bin/run` to `bin/dev`, since this matches what Rails does (sometimes).
    - Remove mention of having to `bundle update` Thor.
    - Added help flags to the various `bin/` scripts.
- Chapter 5
    - Added a new section that references "Patterns of Enterprise Application Architecture", since this where the active record pattern originated.
- Chapter 7
    - Recommend the use of View Components
    - Recommend strict locals for partials
- Chapter 8
    - Clarify that helpers *can* be made to be modular, and discuss configuring Rails to either treat them that way or to not generate falsely-modular helpers.
    - More strongly discourage presenter-like libraries, and remove a lot of content around managing them.
    - In place of presenters, discuss how using Active Model or View Components can manage complexity instead of gobs of helpers.
- Chapter 9
    - Clear warning about Tailwind's lack of built-in design system and what you should consider if adopting it.
- Chapter 11
    - Qualify the recommendation for Hotwire given that 37 Signals have made it clear they will change it however they like whenever they like.

- Chapter 15
    - Reference "Patterns of Enterprise Application Architecture" and its definition of a *service layer*, which is what this chapter describes.
    - Make it clear that the term "Service Objects" is not a service layer and is actually just another name for the command pattern (and that you should not use this pattern).
- Chapter 16
    - Replace use of `before_validation` callback with the new `normalizes` macro
    - Make a stronger case for not using callbacks by clarifying exactly what they do and are for.
- Chapter 17
    - Replace the re-usable partial with a View Component in the example.
- Chapter 23
    - Show code to monkey-patch Thor to make it useful for Rails generators.
    - Discourage the use of app templates in favor of template repositories.
- Chapter 24
    - Use `CurrentAttributes` to store information for the log instead of thread local storage.
    - Discuss the need to revisit security practices, along with an anecdote from a previous job.
- Appendix A
    - Re-work Docker stuff based on updated learnings and code.
    - Explainer on getting your own shell aliases or software into the dev container.

PART
I

introduction

1
Why This Book Exists

Rails can scale. But what does that actually mean? And how do we do it? This book is the answer to both of these questions, but instead of using "scalable", which many developers equate with "fast performance", I'm using the word "sustainable". This is really what we want out of our software: the ability to sustain that software over time.

Rails itself is an important component in sustainable web development, since it provides common solutions to common problems and has reached a significant level of maturity. But it's not the complete picture.

Rails has a lot of features and we may not need them all. Or, we may need to take some care in how we use them. Rails also leaves gaps in your application's architecture that you'll have to fill (which makes sense, since Rails can't possibly provide *everything* your app will need).

This book will help you navigate all of that.

Before we begin, I want to be clear about what *sustainability* means and why it's important. I also want to state the assumptions I'm making in writing this, because there is no such thing as universal advice—there are only recommendations that apply in a given context.

1.1 What is Sustainability?

The literal interpretation of sustainable web development is web development that can be sustained. As silly as that definition is, I find it an illuminating restatement.

To *sustain* the development of our software is to ensure that it can continue to meet its needs. A sustainable web app can easily suffer new requirements, increased demand for its resources, and an increasing (or changing) team of developers to maintain it.

A system that is hard to change is hard to sustain. A system that can't avail itself of the resources it needs to function is hard to sustain. A system that only *some* developers can work on is hard to sustain.

Thus, a sustainable application is one in which changes we make tomorrow are as easy as changes are today, for whatever the application might need to do and whoever might be tasked with working on it.

So this defines *sustainability*, but why is it important?

1.2 Why Care About Sustainability?

Most software exists to meet some need, and if that need will persist over time, so must the software. *Needs* are subjective and vague, while software must be objective and specific. Thus, building software is often a matter of continued refinement as the needs are slowly clarified. And, of course, needs have a habit of changing along the way.

Software is expensive, mostly owing to the expertise required to build and maintain it. People who can write software find their skills to be in high demand, garnering some of the highest wages in the world, even at entry levels. It stands to reason that if a piece of software requires more effort to enhance and maintain over time, it will cost more and more and deliver less and less.

In an economic sense, sustainable software minimizes the cost of the software over time. But there is a human cost to working on software. Working on sustainable software is, well, more enjoyable. They say employees quit managers, but I've known developers that quit codebases. Working on unsustainable software just plain sucks, and I think there's value in having a job that doesn't suck... at least not all of the time.

Of course, it's one thing to care about sustainability in the abstract, but how does that translate into action?

1.3 How to Value Sustainability

Sustainability is like an investment. It necessarily won't pay off in the short term and, if the investment isn't sound, it won't ever pay off. So it's really important to understand the value of sustainability to your given situation and to have access to as much information as possible to know exactly how to invest in it.

Predicting the future is dangerous for programmers. It can lead to over-engineering, which makes certain classes of changes more difficult in the future. To combat this urge, developers often look to the tenets of agile software development, which have many cute aphorisms that boil down to "don't build software that you don't know you need".

If you are a hired consultant, this is excellent advice. It gives you a framework to be successful and manage change when you are in a situation where you have very little access to information. The strategy of "build for only what you 100% know you need" works great to get software shipped with confidence, but it doesn't necessarily lead to a sustainable outcome.

For example, no business person is going to ask you to write log statements so you can understand your code in production. No product owner is going to ask you to create a design system to facilitate building user interfaces more quickly. And no one is going to require that your database have referential integrity.

The features of the software are merely one input into what software gets built. They are a significant one just not the only one. To make better technical decisions, you need access to more information than simply what someone wants the software to do.

Do you know what economic or behavioral output the software exists to produce? In other words, how does the software make money for the people paying you to write it? What improvements to the business is it expected to make? What is the medium or long-term plan for the business? Does it need to grow significantly? Will there need to be increased traffic? Will there be an influx of engineers? Will they be very senior, very junior, or a mix? When will they be hired and when will they start?

The more information you can get access to the better, because all of this feeds into your technical decision-making and can tell you just how sustainable your app needs to be. If there will be an influx of less experienced developers, you might make different decisions than if the team is only hiring one or two experienced specialists.

Armed with this sort of information, you can make technical decisions as part of an overall *strategy*. For example, you may want to spend several days setting up a more sustainable development environment. By pointing to the company's growth projections and your team's hiring plans, that work can be easily justified (see the sidebar "Understanding Growth At Stitch Fix" on the next page for a specific example of this).

If you don't have the information about the business, the team, or anything other than what some user wants the software to do, you aren't set up to do sustainable development. But it doesn't mean you shouldn't ask anyway.

People who don't have experience writing software won't necessarily intuit that such information is relevant, so they might not be forthcoming. But you'd be surprised just how much information you can get from someone by asking.

Whatever the answers are, you can use this as part of an overall technical strategy, of which sustainability is a part. As you read this book, I'll talk about the considerations around the various recommendations and techniques. They might not all apply to your situation, but many of them will.

Which brings us to the set of assumptions that this book is based on. In other words, what *is* the situation in which sustainability is important and in which this book's recommendations apply?

> **Understanding Growth At Stitch Fix**
>
> During my first few months at Stitch Fix, I was asked to help improve the operations of our warehouse. There were many different processes and we had a good sense of which ones to start automating. At the time, there was only one application—called HELLBLAZER—and it served up `stitchfix.com`.
>
> If I hadn't been told anything else, the simplest thing to do would've been to make a `/warehouse` route in HELLBLAZER and slowly add features for the associates there. But I *had* been told something else.
>
> Like almost everyone at the company, the engineering team was told—very transparently—what the growth plans for the business were. It needed to grow in a certain way or the business would fail. It was easy to extrapolate from there what that would mean for the size of the engineering team, and for the significance of the warehouse's efficiency. It was clear that a single codebase everyone worked in would be a nightmare, and migrating away from it later would be difficult and expensive.
>
> So, we created a new application that shared HELLBLAZER's database. It would've certainly been faster to add code to HELLBLAZER directly, but we knew doing so would burn us long-term. As the company grew, the developers working on warehouse software were fairly isolated since they worked in a totally different codebase. We replicated this pattern and, after six years of growth, it was clearly the right decision, even accounting for problems that happen when you share a database between apps.
>
> We never could've known that without a full understanding of the company's growth plans, and long-term vision for the problems we were there to solve.

1.4 Assumptions

This book is prescriptive, but each prescription comes with an explanation, and *all* of the book's recommendations are based on some key assumptions that I would like to state explicitly. If your situation differs wildly from the one described below, you might not get that much out of this book. My hope—and belief—is that the assumptions below are common, and that the situation of writing software that you find yourself in is similar to situations I have faced. Thus, this book will help you.

In case it's not, I want to state my assumptions up front, right here in this free chapter.

1.4.1 The Software Has a Clear Purpose

This might seem like nonsense, but there are times when we don't exactly know what the software is solving for, yet need to write some software to explore the problem space.

Perhaps some venture capitalist has given us some money, but we don't yet know the exact market for our solution. Maybe we're prototyping a potentially complex UI to do user testing. In these cases we need to be nimble and try to figure out what the software should do.

The assumption in this book is that that has already happened. We know generally what problem we are solving, and we aren't going to have to pivot from selling shoes to providing AI-powered podiatrist back-office enterprise software.

1.4.2 The Software Needs To Exist For Years

This book is about how to sustain development over a longer period of time than a few months, so a big assumption is that the software actually *needs* to exist that long!

A lot of software falls into this category. If you are automating a business process, building a customer experience, or integrating some back-end systems, it's likely that software will continue to be needed for quite a while.

1.4.3 The Software Will Evolve

Sometimes we write code that solves a problem and that problem doesn't change, so the software is stable. That's not an assumption I am making here. Instead, I'm assuming that the software will be subject to changes big and small over the years it will exist.

I believe this is more common than not. Software is notoriously hard to get right the first time, so it's common to change it iteratively over a long period to arrive at optimal functionality. Software that exists for years also tends to need to change to keep up with the world around it.

1.4.4 The Team Will Change

The average tenure of a software engineer at any given company is pretty low, so I'm assuming that the software will outlive the team, and that the group of people charged with the software's maintenance and enhancement will change over time. I'm also assuming the experience levels and skill-sets will change over time as well.

1.4.5 You Value Sustainability, Consistency, and Quality

Values are fundamental beliefs that drive actions. While the other assumptions might hold for you, if you don't actually value sustainability, consistency, and quality, this book isn't going to help you.

Sustainability

If you don't value sustainability as I've defined it, you likely didn't pick up this book or have stopped reading by now. You're here because you think sustainability is important, thus you *value* it.

Consistency

Valuing consistency is hugely important as well. Consistency means that designs, systems, processes, components (etc.), should not be arbitrarily different. Same problems should have same solutions, and there should not be many ways to do something. It also means being explicit that personal preferences are not critical inputs to decision-making.

A team that values consistency is a sustainable team and will produce sustainable software. When code is consistent, it can be confidently abstracted into shared libraries. When processes are consistent, they can be confidently automated to make everyone more productive.

When architecture and design are consistent, knowledge can be transferred, and the team, the systems, and even the business itself can survive potentially radical change (see the sidebar "Our Uneventful Migration to AWS" on the next page for how Stitch Fix capitalized on consistency to migrate from Heroku to AWS with no downtime or outages).

Quality

Quality is a vague notion, but it's important to both understand it and to value it. In a sense, valuing quality means doing things right the first time. But "doing things right" doesn't mean over-engineering, gold-plating, or doing something fancy that's not called for.

Valuing quality is to acknowledge the reality that we aren't going to be able to go back and clean things up after they have been shipped. There is this fantasy developers engage in that they can simply "acquire technical debt" and someday "pay it down".

I have never seen this happen, at least not in the way developers think it might. It is extremely difficult to make a business case to modify working software simply to make it "higher quality". Usually, there must be some catastrophic failure to get the resources to clean up a previously-made mess. It's simpler and easier to manage a process by which messes don't get made as a matter of course.

Quality should be part of the everyday process. Doing this consistently will result in predictable output, which is what managers really want to see. On the occasion when a date must be hit, cut scope, not corners. Only the developers know what scope to cut in order to get meaningfully faster delivery, but this requires having as much information about the business strategy as possible.

When you value sustainability, consistency, and quality, you will be unlikely to find yourself in a situation where you must undo a technical decision you made at the cost of shipping more features. Business people may want software delivered as fast as possible, but they *really* don't want to go an extended period without any features so that the engineering team can "pay down" technical debt.

We know what sustainability is, how to value it, what assumptions I'm making going in, and the values that drive the tactics and strategy for the rest of the book. But there are two concepts I want to discuss that allow us to attempt to quantify just how sustainable our decisions are: opportunity costs and carrying costs.

> **Our Uneventful Migration to AWS**
>
> For several years, Stitch Fix used the platform-as-a-service Heroku. We were consistent in how we used it, as well as in how our applications were designed. We used one type of relational database, one type of cache, one type of CDN, etc.
>
> In our run-up to going public, we needed to migrate to AWS, which is *very* different from Heroku. We had a team of initially two people and eventually three to do the migration for the 100+ person engineering team. We didn't want downtime, outages, or radical changes in the developer experience.
>
> Because everything was so consistent, the migration team was able to quickly build a deployment pipeline and command-line tool to provide a Heroku-like experience to the developers. Over several months we migrated one app and one database at a time. Developers barely noticed, and our users and customers had no idea.
>
> The project lead was so confident in the approach and the team that he kept his scheduled camping trip to an isolated mountain in Colorado, unreachable by the rest of the team as they moved `stitchfix.com` from Heroku to AWS to complete the migration. Consistency was a big part of making this a non-event.

1.5 Opportunity and Carrying Costs

An *opportunity cost* is basically a one-time cost to produce something. By committing to work, you necessarily cut off other avenues of opportunity. This cost can be a useful lens to compare two different approaches when trying to perform a cost/benefit analysis. An opportunity cost that we'll take in a few chapters is writing robust scripts for setting up our app, running it, and running its tests. It has a higher opportunity cost than simply writing documentation about how to do those things.

But sometimes an investment is worth making. The way to know if that's true is to talk about the *carrying cost*. A carrying cost is a cost you have to pay all the time every time. If it's difficult to run your app in development, reading the documentation about how to do so and running all the various commands is a cost you pay frequently.

Carrying costs affect sustainability more than anything. Each line of code is a carrying cost. Each new feature has a carrying cost. Each thing we have to remember to do is a carrying cost. This is the true value provided by Rails: it reduces the carrying costs of a lot of pretty common patterns when building a web app.

To sustainably write software requires carefully balancing your carrying costs, and strategically incurring opportunity costs that can reduce, or at least maintain, your carrying costs.

If there are two concepts most useful to engineers, it is these two.

The last bit of information I want to share is about me. This book amounts to my advice based on my experience, and you need to know about that, because, let's face it, the field of computer programming is pretty far away from science, and most of the advice we get is nicely-formatted survivorship bias.

1.6 Why should you trust me?

Software engineering is notoriously hard to study and most of what exists about how to write software is anecdotal evidence or experience reports. This book is no different, but I do believe that if you are facing problems similar to those I have faced, there is value in here.

So I want to outline what my experience is that has led to me recommend what I do in this book.

The most important thing to know about me is that I'm not a software consultant, nor have I been in a very long time. For the past fifteen years I have been a product engineer (or part of a project engineering team), working for companies building one or more products designed to last. I was a rank and file engineer at times, a manager on occasion, an architect responsible for technical strategy and, most recently, Chief Technology Officer (CTO) at a venture-backed startup. I've written a lot of code and set a lot of technical and product strategy.

What this means is that the experience upon which this book is based comes from actually building software meant to be sustained. I have actually done—and seen the long-term results of doing—pretty much everything in this book. I've been responsible for sustainable software several times during my career.

- I spent four years at an energy startup that sold enterprise software. I saw the product evolve from almost nothing to a successful company with many clients and over 100 engineers. While the software was

- Java-based, much of what I learned about sustainability applies to the Rails world as well.
- I spent the next year and half at an e-commerce company that had reached what would be the peak of its success. I joined a team of almost 200 engineers, many of whom were working in a huge Rails monolith that contained thousands of lines of code, all done "The Rails Way". The team had experienced massive growth and this growth was not managed. The primary application we all worked in was wholly unsustainable and had a massive carrying cost simply existing.
- I then spent the next six and half years at Stitch Fix, where I was the third engineer and helped set the technical direction for the team. By the time I left, the team was 200 engineers, collectively managing a microservices-based architecture of over 50 Rails applications, many of which I contributed to. At that time I was responsible for the overall technical strategy for the team and was able to observe which decisions we made in 2013 ended up being good (or bad) by 2019.
- I was CTO of a healthcare startup, having written literally the first line of code, navigating the tumultuous world of finding product/market fit, becoming HIPAA[1]-compliant, and trying to never be a bottleneck for what the company needed to do.

What I don't have much experience with is working on short-term greenfield projects, or being dropped into a mess to help clean it up (so-called "Rails Rescue" projects). There's nothing wrong with this kind of experience, but that's not what this book is about.

What follows is what I tried to take away from the experience above, from the great decisions my colleagues and I made, to the unfortunate ones as well (I pushed hard for both Coffeescript and Angular 1 and we see how those turned out).

But, as they say, your mileage may vary, "it depends", and everything is a trade-off. I will do my best to clarify the trade-offs.

Up Next

This chapter should've given you a sense of what you're in for and whether or not this book is for you. I hope it is!

So, let's move on. Because this book is about Ruby on Rails, I want to give an overview of the application architecture Rails provides by default, and how those pieces relate to each other. From that basis, we can then deep dive into each part of Rails and learn how to use it sustainably.

---

[1] HIPAA is the Health Insurance Portability and Accountability Act, a curious law in the United States related to how healthcare information is managed. Like all compliance-related frameworks, it thwarts sustainability, but it's a fact of life in the U.S.

2
The Rails Application Architecture

This book contains guidelines, tips, and recipes for managing the architecture of your Rails application as it grows over time, so I want to start with a review of the default application architecture you get with Rails. This architecture is extremely powerful, mostly because it exists right after you run `rails new` and it provides a solid way to organize the code in your application.

Rails is often referred to as an "MVC Framework", MVC standing for "Model, View, Controller". Rails does, in fact, have models, views, and controllers, but digging into the history of MVC and trying to sort out how it relates to Rails can create confusion, since the concepts don't exactly match up. This is OK, we don't need them to.

We'll skip the theory and look at the actual parts of Rails and how they contribute to the overall application you build with Rails. Although there are quite a few moving parts, each part falls into one of four categories:

- **Boundaries**, which accept input from somewhere and arrange for output to be rendered or sent. Controllers, Mailers, etc are boundaries.
- **Views**, which present information out, usually in HTML. ERB files, JavaScript, CSS, and even JBuilder files are all part of the view.
- **Models**, which are the Active Record classes that interact with your database.
- **Everything else.**

Rails doesn't talk about the parts this way, but we will, since it allows us to group similar parts together when talking about how they work. The figure "Rails' Default Application Architecture" on the next page shows all the parts of Rails and which of the four categories they fall into. The diagram shows that:

- The boundaries of your Rails app are the controllers, jobs, mailers, mailboxes, channels, and rake tasks, as well as Active Storage.

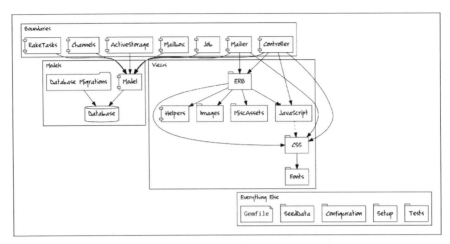

Figure 2.1: Rails' Default Application Architecture

- The view is comprised of ERB, JavaScript, CSS, Images, Fonts, and other assets like PDFs or binary files.
- The models are, well, your models, and they are what talk to your database (though a model does not *have* to talk to a database)
- Anything not mentioned, like configuration files or your Gemfile, are in the catch-all "everything else" bucket.

Let's now go through each layer and talk about the parts of Rails in that layer and what they are all generally for. I'll stay as close as I can to what I believe the intent of the Rails core team is and try not to embellish or assume too much.

First, we'll start with *Boundaries*, which broker input and output.

2.1 Boundaries

The Rails Guide[1] says that controllers are

> ...responsible for making sense of the request, and producing the appropriate output.

When you look at Jobs, Channels, Mailers, Mailboxes, Active Storage, and Rake Tasks, they perform similar functions. In a general sense, no matter what else goes in these areas, they *have* to:

- examine the input to make some sort of sense of it.
- trigger some business logic

---
[1] https://guides.rubyonrails.org/action_controller_overview.html

- examine the output of that business logic and provide some sort of output or effect.

Of course, not all use cases require reading explicit input or generating explicit output, but the overall structure of the innards of any of these classes, at least at a high level, is the same, as shown in the figure below.

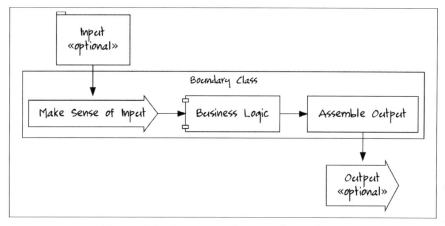

Figure 2.2: Structure of a Boundary Class

This figure shows that:

1. Some input might come in that triggers the Boundary class
2. The Boundary class examines that input to see if it understands it
3. Some business logic happens
4. The result of that logic is examined
5. Explicit output is possibly sent

For now, we're not going to talk about the business logic, specifically if it *should* be directly in the boundary classes or not. The point is that, no matter where the business logic is, these boundary classes are always responsible for looking at the input, initiating the logic, and assembling the output.

We'll talk about these boundary classes in more detail in "Controllers" on page 313, "Jobs" on page 325, and "Other Boundary Classes" on page 349.

Because Rails is for building web applications, the output of many of our boundary classes is a web view or some other dynamic output. And creating the view layer of a web application—even if it's just JSON—can be complex, which is why a big chunk of Rails is involved in these views.

2.2 Views

Rails support for rendering HTML web views is quite sophisticated and powerful. In particular, the coupling between Active Model and Rails' form helpers is very tight (a great example of the power in tightly-coupling components). Actions performed by boundary classes that result in dynamic output (usually controllers and mailers) will initiate the rendering of the view from a template, and that template may pull in JavaScript, CSS, or other templates (partials).

Often the templates are HTML, but they can be pretty much anything, including JSON, text, or XML. Templates also have access to *helpers*, which are free functions in the global namespace. Rails provides many helpers by default, and you can make your own.

View code tends to feel messy, because while a particular template can be isolated pretty well, including decomposing it into re-usable partials, CSS and JavaScript by their nature aren't organized the same way. Often CSS and JavaScript are globally available and taking care to keep them isolated can be tricky.

Rails 7 includes what DHH and the core team believe to be the best ways to manage JavaScript, and most of them boil down to getting JavaScript (and CSS) to the venerable Asset Pipeline.

Rails is also designed for server-rendered views, and this is where the tight-coupling comes into play. Take this pretty standard ERB for rendering an edit form for a widget:

```
<% form_for @widget do |form| %>
  <%= form.label :name %>
  <%= form.text :name %>

  <%= form.submit %>
<% end %>
```

To create the same form in an alternate front-end technology (such as React) would require quite a bit more code, and it would require specific markup in order to be interpreted by the controller this form submits to. Thus, replacing the Rails view layer with a single page application requires both giving up some of the power of Rails and providing your own solution to the problems Rails has already solved.

We'll discuss aspects of the view in "Routes and URLs" on page 73, "HTML Templates" on page 93, "Helpers" on page 119, "CSS" on page 139, "Minimize JavaScript" on page 157, "Carefully Manage the JavaScript You Need" on page 169, and "Testing the View" on page 181. Unlike most other parts of Rails, the view brings together a ton of different technologies, so it requires a more detailed analysis.

The boundaries and views make up most of the plumbing of a Rails application, which leaves us with the models.

2.3 Models

Models are almost always about interacting with the database. Any database table you need access to will assuredly require a model for you to do it, and you likely have one or more database migrations to manage that table's schema.

This isn't to say that everything we call a "model" has to be about a database, but the history of Rails is such that the two are used synonymously. It wasn't until Rails 4 that it become straightforward to make a model that worked with the view layer that was not an Active Record. The result of this historical baggage is that developers almost always use "model" to mean "thing that accesses the database".

Even non-database-table-accessing models (powered by Active Model) still bear a similar mark to the Active Records. They are both essentially data structures whose members are public and can be modified directly. Of course code like `widget.name = "Stembolt"` is actually a method call, but the overall design of Active Records and Active Models is one in which public data can be manipulated and there is no encapsulation.

In addition to providing access to structured data, models also tend to be where all the business logic is placed, mostly because Rails doesn't prescribe any other place for it to go. We'll talk about the problems with this approach in the chapter "Business Logic (Does Not Go in Active Records)" on page 57.

The model layer also includes the database migrations, which create the schema for the database being used. These are often the only artifact in a Rails app other than the database schema itself that tells you what attributes are defined on Active Records, since Rails dynamically creates those attributes based on what it finds in the database.

We'll cover models in "Models, Part 1" on page 203, "The Database" on page 213, and "Models, Part 2 on page 255. We'll discuss business logic specifically in "Business Logic (Does Not Go in Active Records)" on page 57 and "Business Logic Code is a Seam" on page 241.

There are a few other bits of your Rails app that you're less likely to think about, but are still important.

2.4 Everything Else

Although your Rails app in production is going to be running the code in your Boundaries, Views, and Models, there is other code that is critical to the sustainability of your Rails app, and I want to mention it here because it's important and we'll talk about it later.

First are tests, and there are often tests for each class. But there are also both system tests and integration tests, which test user flows across many classes. We'll discuss this in "Helpers Should Be Tested and Testable" on page 130, "Ensure System Tests Fail When JavaScript is Broken" on page 178, "Testing the View" on page 181, "Writing Tests for Database Constraints" on page 237, "Don't Over Test" in the "Controllers" chapter on page 318, and in other parts throughout the book.

There are, of course, your application dependencies as declared in `Gemfile` and either `package.json` or `config/importmap.rb`, as well as the Rails configuration files in `config/` that you might need to modify.

There is also `db/seeds.rb`, which contains data that Rails describes both as useful for production but also for development. We'll talk about that in more detail later, but I don't consider it part of the model layer since it's more of a thing used for development or operations and isn't used in production by default.

Lastly, there is `bin/setup`, which sets up your app. Rails provides a version of this that provides installation of gems and basic database setup. We'll talk about this in detail in "Start Your App Off Right" on page 33.

With our tour of Rails done, let's talk about the pros and cons of what Rails gives you.

2.5 The Pros and Cons of the Rails Application Architecture

It's important to understand just how powerful the Rails Application Architecture is. Working in any other system (at least one that did not just duplicate Rails) requires a team to make a lot of decisions about the internal architecture before they really even get going.

In most situations, teams will end up designing something that looks like Rails anyway (see the sidebar "Maintaining the Architecture of a Java Spring App" on the next page for just how much work there is without having Rails to help).

What this means is that a team working on a Rails app doesn't have to make a bunch of big up-front decisions in order to get started and they don't have to worry about big drifts in the structure of the codebase.

We can also easily work within this architecture to create a sustainable application. We don't need to abstract our code from Rails, or create a framework-within-a-framework. We just need to be intentional in how we use Rails, and fill in a few gaps for cases where Rails doesn't provide guidance for what we should do.

There are two downsides to the Rails Application Architecture. The first is that it's designed to build a particular type of application: a database-backed web application. If you aren't doing that, Rails isn't much help. The second downside is one Rails can't really do much about. Rails provides no guidance about where business logic should go. The result is that every

Rails developer I've ever met has a slightly different take on it, though those same developers also have had a bad experience with a variety of strategies.

We'll talk about this specific problem in several chapters, notably "Business Logic (Does Not Go in Active Records)" on page 57. It's important to understand that while DHH, the creator of Rails, might put business logic in models, the Rails documentation doesn't explicitly say this—developers used to put business logic in their controllers before the "fat model, skinny controller" aphorism became popular.

> ### Maintaining The Architecture of a Java Spring App
>
> I was the tech lead for an application to be built with the Java Spring Framework. Like Rails, Spring is incredibly powerful. Unlike Rails, however, Spring provides little guidance or direction on how to structure your application.
>
> There were many ways to map routes to controllers, you could name your controller methods anything, and you could use any database layer you wanted (and the most common database layer—Hibernate—also provides no presets or guidance and has ultimate flexibility).
>
> The team and I set up a basic structure of where files would go, naming conventions, configuration options, etc. It wasn't hard, but it did take time and required documentation. I even wrote some shell scripts to generate some boilerplate code to help everyone follow the conventions.
>
> The entire build of the product required *constant* vigilance for adherence to the architectural conventions. New developers would deviate, veteran developers would forget, and it ended up being a constant tax on the productivity of the team. I've never experienced this with a team working on a Rails application.

Where We Go From Here

I strongly believe that software should be developed with a user focus, and that the behavior of the software must flow from the user. This means that working "outside in" is preferred. If we know the user experience we want to create, the code we write can then be laser-focused on making that experience happen.

Before we can think about the user, we have to have a working environment first, and we have to have some semblance of a Rails app in which to work.

The next chapter will outline what you need to follow along in the book. The chapter after that will involve creating a new Rails app, all set up for sustainable web development.

3
Following Along in This Book

To follow along in this book, you'll need to know a few things about how it's written as well as to have a working development environment. This chapter will give you an outline of everything you need.

3.1 Typographic Conventions

This book contains both code listings as well as instructions for running commands in a shell.

Code listings will usually be preceded with the filename and either show the entire file or provide enough context to know where in the file I'm referring to. Changes will be highlighted with arrows. Lines to remove, if not obvious from context, are called out with an "x". For example, the following code listing shows a single method of a Rails controller where we have changed two lines and removed one[1]:

```
  # app/controllers/widgets_controller.rb

  def create
    @widget = Widget.create(widget_params)
    if @widget.valid?
x #     puts "debug: #{widget_params}"
→     Rails.logger.info(@widget.inspect)
→     redirect_to widget_path(@widget)
    else
      render :new
    end
  end
```

For shell commands, the command you need to type is preceded by a greater-than sign (>), and the output of that command is shown without any prefix, like so:

---

[1] For reasons beyond my understanding, the code listings in the book are difficult to copy and paste. You can always download the code if you don't want to type it in.

```
> ls app
controllers models views
```

On occasion, the output will be very long or otherwise too verbose to include. In that case, I'll use guillemets around a message indicating the output was elided, like so:

```
> yarn install
«lots of output»
```

Sometimes the output is useful but is too wide to fit on the page. In *that* case, the lines will be truncated with an ellipsis (...) like so:

```
> bin/rails test
A very very long line that is not that important for you to see, bu...
Followed by some possibly short lines
And then maybe some much much longer lines that will have to be tru...
```

Sometimes a command needs to be on more than one line, due to the constraints of the medium. In that case, I'll use the standard Unix mechanism for this, which is the backslash character (\):

```
> bin/rails g model Widget \
    name:string \
    quantity:int \
    description:text
```

If you are using a UNIX shell, these backslashes will work and you can type the command in just like it is.

Unless otherwise stated, *all* shell commands are assumed to be running in your development environment. Sometimes, however, we need to run commands inside the Rails console or inside the database. In those cases, I'll show the command to start the console/connect to the database, and then a change in prompt.

Here is how you would start a Rails console and then count the number of Widgets with a quantity greater than 1:

```
> bin/rails c
console> Widget.where("quantity > 1").count
99
```

Here is how you'd do that in SQL:

```
> bin/rails dbconsole
db> select count(*) from widgets where quantity > 1;

+-------+
| count |
|-------|
|    99 |
+-------+
```

Finally, note that when Rails console or SQL statements require more space than can fit on one line I *won't* be using the backslash notation, because that notation won't work in those environments. Sometimes the output will be formatted to fit this medium and won't match exactly, but hopefully it'll all make sense.

Next you need to make sure you have the same versions of the software I do.

3.2 Software Versions

Most of the code in this book is executed by a script as the book itself is compiled from the original source Markdown. This means that, hopefully, any issues with it were sorted out by me before they got to you. If you *do* have problems, the best way to figure them out is if you and I are using the same environment.

Those versions are:

- Ruby 3.2.2, specifically:

    ```
    > ruby --version
    ruby 3.2.2 (2023-03-30 revision e51014f9c0) [aarch64-linux]
    ```

- Ruby on Rails 7.1.1

- Postgres 15

- Redis 6.2.6

- Bundler 2.4.13

- RubyGems 3.4.13

- Debian bookworm, specifically:

```
> lsb_release -a
No LSB modules are available.
Distributor ID: Debian
Description:    Debian GNU/Linux 12 (bookworm)
Release:    12
Codename: bookworm
```

In Setting Up Docker for Local Development on page 445, I'll walk you through setting up an environment identical to mine, but if you already have a setup you prefer, by all means use that. Try to match versions as much as possible so if you run into any problems, it'll eliminate at least a few sources of errors.

3.3 Sample Code

Most of the code shown in this book is generated by the source code of the book. At the end of each section a snapshot is taken of the status of the app being built. You can download the code directly from the book's website at `https://sustainable-rails.com/assets/sample-code.zip`[2]

In each section where there is sample code available, there will be a note at the start of the section that indicates where to find the code, like so:

> This section's code is in the folder 03-02 of the sample code.

When you unzip `sample-code.zip`, you'll see a bunch of folders with numeric names. The message above says that the code in the section you are about to read is in the folder named 03-02. In almost every case, each folder contains the folder `widgets/`, which contains the entire state or the sample app *after* that section is completed.

The folders have numeric names that are ordered in the same way the book is. Thus, all changes would be against the version of the app in 03-01 in the example above.

If you are reading this as a PDF or a print book, the numbers should match the chapters and sections. If you are reading an ePub version on an eReader, the chapter numbers are unfortunately out of my control, so please pay attention to the notes at the start of each section.

Note that some sample code is just shown in the book as an example. The code in the downloadable `.zip` file is only the code for the example app you'll build in this book. But, that's a significant portion of the code!

---

[2] https://sustainable-rails.com/assets/sample-code.zip

Up Next

Now that you're oriented on the book and ready to write code, let's start where everyone has to start with Rails, which is setting up a new app. There's more than just running `rails new` if you want to get set up for sustainable development.

4
Start Your App Off Right

> This section's code is in the folder 04-01/ of the sample code.

`rails new` is pretty powerful. It gives you a ready-to-go Rails application you can start building immediately. But it doesn't completely set us up for sustainable development.

We know a few things about our app right now:

- Other developers will work on it, and need to be able to set it up, run its tests, and run it locally.
- It will eventually have security vulnerabilities (in our code and in our dependencies).
- It will be deployed into production via a continuous integration pipeline and require operational observability.

Given the assumptions we listed in the first chapter, we are also quite confident that the app will get more complex over time and more and more developers will work on it.

Before we start writing code, we're going to take a few minutes to consider how we create our app, how developers will set it up and work with it, and how we'll manage it in production. In other words, we need to consider *developer workflow*, which starts with setup and ends with maintaining the app in production.

The figure "Developer Workflow" on the next page shows this workflow and the parts of it that we'll create in this chapter.

The diagram shows:

- `bin/setup` will set up our app after we've pulled it down from version control.
- `bin/dev` will be used to run our app locally, with the dotenv gem providing runtime configuration for development and testing.
- `bin/ci` will run all of our quality checks, suitable for running in CI, which will include both tests and security analysis via Brakeman and `bundle audit`.

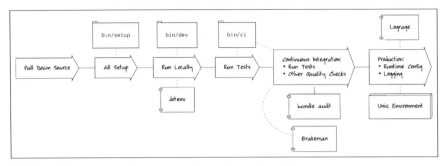

Figure 4.1: Developer Workflow

- In production, we'll get all runtime configuration from the UNIX environment, and we'll use the lograge gem to configure more production-friendly log output.

This won't take a lot of code or configuration, and we'll end up with automation, which is far more effective and easier to maintain than documentation (see the sidebar "Automating Alert Setup" on the next page to learn how powerful automation can be).

Before any of this, however, we need an app to work in.

4.1 Creating a Rails App

This book is intended to be easily referred to after you're done reading it, so we won't be embarking on a hero's journey to build an app together. That said, it's helpful to have a single running example, so we'll create that now. It'll be called "widgets" because it will manage the sale of widgets. Boring, I know, but I don't want you getting distracted by something more fanciful.

I recommend tailoring your `rails new` command as little as possible. It can be hard to add back parts of Rails you initially skip, and for the most part, the parts of Rails you don't use can sit there, inert, not bothering anyone.

Since we're using Postgres as our database, we can specify that to `rails new` so we have the right gems and configuration. This gives the following invocation to create our app:

```
> rails new --database=postgresql widgets
«lots of output»
```

We aren't yet ready to run our app or its tests because Rails needs to know how to connect to Postgres. This leads us nicely to our next topic on managing runtime configuration.

> **Automating Alert Setup**
>
> When Stitch Fix was deploying to Heroku, we had a battery of monitors and alerts that each application needed to have. Setting all of these up was critical to understanding the behavior of our apps, but the setup was lengthy and complex.
>
> Almost everyone that had to do this setup messed up some part of it. Some developers would skip it entirely. But the documentation was updated, correct, and made a strong case for why the steps had to be followed. It was just too complex to do well, and too important to leave to documentation alone.
>
> Eventually, we implemented automation in our deployment pipeline that detected an app's structure and automatically set up all the monitoring and alerting it would need. This "documentation" was always up to date, and was always followed because we automated it.

4.2 Using The Environment for Runtime Configuration

> This section's code is in the folder 04-02/ of the sample code.

Runtime configuration is information Rails cannot properly determine on its own, but that is critical for your app to be able to start up and run. This information also tends to be different in development, test, and production. Database credentials are a great example.

Rails provides three mechanisms that all work together to manage runtime configuration: the UNIX environment, `config/database.yml`, and an encrypted YAML file called `config/credentials.yml.enc` (encrypted with `config/master.key`). In my experience, this creates a lot of confusion and makes scripting a consistent environment difficult. We value consistency, so we want *one* way to manage runtime configuration, not three.

Managing files in production is becoming both increasingly difficult (due to ephemeral, containerized deployment systems), and increasingly risky, since runtime configuration is often secret information like credentials and API keys.

To that end, we'll follow the architecture of a 12-Factor App[1] and standardize on the UNIX environment. The UNIX environment is a set of key/value pairs provided by the operating system to the application. In a Ruby application, you can access it via the `ENV` constant.

For example, if your API key to your payment processor is "abcdefg1234", you would arrange to have that value set in the UNIX environment, under a key, such as `PAYMENTS_API_KEY`. You can then access it at runtime via `ENV["PAYMENTS_API_KEY"]`.

---

[1] http://12factor.net

Rails already uses this mechanism for database credentials (looking at the key DATABASE_URL) as well as the general secret key used for encrypting cookies (under the key SECRET_KEY_BASE).

Because of this, there's nothing special we need to do in our app about this—we just need to use ENV to access runtime credentials (see the sidebar "Be Careful with ENV" on the next page for how to do this safely). That said, the existence of the other mechanisms in our app will be confusing, so we should delete those files now:

```
> rm config/database.yml config/credentials.yml.enc \
    config/master.key
```

When we deploy, we'll need to make sure that both DATABASE_URL and SECRET_KEY_BASE have values in the production UNIX environment (see the section "Managing Secrets, Keys, and Passwords" on page 440 for some production and deployment considerations).

This does lead to the question of how to manage this in our local development environment. We don't want to set these values in *our* UNIX environments for two reasons: 1) it is hard to automate across the team, and 2) we may work on multiple apps which will have different runtime configuration values.

To manage the UNIX environment for our local development, we'll use a tool called "dotenv".

4.3 Configuring Local Development Environment with dotenv

> This section's code is in the folder 04-03/ of the sample code.

dotenv[2] merges the existing UNIX environment with a set of key/value pairs stored in files. These files are named for the Rails environment they apply to, so .env.development is used to store development environment variables, and .env.test for test.

---
[2]https://github.com/bkeepers/dotenv

> **Be Careful with ENV**
>
> Ruby's ENV constant behaves like a `Hash`, but it's actually a special object implemented in C. It may only contain strings (or objects that implement `to_str`, which is used to store the object inside ENV):
>
> ```
> puts ENV.class # => Object
> ENV["foo"] = true
> ## => TypeError (no implicit conversion of true into String)
> ```
>
> This means when you access it, you need to coerce the string value to whatever type you need. A very common error developers make is assuming the strings `"true"` and `"false"` are equivalent to their boolean counterparts. This leads to code like so:
>
> ```
> if ENV["PAYMENTS_DISBLED"]
>   give_free_order
> end
> ```
>
> The problem is that *every* non-nil value for PAYMENTS_DISBLED is truthy, including the string `"false"`. Instead, always use == to compare the value from ENV:
>
> ```
> if ENV["PAYMENTS_DISBLED"] == "true"
>   give_free_order
> end
> ```

Storing configuration keys and values in files means we avoid having to document what variables a developer must set and how to get the right value. Using dotenv means that our app can still access its runtime information from ENV, so our code won't be littered with checks for the Rails environment.

Since our development and test runtime configuration values aren't actual secrets, we can safely check them into version control. We also won't allow dotenv to run in production, so there's no chance of files containing secrets creeping into our app and being used.

This also has the added benefit of pushing more consistency into our developer workflow. There's really no reason developers should have different Postgres configurations, and putting the credentials inside files checked into version control makes being consistent much easier.

First, we'll install dotenv by adding `dotenv-rails` it to our `Gemfile`:

```
# Gemfile

source "https://rubygems.org"

ruby "3.2.2"

# All runtime config comes from the UNIX environment
# but we use dotenv to store that in files for
# development and testing
gem "dotenv-rails", groups: [:development, :test]

# Bundle edge Rails instead: gem "rails", github: "rails/rail...
gem "rails", "~> 7.1.2"
```

Notice how we've preceded it with a comment explaining its purpose? This is a good practice to document why gems are there and what they do. Ruby gems don't have a great history of self-explanatory naming, so taking a few seconds to document what a gem is for will help everyone in the future when they need to understand the app. Rails 7 uses this convention and you should, too.

We can now install dotenv with Bundler:

```
> bundle install
«lots of output»
```

When Bundler loads the dotenv-rails gem, the gem activates itself automatically. There's no further action we need to take for our app to use it (other than creating the files containing the environment variables). Because we've specified it only in the :development and :test group, it *won't* be used in production.

The last step is to create our initial .env.development and .env.test files. All they need to specify right now are the database credentials. If you followed the Docker-based setup on page 445, the Postgres we are using has a username and password of "postgres", runs on port 5432, and is available on the host named db. We also follow Rails' convention for our database names (widgets_development and widgets_test).

Create .env.development as follows.

```
# .env.development
```

```
DATABASE_URL="
  postgres://postgres:postgres@db:5432/widgets_development"
```

Now create `.env.test` similarly:

```
# .env.test

DATABASE_URL=postgres://postgres:postgres@db:5432/widgets_test
```

Note if you are not using the Docker-based set up described in the Appendix on page 445, you'll need to use whatever credentials you used when setting up Postgres yourself. *Also* note that you don't need to quote this value—I'm doing that to avoid a long line extending off the edge of the page.

dotenv recognizes more files than just the two we've made. Three of them would be very dangerous to accidentally check into version control, so we're going to modify our local `.gitignore` file right now to make sure no one ever adds them.

The first file is named `.env`, and it's used in *all* environments. This leads to a lot of confusion, and in my experience it is better to have development and testing completely separated, even if that means some duplication in the two files. The second two files are called `.env.development.local` and `.env.test.local`. These two files override what's in `.env.development` and `.env.test`, respectively.

Convention dictates that these two `.local` files are used when you need an actual secret on your development machine, such as an AWS key to a development S3 bucket. Unlike our local database credentials, you don't want to check that into version control since they are actual secrets you want to keep protected.

Although we don't have any such secrets yet, ignoring `.env.development.local` and `.env.test.local` *now* will prevent mishaps in the future (and codify our decision to use those files for local secrets when and if needed).

We'll also follow the convention established in our `Gemfile` by putting comments in `.gitignore` about why files are being ignored.

```
# .gitignore


  # Ignore master key for decrypting credentials and more.
  /config/master.key
```

```
→
→ # The .env file is read for both dev and test
→ # and creates more problems than it solves, so
→ # we never ever want to use it
→ .env
→
→ # .env.*.local files are where we put actual
→ # secrets we need for dev and test, so
→ # we really don't want them in version control
→ .env.*.local
```

With that done, our Rails app should be able to start up, however any attempt to use it will generate an error because we have not set up our database. We could do that with `bin/rails db:setup`, but this would then require documenting for future developers and we'd rather maintain automation than documentation.

The place to do this is in `bin/setup`.

4.4 Automating Application Setup with `bin/setup`

> This section's code is in the folder 04-04/ of the sample code.

Rails provides a `bin/setup` script that is decent, but not perfect. We want our `bin/setup` to be a bit more user friendly, but we also want it to be idempotent, meaning it has the exact same effect every time it's run. Right now, that means it must blow away and recreate the database.

Many developers infrequently reset their local database. The problem with this is that your local database builds up cruft, which can inadvertently create dependencies with tests or local workflows, and this can lead to complicated and fragile setups just to get the app working locally.

Worse, you might use a copy of the production database to seed local development databases. This is a particularly unsustainable solution, since it puts potentially personal user information on your computer and becomes slower and slower to copy over time as the database size increases.

Instead we want to create a culture where the local development database is blown away regularly. This, becomes a forcing function to a) not depend on particular data in our database to do work, and b) motivate us to script any such data we *do* need in the `db/seeds.rb` file so that everyone can have the same setup.

The situation we want to create is that developers new to the app can pull it down from version control, set up Postgres, run `bin/setup`, and be good to go. We also want existing developers to get into the habit of doing this frequently. As the app gets more and more complex to set up, this script can automate all of that, and we don't need to worry about documentation going out of date.

Let's replace the Rails-provided `bin/setup` with one of our own. Remember, this script runs before any gems are installed, so we have to write it with only the Ruby standard library. This script also won't be something developers work on frequently, so our best approach is to make it explicit and procedural, free of clever DSLs or other complicated constructs.

We'll create a main method called `setup` that performs the actual setup steps. That will go at the top of the script. We'll also need to add the shebang line to indicate this is a Ruby script. We'll also require Ruby's `OptionParser` library, which we'll use to allow `-h` and `--help` to trigger a help message. Here's how this should look:

```ruby
# bin/setup

#!/usr/bin/env ruby

require "optparse"

def setup
  log "Installing gems"
  # Only do bundle install if the much-faster
  # bundle check indicates we need to
  system! "bundle check || bundle install"

  log "Dropping & recreating the development database"
  # Note that the very first time this runs, db:reset
  # will fail, but this failure is fixed by
  # doing a db:migrate
  system! "bin/rails db:reset || bin/rails db:migrate"

  log "Dropping & recreating the test database"
  # Setting the RAILS_ENV explicitly to be sure
  # we actually reset the test database
  system!({ "RAILS_ENV" => "test" }, "bin/rails db:reset")

  log "All set up."
  log ""
  log "To see commonly-needed commands, run:"
  log ""
  log "    bin/setup help"
  log ""
end
```

`log` and `system!` are not in the standard library, and we'll define them in a moment. `system!` executes a shell command (similar to the built-in `system` method) and `log` prints output (similar to `puts`).

Note how we've written this script. Because it's not something developers will edit frequently, we've written comments about why and how each command works so that if someone needs to go into it, they can quickly understand what's going on. And since these comments explain *why* and not *what*, they are unlikely to go out of date.

Comments like this are particularly useful for complicated scripting and setup. The fact that `bin/rails db:reset` will fail the first time it's run isn't obvious, and there's no sense forcing someone to search the web in a moment of stress as they navigate unfamiliar code.

Before we define `log` and `system!`, let's create a method called `help` that will print out help text (note that in Ruby, `$0` contains the name of the script being executed).

```
# bin/setup
    log "   bin/setup help"
    log ""
  end

→
→ def help
→   puts "Usage: #{$0}"
→   puts ""
→   puts "Installs gems, recreates dev database, and generally"
→   puts "prepares the app to be run locally"
→   puts ""
→   puts "Other useful commands:"
→   puts ""
→   puts "  bin/dev"
→   puts "     # run app locally"
→   puts ""
→   puts "  bin/ci"
→   puts "     # runs all tests and checks as CI would"
→   puts ""
→   puts "  bin/rails test"
→   puts "     # run non-system tests"
→   puts ""
→   puts "  bin/rails test:system"
→   puts "     # run system tests"
→   puts ""
→   puts "  bin/setup help"
→   puts "     # show this help"
```

```
↪    puts ""
↪  end
↪
↪  # start of helpers
```

We'll define bin/dev and bin/ci in the next section. We've documented bin/rails test and bin/rails test:system here to be helpful to new or inexperienced developers. They might not realize that bin/rails -T will produce a documented list of all rake tasks, and even if they did, it might not be clear which ones run the tests.

Next, let's create our two helper methods. First is log, which wraps puts but prepends a message to the user that bin/setup is where the message originated. This can be helpful when interpreting a lot of terminal output.

```
# bin/setup

  end

  # start of helpers
↪
↪ # It's helpful to know what messages came from this
↪ # script, so we'll use log instead of `puts`
↪ def log(message)
↪   puts "[ bin/setup ] #{message}"
↪ end
↪
↪ # end of helpers
```

Next, system! will defer to Kernel#system[3], but handle checking the return value and aborting if anything goes wrong. It will also log what it's doing explicitly.

```
# bin/setup

  end

  # start of helpers
↪
↪ # We don't want the setup method to have to do all this error
```

---

[3]https://ruby-doc.org/core-3.1.0/Kernel.html

```
→ # checking, and we also want to explicitly log what we are
→ # executing. Thus, we use this method instead of Kernel#system
→ def system!(*args)
→   log "Executing #{args}"
→   if system(*args)
→     log "#{args} succeeded"
→   else
→     log "#{args} failed"
→     abort
→   end
→ end

  # It's helpful to know what messages came from this
  # script, so we'll use log instead of `puts`
```

The last part of bin/setup is to actually call either setup or help, depending on what the user has asked for. We want our script to respond to -h and --help, as these are somewhat standard ways to ask a program what it does without doing anything. Ideally, our script will also produce an error if the user provides other flags that aren't known. This can be achieved with Ruby's OptionParser.

Lastly, we'll also respect bin/setup help as a way to get help, as this is often expected to work. We can check ARGV[0] to see if the user specified that. Here's how it all looks:

```
# bin/setup

  end

  # end of helpers
→
→ OptionParser.new do |parser|
→   parser.on("-h", "--help") do
→     help
→     exit
→   end
→ end.parse!
→
→ if ARGV[0] == "help"
→   help
→ elsif !ARGV[0].nil?
→   puts "Unknown argument: '#{ARGV[0]}'"
→   exit 1
```

```
→ else
→   setup
→ end
```

With that done, we want to make sure the file is executable (it should be, since Rails created it that way, but if you deleted the file before editing, it won't be):

```
> chmod +x bin/setup
```

And *now* we can run it to complete our setup:

```
> bin/setup
[ bin/setup ] Installing gems
[ bin/setup ] Executing ["bundle check || bundle install"]
The Gemfile's dependencies are satisfied
[ bin/setup ] ["bundle check || bundle install"] succeeded
[ bin/setup ] Dropping & recreating the development database
[ bin/setup ] Executing ["bin/rails db:reset || bin/rails db...
/root/widgets/db/schema.rb doesn't exist yet. Run `bin/rails...
Dropped database 'widgets_development'
Created database 'widgets_development'
[ bin/setup ] ["bin/rails db:reset || bin/rails db:migrate"]...
[ bin/setup ] Dropping & recreating the test database
[ bin/setup ] Executing [{"RAILS_ENV"=>"test"}, "bin/rails d...
Dropped database 'widgets_test'
Created database 'widgets_test'
[ bin/setup ] [{"RAILS_ENV"=>"test"}, "bin/rails db:reset"] ...
[ bin/setup ] All set up.
[ bin/setup ]
[ bin/setup ] To see commonly-needed commands, run:
[ bin/setup ]
[ bin/setup ]     bin/setup help
[ bin/setup ]
```

We can also see that bin/setup --help produces some useful help:

```
> bin/setup --help
Usage: bin/setup

Installs gems, recreates dev database, and generally
prepares the app to be run locally

Other useful commands:
```

45

```
bin/dev
    # run app locally

bin/ci
    # runs all tests and checks as CI would

bin/rails test
    # run non-system tests

bin/rails test:system
    # run system tests

bin/setup help
    # show this help
```

This file will stand in for any documentation about setting up the app. To keep it always working and up to date, it will also be used to set up the continuous integration environment. That way, if it breaks, we'll have to fix it.

Before that, we need to run the app locally.

4.5 Running the Application Locally with `bin/dev`

> This section's code is in the folder 04-05/ of the sample code.

Currently, we can run our Rails app like so:

```
> bin/rails server --binding=0.0.0.0
```

While this is easy enough to remember, our app will one day require more complex commands to run it locally. Following our pattern of using scripts instead of documentation, we'll create `bin/dev` to wrap `bin/rails server`.

We're calling it `bin/dev` (instead of, say, `bin/run`) for two reasons. First, Rails has somewhat standardized on `bin/dev` for situations where you have to run more than one process to run your app locally (and we'll need to do that in when we learn about background jobs on page 331). Secondly, *running* is something the app does in production as well, and this script *is not* for doing that. Calling it `bin/dev` makes it clear it's just for our local dev environment.

This will be a Bash script since it currently just needs to run one command. The first line indicates this to the operating system. We'll then call `set -e` to make sure the script fails if any command it calls fails. We'll also add some code to check for -h, --help, and help to show a brief help message. After that, we call bin/rails server.

```bash
# bin/dev

#!/usr/bin/env bash

set -e

if [ "${1}" = -h ]     || \
   [ "${1}" = --help ] || \
   [ "${1}" = help ]; then
  echo "Usage: ${0}"
  echo
  echo "Runs app for local development"
  exit
else
  if [ ! -z "${1}" ]; then
    echo "Unknown argument: '${1}'"
    exit 1
  fi
fi

# We must bind to 0.0.0.0 inside a
# Docker container or the port won't forward
bin/rails server --binding=0.0.0.0
```

Bash is weird. You are reading this right that the way to end an if statement is to use the word if spelled backward: fi. And yes, if we created a case statement, we would end it in esac. I wish I were making that up.

bin/dev will need to be executable:

```
> chmod +x bin/dev
```

Let's try it out:

```
> bin/dev
=> Booting Puma
=> Rails 7.1.1 application starting in development
=> Run `bin/rails server --help` for more startup options
Puma starting in single mode...
* Puma version: 6.4.0 (ruby 3.2.2-p53) ("The Eagle of Durango")
```

```
*  Min threads: 5
*  Max threads: 5
*  Environment: development
*          PID: 782
* Listening on http://0.0.0.0:3000
Use Ctrl-C to stop
```

Now, if you visit `http://localhost:9999` (this is where the app will be available if you followed the Docker-based setup), you should see your app as shown in the screenshot below.

Figure 4.2: App Running

If you can keep `bin/setup` and `bin/dev` maintained, you have a shot at a sustainable developer workflow, and this will be a boon to the team. Nothing demoralizes developers more than having a constantly broken dev environment that no one seems capable of fixing. And the bigger the team gets and the more important the app becomes, the harder it will be to justify taking precious developer time away to fix the development environment.

This leaves two things left: scripting all the app's quality checks and creating a production-ready logging configuration.

4.6 Putting Tests and Other Quality Checks in bin/ci

> This section's code is in the folder 04-06/ of the sample code.

In the output of bin/setup help, you saw a reference to bin/ci, which is what we'll create now. This script runs whatever tests and quality checks the app might need and is named ci for "continuous integration". Once this script is created, you should be able to configure your CI environment to use bin/setup and bin/ci as your entire check. This is also where you can run bin/setup twice in a row to make sure it's idempotent. This is the key to ensuring your bin/setup stays working, even if developers don't use it every day.

```
bin/setup  # perform the actual setup
bin/setup  # ensure setup is idempotent
bin/ci     # perform all checks
```

We already have bin/rails test and bin/rails test:system to run our application's tests. Beyond these, we want to automate some security vulnerability checks as well. Since we have not written any code yet, we should not have any security issues.

By setting up an automated check now, we make it much easier to avoid introducing known issues into the codebase in the future. This sort of policy-as-automation can be hugely impactful for keeping a team consistent in their approach to best-practices.

Brakeman[4] can perform audits on the code we write, and Bundler can audit our dependencies, though it requires the bundler-audit gem. Let's install that and Brakeman now.

```
# Gemfile

  # but we use dotenv to store that in files for
  # development and testing
  gem "dotenv-rails", groups: [:development, :test]
→
→ # Brakeman analyzes our code for security vulnerabilities
→ gem "brakeman"
→
→ # bundler-audit checks our dependencies for vulnerabilities
```

---
[4]https://brakemanscanner.org

```
→ gem "bundler-audit"

  # Bundle edge Rails instead: gem "rails", github: "rails/rail...
  gem "rails", "~> 7.1.2"
```

We'll install this via `bundle install`:

```
> bundle install
«lots of output»
```

Brakeman includes the brakeman command line app. bundler-audit allows us to run `bundle audit check --update` which will refresh the database of known vulnerabilities and then analyze our `Gemfile.lock` to see if we are running any vulnerable versions. Note that this only works if bundle-audit is installed in your system gems, but since we have installed it in the app's `Gemfile`, we have to use `bundle exec bundle audit check --update`. I know.

We'll put all this, plus our test invocations, into `bin/ci`. The order matters, however. We want the checks to be ordered based on how useful their feedback is to local development. There's no sense in analyzing our code for security issues using Brakeman if the code doesn't pass its tests.

Here's what `bin/ci` looks like (note the inclusion of similar logic from bin/dev to provide help on the command line):

```
# bin/ci

#!/usr/bin/env bash

set -e

if [ "${1}" = -h ]        || \
   [ "${1}" = --help ]    || \
   [ "${1}" = help ]; then
  echo "Usage: ${0}"
  echo
  echo "Runs all tests, quality, and security checks"
  exit
else
  if [ ! -z "${1}" ]; then
    echo "Unknown argument: '${1}'"
    exit 1
  fi
```

```
    fi

    echo "[ bin/ci ] Running unit tests"
    bin/rails test

    echo "[ bin/ci ] Running system tests"
    bin/rails test:system

    echo "[ bin/ci ] Analyzing code for security vulnerabilities."
    echo "[ bin/ci ] Output will be in tmp/brakeman.html, which"
    echo "[ bin/ci ] can be opened in your browser."
    bundle exec brakeman -q -o tmp/brakeman.html

    echo "[ bin/ci ] Analyzing Ruby gems for"
    echo "[ bin/ci ] security vulnerabilities"
    bundle exec bundle audit check --update

    echo "[ bin/ci ] Done"
```

Note again that we print a message for each step of the process and prepend those messages with [bin/ci] so that it's obvious where the messages came from. These messages also serve as documentation for why the commands exist.

We'll need to make this executable:

```
> chmod +x bin/ci
```

And, since we just created our app and have written no code, all the checks should pass:

```
> bin/ci
[ bin/ci ] Running unit tests
Running 0 tests in a single process (parallelization thresho...
Run options: --seed 57185

# Running:



Finished in 0.000210s, 0.0000 runs/s, 0.0000 assertions/s.
0 runs, 0 assertions, 0 failures, 0 errors, 0 skips
[ bin/ci ] Running system tests
Run options: --seed 19317
```

```
# Running:



Finished in 0.001059s, 0.0000 runs/s, 0.0000 assertions/s.
0 runs, 0 assertions, 0 failures, 0 errors, 0 skips
[ bin/ci ] Analyzing code for security vulnerabilities.
[ bin/ci ] Output will be in tmp/brakeman.html, which
[ bin/ci ] can be opened in your browser.
[ bin/ci ] Analyzing Ruby gems for
[ bin/ci ] security vulnerabilities
Download ruby-advisory-db ...
Cloning into '/root/.local/share/ruby-advisory-db'...
ruby-advisory-db:
  advisories:    827 advisories
  last updated: 2023-11-30 12:36:04 -0800
  commit:    d821bf162550302abd1fa1fe15007f3012b76f32
No vulnerabilities found
[ bin/ci ] Done
```

Note that the extremely verbose lecture from git above is a factor of my development environment and the way bundler-audit works (it does a `git clone` to get the latest security vulnerabilities). Like much of git's UI, this information is useless, confusing, and can be ignored.

The last thing is to get ready for production by changing how Rails does logging

4.7 Improving Production Logging with lograge

> This section's code is in the folder 04-07/ of the sample code.

Rails' application logs have colored text and appear on multiple lines. This might be nice for local development, but wreaks havoc with most log aggregation tools we may use in production to examine our application logs. Even if we download the files and grep them, we need each logged event to be on a single line on its own.

lograge[5] is a gem that provides this exact feature. It requires only a short initializer in `config/initializers` as configuration.

Let's install the gem first:

---

[5]https://github.com/roidrage/lograge

```
# Gemfile

  # bundler-audit checks our dependencies for vulnerabilities
  gem "bundler-audit"
→
→ # lograge changes Rails' logging to a more
→ # traditional one-line-per-event format
→ gem "lograge"

  # Bundle edge Rails instead: gem "rails", github: "rails/rail...
  gem "rails", "~> 7.1.2"
```

Install it:

```
> bundle install
«lots of output»
```

To enable lograge, we must set `config.lograge.enabled` to `true` inside a `Rails.application.configure` block. Most of the time, we only want lograge's formatting for production, but sometimes we might want it for local development. To make this work, we'll enable lograge if we *aren't* in the Rails development environment *or* if the environment variable `LOGRAGE_IN_DEVELOPMENT` is set to `"true"`.

This can all be done in `config/initializers/lograge.rb`, like so:

```
# config/initializers/lograge.rb

Rails.application.configure do
  if !Rails.env.development? ||
      ENV["LOGRAGE_IN_DEVELOPMENT"] == "true"
    config.lograge.enabled = true
  else
    config.lograge.enabled = false
  end
end
```

We should document this in `bin/setup`:

```
# bin/setup
```

```
    puts ""
    puts "  bin/dev"
    puts "    # run app locally"
→   puts ""
→   puts "  LOGRAGE_IN_DEVELOPMENT=true bin/dev"
→   puts "    # run app locally using"
→   puts "    # production-like logging"
→   puts ""
    puts ""
    puts "  bin/ci"
    puts "    # runs all tests and checks as CI would"
```

Now, if you restart your app setting LOGRAGE_IN_DEVELOPMENT to true, then go to localhost:9999, you should see the log message on one line (note it's truncated in this medium):

```
  => Booting Puma
  => Rails 7.1.1 application starting in development
  => Run `bin/rails server --help` for more startup options
  Puma starting in single mode...
  * Puma version: 6.4.0 (ruby 3.2.2-p53) ("The Eagle of Durango")
  *  Min threads: 5
  *  Max threads: 5
  *  Environment: development
  *          PID: 782
  * Listening on http://0.0.0.0:3000
  Use Ctrl-C to stop
→ method=GET path=/ format=html controller=Rails::WelcomeController...
```

Before we finish, we should update the app's README so it's consistent with everything we just did. Replace README.md with the following:

```
<!-- README.md -->

# Widgets - The App For Widgets

## Setup

1. Pull down the app from version control
2. Make sure you have Postgres running
3. `bin/setup`

## Running The App
```

1. `bin/dev`

Tests and CI

1. `bin/ci` contains all the tests and checks for the app
2. `tmp/test.log` will use the production logging format
   not the development one.

Production

* All runtime configuration should be supplied
  in the UNIX environment
* Rails logging uses lograge. `bin/setup help`
  can tell you how to see this locally

This minimal README won't go out of date, because we now have three scripts that automate setup, running, and CI. Because we'll be using these scripts every day, they will *have* to be kept up to date, since when they break, we can't do our work.

If you can get your app into a production-like environment now, you should try to do so before writing too much code. You should also actually configure continuous integration to make sure all this automation is working for you. See the section "Continuous Integration" on page 405 for some tips and tricks on how to do this if you don't have much flexibility in your CI environment.

Up Next

That might've felt like a lot of steps, but it didn't take *too* long and this minor investment now will pay dividends later. Instead of an out-of-date README, we have scripts that we can keep up to date and can automate the setup and execution of our development environment. It works the same way for everyone (as well as in the CI environment), so it's one less thing to go wrong, break, or have to be maintained.

It's almost time to dive into the parts of Rails, but before we do that, I want to talk about what makes your app special: the business logic. In the next chapter I'll define what I mean by business logic, why it's critical to manage properly, and the one strategy you need to manage it: don't put it in your Active Records.

5
Business Logic (Does Not Go in Active Records)

Much of this book contains strategies and tactics for managing each part of Rails in a sustainable way. But there is one part of every app that Rails doesn't have a clear answer for: the *business logic*.

Business logic is the term I'm going to use to refer to the core logic of your app that is specific to whatever your app needs to do. If your app needs to send an email every time someone buys a product, but only if that product ships to Vermont, unless it ships from Kansas in which case you send a text message… this is business logic.

The biggest question Rails developers often ask is: where does the code for this sort of logic go? Rails doesn't have an explicit answer. There is no `ActiveBusinessLogic::Base` class to inherit from nor is there a `bin/rails generate business-logic` command to invoke.

This chapter outlines a simple strategy to answer this question: do not put business logic in Active Records. Instead, put each bit of logic in its own class, and put all those classes somewhere inside app/ like `app/services` or `app/businesslogic`.

The reasons don't have to do with moral purity or adherence to some object-oriented design principles. They instead relate directly to sustainability by minimizing the impact of bugs found in business logic. That said, Martin Fowler—who popularized the active record pattern upon which Active Record is based—does not recommend putting all business logic in active records, either.

We'll learn that business logic code is both more complex and less stable than other parts of the codebase. We'll then talk about *fan-in* which is a rough measure of the inter-relations between modules in our system. We'll bring those concepts together to understand how bugs in code used broadly in the app—such as Active Records—can have a more serious impact than bugs in isolated code.

So, let's jump in. What's so special about business logic?

5.1 Business Logic Makes Your App Special... and Complex

Rails is optimized for so-called *CRUD*, which stands for "Create, Read, Update, and Delete". In particular, this refers to the database: we create database records, read them back out, update them, and sometimes delete them.

Of course, not every operation our app needs to perform can be thought of as manipulating a database table's contents. Even when an operation requires making changes to multiple database tables, there is often other logic that has to happen, such as conditional updates, data formatting and manipulation, or API calls to third parties.

This logic can often be complex, because it must bring together all sorts of operations and conditions to achieve the result that the domain requires it to achieve.

This sort of complexity is called *necessary complexity* (or *essential* complexity) because it can't be avoided. Our app has to meet certain requirements, even if they are highly complex. Managing this complexity is one of the toughest things to do as an app grows.

5.1.1 Business Logic is a Magnet for Complexity

While our code has to implement the necessary complexity, it can often be even more complex due to our decisions about how the logic gets implemented. For example, we may choose to manage user accounts in another application and make API calls to it. We didn't *have* to do that, and our domain doesn't require it, but it might be just the way we ended up building it. This kind of complexity is called *accidental* or *unnecessary* complexity.

We can never avoid *all* accidental complexity, but the distinction to necessary complexity is important, because we do have at least limited control over accidental complexity. The better we manage that, the better able we are to manage the code to implement the necessarily complex logic of our app's domain.

What this means is that the code for our business logic is going to be more complex than other code in our app. It tends to be a magnet for complexity, because it usually contains the necessarily complex details of the domain as well as whatever accidentally complexity that goes along with it.

To make matters worse, business logic also tends to change frequently.

5.1.2 Business Logic Experiences Churn

It's uncommon for us to build an app and then be done with it. At best, the way we build apps tends to be iterative, where we refine the implementation using feedback cycles to narrow in on the best implementation. Software is notoriously hard to specify, so this feedback cycle tends to work the best. And that means changes, usually in the business logic. Changes are often called *churn*, and areas of the app that require frequent changes have *high churn*.

Churn doesn't necessarily stop after we deliver the first version of the app. We might continue to refine it, as we learn more about the intricacies of the problem domain, or the world around might change, requiring the app to keep up.

This means that the part of our app that is special to our domain has high complexity and high churn. *That* means it's a haven for bugs.

North Carolina State University researcher Nachiappan Nagappan, along with Microsoft employee Richard Ball demonstrated this relationship in their paper "Use of Relative Code Churn Measures to Predict System Defect Density"[1], in which they concluded:

> Increase in relative code churn measures is accompanied by an increase in system defect density [number of bugs per line of code]

Hold this thought for a moment while we learn about another concept in software engineering called *fan-in*.

5.2 Bugs in Commonly-Used Classes Have Wide Effects

Let's talk about the inter-dependence of pieces of code. Some methods are called in only one place in the application, while others are called in multiple places.

Consider a controller method. In most Rails apps, there is only one way a controller method gets called: when an HTTP request is issued to a specific resource with a specific method. For example, we might issue an HTTP GET to the URL /widgets. That will invoke the index method of the WidgetsController.

Now consider the method find on User. *This* method gets called in *many* more places. In applications that have authentication, it's possible that User.find is called on almost every request.

Thus, if there's a problem with User.find, most of the app could be affected. On the other hand, a problem in the index method of WidgetsController will only affect a small part of the app.

We can also look at this concept at the class level. Suppose User instances are part of most pieces of code, but we have another model called WidgetFaxOrder that is used in only a few places. Again, it stands to

---

[1] https://www.st.cs.uni-saarland.de/edu/recommendation-systems/papers/ICSE05Churn.pdf

reason that bugs in User will have wider effects compared to bugs in WidgetFaxOrder.

While there are certain other confounding factors (perhaps WidgetFaxOrder is responsible for most of our revenue), this lens of class dependencies is a useful one.

The concepts here are called *fan-out* and *fan-in*. Fan-out is the degree to which one method or class calls into other methods or classes. Fan-in is what I just described above and is the inverse: the degree to which a method or class is *called* by others.

What this means is that bugs in classes or methods with a high fan-in—classes used widely throughout the system—can have a much broader impact on the overall system than bugs in classes with a low fan-in.

Consider the system diagrammed in the figure below. We can see that WidgetFaxOrder has a low fan-in, while Widget has a high one. WidgetFaxOrder has only one incoming "uses" arrow pointing to it. Widget has two incoming "uses" arrows, but is also related via Active Record to two other classes.

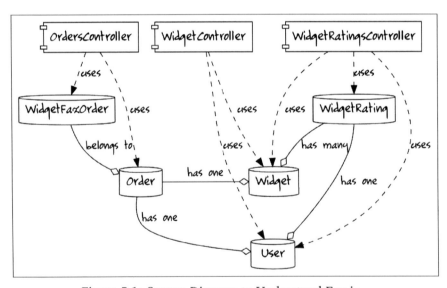

Figure 5.1: System Diagram to Understand Fan-in

Consider a bug in WidgetFaxOrder. The figure "Bug Effects of a Low Fan-in Module" on the next page outlines the effected components. This shows that because WidgetFaxOrder has a bug, it's possible that OrdersController is also buggy, since it relies on WidgetFaxOrder. The diagram also shows that it's highly unlikely that any of the rest of the system is affected, because those parts don't call into WidgetFaxOrder or any class that does. Thus, we are seeing a worst case scenario for a bug in WidgetFaxOrder.

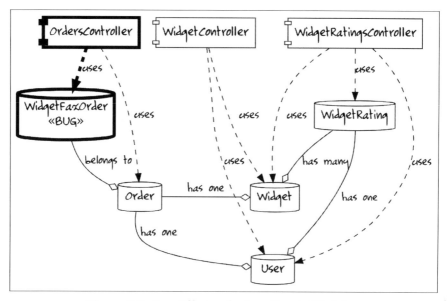

Figure 5.2: Bug Effects of a Low Fan-in Module

Now consider if instead `Widget` has a bug. The figure "Bug Effects of a High Fan-in Module" on the next page shows how a broken `Widget` class could have serious effects throughout the system in the worst case. Because it's used directly by two controllers and possibly indirectly by another through the Active Record relations, the potential for the Widget class to cause a broad problem is much higher than for `WidgetFaxOrder`.

It might seem like you could gain a better understanding of this problem by looking at the method level, but in an even moderately complex system, this is hard to do. The system diagrammed here is vastly simplified.

What this tells me is that the classes that are the most central to the app have the highest potential to cause serious problems. Thus it is important to make sure those classes are working well to prevent these problems.

A great way to do that is to minimize the complexity of those classes as well as to minimize their churn. Do you see where I'm going?

5.3 Business Logic in Active Records Puts Churn and Complexity in Critical Classes

We know that the code that implements business logic is among the most complex code in the app. We know that it's going to have high churn. We know that these two factors mean that business logic code is more likely to have bugs. And we also know that bugs in classes widely used throughout the app can cause more serious systemic problems.

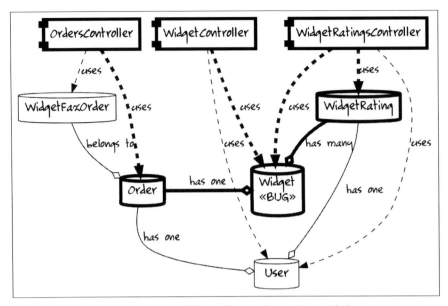

Figure 5.3: Bug Effects of a High Fan-in Module

So why would we put the code most likely to have bugs in the classes most widely used in the system? Wouldn't it be extremely wise to keep the complexity and churn on high fan-in classes—classes used in many places—as low as possible?

If the classes most commonly used throughout the system were very stable, and not complex, we minimize the chances of system-wide bugs caused by one class. If we place the most complex and unstable logic in isolated classes, we minimize the damage that can be done when those classes have bugs, which they surely will.

Let's revise the system diagram to show business logic functions on the Active Records. This will allow us to compare two systems: one in which we place all business logic on the Active Records themselves, and another where that logic is placed on isolated classes.

Suppose that the app shown in the diagram has these features:

- Purchase a widget
- Purchase a widget by fax
- Search for a widget
- Show a widget
- Rate a widget
- Suggest a widget rated similar to another widget you rated highly

I've added method names to the Active Records where these might go in the figure "System with Logic on Active Records" on the next page. You might put these methods on different classes or name them differently, but this should look pretty reasonable for an architecture that places business logic on the Active Records.

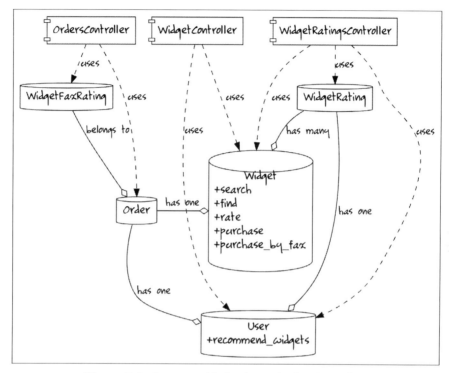

Figure 5.4: System with Logic on Active Records

Now consider an alternative. Suppose that each bit of business logic had its own class apart from the Active Records. These classes accept Active Records as arguments and use the Active Records for database access, but they have all the logic themselves. They form a *service layer* between the controllers and the database. We can see this in the figure below.

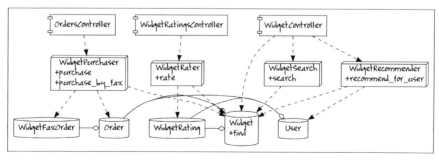

Figure 5.5: System with Business Logic Separated

Granted, there are more classes, so this diagram has more paths and seems more complex, but look at the fan-in of our newly-introduced service layer (the classes in 3-D boxes). All of them have low fan-in. This means that a bug in those classes is likely to be contained. And because those classes are the ones with the business logic—by definition the code likely to contain the most bugs—the effect of those bugs is minimized.

And *this* is why you should not put business logic in your Active Records. There's no escaping a system in which a small number of Active Records are central to the functionality of the app. But we can minimize the damage that can be caused by making those Active Records stable and simple. And to do that, we simply don't put logic on them at all.

There are some nice knock-on effects of this technique as well. The business logic tends to be in isolated classes that embody a domain concept. In our hypothetical system above, one could imagine that `WidgetPurchaser` encapsulates all the logic about purchasing a widget, while `WidgetRecommender` holds the logic about how we recommend widgets.

Both use `Widget` and `User` classes, which don't represent any particular domain concept beyond the attributes we wish to store in the database. And, as the app grows in size and features, as we get more and more domain concepts which require code, the `Widget` and `User` classes won't grow proportionally. Neither will `WidgetRecommender` nor `WidgetPurchaser`. Instead, we'll have new classes to represent those concepts.

In the end, you'll have a system where churn is isolated to a small number of classes, depended-upon by a few number of classes. This makes changes safer, more reliable, and easier to do. That's sustainable.

But don't take my word for it. Martin Fowler, the person who coined and first described the active record pattern that was inspiration for this part of Rails encourages this as well, when your application is complex.

5.4 Active Records Were Never Intended to Hold All the Business Logic

You may think that since Rails includes an implementation of the active record *pattern*, and that pattern is loosely defined as an object that adds domain logic to database data, we should follow the pattern the Rails Way and put our logic on our Active Records.

Let's set aside that this is an appeal to authority and let's also set aside that 99% of Active Record's documentation and 100% of its API are about database access. Is this actually what Martin Fowler, the author of *Patterns of Enterprise Application Architecture*, intended? No.

Early in the book, Fowler talks about business logic:

> Many designers, including me, like to divide "business logic" into two kinds: "domain logic," having to do purely with the problem domain (such as strategies for calculating revenue recognition on a contract), and "application logic," having to do with application responsibilities... sometimes referred to as "workflow logic".

Later, when talking about the active record pattern, he is clear that the logic you'd couple to your database schema is *domain* logic only:

> Each Active Record is responsible for saving and loading to the database and also for any domain logic that acts on the data.

"Domain logic that acts on the data" is certainly a subset of your application's business logic. For one, it doesn't include application logic, as defined by Fowler. Secondly, it doesn't include domain logic that doesn't "act on data". Fowler goes on to clarify this point:

> Active Record is a good choice for domain logic that isn't too complex, such as creates, reads, updates, and deletes. Derivations and validations based on a single record work well in this structure... If your business logic is complex, you'll soon want to use your object's direct relationships, collections, inheritance, and so forth. These don't map easily onto Active Record, and adding them piecemeal gets very messy.

I have never worked on an application that was so simple it could keep all of its logic in the Active Records. But I have definitely worked on applications where application logic and database-agnostic domain logic were crammed into the Active Records. It was not sustainable.

I mention this to really underscore that it's not just me telling you not to put all your business logic in Active Records. The guy that came up with it also doesn't think you should do that.

OK, let's see an example of some code that doesn't put business logic in the Active Records.

5.5 Example Design of a Feature

Suppose we are building a feature to edit widgets. Here is a rough outline of the requirements around how it should work:

1. A user views a form where they can edit a widget's metadata.
2. The user submits the form with a validation error.
3. The form is re-rendered showing their errors.
4. The user corrects the error and submits the edit again.
5. The system then updates the database.

6. When the widget is updated, two things have to happen:
   1. Depending on the widget's manufacturer, we need to notify an admin to approve of the changes
   2. If the widget is of a particular type, we must update an inventory table used for reporting.
7. The user sees a result screen.
8. Eventually, an email is sent to the right person.

This is not an uncommon amount of complexity. We will have to write a bit of code to make this work, and it's necessarily going to be in several places. A controller will need to receive the HTTP request, a view will need to render the form, a model must help with validation, a mailer will need to be created for the emails we'll send and somewhere in there we have a bit of our own logic.

The figure below shows the classes and files that would be involved in this feature. `WidgetEditingService` is probably sticking out to you.

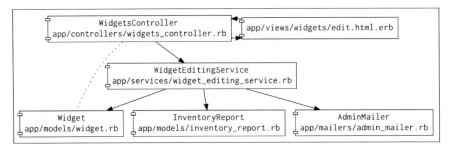

Figure 5.6: Class Design of Feature

Here's what that class might look like:

```
class WidgetEditingService
  def edit_widget(widget, widget_params)
    widget.update(widget_params)

    if widget.valid?
      # create the InventoryReport
      # check the manufacturer to see who to notify
      # trigger the AdminMailer to notify the right person
    end

    widget
  end
end
```

The code in the other classes would be more or less idiomatic Rails code you are used to.

Here's `WidgetsController`:

```ruby
class WidgetsController < ApplicationController
  def edit
    @widget = Widget.find(params[:id])
  end

  def update
    widget  = Widget.find(params[:id])
    @widget = WidgetEditingService.new.edit_widget(
                widget, widget_params
              )
    if @widget.valid?
      redirect_to widgets_path
    else
      render :edit, status: :unprocessable_entity
    end
  end
private
  def widget_params
    params.require(:widget).permit(:name, :status, :type)
  end
end
```

`Widget` will have a few validations:

```ruby
class Widget < ApplicationRecord
  validates :name, presence: true
end
```

`InventoryReport` is almost nothing:

```ruby
class InventoryReport < ApplicationRecord
end
```

`AdminMailer` has methods that just render mail:

```ruby
class AdminMailer < ApplicationMailer
  def edited_widget(widget)
    @widget = widget
  end

  def edited_widget_for_supervisor(widget)
    @widget = widget
  end
end
```

Note that just about everything about editing a widget is in `WidgetEditingService` (which also means that the test of this class will almost totally specify the business process in one place). `widget_params` and the validations in `Widget` *do* constitute a form of business logic, but to co-locate those in `WidgetEditingService` would be giving up a *lot*. There's a huge benefit to using strong parameters and Rails' validations. So we do!

Let's see how this survives a somewhat radical change. Suppose that the logic around choosing who to notify and updating the inventory record are becoming too slow, and we decide to execute that logic in a background job—the user editing the widget doesn't really care about this part anyway.

The figure below shows the minimal change we'd make. The highlighted classes are all that needs to change.

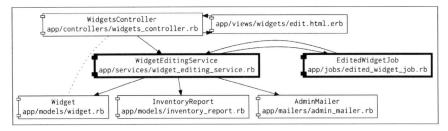

Figure 5.7: Design with a Background Job Added

We might imagine that `WidgetEditingService` is now made up of two methods, one that's called from the controller and now queues a background job and a new, second method that the background job will call that contains the logic we are backgrounding.

```ruby
class WidgetEditingService
  def edit_widget(widget, widget_params)
    widget.update(widget_params)
```

```
      if widget.valid?
        EditedWidgetJob.perform_later(widget.id)
      end

      widget
    end

    def post_widget_edit(widget)
      # create the InventoryReport
      # check the manufacturer to see who to notify
      # trigger the AdminMailer to notify whoever
      # should be notified
    end
  end
```

The `EditedWidgetJob` is just a way to run code in the background:

```
class EditedWidgetJob < ApplicationJob
  def perform(widget_id)
    widget = Widget.find(widget_id)
    WidgetEditingService.new.post_widget_edit(widget)
  end
end
```

As you can see, we're putting only the code in the background job that *has* to be there. The background job is given an ID and must trigger logic. And that's all it's doing.

I'm not going to claim this is beautiful code. I'm not going to claim this adheres to object-oriented design principles… whatever those are. I'm also not going to claim this is how DHH would do it.

What I will claim is that this approach allows you to get a *ton* of value out of Rails, while also allowing you to consolidate and organize your business logic however you like. And this will keep that logic from getting intertwined with HTTP requests, email, databases, and anything else that's provided by Rails. And *this* will help greatly with sustainability.

Do note that the "service layer" a) can be called something else, and b) can be designed any way you like yet still reap these benefits. While I would encourage you to write boring procedural code as I have done (and I'll make the case for it in "Business Logic Class Design" on page 241), you can use any design you like.

Up Next

This will be helpful context about what's to come. Even when isolating business logic in standalone classes, there's still gonna be a fair bit of code elsewhere in the app. A lot of it ends up where we're about to head: the view. And the first view of your app that anyone ever sees is the URL, so we'll begin our deep-dive into Rails with routes.

PART
II
———

deep dive into rails

6

Routes and URLs

Routes serve two purposes. Their primary purpose is to connect the view to the controller layer. Routes let you know what code will be triggered when an HTTP request is made to a given URL. The second (and unfortunate) purpose of routes is as a user interface element. URLs have a tendency to show up directly in social media, search results, and even newspaper articles. This means that a user will see them. This means they matter.

It can be hard to design routes that serve both purposes. If your routes are designed first around aesthetic concerns, you will quickly have a sea of inconsistent and confusing URLs, and this will create a carrying cost on the team every time a new feature has to be added. But you also can't insist that your app is only available with conventional Rails routes. Imagine someone reading a podcast ad with a database ID in it!

The marketing department isn't the only source of complexity with your routes, however. The more routes you add and the more features your app supports, the harder it can be to keep the routes organized. If routes become messy, inconsistent, or hard to understand, it adds carrying costs with every new feature you want to implement.

Fortunately, with a bit of discipline and a few simple techniques, you can keep your routes file easy to navigate, easy to understand, and still provide the necessary human-friendly URLs if they are called for.

The five conventions that will help you are:

- Always use canonical routes that conform to Rails' defaults.
- Never configure a route in `config/routes.rb` that is not being used.
- User-friendly URLs should be added *in addition* to the canonical routes.
- Avoid custom actions in favor of creating new resources that use Rails' default actions.
- Use nested routes strategically.

Let's dig into each of these to learn how they help sustainability.

6.1 Always Use Canonical Routes that Conform to Rails' Defaults

> This section's code is in the folder `06-01/` of the sample code.

With just a single line of code, Rails sets up eight routes (seven actions) for a given resource.

```
resources :widgets
```

This simple declaration in `config/routes.rb` is the basis for a consistency that provides a lot of leverage. You get URL helpers to generate canonical URLs without string-building, you get a clear and easy to understand connection to your controllers, and there's some nice documentation available via `bin/rails routes`.

If the app's routes are made up entirely of calls to `resources`, it becomes easy to understand the app at a high level. Developers can begin each feature by identifying the right resource, and choosing which of the seven conventional actions need to be supported. It also means that looking at the URL of a browser is all you need to figure out what code is triggering the view you're seeing.

Even though it might not seem like a major architectural decision, sticking with Rails conventions for routing can reduce real friction during development. Let's make two routes: one will be conventional using `resources` and the other will diverge from this standard and use `get`.

The first route will be for showing the information about a given widget. We'll add the "widgets" resource to `config/routes.rb`:

```
# config/routes.rb

Rails.application.routes.draw do
→   resources :widgets
→

  # Reveal health status on /up that returns 200 if the app b...
  # Can be used by load balancers and uptime monitors to veri...
```

With just this one line, when we run `bin/rails routes` we get a glimpse of what Rails gives us:

```
> bin/rails routes -g widgets
       Prefix Verb   URI Pattern                  Controller#Ac...
      widgets GET    /widgets(.:format)           widgets#index
              POST   /widgets(.:format)           widgets#creat...
   new_widget GET    /widgets/new(.:format)       widgets#new
  edit_widget GET    /widgets/:id/edit(.:format)  widgets#edit
       widget GET    /widgets/:id(.:format)       widgets#show
              PATCH  /widgets/:id(.:format)       widgets#updat...
              PUT    /widgets/:id(.:format)       widgets#updat...
              DELETE /widgets/:id(.:format)       widgets#destr...
```

This has set up the eight different routes and also created some URL helpers. The value under "Prefix" is what we use with either _path or _url to generate routes without string-building. The helpers that take arguments (such as widget_path) can also accept an Active Model instead of an ID. Those helpers will intelligently figure out how to build the URL for us.

Before we make the second route, let's fill in the controller and view here just to have something working. Since we don't have any database tables, we'll use the Ruby standard library's OpenStruct class to make a stand-in widget. The code below should be in app/controllers/widgets_controller.rb. Note that the OpenStruct used in the show method creates an object that responds to id, name, and manufacturer_id.

```ruby
# app/controllers/widgets_controller.rb

class WidgetsController < ApplicationController
  def show
    @widget = OpenStruct.new(id: params[:id],
                             manufacturer_id: rand(100),
                             name: "Widget #{params[:id]}")
  end
end
```

The default behavior of our show method is to render the template in app/views/widgets/show.html.erb, so we'll make a barebones version of that.

```erb
<%# app/views/widgets/show.html.erb %>

<h1><%= @widget.name %></h1>
<h2>ID #<%= @widget.id %></h2>
```

See the screenshot "Initial Widget 'show' page" below for what this looks like[1].

Now, let's create a route for the manufacturer's page, but use get instead of resources. This will illustrate the difference in the approaches.

We'll add the route to `config/routes.rb`:

```
# config/routes.rb


    # Defines the root path route ("/")
    # root "posts#index"
→   get "manufacturer/:id", to: "manufacturers#show"
  end
```

Figure 6.1: Initial Widget 'show' page

We can already start to smell a problem when we look at `bin/rails routes`.

```
> bin/rails routes -g manufacturers
Prefix Verb URI Pattern                  Controller#Action
       GET  /manufacturer/:id(.:format)  manufacturers#show
```

Whereas our widgets resource had helpers defined for us, using get doesn't do that. This means that if we have to create a URL for our manufacturer, we either need to create our own implementations of `manufacturer_path` and `manufacturer_url`, or we have to build the URL ourselves, like so:

---

[1] Just don't forget to nominate me for a Webby.

```erb
<h1><%= @widget.name %></h1>
<h2>ID #<%= @widget.id %></h2>
<%= link_to "/manufacturers/#{ @widget.manufacturer_id }" do %>
  View Manufacturer
<% end %>
```

This might seem like only a minor inconsistency, but it can have a real carrying cost. If your routes file only has these two lines in it, you're already sending a message to developers that each new feature requires making unnecessary decisions about routing:

- Should they use the standard `resources` or should they make a custom route with `get`, `post`, etc.?
- Should they build URLs with string interpolation, or should they make their own helper in `app/helpers/application_helper.rb`, or should it go in `app/helpers/manufacturer_helper.rb`?
- Should they use `as:` to give the route a name to make the helper, and what should that name be?

There's just no benefit to hand-crafting routes like this. These are the sort of needless decisions Rails is designed to save us from having to make. And it won't end here. Rails provides a *lot* of ways to generate routes, and some developers, when they see two ways to do something, create a third.

Of course, using `resources` on its own isn't perfect. We've created inconsistency around our routes file, controllers, and views. The output of `bin/rails routes` shows eight routes that our app supports, but in reality, our app only responds to one of them.

6.2 Never Configure Routes That Aren't Being Used

> This section's code is in the folder 06-02/ of the sample code.

Running `bin/rails routes` on an app is a great way to get a sense of its size, scope, and purpose. If the output of that command lies—as ours currently does—it's not helpful. It creates confusion. More than that, it allows you to use a URL helper that will happily create a route that will never, ever work.

The solution is to use the optional `only:` parameter to `resources`. This parameter takes an array of actions that you intend to support.

Doing this ensures that if you try to create a route you don't support using a URL helper, you get a nice `NameError` (as opposed to a URL that will generate a 404). I mistype URL helpers all the time, and it's much nicer to find out about this mistake locally with a big error screen than to scratch my head wondering why I'm getting a 404 for a feature I *just* implemented.

A nice side-effect of explicitly listing your actions with `only:` is that `bin/rails routes` provides a clean and accurate overview of your app. It lists out the important nouns related to your app and what it does, and this can be a nice jumping-off point for building new features or bringing a new developer onto the team.

This might not seem like a big win for a small app, but remember, we're setting the groundwork for our app to grow. If you start off using `resources` and adopt the use of `only:` when your app gets larger, you now have needless inconsistency and confusion. You create another decision developers have to make when creating routes: Do I use `only:` or not?

The Rails Guide[2] even tells you to avoid creating non-existent routes if your app has a lot of them:

> If your application has many RESTful routes, using :only and :except to generate only the routes that you actually need can cut down on memory use and speed up the routing process.

The simplest way to solve this problem is to not create it in the first place. Let's fix our routes file now by changing the previous call to `resources` in `config/routes.rb` with this:

```
# config/routes.rb

Rails.application.routes.draw do
→   resources :widgets, only: [ :show ]


    # Reveal health status on /up that returns 200 if the app b...
```

Now, `bin/rails routes` is accurate.

```
> bin/rails routes -g widgets
Prefix Verb URI Pattern              Controller#Action
widget GET  /widgets/:id(.:format)   widgets#show
```

You might also be aware of `except:`, which does the opposite of `only:`. It tells Rails to create all of the standard routes *except* those listed. For example,

---
[2] https://guides.rubyonrails.org/routing.html

if we wanted all the standard routes except `destroy`, we could use `except: [ :destroy ]` in our call to `resources`.

This technique certainly achieves the goal of making the routes file accurate, but I find it confusing to have to work out negative logic in my head to arrive at the proper value. I would advise sticking with `only:` because it's much simpler to provide the correct value. It also means you only have a single technique for creating routes, which reduces the overhead needed to work on the app.

The routes in your app are primarily there for developers, and using canonical routes, explicitly listed, creates a consistency that the developers will benefit from. This works great until the marketing department wants to plaster a URL on a billboard. Sometimes, we need so-called *vanity URLs* that are more human-friendly than our standard Rails routes.

6.3 Vanity URLs Should Redirect to a Canonical Route

> This section's code is in the folder `06-03/` of the sample code.

Like it or not, URLs are public-facing, and so they are subject to the requirements of people outside the engineering team. Because they show up in search results, social media posts, and even podcast ads, we really do need a way to make human-friendly URLs. But, we don't want to create a ton of inconsistency with the canonical URLs created by `resources`.

The way to think about this is that the canonical URLs you create with `resources` are *for developers* and should serve the needs of the team and app so that all the various URLs can be created easily and correctly. If user-facing URLs are needed, those should be created *in addition* to the canonical URLs and, of course, only if you actually need them.

Let's suppose the marketing team is creating a big campaign about our widget collection, all based around the word "amazing". They are initially going to buy podcast ads that ask listeners to go to `example.com/amazing`. The marketing team wants that URL to show the list of available widgets.

We don't have that page yet, but we should *not* make the route `/amazing` be the canonical URL for that page. For consistency and simplicity, we want a canonical URL, which is `/widgets`. Because we already have the `resources` call for the `show` action, we'll modify the array we give to `only:` to include `:index`:

```
# config/routes.rb

  Rails.application.routes.draw do
→   resources :widgets, only: [ :show, :index ]
```

```
# Reveal health status on /up that returns 200 if the app b...
```

Just to get something working, we'll create a basic `index` method in `app/controllers/widgets_controller.rb` using OpenStruct again:

```
# app/controllers/widgets_controller.rb

                            manufacturer_id: rand(100),
                            name: "Widget #{params[:id]}")
    end
→   def index
→     @widgets = [
→       OpenStruct.new(id: 1, name: "Stembolt"),
→       OpenStruct.new(id: 2, name: "Flux Capacitor"),
→     ]
→   end
  end
```

Our `app/views/widgets/index.html.erb` can be pretty simple for now:

```
<%# app/views/widgets/index.html.erb %>

<h1>Our Widgets</h1>
<ul>
  <% @widgets.each do |widget| %>
    <li>
      <%= link_to widget.name, widget_path(widget.id) %>
    </li>
  <% end %>
</ul>
```

Everything works as expected as shown in the screenshot "Initial Widgets index page" on the next page.

This route was created for us, the developers. Any time we need to create a link to the widgets index page, we use `widgets_path`, which will create the url `/widgets`. *Now* we can create our custom URL for the marketing team.

To do that, we'll use the `redirect` method in `config/routes.rb`. We'll also use comments to set these new routes off from the canonical ones.

Our Widgets

- <u>Stembolt</u>
- <u>Flux Capacitor</u>

Figure 6.2: Initial Widgets index page

```
# config/routes.rb

    # Defines the root path route ("/")
    # root "posts#index"

    ####
    # Custom routes start here
    #
    # For each new custom route:
    #
    # * Be sure you have the canonical route declared above
    # * Add the new custom route below the existing ones
    # * Document why it's needed
    # * Explain anything else non-standard

    # Used in podcast ads for the 'amazing' campaign
    get "/amazing", to: redirect("/widgets")

  end
```

That's a lot of code and it's mostly comments! The first few lines indicate that we are in a special section of the routes file for vanity URLs, which I'm calling "custom routes" because that's a bit more inclusive of what we might need here. Next, we document our policy around creating these routes. It makes more sense to put the policy right in the file where it applies than hide it in a wiki or other external document.

Then, we use the `to: redirect(...)` parameter for the `get` method to implement the redirect, along with a comment about what it's for. Unfortunately, we can't directly use `widgets_path` inside the routes file, so we have to hard-code the route, but it's a minor duplication. In reality, our canonical routes aren't likely to change, so this should be OK.

If you *do* need to make a lot of custom routes, you could do something more sophisticated, like use route globbing to a custom controller that uses the URL helpers, but I would advise against this unless you really need it.

Note that `redirect(...)` will use an HTTP 301 to do the redirect. You can provide an additional parameter to get named `status:` that can override this HTTP status to use a 302 for example.

Once this route is set up, you should be able to navigate to `/amazing` and see your handiwork, just as in the screenshot below.

Our Widgets

- Stembolt
- Flux Capacitor

Figure 6.3: A Basic Vanity URL

You'll also notice that Rails made a URL helper for the custom route, so you can use `amazing_url` in a mailer view to put the custom route into an email or other external communications.

If, for whatever reason, it's really important that no redirects happen, you can always use get in the more conventional way:

```
# config/routes.rb

    # * Explain anything else non-standard

    # Used in podcast ads for the 'amazing' campaign
```

```
    get "/amazing", to: "widgets#index"

end
```

If you check that in your browser, you'll see the vanity URL render the widget index page without any redirects.

The key thing here is that every single route in the application has a canonical route, consistent with Rails' conventions. Our vanity URLs are created *in addition* to those routes. This consistency means that each time a new route is needed, you always use `resources` to create it in the normal Rails way. If you have a need for a vanity route, you *also* create that using `get` and `redirect(...)`.

Playing this technique forward a year or two from now, the routes file might be large, but it should be relatively well-organized. It will mostly be made up of a bunch of calls to `resources`, followed by that big comment block, and then any custom URLs you may have added over that time (along with up-to-date comments about what they are for).

Comments often get a bad rap, but the way they are used here is defensible and important. Routes are one of the most stable parts of the app (they might even outlive the app itself!). This means that comments about those routes are equally stable, meaning they won't get out of date. Because of that, we can take advantage of the proximity of these comments to the code they apply to. Don't underestimate how helpful it can be when a comment about a piece of code exists and is accurate.

The comments also serve to call out the inconsistency vanity URLs create. As you scroll through the routes file and come across a big, fat comment block, your mind will immediately think that something unusual is coming up. That's because it is!

Vanity URLs are a design challenge imposed on us by product stakeholders. But we developers can create our own design challenges with routes. Let's talk about one of them next, which is what happens when you feel the need for a custom action.

6.4 Don't Create Custom Actions, Create More Resources

> This section's code is in the folder `06-04/` of the sample code.

Suppose we want to allow users to give a widget a rating, say one to five stars. Let's suppose further that we store these ratings aggregated on the widget itself, using the fields current_rating and num_ratings[3].

This example is contrived to create the problem whose solution I want to discuss, but I'm sure you've encountered a similar situation where you have a new action to perform on an existing resource and it doesn't *quite* fit with one of the standard actions.

We know what parameters we need—a widget ID and the user's rating—but we don't know what route should receive them because it's not exactly clear what resource and what action are involved.

We could use the update action on a widget, triggered by a PATCH to the /widgets/1234 route. This would be mostly conventional, since a PATCH is "partial modification" to a resource. The problem arises if we have lots of different ways to update a widget. Our controller might get complicated since it would need to check what sort of update is actually happening:

```
def update
  if params[:widget][:rating].present?
    # update the rating
  else
    # do some other sort of update
  end
end
```

The more types of updates we have to a widget, the more complicated this becomes. Developers often seek to solve this problem by avoiding the generic update action and creating a more specific one. For example, we might implement update_rating in the WidgetsController, with a route like so:

```
resources :widgets, only: [ :show ] do
  post "update_rating"
end
```

This creates a decent URL *and* a route helper, but I don't recommend this approach. In my experience, this leads to a proliferation of custom actions,

---

[3]Yes, you can maintain a correct running average with just these two fields. If you'd like to work out exactly how to do that, the best way is to apply for some jobs in Silicon Valley where eventually some smug mid-level engineer will make you solve this on a whiteboard, then scoff at your inability to do so before quickly writing the answer he memorized prior to interviewing you.

where a scant number of resources start to have a growing set of custom actions in the routes and controllers.

When this happens, the process for making a new feature requires deciding on a custom action name for an existing resource, rather than considering what resource is really involved. It also further diverges the app's codebase from Rails' standards and doesn't provide much value in return.

Rails works best when you are *resource-focused*, not action-focused. When you think about common techniques around software design, many involve starting with a domain model, which is essentially the list of nouns that the app deals with. Rails intends these to be your resources.

Thus, you should reframe your process to one that is resource-focused, not action-focused. Doing so results in many different resources that all support the same small number of actions. Because your app is a web app, and because HTTP is—you guessed it—resource-based supporting a limited number of actions on any given resource, this creates consistency and transparency in your app's behavior.

It allows you to mentally translate URLs through routes to the controller without having to do a lot of lookups to see how things are wired together. As we'll talk about in the chapter on controllers on page 313, controllers are the boundary between HTTP and whatever makes your app special. Sticking with a resource-based approach with standard actions for routes and controllers reinforces that boundary and keeps your app's complexity out of the controllers.

So what do we do about our widget ratings problem? If we stop thinking about the action of "rating" and start thinking about the resource of "a widget's rating", the simplest thing to do is create a resource called `widget_rating`. When the user rates a widget, that creates a new instance of the `widget_rating` resource.

This is how that looks in `config/routes.rb`:

```
# config/routes.rb

  Rails.application.routes.draw do
    resources :widgets, only: [ :show, :index ]
→   resources :widget_ratings, only: [ :create ]


    # Reveal health status on /up that returns 200 if the app b...
```

This will assume the existence of a `create` method in `WidgetRatingsController`, so we can create that in `app/controllers/widget_ratings_controller.rb` like so:

```ruby
# app/controllers/widget_ratings_controller.rb

class WidgetRatingsController < ApplicationController
  def create
    if params[:widget_id]
      # find the widget
      # update its rating
      redirect_to widget_path(params[:widget_id]),
        notice: "Thanks for rating!"
    else
      head :bad_request
    end
  end
end
```

We don't need a view for this new action, but let's add the new flash message to the existing widget view in `app/views/widgets/show.html.erb`, along with a form to do the rating, so we can see it all working.

```erb
<%# app/views/widgets/show.html.erb %>

  <h1><%= @widget.name %></h1>
  <h2>ID #<%= @widget.id %></h2>
→ <% if flash[:notice].present? %>
→   <aside>
→     <%= flash[:notice] %>
→   </aside>
→ <% end %>
→ <section>
→   <h3>Rate This Widget</h3>
→   <ol>
→     <% (1..5).each do |rating| %>
→       <li>
→         <%= button_to rating,
→                       widget_ratings_path,
→                       params: { widget_id: @widget.id,
→                                 rating: rating } %>
→       </li>
→     <% end %>
→   </ol>
→ </section>
```

Notice how all the code still looks very Rails-like? Our controller has a canonical action, our routes file uses the most basic form of `resources`, and our view uses standard-looking Rails helpers. There is huge power in this as the app (and team) gets larger.

Don't worry (for now) that "widget ratings" isn't a database table. We'll talk about that more in the database chapter on page 213. Just know for now that this doesn't create a problem we can't easily handle.

As we did with custom routes, play this technique forward a few years. You'll have lots of resources, each an important name in the domain of your app, and each will have at most seven actions taken on them that map precisely to the HTTP verbs that trigger those actions.

You'll be able to go from URL to route to controller easily, even if your app has hundreds of routes! *That's* sustainability.

This brings us to the last issue around routing, which is nested routes.

6.5 Use Nested Routes Strategically

> This section's code is in the folder 06-05/ of the sample code.

The Rails Routing Guide[4] says:

> Resources should never be nested more than [one] level deep

This is for good reason, as it starts to blur the lines about what resource is actually being manipulated *and* it creates highly complex route helpers like `manufacturer_widget_order_url` that then take several positional parameters.

Nested routes do solve some problems, so you don't want to entirely avoid them. There are three main reasons to consider a nested route: sub-resource ownership, namespacing, and organizing content pages.

6.5.1 Create Sub-Resources Judiciously

A sub-resource is something properly owned by a parent resource. Using our widget rating example from the previous section, you might think that a widget "has many" ratings, and thus the proper URL for a widget's ratings would be `/widget/:id/ratings`.

You could create that route like so:

---
[4]https://guides.rubyonrails.org/routing.html

```
resources :widgets, only: [ :show ] do
  resources :ratings, only: [ :create ]
end
```

This design is making a very strong statement about how your domain is modeled. Consider that a route is creating a URI—Uniform Resource Identifier—for a resource in your system. A route like `/widget/:id/ratings` says that to identify a widget rating, you *must* have a widget. It means that a rating doesn't have any meaning outside of a specific widget. This might not be what you mean, and if you create this constraint in your system, it might be a problem later.

Consider a feature where a user wants to see all the ratings they've given to widgets. What would be the route to retrieve these? You couldn't use the existing `/widgets/:id/ratings` resource, because that requires a widget ID, and you want all ratings for a *user*.

If you made a new route like `/users/:id/widget_ratings`, you now have two routes to what sounds like the same conceptual resource. This will be confusing. Consider the names of the controllers Rails would use for these two routes: `RatingsController` and `WidgetRatingsController`. Which is the controller for widget ratings? What is a plain "rating"? This is confusing.

This comes back to routes as URIs and routes being for developers' use. If a rating can exist, be linked to, or otherwise used on its own, independent of any given widget, making ratings a sub-resource of widgets is wrong. This is because a sub-resource is creating an identifier for a rating that requires information (a widget's ID) that the domain does not require.

Of course, you might not actually know enough about the domain at the time you have to make your routes. Because of this lack of knowledge, making ratings its own resource (as we did initially) is the safer bet. While a URL like `/widget_ratings?widget_id=1234` might feel gross, it's much more likely to allow you to meet future needs without causing confusion than if you prematurely declare that a rating is always a sub-resource of a widget.

Remember, these URLs are for the developers, and aesthetics is not a primary concern in their design. They should be chosen for consistency and simplicity. If you really do need a nicer URL to locate a widget's rating, you can use the custom URL technique described above to do that. Just be clear about *why* you're doing that.

Another use for nested resources is to namespace parts of the application.

6.5.2 Namespacing Might (or Might Not) be an Architecture Smell

Namespacing in the context of routes is a technique to disambiguate resources that have the same name but are used in completely different contexts.

Perhaps our app needs a customer service interface to view, update, and delete widgets—the same resources accessed by users—but requires a totally different UI.

While you could complicate `WidgetsController` and its views to check to see if the user is a customer service agent, it's often cleaner to create two controllers and two sets of views.

While you could do something like `UserWidgetsController` and `CustomerServiceWidgetsController`, it's cleaner to use namespaces. We can assume `WidgetsController` is our default view for our users, and create a `CustomerService` namespace so that `CustomerService::WidgetsController` handles the view of widgets for customer service agents.

The `namespace` method available in `config/routes.rb` can set this up, like so:

```
# config/routes.rb

    # Defines the root path route ("/")
    # root "posts#index"

    namespace :customer_service do
      resources :widgets, only: [ :show, :update, :destroy ]
    end

    ####
    # Custom routes start here
    #
```

This will create canonical Rails-like routes, nested under `/customer_service`:

```
> bin/rails routes -g customer_service -E
--[ Route 1 ]------------------------------------------- ...
Prefix            | customer_service_widget
Verb              | GET
URI               | /customer_service/widgets/:id(.:format)
Controller#Action | customer_service/widgets#show
Source Location   | config/routes.rb:15
```

```
--[ Route 2 ]---------------------------------------...
Prefix            |
Verb              | PATCH
URI               | /customer_service/widgets/:id(.:format)
Controller#Action | customer_service/widgets#update
Source Location   | config/routes.rb:15
--[ Route 3 ]---------------------------------------...
Prefix            |
Verb              | PUT
URI               | /customer_service/widgets/:id(.:format)
Controller#Action | customer_service/widgets#update
Source Location   | config/routes.rb:15
--[ Route 4 ]---------------------------------------...
Prefix            |
Verb              | DELETE
URI               | /customer_service/widgets/:id(.:format)
Controller#Action | customer_service/widgets#destroy
Source Location   | config/routes.rb:15
```

You get nicely named URL helpers as well as a namespaced controller, in this case `CustomerService::WidgetsController`. The views are similarly expected to be in `app/views/customer_service/widgets`. As you get more and more resources under `customer_service`, your code is nicely separated.

If this is the outcome you want, namespacing is the proper technique. It should *not* be used for aesthetic reasons. Create custom URLs as previously discussed if you need that.

The only thing to watch out for is overuse. If you find yourself needing a lot of namespaces, this means that you have many disparate uses for your resources and *this* could indicate that your app is doing too many things and might benefit from being broken up. We'll talk about this exact problem in the appendix "Monoliths, Microservices, and Shared Databases" on page 453. For now, just keep an eye on your namespaces and if you start to see more than a couple of them, take a fresh look at your roadmap and architecture to see if you might need to make more apps that each do fewer things.

The last use for nested routes is similar to namespacing, but it's when you have a lot of non-interactive content pages.

6.6 Nested Routes Can Organize Content Pages

In addition to the main features of your web app, web sites that are accessible by the general public or a very wide audience often have non-interactive pages that serve up content. These could be pages like a privacy policy, a marketing landing page, or documentation.

Where possible, you should try to model these as resources, but doing so can often be awkward. For example, you could use `resource :privacy_policy, only: [ :show ]` to manage you privacy policy, using the singular `resource`, since you don't have many privacy policies. Confusingly, Rails wants this served from the `PrivacyPoliciesController`. It's even more difficult when you have landing pages for marketing that don't map naturally to a resource at all.

In these cases, it can be better to create a namespace for such pages and then have non-standard routes used simply as a way to serve up content. While some organizations might serve such content from a static web server or content management system, you may not have the ability to do this and might be served well by organizing these pages away from the core resources that make up your app.

Up Next

Bet you didn't think routing was such a deep topic! I want you to reflect on the lessons here, however. If you follow these guidelines, you really aren't using anything but the most basic features of the Rails router. That's a good thing! It means anyone can easily understand your routes, and even the most inexperienced developer can begin adding features. This is sustainable over many years.

And with this, let's move onto the next layer of the view: HTML templates.

7 HTML Templates

Now that we've learned about some sustainable routing practices let's move on to what is usually the bulk of the work in any Rails view: HTML templates.

HTML templates feel messy, even at small scale, and the way CSS and JavaScript interact with the view can be tricky to manage. And, even though you *can* de-couple HTML templates and manage their complexity with layouts and partials, it's not quite the same as managing Ruby code, so the entire endeavor often feels awkward at best.

This chapter will help you get a hold of this complexity. It boils down to these guidelines:

- Mark up all content and controls using semantic HTML; use `div` and `span` to solve layout and styling problems.
- Build templates around the controller's resource as a single instance variable.
- Extract shared components into partials.
- The View Components gem helps manage complex views far better than partials.
- ERB is fine.

Remember, these are guidelines. It's OK to "violate" these rules as long as you have a good reason and understand the reason for their existence.

Let's start with the HTML itself.

7.1 Use Semantic HTML

> This section's code is in the folder 07-01/ of the sample code.

HTML5 contains many tags and attributes to mark up whatever UI or content you need. Mozilla's reference[1] is something you should have bookmarked. It has everything you need to know about what tags exist and what they are for.

---

[1] https://developer.mozilla.org/en-US/docs/Web/HTML

The process you follow for building a UI should start by marking up all the content and controls with specific HTML elements appropriate to the purpose of the content or control. *Do not* choose HTML tags based on their appearance or other layout characteristics. *After* you have applied semantic tags, use `<div>` or `<span>` elements only to solve layout and styling problems. This two-step technique will make it much simpler to build views and also result in sustainable views that are easier to understand and change later.

Let's start with marking up the view with tags.

7.1.1 Build Views by Applying Meaningful Tags to Content

We have seen this technique in the book already. We created an index page to list all the widgets in the system. Regardless of how that page is ultimately supposed to appear, it had these elements:

- A header explaining what was on the page. We used an `<h1>` for this.
- A list of widgets that was not ordered. We used a `<ul>` for this.
- Each widget has a name and a link. We used an `<li>` for this as well as an `<a>` (as provided by Rails `link_to` helper).

While we can absolutely create the visual appearance we need with just `<div>`s, we used tags the way they were intended to create the initial version of our UI.

Doing this has three advantages:

- HTML code is easier to navigate when it uses tags appropriately. Opening up a view file to a sea of `div`s can be jarring, and code like that will be hard to understand and change.
- Semantic markup used to tag content and controls tends to be more stable, so your views' overall structure is unlikely to change, even in the face of drastic changes to look and feel.
- Assistive devices will provide their users a *much* better experience when tags are used appropriately.

The first two advantages speak directly to sustainability. When you can open up the code for a view and easily navigate it to find the parts you need to change or add, your job working on the app is easier. The decision-making process for dealing with the view is simpler when you begin by using semantic markup.

Semantic tags are also more stable. Our widget index page might go through many redesigns, but none of them will change the fact that an un-ordered list uses the `<ul>` tag. That means that tests that involve the UI can rely on this and thus be more stable.

The third advantage only tangentially helps with sustainability, mostly when someone decides to care about assistive devices. When that happens, semantically marked-up UIs will be a better experience and thus require less overall work to bridge any gaps in what you've done with what is needed for a great experience with assistive devices.

Even if no stakeholder decides to explicitly target assistive devices, I still do think it's important that we make our UIs work with them where we can. There are more people than you might think that don't use a traditional web browser, and if you can be inclusive to their needs with minimal to no effort, you should be.

There is a practical concern about when to use each tag, because not every piece of content or UI element will map exactly to an existing tag. You may have noticed when we added the flash message to our widget show page that I used the <aside> tag. That tag's explanation[2] is as follows:

> The HTML <aside> element represents a portion of a document whose content is only indirectly related to the document's main content.

That sounds like a flash message to me, but it might not to you. As you build your app, you should develop a set of conventions about how to choose the proper tags. Agreeing to not use <div> or <span> for semantic meaning will go a long way. Ensconcing these decisions in code also helps.

When you identify re-usable components, *that* is when to have the design discussion about which tags are appropriate, and the result of that discussion is the re-usable partial that gets extracted. We'll talk about that in the next section.

So, if we aren't using <div> or <span> to convey semantic meaning (since they cannot), what are they for? The answer is for styling.

7.1.2 Use <div> and <span> for Styling

Once our UI is laid out with semantic tags, thus providing a holder for each element, the next step is to actually style those views. In a subsequent chapter we'll talk about CSS, but to make the point about <div> and <span>, let's create a design problem we can't solve by styling the existing semantic tags.

Our widget show page is just semantic markup right now. Suppose our designer wants the rating section to look like "Rating UI Mockup" below.

When we try to style the view, we will eventually hit a wall preventing us from completely achieving this design without adding more tags. Let's see that in action.

---

[2]https://developer.mozilla.org/en-US/docs/Web/HTML/Element/aside

Figure 7.1: Rating UI Mockup

First, since we have a new element, we need to add that using a semantic tag before styling. We'll use a <p> tag at the bottom of the existing <section>:

```
<%# app/views/widgets/show.html.erb %>

        </li>
      <% end %>
    </ol>
→   <p>Your ratings help us be amazing!</p>
  </section>
```

To get the <h3> and the rating buttons all on one line, we'll float everything left. I'm going to use inline styles so that you can see exactly what styles are being applied (I do not recommend inline styles as a real approach).

First, we'll float the <h3> as well as adjust the margin and padding so it eventually lines up with the rating buttons.

```
<%# app/views/widgets/show.html.erb %>

      </aside>
    <% end %>
    <section>
→     <h3 style="float: left; margin: 0; padding-right: 1rem;">
→       Rate This Widget:
→     </h3>
      <ol>
        <% (1..5).each do |rating| %>
          <li>
```

Next, we need to remove the default styling from the <ol>

```erb
<%# app/views/widgets/show.html.erb %>

    <h3 style="float: left; margin: 0; padding-right: 1rem;">
      Rate This Widget:
    </h3>
→   <ol style="list-style: none; padding: 0; margin: 0">
      <% (1..5).each do |rating| %>
        <li>
          <%= button_to rating,
```

Finally, we'll float the <li> elements left:

```erb
<%# app/views/widgets/show.html.erb %>

    </h3>
    <ol style="list-style: none; padding: 0; margin: 0">
      <% (1..5).each do |rating| %>
→       <li style="float: left">
          <%= button_to rating,
                        widget_ratings_path,
                        params: { widget_id: @widget.id,
```

We can see the problem if we look at the page now, as shown in the screenshot below.

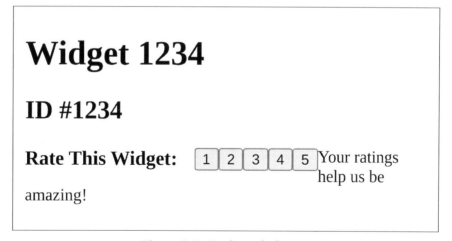

Figure 7.2: Uncleared Floats

We need to clear the floats before the <p> tag. One way to do this is to use a <br> tag. However, this is not what the <br> tag is for[3], since it is designed to help format text that requires line breaks, such as poetry or addresses.

We could put the `clear: all` style on the <p> tag itself, but this creates an odd situation with margin collapsing[4] that will be very confusing when applying other styles to it later[5].

Ideally, we could wrap the floated elements in a tag whose sole purpose is to clear those floats. Since this is a visual styling concern, there isn't such a tag. This is what a <div> is for!

A common way to do this is to create a CSS class with a name like "clear-fix" or "clear-floats" and apply that class to the <div> which we wrap around floated elements.

We can do that by adding this class to `application.css`:

```
/* app/assets/stylesheets/application.css */

 *= require_tree .
 *= require_self
 */
.clear-floats:after {
  content: "";
  display: table;
  clear: both;
}
```

Now, we can surround our code with `<div class="clear-floats">`. We'll start the tag right after the `<section>`:

```
<%# app/views/widgets/show.html.erb %>

    </aside>
  <% end %>
  <section>
    <div class="clear-floats">
      <h3 style="float: left; margin: 0; padding-right: 1rem;">
        Rate This Widget:
      </h3>
```

---

[3]https://developer.mozilla.org/en-US/docs/Web/HTML/Element/br
[4]https://developer.mozilla.org/en-US/docs/Web/CSS/CSS_Box_Model/Mastering_margin_collapsing
[5]Margin collapsing explains *a lot* about why CSS behaves counter to your intuition.

We'll close it after the ordered list:

```
<%# app/views/widgets/show.html.erb %>
        </li>
      <% end %>
    </ol>
→   </div>
    <p>Your ratings help us be amazing!</p>
  </section>
```

The problem is now fixed, as shown in the screenshot below.

Figure 7.3: Cleared Floats

We could certainly have done this by using a new <section> tag to contain the <h3> and the rating buttons, but there is no semantic reason to. If we didn't have the visual styling requirement, there would be no need to add an additional wrapper.

If you apply this technique broadly, what will happen is that every view you open that contains a <div> (or <span>), you can know with certainty that those tags are there to make some visual styling work. This is a strong cue to how the overall view works, which is the first thing you need to know in order to make changes.

It also provides a clear indication for assistive devices that the tag holds no meaning. If we'd used a <section> tag instead, assistive devices would tell their users that there is a new section, even though there really isn't.

This might feel a bit dense right now, but after the chapter on CSS, I hope everything will fall into place about how to apply visual styling in a sustainable way.

The main thing to take away here is that your view code should be treated with the same reverence and care as your Ruby code, even though the view code will be verbose and ugly. If you are disciplined with the HTML in your view code, it will be easier to work with.

There's more to say about our HTML templates, so we'll leave styling for now and talk about how to communicate data from the controllers to the templates.

7.2 Ideally, Expose One Instance Variable Per Action

> This section's code is in the folder 07-02/ of the sample code.

The way Rails makes data from controllers available to views is by copying the instance variables of the controller into the code for the view as instance variables with the same name. I highly suggest being OK with this design. We'll talk about object-orientation and controllers more in the chapter on controllers on page 313, but I don't think there is high value in circumventing this mechanism with something that feels "cleaner" or "more object-oriented".

That said, it's possible to create quite a mess with instance variables, so that's what I want to talk about here. The way to get the most of Rails' design without creating a problem is to adopt two conventions:

- Expose exactly one instance variable from any given action, ideally named for the resource or resources being manipulated by the route to that action. For example, the widget show page should only expose `@widget`.
- There are three exceptions: when a view requires access to reference data, like a list of country codes, when the view needs access to global context, like the currently logged-in user, or when there is UI state that is persisted across page refreshes, such as the currently selected tab in a tab navigation control.

If you follow the advice in the chapter "Routes and URLs" on page 73, these conventions are surprisingly easy to follow, but it does require doing a good job modeling your domain and resources.

The key situation to avoid is exposing multiple instance variables that collectively represent the resource rather than creating a single instance variable—and perhaps a new model class—to do so.

7.2.1 Name the Instance Variable After the Resource

As a reminder, my suggestion is to create routes based on resources that use the Rails conventional actions. This results in an application with many resources. Each controller would then expose a single instance variable named for that resource (for example `@widget` or `@widgets`).

The primary prerequisite of this guideline is that your resources be well-designed. Whatever information is needed to render a given view, the resource for that view must have access to all of it.

How you do this is a design decision with many subtleties, particularly around the so-called Law of Demeter[6], which warns against coupling domain concepts too tightly. Most developers interpret the Law of Demeter (for better of for worse) as avoiding nested method calls like `@widget.manufacturer.address.country`.

I would not have a huge problem with the *Guideline* of Demeter, but as a *Law*, I find it over-reaches, especially given how it is often interpreted. In many cases, it's perfectly fine—and often better—to dig into the object hierarchy for the data you need.

Let's add some code to our widget show page to see the exact problem created by the "single instance variable" approach and the Law of Demeter.

For the purposes of this example, we'll assume our domain model in the figure on the next page describes our domain, which is:

- A widget always has a manufacturer.
- A manufacturer can manufacture many widgets.
- A manufacturer always has an address.
- An address always a country.

Let's update `WidgetsController` so that our `OpenStruct`-based placeholder mimics this domain model.

We can nest OpenStructs for now to create a fake manufacturer. I promise this nastiness will go away when we create real database tables (though faking out the back-end for the sake of the front-end does have other benefits as we'll learn later).

```
# app/controllers/widgets_controller.rb

  class WidgetsController < ApplicationController
    def show
→     manufacturer = OpenStruct.new(
```

---

[6]https://en.wikipedia.org/wiki/Law_of_Demeter

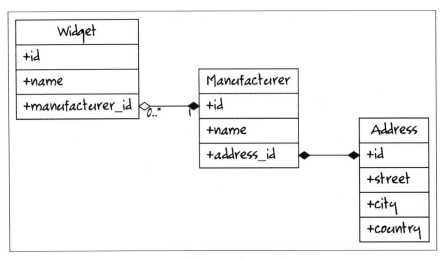

Figure 7.4: Widgets and Manufacturers

```
→        id: rand(100),
→        name: "Sector 7G",
→        address: OpenStruct.new(
→          id: rand(100),
→          country: "UK"
→        )
→      )
      @widget = OpenStruct.new(id: params[:id],
                               manufacturer_id: rand(100),
                               name: "Widget #{params[:id]}")
```

We can now use that in the OpenStruct we are returning as @widget:

```
# app/controllers/widgets_controller.rb

        )
      )
      @widget = OpenStruct.new(id: params[:id],
→                              manufacturer_id: manufacturer.id,
→                              manufacturer: manufacturer,
                               name: "Widget #{params[:id]}")
    end
    def index
```

Since this is available from the `@widget` we're exposing, we can add this to the view like so:

```
<%# app/views/widgets/show.html.erb %>

      <%= flash[:notice] %>
    </aside>
  <% end %>
→ <h3>
→   Built by <%= @widget.manufacturer.name %>
→   out of <%= @widget.manufacturer.address.country %>
→ </h3>
  <section>
    <div class="clear-floats">
    <h3 style="float: left; margin: 0; padding-right: 1rem;">
```

Set aside how gnarly our placeholder code is. When widgets and manufacturers become real models, that code will go away and be simpler, but the view will still look like this, at least if we do the simplest thing and navigate the relationships created by Active Record.

The first thing to understand is that the view's requirements couple the widget to its manufacturer's name and country by design. This is not a coupling created by us developers, but one that naturally occurs in the domain itself.

To me, this makes the code above perfectly fine, and I don't believe the Law of Demeter applies here.

For the sake of argument, however, let's say that we don't like this coupling. If we solve it by creating a new `@manufacturer` instance variable, we create a less sustainable solution. Our view would have code like this in it:

```
<h3>
  Built by <%= @manufacturer.name %>
  out of <%= @manufacturer.address.country %>
</h3>
```

This view is intended to show the widget's manufacturer's name and country. *This* implementation—that uses a second instance variable—means we cannot verify that the view is correct just by looking at the view code. We have to go into the controller to figure out how `@manufacturer` gets its value.

Even if we assume widgets and manufacturers are modeled correctly, we can't know if the correct manufacturer is being used in this view.

Using a second instance variable also creates a practical problem around consistency. Once code with multiple instance variables becomes prolific, developers now have to make a decision every single time they build a controller action: How many instance variables to expose and which ones should they be? This can be a hard question to answer.

The alternative is to modify the way we've modeled our widget. The widget show view's requirements are a big input into what a widget fundamentally *is*. So if a widget really is a thing that has a manufacturer name and country, it would not be unreasonable to model it like so:

```
@widget = OpenStruct.new(
  id: params[:id],
  name: "Widget #{params[:id]}",
  manufacturer_name: "Sector 7G",
  manufacturer_country: "UK",
)
```

Which would make our view code:

```
<h3>
  Built by <%= @widget.manufacturer_name %>
  out of <%= @widget.manufacturer_country %>
</h3>
```

Because the view is using a single instance variable, we know the view is showing the correct data—assuming the resource has been modeled correctly. We can't make that assumption with the multiple instance variable implementation.

This may feel like we've overloaded our Active Record with "view concerns". I would push back on this for three reasons. First, "view concerns" are a requirement to what your domain should actually be, so they should not be dismissed simply because they don't make sense in a relational data model. Second, when your app is made up of many more resources than database tables, you *won't* end up with tons of methods on your small set of core models.

Lastly, however, the various solutions to the problem of separating so-called view concerns mostly result in unsustainable code. Two common solutions are to create presenters (or view models)—classes that just encapsulate whatever the view needs—or to use decorators—classes that proxy what is needed for a view to the real Active Records.

Both of these approaches can mask over problems with domain modeling, especially given Ruby's highly dynamic nature. I've seen code that dynamically changes the methods available on a model depending on the context, and I can't think of a more confusing way to build an app:

```ruby
module WidgetDecorator
  def manufacturer_name
    manufacturer.name
  end

  def manufacturer_country
    manufacturer.address.country
  end
end

## app/controllers/widgets_controller.rb
def show
  @widget = Widget.find(params[:id]).include(WidgetDecorator)
end
```

This adds two methods to the `Widget` passed to the view. Figuring out how this works is not necessarily easy. The view code will appear to call `manufacturer_name` on a `Widget`, and figuring out where that method comes from requires following a circuitous route through the code. I would argue that if the user thinks about a widget as having a manufacturer name, but we don't model that explicitly in our code, we have not done a good job designing.

When controllers sometimes expose Active Records, sometimes mix in concerns, sometimes create presenters, and sometimes do something else, it becomes more difficult than necessary to design new views and features. Even if the team diligently documents how to make those decisions, documentation is rarely found or interpreted in the way intended. This mental overhead makes each new feature harder to deliver.

It's worth re-iterating that if two domain concepts are tightly coupled by design, having the code tightly couple them can actually be an advantage. Our original code that navigated from widget to manufacturer to address mimics the domain.

That being said, I mentioned three exceptions above.

7.2.2 Reference Data, Global Context, and UI State are Exceptions

Almost every Rails app has a method called `current_user` that exposes an object representing who is logged in. It's also common to need a list of reference data, such as country codes, in order to build a drop-down menu or other piece of UI. Lastly, it's common to need to persist UI state between requests, such as for a tabbed-navigation control. None of these make sense as part of an existing resource, because you'd end up with every single model providing access to this data.

These are the exceptions to the "one instance variable per view" guideline. You can certainly provide access to data like this in helpers, and `current_user` is a very common one. We'll talk about helpers in the next chapter, but too many helpers can create view code that is hard to understand. When a piece of view code *only* uses instance variables, it becomes very easy to trace back where those instance variables got their values: the controller.

We don't have any drop-downs in our app yet, but this is what it would look like to expose a list of country codes on a hypothetical manufacturer edit page:

```
class ManufacturersController < ApplicationController
  def edit
    @manufacturer = Manufacturer.find(params[:id])
    @country_codes = CountryCode.all
  end
end
```

Further, we might have a tabbed navigation on the page and need to know which tab is active *and* make that state persist by encoding it in the url, like `/widgets?tab=advanced`. The controller might look like so:

```
class WidgetsController < ApplicationController
  def show
    @tab = if params[:tab] == "advanced"
      :advanced
    else
      :basic
    end
    @widget = Widget.find(params[:id])
  end
end
```

If you end up needing access to country codes or UI state in many places, you can extract the lookup logic at the controller level. I'd still recommend passing this information to the view as an instance variable, for the reasons stated above: instance variables pop out and can only come from the controller. Helpers can come from, well, anywhere.

As your app takes shape, you may start to see patterns of data or markup common to some views. We'll talk about that in the next few sections.

7.3 Wrangling Partials for Simple View Re-use

> This section's code is in the folder 07-03/ of the sample code.

When your app's views are relatively self-contained and display data in a straightforward way, they are easily managed with ERB and helpers. There aren't many apps that don't have more complex needs that would benefit from the re-use of markup or logic from the view. Rails provides one way to do this, which is the use of partials.

We'll talk about partials in this chapter, since they are a lightweight, low-ceremony way to manage complexity. Partials aren't great when you have complex view logic. We'll talk about that in the next section.

7.3.1 Partials Allow Simple Code for Simple Re-use

For sharing markup with little or no logic, partials work great. They are easy to extract, easy to reference, and easy to manage.

Let's suppose our markup for rating a widget needs to be used on more than one page. To that end, let's extract it as partial so we can talk about the potential pitfalls you can run into.

First, we'll copy the ERB to its own file in app/views/widgets/, called _rating.html.erb:

```erb
<%# app/views/widgets/_rating.html.erb %>

<section>
  <div class="clear-floats">
    <h3 style="float: left; margin: 0; padding-right: 1rem;">
      Rate This Widget:
    </h3>
    <ol style="list-style: none; padding: 0; margin: 0">
      <% (1..5).each do |rating| %>
        <li style="float: left">
          <%= button_to rating,
```

```
                        widget_ratings_path,
                        params: {
                                widget_id: @widget.id,
                                rating: rating
                        }
        %>
      </li>
    <% end %>
   </ol>
  </div>
  <p>Your ratings help us be amazing!</p>
</section>
```

We can remove that markup from the widget show page and reference the partial:

```
<%# app/views/widgets/show.html.erb %>

  <h1><%= @widget.name %></h1>
  <h2>ID #<%= @widget.id %></h2>
  <% if flash[:notice].present? %>
    <aside>
      <%= flash[:notice] %>
    </aside>
  <% end %>

→ <%= render partial: "rating" %>
```

This works great, under certain conditions. I'm not showing the hypothetical other view that needs this, but it's not hard to imagine that that view won't expose @widget as an instance variable. If following the guidelines in the previous section, it definitely won't be. That means, this partial won't work, since it would try to call id on nil (the default value of any instance variable).

We need to make this partial more of a re-usable component.

7.3.2 Reference Only Locals in Partials

Partials can be given *locals*—variables declared when the partial is referenced that are only available to that partial. Let's do that, using a local named widget:

```erb
<%# app/views/widgets/show.html.erb %>

    </aside>
  <% end %>

→ <%= render partial: "rating", locals: { widget: @widget } %>
```

Then, in _rating.html.erb, we use widget instead of @widget:

```erb
<%# app/views/widgets/_rating.html.erb %>

          <%= button_to rating,
                        widget_ratings_path,
                        params: {
→                                 widget_id: widget.id,
                                  rating: rating
                                }
          %>
```

This results in a better system. If someone tries to use the partial without setting `widget`, they won't get an error about `nil`, or `NoMethodError`, but instead get an error saying that `widget` is not defined. This is a stronger clue that `widget` is required.

But, as of Rails 7.1, we can do even better by using *strict locals*

7.3.3 Partials Should Use Strict Locals

Rails 7.1 introduced a feature to partials called *strict locals*. What this feature allows you to do is declare the locals that are required by the partial. If someone attempts to use the partial without setting that local, Rails will produce a very clear error message: "missing local widgets".

This feature *also* generates an error for any un-declared local, meaning if someone mis-types the local and uses `widget`, Rails will produce an error message that this local is not accepted. This is a huge benefit for sustainable use of locals.

Let's do this right now in our _rating.html.erb:

```erb
<%# app/views/widgets/_rating.html.erb %>
```

```
→ <%# locals: (widget:) %>
  <section>
    <div class="clear-floats">
      <h3 style="float: left; margin: 0; padding-right: 1rem;">
```

You can see this in action by omitting the local in app/views/widgets/show.html.erb and reloading the page.

Note that this feature is implemented as a magic comment parsed with a regular expression. This means if you mis-type it, Rails will not realize you are intending to use strict locals and treat the syntax error as a comment. Two steps forward and one step back is still a step forward.

Strict locals provides another benefit when we need logic driven by optional parameters. Suppose we want to allow users of the new ratings component to omit the "Your ratings help us be amazing" call-to-action. Further suppose we don't want any existing users of this component to have to specify this— we want them to default to the current behavior without changing their call to render.

Strict locals allow default values for any declared local. No more using local_assigns.

7.3.4 Use Default Values for Strict Locals to Simplify Partial APIs

Without using strict locals, to achieve a default value for a local, you had to use local_assigns. Suppose our new local is going to be called show_cta, with a default value of true. To make this work, here is what you have to do if you *aren't* using strict locals:

```
<%
  if !local_assigns.key(:show_cta)
    show_cta = true
  end
%>
```

This is clunky. Strict locals allows setting a default value, like so:

```
<%# app/views/widgets/_rating.html.erb %>

→ <%# locals: (widget:, show_cta: true) %>
  <section>
```

```
<div class="clear-floats">
  <h3 style="float: left; margin: 0; padding-right: 1rem;">
```

Now, we can add the conditional logic without worrying about `local_assigns` or any other error-checking:

```
<%# app/views/widgets/_rating.html.erb %>

      <% end %>
    </ol>
  </div>
→ <% if show_cta %>
→   <p>Your ratings help us be amazing!</p>
→ <% end %>
</section>
```

Although our new bit of logic is relatively simple, you don't have to work on web apps very long before you end up having to build a complex bit of UI that has lots of different possible UI states. In this situation, partials become unwieldy, both in terms of implementation, but also for testing.

The only way to completely cover a complex bit of UI logic with tests is to use system tests. As we'll discuss later in the book, these are slow and brittle. Unfortunately, Rails doesn't provide anything other than partials and helpers to manage complex views.

This is why I'd recommend a third-party library for this case: View Components.

7.4 Use the View Component Library for Complex UI Logic

> This section's code is in the folder 07-04/ of the sample code.

Our widget rating component is pretty simple, and if how it is now is all it needs to be, partials work great. But suppose our widget rating component became more complex? What if ratings below 3 warranted a different visual design? What if admins looking at the page shouldn't see the rating controls? What if are running an A/B test on a different way of gathering ratings?

All of these hypothetical situations will result in complex logic in the ERB that requires management and testing. If you've ever had to do this, it can be difficult. You don't have a way to test it outside of a system test, and complex `if` statements inside a markup language creates a lot of friction.

View Component[7] is a library that can solve these problems in a Rails-like way. View Component can manage server-rendered HTML fragments with Ruby and ERB code together. A fragment of ERB is connected to a Ruby class, and the two are used to render HTML. View Component was developed at GitHub where it is widely used, and is otherwise popular and well-maintained. And, it's a small API that can be learned quickly.

Here's how you'd render a view component named `WidgetRatingComponent` in any ERB file:

```erb
<%= render(WidgetRatingComponent.new(widget: @widget)) %>
```

By default, the file `app/components/widget_rating_component.html.erb` is rendered in the context of an instance of `WidgetRatingComponent`, which is defined in `app/components/widget_rating_component.rb`. The result of that render is inserted into the ERB file, just like with a partial.

Let's see this in action by converting our widget rating component to use View Component.

7.4.1 Creating a View Component

First, we'll add the gem to our `Gemfile`:

```ruby
# Gemfile

  # lograge changes Rails' logging to a more
  # traditional one-line-per-event format
  gem "lograge"

  # View Component is used to manage
  # and test complex view logic
  gem "view_component"

  # Bundle edge Rails instead: gem "rails", github: "rails/rail...
  gem "rails", "~> 7.1.2"
```

We'll install it with `bundle install`:

---

[7] https://viewcomponent.org

```
> bundle install
«lots of output»
```

View Component comes with a generator to create a scaffold for us via bin/rails generate component. We'll use that to create our new component. It takes a required argument for the name of the component, and then any number of optional arguments that represent the parameters to pass to a constructor. We'll set those as the locals we used earlier: widget and show_cta:

```
> bin/rails generate component WidgetRating widget show_cta
      create    app/components/widget_rating_component.rb
      invoke  test_unit
      create    test/components/widget_rating_component_test...
      invoke  erb
      create    app/components/widget_rating_component.html....
```

This created a component Ruby class, an ERB template, and a test. We'll populate the ERB template first.

It's located in app/components/widget_rating_component.html.erb and should look pretty similar to the partial we extracted:

```erb
<%# app/components/widget_rating_component.html.erb %>

<section>
  <div class="clear-floats">
    <h3 style="float: left; margin: 0; padding-right: 1rem;">
      Rate This Widget:
    </h3>
    <ol style="list-style: none; padding: 0; margin: 0">
      <% (1..5).each do |rating| %>
        <li style="float: left">
          <%= button_to rating,
                        widget_ratings_path,
                        params: {
                                  widget_id: widget.id,
                                  rating: rating
                                }
          %>
        </li>
      <% end %>
    </ol>
  </div>
  <% if show_cta %>
```

```erb
    <p>
      Your ratings help us be amazing!
    </p>
  <% end %>
</section>
```

When using View Component, any method called from the ERB must be available from the component's class as an instance method. Thus, we'll need to define both `widget` and `show_cta` in the component class. Since we don't need any other logic for now, we can do that by declaring them both as `attr_readers` in app/components/widget_rating_component.rb. We'll also change the initializer to default `show_cta` to true:

```ruby
# app/components/widget_rating_component.rb

  # frozen_string_literal: true

  class WidgetRatingComponent < ViewComponent::Base
→   attr_reader :widget, :show_cta
→   def initialize(widget:, show_cta: true)
      @widget = widget
      @show_cta = show_cta
    end
```

Now, we can remove the partial and use the component. First, we'll delete app/views/widgets/_rating.html.erb:

```
> rm app/views/widgets/_rating.html.erb
```

Next, we'll change app/views/widgets/show.html.erb to use the component instead. We'll set `show_cta` to false to demonstrate that it's using the logic:

```erb
<%# app/views/widgets/show.html.erb %>

    </aside>
  <% end %>

→ <%= render(WidgetRatingComponent.new(widget: @widget,
→                                     show_cta: false)) %>
```

If you restart your server, you can see that the page is working (and the CTA is omitted):

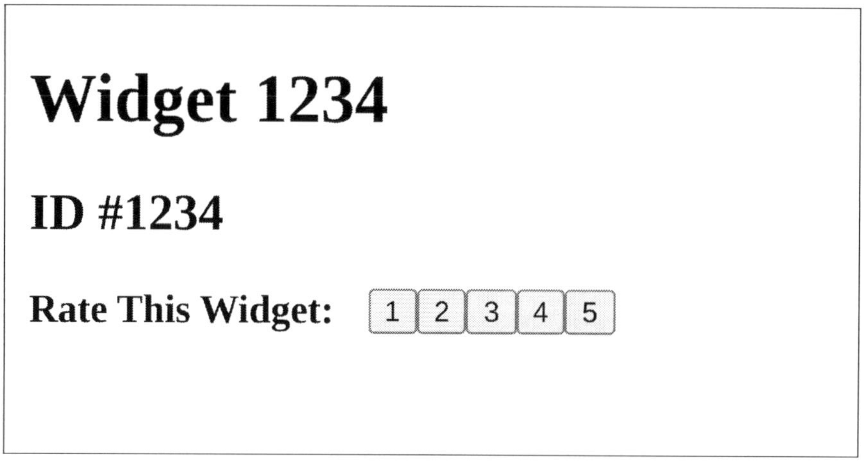

Widget 1234

ID #1234

Rate This Widget: [1] [2] [3] [4] [5]

Figure 7.5: Using a View Component

Based on the markup alone, this is a moderate improvement over ERB. If the logic for what should be in the view becomes complex, most of that logic can be managed in the View Component's class. And, to be fair, without View Component, you could achieve this by creating an Active Model or other Ruby class that the controller exposes.

Where View Component really shines is testing.

7.4.2 Testing Markup from a Unit Test

A regular Ruby class can be tested by creating a test in test/«whatever». For a bit of re-usable ERB, however, you can't just test the logic, you also need to make sure the ERB code itself is working. By default, the only part of Rails that actually executes and renders the view templates is a system test.

View Component provides the best of both worlds by allow the template logic to be rendered in a unit test that runs quickly. You can set up your test the same as any other test in Rails, but then assert on the rendered HTML, like you would in a system test. This provides a lot of confidence that your view logic is working—confidence that is difficult to get otherwise.

The scaffold generated an empty test named widget_rating_component_test.rb in test/components/. Let's modify that to test our ratings component. The component has two states: showing the CTA and hiding it. We'll write two tests, each which will instantiate the View Component, call render_inline, then make assertions that are similar to those you'd make in any system test.

Here's how it will look:

```
# test/components/widget_rating_component_test.rb

require "test_helper"

class WidgetRatingComponentTest < ViewComponent::TestCase
  def test_show_cta
    render_inline(
      WidgetRatingComponent.new(
        widget: OpenStruct.new(id: 1234),
        show_cta: true
      )
    )
    assert_text("Your ratings help us be amazing")
  end
  def test_no_cta
    render_inline(
      WidgetRatingComponent.new(
        widget: OpenStruct.new(id: 1234),
        show_cta: false
      )
    )
    refute_text("Your ratings help us be amazing")
  end
end
```

Now, we can test this component, and it'll execute just as fast as a unit test:

```
> bin/rails test \
  test/components/widget_rating_component_test.rb
Running 2 tests in a single process (parallelization thresho...
Run options: --seed 30458

# Running:

..

Finished in 0.028657s, 69.7916 runs/s, 69.7916 assertions/s.
2 runs, 2 assertions, 0 failures, 0 errors, 0 skips
```

Nice! In my most recent job, I maintained a customer service app that had a lot of complex UI states. View Component, in particular this method of testing, allowed me to quickly build the UI and have confidence that it was working.

Why not always use View Component? Why even use partials?

7.4.3 Deciding Between a Partial or a View Component

As you can see from our simple example, a partial just requires moving markup from one file to another, adding a single line of code to declare the locals, and that's it. A View Component requires the same sort of file, plus a class, plus a test. And, as you create more and more View Components, your `app/components` folder will get messy and require organization.

Although there is virtue in having exactly one way to do something, I think there is value in using both partials and View Component. Partials work great when you need to re-use markup that has very little or no logic. Using a View Component for that situation would result in an empty class and an empty test.

And, as we saw, converting a partial to a View Component is relatively straightforward. So, if a partial today becomes complex, you can quickly make it into a View Component when needed.

Another rule of thumb is if your partial has logic you wish you could test outside of a system test, make it a View Component. And, if you grow tired of typing out class names in your view templates, you can always create a helper to call `render`.

We'll talk about helpers next, but before we leave, I want to urge you to avoid alternative templating mechanisms and stick with ERB.

7.5 Just Use ERB

The default templating mechanism in Rails is HTML using ERB (which I'm going to refer to simply as "ERB" even though ERB is a general templating system that can template anything). Some developers strongly believe ERB to be problematic and seek to use alternatives like HAML[8] or Slim[9]. I don't believe the benefits ascribed to these technologies outweigh the downsides, and I want to talk briefly about why.

There are two reasons I believe ERB is the sustainable choice:

- It's the default in Rails, so its behavior is managed and updated with Rails and thus more stable and reliable.
- It is based on HTML, which is widely understood by almost every web developer, even those unfamiliar with Rails.

---

[8] http://haml.info
[9] http://slim-lang.com

Sticking with Rails' default choices is a sustainable decision, because you will need to update your version of Rails over the life of the app. The fewer dependencies your app has, the easier that process is going to be. I'm sure HAML and Slim are well-updated and maintained, but if incompatibilities exist between these technologies and Rails, it's not going to delay a Rails release. Incompatibilities with ERB will. This means that HAML and Slim (like any dependency) can prevent you from updating to the latest version of Rails.

As to the broad mindshare of HTML, while it's not hard to learn HAML or Slim, neither technology actually makes it easier to write HTML. They are both translators, not abstractions, so you still need to think about what HTML is going to be generated. I don't enjoy writing code that I must mentally translate as I write it. I find it difficult to both understand how the dynamic nature of the template affects the resulting markup *while also* translating HAML or Slim mentally into HTML.

A non-default templating language is also one more thing to learn in order to be productive (especially since Slim and HAML use a modified version of embedded Ruby that doesn't need end statements). While any single non-standard thing may not be hard to learn, these tend to add up. Anything you add to your app should provide a clear benefit to justify its existence. For non-default templating languages, there really isn't a strong benefit.

Consider also the use of advanced front-end technologies like React or Vue. Those use HTML by default, too. Adopting HAML or Slim for HTML templates means you either have inconsistency with your JavaScript components, or you need a JavaScript dependency to change the markup language there, too. While RubyGem dependencies carry risk, JavaScript dependencies carry a higher risk (as we'll discuss later).

It's just not worth it. HAML and Slim simply don't solve a serious enough problem to justify the cost of their adoption. Arguments about "cleanliness" are subjective, and I prefer to limit the number of technical decisions made based on subjective measures. Subjective or aesthetic arguments can be decent tiebreakers, but as the foundation of a technical decision, I find them wanting[10].

Up Next

We've talked about HTML templates and how to manage them. As we work our way into the app, the next view technology to look at is the helper. Helpers are used to extract logic needed in templates to Ruby code, where they can be more easily managed and tested. But we can make an awful mess with them.

---

[10]I want to point out that I have made no argument related to the whitespace-significance of HAML or Slim. I believe their lack of appropriateness can be understood on technical merits alone.

8
Helpers

Ah helpers! So handy, yet also a magnet for mess and unsustainability. I am not going to give you a clean, perfect, sustainable solution here, but I *can* help clarify the issues with helpers, explain the best way to use them, and help ease some of the pain.

Helpers are a way (well, the *only* way included with Rails) to export methods to be available to a view. Any method defined in `app/helpers/application_helper.rb` will be included and available to all your views. Helpers can also be added via the `helper` method in a controller, which will import methods from a class, module, block of code, or really anywhere.

The main problem that comes up around helpers is the sheer volume of them. Because they exist in a single global namespace by default, the more helpers there are, the harder it is to avoid name clashes and the harder it is to find helpers to reuse. It's just not feasible to expect engineers to read through tons of helpers to figure out if what they need exists or not.

An extreme way to deal with this problem is to ban the use of helpers entirely. You could be successful with this approach, but you'd then need an answer for where code goes that does what a helper would normally do. Those approaches, usually called *presenters*, have their own problems, which we'll talk about.

But even a nuanced approach that clearly defines what code should be in a helper and what shouldn't still requires answering questions about where all the code you need should end up. And, of course, helpers generate HTML, making them a great place to inject security vulnerabilities.

The reality is, there's going to be a lot of code to handle view logic and formatting. Whether that code is in helpers or not, it doesn't change the fact that we have a code management problem, and there's no perfect solution.

To deal with this reality, we'll look at the following techniques:

- Reduce the number of helpers you need by properly modeling your domain.
- Concentrate helpers on what they do best: producing inline markup.

- When generating markup (in a helper or not), use Rails APIs to avoid security issues.
- Helpers with logic should be tested, but take care not to over-couple them to the markup being generated.
- Presenters (or other proxies where you might put helper-like methods) aren't needed given Active Model and View Components.

We'll start with the most important technique for managing helpers, which is to make sure you are putting domain concerns in the domain objects where they belong, not in your helpers.

8.1 Don't Conflate Helpers with Your Domain

> This section's code is in the folder `08-01/` of the sample code.

Helpers are often used for so-called *view concerns*, which is the transformation of canonical data to something only needed for a view. Rails' `number_to_currency` is a great example. Therefore, to understand helpers is to understand view concerns. What are they?

A common convention for identifying view concerns is to assume any piece of data that doesn't come from the database, and is thus aggregated or derived from the database, is a view concern. While easy to follow, this convention is overly simplistic and ends up pushing too many actual domain concepts out of the domain.

Instead, you should think more deeply about what really is part of the domain. The resource upon which your view is based isn't just an aggregation of data from the database but instead is *everything* that's part of that domain concept, *including* data that might be derived or aggregated from the database.

Let's suppose our widget IDs are meaningful to users. There are a lot of good reasons for this to be true. In our imagined domain of widget sales, we can assume we're migrating some legacy widget database into our own, and we'll suppose that users are used to seeing widget IDs in general, and specifically, they are accustomed to seeing them formatted with the last two digits separated by a dot. So the widget with ID 12345 would be shown as 123.45.

This might seem like a view concern. It's a formatting of canonical data in our database. But *why* do we need to do this? Because it's meaningful to users. This formatted ID represents a meaningful concept to the users of our system. That feels fundamentally different than, say, using a monospaced font to render the ID.

I'd argue that something like this is *not* a view concern and *should* be part of the domain. That doesn't mean we have to store it in our database, but what it *does* mean is that it's part of the widget resource and not something we'd put in a partial template component or helper. See the sidebar "Formatting Item IDs" on page 123 for a real-world example of this.

We don't have a `Widget` class yet, but we can still add this derived data to our stand-in `OpenStruct`. Let's do that now in `widgets_controller.rb`:

```
# app/controllers/widgets_controller.rb

                                    manufacturer_id: manufacturer.id...
                                    manufacturer: manufacturer,
                                    name: "Widget #{params[:id]}")
→     def @widget.widget_id
→       if self.id.to_s.length < 3
→         self.id.to_s
→       else
→         self.id.to_s[0..-3] + "." +
→           self.id.to_s[-2..-1]
→       end
→     end
    end
    def index
      @widgets = [
```

If you haven't done this sort of hacky metaprogramming, don't worry. It's not a technique you should use often, but essentially this is defining the method `widget_id` on the `@widget` object itself. Note that this code won't last long, as we'll turn `Widget` into a real class later in the book.

We can use this in the view:

```
<%# app/views/widgets/show.html.erb %>

  <h1><%= @widget.name %></h1>
→ <h2>ID #<%= @widget.widget_id %></h2>
  <% if flash[:notice].present? %>
    <aside>
      <%= flash[:notice] %>
```

This should work great as shown in the screenshot "Formatted Widget ID" below.

```
┌─────────────────────────────────────────┐
│                                         │
│   Widget 12345                          │
│                                         │
│   ID #123.45                            │
│                                         │
│   Rate This Widget:   [1][2][3][4][5]   │
│                                         │
│                                         │
└─────────────────────────────────────────┘
```

Figure 8.1: Formatted Widget ID

```
> rm -f log/development.log
```

```
> cat log/development.log
Started GET "/widgets/12345" for 172.18.0.3 at 2023-12-04 23...
   ActiveRecord::SchemaMigration Load (0.4ms)  SELECT "schema...
Processing by WidgetsController#show as HTML
   Parameters: {"id"=>"12345"}
   Rendering layout layouts/application.html.erb
   Rendering widgets/show.html.erb within layouts/application
   Rendered widgets/show.html.erb within layouts/application ...
   Rendered layout layouts/application.html.erb (Duration: 33...
Completed 200 OK in 47ms (Views: 38.4ms | ActiveRecord: 0.0m...
```

When you start to critically examine your domain, and take into account all the inputs to what should define it, you'll find that there are many pieces of data that you won't store in your database. These aren't view concerns.

Nevertheless, you will still encounter the need to render data or perform logic specific to how data is viewed. Formatting numbers or currency based on locale is one. Another is UI logic based on global state or context, such as showing or hiding parts of a view based on what the current logged-in user is authorized to do. This means we'll need *some* code between our resources and our views to manage this. Helpers can do this, and so let's talk about what helpers can do, specifically what *only* helpers can do.

> **Formatting Item IDs**
>
> The Stitch Fix warehouses were organized in a seemingly chaotic, random fashion. This was by design as it helped the efficiency of the fulfillment process greatly. We initially had 1,000 locations or *bins*, and we assigned an item's location based on the last three digits of its primary key in the database.
>
> When you looked at any app, any tag, or any packing slip, item IDs would render like 1234-567, and this would tell you that bin 567 is where that item should go. The code to format the IDs originally lived in a helper. Of course, we ended up needing it in a lot of places over the years. The result was a ton of duplicate code spread across the app (and later, many apps), all because we considered it a view concern.
>
> The reality is, this formatted ID was meaningful to everyone, and the fact that it came from the database primary key was irrelevant. It was part of the domain model that we missed.

8.2 Helpers are Best at Exposing Global UI State and Generating Markup

> This section's code is in the folder 08-02/ of the sample code.

Rails built-in helpers format data for the view, often by generating markup. For situations where little or no markup is needed, helpers can be a good solution, since they are lighter-weight than a partial or View Component. Helpers can also provide access to global state without requiring instance variables. As long as there's not too much global state, helpers can work well.

8.2.1 Global UI Logic and State

Almost every Rails app has a `current_user` method that exposes the logged-in user. It's common to use this on many views, either to access user-specific information or to check that the user is authorized to view different aspects of the UI. Setting a `@current_user` instance variable in every controller method would be cumbersome. Thus, a `current_user` helper is common and makes sense.

Another example is feature flags. You might be rolling out a new feature to a subset of users and want to modify the UI for only those users. You may need to check if the user has been granted access to the new feature from anywhere, and an instance variable might be inconvenient or hard to maintain. You might expose a `feature_enabled?` helper to handle this.

Helpers are also a good tool for managing markup generation. You could think of these needs as small inline components that don't warrant a partial and definitely don't warrant a View Component.

8.2.2 Small, Inline Components

Suppose we wish to render our widget ID in a monospace font, and let's suppose we need to do this everywhere in the app. While the formatting of our ID using dots is not a view concern but part of our domain, the specific font we're using really *is* a view concern.

If we want a re-usable component for this, we need something to produce this HTML:

```
<span style="font-family: monospace">123.45</span>
```

Note again I'm using inline styles merely to show what styles are being applied. In reality you'd use CSS for this, but the overall point will stand (we'll talk about CSS later). *Also* note the use of <span>. Certainly, <code> would achieve the look we want, but our widget ID is not a piece of computer code, so using <code> would be semantically incorrect.

To create this inline component, we'll create a new helper in app/helpers/application_helper.rb.

```
# app/helpers/application_helper.rb

  module ApplicationHelper
→
→   def styled_widget_id(widget)
→     content_tag(:span,
→                 widget.widget_id,
→                 style: "font-family: monospace")
→   end
  end
```

We can use this helper in app/views/widgets/show.html.erb:

```
<%# app/views/widgets/show.html.erb %>

  <h1><%= @widget.name %></h1>
→ <h2>ID #<%= styled_widget_id(@widget) %></h2>
  <% if flash[:notice].present? %>
```

```
<aside>
  <%= flash[:notice] %>
```

It works, as you can see in the screenshot "Widget ID Component" on the next page.

Figure 8.2: Widget ID Component

If we'd used a partial template for this, it would be super cumbersome:

```
<h2>
ID #<%= render partial: "styled_widget_id",
           locals: { widget: @widget } %>
</h2>
```

A View Component would be equally clunky.

```
<h2>
ID #<%= render(StyledWidgetIdComponent.new(widget: @widget) %>
</h2>
```

Even with a disciplined approach that minimized helpers to only those that are necessary and beneficial, your app will end up with a lot of them. Thus, you need a strategy for where they are defined.

8.3 Configure Rails based on Your Strategy for Helpers

By default, all files in app/helpers are included in every view. This creates a huge global namespace that gives the appearance of modularity, but without actually achieving it. There are two ways to deal with this: only use app/helpers/application_helper.rb or configure Rails to use helpers in a modular way.

8.3.1 Consolidating Helpers in One File

If you are using View Component (whose relation to helpers we'll discuss later in this chapter), you can probably survive on a single global namespace for helpers, all of which would be defined in app/controllers/application_helper.rb. This is what I have done and is a simple pattern to understand and conform to.

If you want to do that, you should configure Rails to not create per-controller helper files. You can do this by placing code like so in config/application.rb:

```
# config/application.rb

    #
    # config.time_zone = "Central Time (US & Canada)"
    # config.eager_load_paths << Rails.root.join("extras")
→   config.generators do |g|
→     # Prevent generators from creating
→     # per-controller helpers
→     g.helper false
→   end
  end
end
```

After configuring this, when you do something like `bin/rails g resource` Rails will not create a helper for that resource, which codifies your decision to use a single namespace for all helpers.

If you *do* want modularity, there is a different configuration for this:

8.3.2 Configure Helpers to Be Actually Modular

If you aren't using View Component, a way to manage view-specific helpers is to make Rails treat the per-controller helper files as actually separate. By default, if you have the file app/helpers/widgets_helper.rb, that would be included in all views. This behavior can be confusing and error-prone, because you cannot easily manage the global namespace and avoid name clashes.

If you wanted actual modularity, meaning app/helpers/widgets_helper.rb would *only* be included on views rendered from the WidgetsController, you can achieve this by configuring Rails like so:

```ruby
# config/application.rb
require_relative "boot"

require "rails/all"

# Require the gems listed in Gemfile, including any gems
# you've limited to :test, :development, or :production.
Bundler.require(*Rails.groups)

module Widgets
  class Application < Rails::Application

    # existing configuration...

→   # Only include controller-specific helpers for that
→   # controller's views.
→   config.action_controller.include_all_helpers = false
  end
end
```

I find the use of View Component for consolidating view-specific logic easier to manage than helpers, but modularizing the helpers system isn't a bad solution. It does allow you to keep within vanilla Rails and reduce the dependencies your project has.

One caveat with this approach is the use of helpers in partials. If a partial using a helper is rendered by a view from the WidgetsController, but then is re-used from, say, the ManufacturersController, the helper won't be available. This can be confusing, so ensure you have good test coverage to detect these issues.

Another consideration for defining helpers is when you have logic that must be shared between a controller and a view.

8.3.3 Use `helper_method` to Share Logic Between Views and Controllers

A common need in applications is to access the currently logged-in user, which is typically available via a method named `current_user`, defined in `ApplicationController` (or a module that it includes). The view often needs access to this method as well. This can be arranged without duplicating the method by using `helper_method` in `ApplicationController`, like so:

```ruby
class ApplicationController < ActionController::Base

private

  def current_user
    User.find_by(id: session[:current_user_id])
  end
  helper_method :current_user

end
```

Any controller can use `helper_method` to expose a method as a helper to the views that are rendered. I would caution the extensive use of this feature as it can quickly become difficult to know which helper methods truly are available to a view, and make view refactoring difficult. Imagine extracting a partial or View Component that relies on a controller-specific helper, and then using that as part of a view that renders a partial that renders another partial that calls a View Component that relies on that helper. This is not sustainable.

As messy as this all seems, helpers are the only feature of Rails to allow calling a method inside a view. View Component, which we discussed in the previous chapter on page 111 provide true scoped methods accessible by ERB.

We'll talk about more involved use-cases later in this chapter, but next, let's go a bit deeper on generating markup without creating security vulnerabilities.

8.4 Use Rails' APIs to Generate Markup

The view is a magnet for security issues, because it's code that gets executed in the user's browser and not on your servers. If you aren't familiar with the OWASP Top Ten[1], it's a list of the ten most problematic security risks

---

[1] https://owasp.org/www-project-top-ten/

for a web application. Several of these vulnerabilities can be exploited by allowing unsafe content to be sent to a user's browser in HTML, CSS, or JavaScript.

When we just use ERB templates and Rails view helpers, Rails does a great job of preventing these problems. If a user creates a Widget named "<strong>HACKED</strong> Stembolts", Rails would escape those <strong> tags so the browser doesn't render them.

Problems can occur when we generate markup in Ruby code, which is often what our helpers need to do.

For example, we could've implemented our styled widget ID helper like so:

```ruby
def styled_widget_id(widget)
  %{
    <span style="font-family: monospace">
      #{ widget.widget_id }
    </span>
  }
end
```

Rails does not consider this string to be HTML safe, so it would escape all of that HTML and the result would be that the user would see raw un-rendered HTML in their browser.

We can tell Rails that the string *is* safe to render in the browser by calling html_safe on it.

```ruby
  def styled_widget_id(widget)
    %{
      <span style=\"font-family: monospace\">
        #{ widget.widget_id }
      </span>
→   }.html_safe
  end
```

Rails will then skip escaping this string thus allowing the browser to render it. For the <span> tags in this method, that's fine. We can easily see that we have not introduced a security vulnerability. But what about widget.widget_id? Figuring out where that value comes from, and if it could contain markup or JavaScript, is not easy. We can't really be sure this implementation won't introduce a vulnerability.

If instead, our helper absolutely prevents this problem, we don't have to worry about any of that. We need to generate HTML-safe markup, but we need to escape anything we can't trust, such as the `widget_id`. While we could handle that by calling `CGI.escapeHTML` from the standard library, it's much better to use Rails' APIs like `content_tag`.

When our helper code sometimes uses `html_safe` and sometimes doesn't, it creates confusion. Developers will wonder when they have to use it and when they shouldn't. They will have to know the nuances of injection attacks and know when to escape values and when not to. And they will have to do it correctly. This is exceedingly difficult to manage. I've seen very senior developers—myself included—mess this up, even after thinking it through and getting peer feedback.

Instead, Rails provides `content_tag` (along with all the other various form helpers), which will safely build strings with dynamic content.

Thus, when authoring helpers, *never* build strings using interpolation or concatenation. Try to *always* use Rails' helper methods to create your markup. I would even recommend using our old friend code comments if you have to use `html_safe`. Explaining in words why you think the string is safe to send to the browser at least captures your thinking at the time the code was written while sending a warning to others that `html_safe` is not something to reach for by default.

Helpers, being Ruby code, can be tested, and it can be worth testing them via unit tests.

8.5 Helpers Should Be Tested and Thus Testable

> This section's code is in the folder 08-04/ of the sample code.

Helpers are Ruby code, and if one of them is broken, the only way to know that is to hope that a system test catches it. Since helpers are relatively easy to test, there is value in testing them in isolation, at least when they have nontrivial logic in them. We have to be careful not to overly specify our tests for helpers, however, because we don't want our helpers' tests to fail if we change immaterial things like styling.

The testing strategy I recommend for helpers is:

- If there is no logic, it may be OK to skip writing a test, especially if the helper is called from a view exercised by a system test.
- If there *is* logic, a unit test can be beneficial, but you should not over-specify the assertions in case the markup needs to change.
- Testing for HTML-safety can be useful if you are already writing a test.

Given the way `styled_widget_id` is implemented, there isn't any logic to it, and thus I'm not sure there is a lot of value in testing it. But, as a demonstration, let's make it more involved. Suppose that the business rules are such that if the widget ID is less than 10,000 (which indicates it's a legacy widget imported from the old system), we prefix the value with zeros to make it six digits. The widget with ID 1234 would render `0012.34`, whereas widget with ID 987654 would render as `9876.54`.

We don't want to over-couple our test to the markup in question, so let's try to assert only on the content, since that is what will change based on the business rules.

We'll write two tests, both of which go in `application_helper_test.rb`, located in `test/helpers/`. The first will test that a widget with ID 1234 prefixes the value with two zeros. The second will check that widget 987654 does not.

We'll do these checks using regular expressions, asserting that the rendered widget id is present. Our regular expressions will also use \D to ensure that no additional digits are present around the rendered ID.

Since we're testing the output, we can also assert that it is HTMl safe. It's not worth testing just for this, but since we are testing the output, it's good to include.

```ruby
# test/helpers/application_helper_test.rb

require "test_helper"

class ApplicationHelperTest < ActionView::TestCase
  test "styled_widget_id < 6 digits, pad with 0's" do
    widget = OpenStruct.new(widget_id: "12.34")
    rendered_markup = styled_widget_id(widget)

    assert_match /\D0012\.34\D/, rendered_markup
    assert rendered_markup.html_safe?
  end

  test "styled_widget_id >= 6 digits, no padding" do
    widget = OpenStruct.new(widget_id: "9876.54")
    rendered_markup = styled_widget_id(widget)

    assert_match /\D9876\.54\D/, rendered_markup
    assert rendered_markup.html_safe?
  end
end
```

This test should fail, since we haven't made the change yet:

```
> bin/rails test test/helpers/application_helper_test.rb || \
  echo Test failed
Running 2 tests in a single process (parallelization thresho...
Run options: --seed 18356

# Running:

F

Failure:
ApplicationHelperTest#test_styled_widget_id_<_6_digits,_pad_...
Expected /\D0012\.34\D/ to match "<span style=\"font-family:...

bin/rails test test/helpers/application_helper_test.rb:4


.

Finished in 0.003475s, 575.4705 runs/s, 1438.6763 assertions...
2 runs, 5 assertions, 1 failures, 0 errors, 0 skips
Test failed
```

Let's change the implementation to match our test using Ruby's `rjust` method, which does basically what we want:

```
# app/helpers/application_helper.rb


    def styled_widget_id(widget)
      content_tag(:span,
→                 widget.widget_id.to_s.rjust(7,"0"),
                  style: "font-family: monospace")
    end
  end
```

Now, the test should pass:

```
> bin/rails test test/helpers/application_helper_test.rb
Running 2 tests in a single process (parallelization thresho...
Run options: --seed 34155

# Running:
```

```
..
Finished in 0.007018s, 284.9781 runs/s, 854.9343 assertions/...
2 runs, 6 assertions, 0 failures, 0 errors, 0 skips
```

If we change the styling of the component in the future, the test will continue to pass as long as the ID is formatted properly.

Before we move on, let's talk about handling situations where you have more complex view logic. By default, helpers are the *only* way in Rails to invoke a method directly in a view. Given that helpers are in a global namespace, it can be come quite hard to manage them over time, and if you have complex view-specific methods you want to write, you have to put them into the global namespace and hope no one re-uses them.

Presenter frameworks are historically used to manage this, but in my experience, you can handle this with better resource modeling and/or View Components.

8.6 Tackle Complex View Logic with Better Resource Design or View Components

Often, a view requires highly complex logic that you may not want to be implemented in ERB, and is too use-case-specific to be in a helper. Historically, Rails developers have used presenter frameworks (also called *view models*, *proxies*, or *decorators*) to try to wrangle this.

This section is going to make the case for *not* using such frameworks and instead rely on either new resources and Active Model or View Components.

8.6.1 Presenters Obscure Reality and Breed Inconsistency

Most presenter frameworks work by creating proxy objects around an existing Active Record. For example, if you needed to show a flag on the widget show page that indicated that widget's manufacturer was local to the user's locality, you could implement that by creating a wrapper or proxy object like so:

```
class WidgetPresenter
  delegate_missing_to :@widget

  def initialize(widget)
    @widget = widget
  end
```

```ruby
  def local_to_user?(user)
    widget.manufacturer.address.us_state == user.address.us_state
  end

end
```

If you've never used `delegate_missing_to`, it allows the object that calls it to send all missing methods to the underlying object. In this case, if you call name on a `WidgetPresenter`, that method is missing, so it will delegate it to `@widget`, effectively calling `@widget.name`. It makes `WidgetPresenter` appear to be a `Widget` with extra methods.

Even at moderate complexity, this will be confusing for several reasons:

- Do you call the instance variable `@widget`, thus making it unclear what the actual class is, or do you call it `@widget_presenter`, making it diverge from the convention of naming a resource and instance variable the same?
- Do you always create a presenter? If not, when do you? When don't you?
- Do re-usable components, partials, or helpers expect a `Widget` or a `WidgetPresenter`? How do you know which to use when?

There are many ways to decorate one object with additional behavior, but they all create the same problems. Managing these problems can be difficult, and often requires code review to avoid a convoluted mess.

Because of this, I would caution against the use of presenters or proxies and instead use one of the two techniques described below, starting with resource modeling.

8.6.2 Custom Resources and Active Model Create More Consistent Code

In the chapter on routes on page 83, we talked about using resources instead of custom routes. Rails allows you to create any resource you like, even if it's not an Active Record. Rails also provides you with the module `ActiveModel::Model` that allows you to create a class that works with the Rails view in the same way an Active Record does.

When faced with the need to make a complicated view for a resource, it may be helpful to give that view a more specific name, and then create an Active Model to represent it. For example, we may decide that instead of the widget show resource, our need to show the locality of a widget will be called a `GeographicLocalWidget`. Not the best name, but it will be hard to mis-use.

First, we'd create a canonical Rails route for this:

```
# config/routes.rb
resources :geographic_local_widgets, only: [ :index, :show ]
```

This means that the controller `GeographicLocalWidgetsController` will have an `index` and a `show` method. `index` will expose the instance variable `@geographic_local_widgets`, and `show` will expose `@geographic_local_widget`. What we want is for those instance variables to behave like Active Records. We want to write code like so:

```
<ul>
<% @geographic_local_widgets.each do |geographic_local_widget| %>
  <li>
    <%= link_to geographic_local_widget do %>
      Widget <%= geographic_local_widget.id %>
    <% end %>
  </li>
<% end %>
</ul>
```

But, of course, we also need to be able to call `local_to_user?(current_user)` on whatever a `geographic_local_widget` is. We can achieve both with Active Model. We'll talk more about Active Model in chapter 13 on page 209, but if we create `GeographicLocalWidget` like so, it will work:

```
class GeographicLocalWidget
  include ActiveModel::Model

  attr_accessor :id, :name, :manufacturer

  def persisted? = true
  def to_key = [ self.id ]

  def local_to_user?(user)
    manufacturer.address.us_state == user.address.us_state
  end
end
```

This can be used in our controller as if it were an Active Record:

```ruby
def show
  widget = Widget.find(params[:id])
  @geographic_local_widget = GeographicLocalWidget.new(
    id: widget.id,
    name: widget.name,
    manufacturer: widget.manufacturer
  )
end
```

Essentially, this creates a new domain concept based on an existing Active Record, and includes the methods you need on it. It's *similar* to a presenter, but works better with Rails and creates more consistent code. View code that uses an Active Record will look almost exactly like view code that uses an Active Model. You won't mistake what a `@geographic_local_widget` is, because it's a well-defined class just like `Widget`.

Sometimes, however, the logic you need is not really a new domain concept or resource. In that case, you can have a View Component take over the entire page.

8.6.3 View Components can Render Entire Pages When Logic is Complex

Although View Components, which we discussed in chapter 7 on page 111, are primarily used to create re-usable bits of view logic, they can certainly render the entire page. The View Component class could include all the logic you might otherwise put into a presenter.

For example, we could create `WidgetShowPageComponent` and place all of `app/views/widgets/show.html.erb` into its ERB, leaving `widgets.show.html.erb` looking like so:

```erb
<%= render(WidgetShowPageComponent.new(widget: @widget)) %>
```

Then, `WidgetShowPageComponent` could implement `local_to_user?`, like so:

```ruby
# app/components/widget_show_page_component.rb
class WidgetShowPageComponent < ViewComponent::Base
  def initialize(widget: )
    @widget = widget
  end
```

```
    def local_to_user?(current_user)
      @widget.manufacturer.address.us_state ==
        current_user.address.us_state
    end
end
```

The ERB code can call `local_to_user?`.

Like using an Active Model, this technique is similar to using presenters, however it doesn't have the issues presenters have. There is no conflation of objects (`Widget` vs `WidgetPresenter`) and the component is a well-defined class using a pattern you would already have in your app.

Up Next

Helpers are problematic, but so are the alternatives. Of course, you could just live with some duplication in your markup, and this isn't the worst idea in the world. The "Don't Repeat Yourself" (DRY) Principle isn't any more of a real rule than the Law of Demeter. It's all trade-offs.

The news is about to get worse. All the problems that exist with helpers are exacerbated by our next topic: CSS.

9

CSS

> This section's code is in the folder 09-01/ of the sample code.

Like helpers, the problem with CSS is how to manage the volume of code. CSS, by its nature, makes the problem worse, because of the way CSS can interact with itself and the markup. It's not unheard of for a single line of CSS to break an entire website's visuals.

When CSS is unmanaged, developer productivity can go down, and the app becomes less sustainable. There are two main factors that lead to this that you must control:

- Some CSS must be written for each new view or change to a view. The more required, the slower development will be.
- The more CSS that exists, that harder it is to locate re-usable classes, which leads to both duplication *and* even more CSS. As with helpers, there is a volume at which no developer can reasonably understand all the CSS to locate re-usable components, and the safest route is to add more CSS.

Therefore, to keep CSS from making your app unsustainable, you must manage the volume. Ideally, the rate of growth in CSS is lower than the rate of growth of the codebase. Thus, the more re-usable CSS you have, the less CSS we will need.

To achieve this, you need three things:

- A Design System, which specifies font sizes, spacing, and colors (among other things).
- A CSS Strategy, which implements the design system, but also provides a single mechanism for styling components and re-using them when needed.
- A Style Guide, which is a living document of your Design System and CSS Strategy.

The absolute biggest boon to any team in wrangling CSS is to adopt a *design system*.

9.1 Adopt a Design System

A *design system* is a set of elemental units of the design of your app. At its base, it is:

- A small set of font-sizes, usually around eight.
- A small set of pre-defined spacings, again usually around eight.
- A color palette of a finite number of colors.

Any design for any part of the app uses these elemental units. For example, any text in the app should be in one of the eight available sizes.

Many designers create a design system before doing a large project, because it reduces the number of design decisions they have to make. Most apps can be very well designed without needing an infinite number of font sizes, spacing, or colors. For example, when a designer is laying out a page, they can literally audition all eight font sizes and choose the best one.

You can leverage this by replicating the design system in your code. So instead of specifying the font-size directly in pixels or rems, you specify "font size 3" or "font size 5" (for example).

The design system can also contain reusable components like buttons, form fields, or other complex layouts. These reusable components might not all be known up front, so some emergent additions to the design system will appear over time.

If your app is designed based on a design system, this will vastly reduce the amount of CSS you have to write, and the CSS you *do* write will be easier to understand and predict. Ideally, entire views can be created using the design system's classes without creating any new CSS.

Talk to your design team, if you have one, and ask about the design system. Even if all they have is a set of font-sizes, that's something. Encourage them to standardize colors and spacings if they haven't, and explain to them (plus whatever manager might be around making decisions) that a stable design system will boost your team's productivity. You can always—if you are feeling subversive—implement their designs using a design system you reverse engineer. Many designers don't want pixel-perfect designs.

Of course, not everything will conform to the design system. Some designs will require something custom, but this should be a small percentage of the designs and pages. Writing some CSS is OK, as long most of what you do conforms to the design system.

If you don't have a design team, which is common when building so-called "internal" software (for example, a customer service app), you can use a CSS framework which will be based on its own design system. We'll talk about that in the next section.

9.2 Adopt a CSS Strategy

A design system is great, but if you don't have a way to manage your CSS and leverage that system, your CSS will be a huge mess. Unfortunately, Rails does not provide any guidance on how to manage CSS. Before Rails 7, Rails' generators create per-controller .css files, creating confusion. These files gave the illusion of modularity, but those .css files were rolled up into one application.css and you ended up with a global namespace of classes spread across many files.

When deciding on a strategy, remember that we are building server-rendered views. We'll talk about that a bit more in the next chapter on page 161, but the important thing to understand is that a strategy that doesn't work with Rails views is not a viable strategy.

This leaves three main strategies: a framework, Object-Oriented CSS (OOCSS), and Functional CSS.

I do want to be explicit about a strategy you should *not* use, which is likely the strategy you learned when you first learned web development: semantic CSS.

There is no value in giving markup a class that has some semantic meaning. Users using a web browser won't see this class, and assistive technologies rely on ARIA Roles[1] when more meaning is needed for some markup. If you need to provide a hook for a piece of the DOM for non-presentational purposes, data- attributes are more effective.

Thus, the front-end engineering ecosystem has largely embraced using classes with presentational meanings, since the only reason to use a class is to attach CSS to it. For example, here is the markup for a button in the Bootstrap framework that uses an outline look and a large font:

```
<button class="btn btn-outline-success btn-lg">
  OK
</button>
```

Both OOCSS and Functional CSS take the approach of using classes in markup to have presentational meaning. They differ in exactly how they do that. Both approaches are ways to manage CSS and thus create your design system in code. A framework does all this for you, but it's not always the right choice.

---

[1] https://developer.mozilla.org/en-US/docs/Web/Accessibility/ARIA/Roles

9.2.1 A CSS Framework

A CSS Framework is something like Bootstrap[2] or Bulma[3]. These contain a wide variety of pre-styled components, from font-sizes to complex forms and dialog boxes. For an internally-facing app, a framework is going to make your team far more productive than hand-styling views, because the design doesn't matter *as much* as for a public-facing app, *and*, you rarely need highly-branded visual styling for internal apps.

Using something like Bootstrap means you don't need to create a design system (Bootstrap and other frameworks have a set of defaults built-in), and without writing any CSS, anyone on the team can design and build UIs that look pretty good. CSS Frameworks aren't replacements for real designers or user-experience experts, but if you have internal apps that can use a framework as its design system, you have fewer decisions to make and will have an easier time building views.

Also, there will be *far* less CSS to manage, and you won't need to write much, if any. This is highly sustainable.

That said, most public-facing apps need more customization, more specialized branding, and have more functionality than the simple web forms and info dumps present in an internal app.

In those cases, you will want more control over CSS and you will want to implement and grow the design system yourself. Thus, you need a single convention on how to use CSS, which comes down to deciding what the classes should be on your markup.

There are many popular approaches that I'm going to group together as *object-oriented CSS*, which we'll discuss first.

9.2.2 Object-Oriented CSS

Object-oriented CSS (OOCSS) is not strictly defined, and it's a confusing name if you come from object-oriented programming. In OOCSS, there are no classes, objects, or methods like there are in Ruby. The *object* being referred to in the name is what we've been calling a component, or might be called a module. It is markup plus CSS to achieve some particular design. A button with rounded corners and a large font in all caps is an object/component/module. I'm going to use the word *component*, since that's what we've been using thus far.

In OOCSS, markup is assigned a name as to what visual component it is supposed to be. OOCSS methodologies employ naming conventions based on that to attach classes to any part of the component's markup that needs styling. There is typically no deep nesting of CSS, no styling directly on elements, and often a delineation between base styles to achieve a layout

---

[2]https://getbootstrap.com
[3]https://bulma.io

and modifiers which tweak it. For example, a button always has rounded corners, but a dangerous button will additionally have red text.

Two common strategies for OOCSS are Block-Element-Modifier (BEM)[4] and SMACCS[5]. If you like the OOCSS approach, I strongly recommend adopting one of these two, with BEM being slightly easier to understand in my experience.

For example, suppose we want to enhance the <h1> and <h2> in our widget show page. We want the widget's name to be bold and in all-caps, and we want the ID to be in a monospace font. In an OOCSS approach, you might do something like this:

```
<header class="widget-title">
  <h1 class="widget-title__name">Stembolt</h1>
  <h2 class="widget-title__id">123.45</h2>
</header>
```

The classes demarcate each part of the component. The CSS might look like so:

```
.widget-title__name {
  font-weight: bold;
  text-transform: uppercase;
}

.widget-title__id {
  font-weight: normal;
  font-family: monospace;
}
```

Although the widget-title class doesn't get styling in this example, you can begin to see the theory here. Components have a class indicating what they are (not semantically, but presentationally), and we use a naming convention to create classes as needed for the parts of the component. Note that we *don't* prescribe the HTML tags to use; the CSS is agnostic. This allows us to re-use this component's styling in a situation where perhaps an <h3> is more appropriate than an <h1>.

This approach is sustainable, mostly because it provides a clear and simple way to keep CSS isolated. CSS can get very complicated when there is deep

---

[4]https://getbem.com
[5]http://smacss.com

nesting and stacking of styles, and an OOCSS approach instead keeps them flat

But, it's not perfect. There are a few downsides:

- Everything you style has to be a component with a name, even if that component is never re-used. This means that you have to make a *lot* of naming decisions. It also means that it's not clear from your CSS what components are actually intended for re-use.
- When you *do* identify re-usable components, you need an additional strategy for how to manage that. For example, if it turns out that components `widget_title`, `manufacturer_name`, and `shipping_location` are all what should be called a `title_component`, you now have to either rename the classes, or configure a CSS pre-processor to re-use the common styling.
- To predict how a view will render, you must mentally merge the `.css` file and the view. You cannot just look at the markup to know what styles will be applied.

The result is that you will read and write a lot of CSS. The CSS you write will more or less grow linearly with your markup and views, and the more of it that exists, the less likely you and your team are to re-use it without careful grooming and documentation.

Another approach is functional CSS.

9.2.3 Functional CSS

Functional CSS (sometimes called *atomic* CSS) is a strategy where you have a largely static set of small, single purpose, highly-presentational classes that you combine to achieve a certain look. For example, there might be a class named `fwb` that does nothing but set `font-weight` to `bold` and another called `ttu` which does nothing but sets `text-transform` to `uppercase`. To style some content in bold uppercase, you'd use `class="ttu fwb"`.

It's called *functional* in a nod to mathematical functions, which produce the same output for the given input. Classes in a functional CSS system have completely predictable and unambiguous behavior. They can feel like short-hand for using CSS directly in your markup.

Our widget title component would look like so:

```
<h1 class="fwb ttu">Stembolt</h1>
<h2 class="normal courier">123.45</h2>
```

The CSS for this code (which, remember, you don't have to write) might look like so:

```
.fwb     { font-weight: bold }
.normal  { font-weight: normal }
.ttu     { text-transform: uppercase }
.courier { font-family: Courier, monospace }
```

These terse classes are based on Tachyons[6]. When you use functional CSS, you typically use a library like Tachyons or Tailwind[7] which provide all the CSS classes you need. There are usually several CSS classes for each CSS attribute.

For example, there might be 10 classes for 10 common values for font-weight: 100, 200, 300, 400, 500, 600, 700, 800, 900, and bold. Tachyons uses extremely terse names like fw4 or fwb, whereas Tailwind uses more semantic names like font-thin or font-bold.

In my experience, Tachyons becomes easier to use over time, because most of the classes are terse initialisms and mnemonics. For example ttu is a way to set text-transform to uppercase. In Tailwind, the class to accomplish this is uppercase, which might read better but has zero connection to the underlying CSS it produces.

Functional CSS is not the Same as Inline Styles

Note that this approach is not identical to using inline styles, because you cannot style pseudo elements with inline styles, nor can you achieve different breakpoints and media queries with inline styles. Inline styles also have a higher specificity, so using classes for styling allows you to use inline styles if needed to solve a particular problem.

Functional CSS *is* highly sustainable, even if it doesn't seem so at first glance. Consider the markup examples we've seen so far in the book. I used inline styles to demonstrate what styling was being applied without having to actually discuss CSS. This was merely to keep us focused, but did you notice how you could look at *just* the markup and understand the intended visual presentation of the view?

Functional CSS provides this without using inline styles. It means that you can look at *just* the markup in order to understand how a page will be styled. It also means you rarely write CSS and thus have almost no CSS to actually manage.

---

[6] http://tachyons.io
[7] https://tailwindcss.com

Re-use with Functional CSS Leverages your HTML Templates

Unlike using a framework or OOCSS, functional CSS does not include an obvious way to extract re-usable components. If we have red bold text, set in the second largest font, all in uppercase with wide letter spacing, we'd have to write `<p class="red fwb f2 ttu tracked">` everywhere we wanted to re-use that.

Functional CSS approaches assume that the unit of re-use is not the CSS class, but your templating system. We discussed in the chapter "HTML Templates" on page 93 how to re-use markup using partials or View Components. Because that markup has classes that represent all the needed styles, this naturally allows re-use of styling as well.

Thinking of markup as the unit of re-use also provides one way to manage re-usable components, not two. That said, when you do need to create your own classes, you may want to re-use aspects of your functional CSS framework. Some frameworks make this easy—by providing CSS custom properties—and some make it more difficult, requiring a complex toolchain of configuration files and pre-processors.

Downsidies to Functional CSS

There are downsides to this approach:

- If your UI must be highly configurable, beyond just sizing, fonts, and colors, functional CSS pretty much won't work. This is not a common need, but if it is a real need, OOCSS will work better.
- If you have a split back-end and front-end team, you will need to adopt a workflow to allow both teams to work, since both teams would do the bulk of their work in the HTML templates. An OOCSS approach allows the front-end team to work mostly inside `.css` files.
- Complex styling such as custom form elements can't easily be done with functional CSS, so you would need a way to manage that. I would recommend you adopt something like BEM whenever you need to write a lot of `.css`.

Note on Tailwind's Lack of Design System

Since I first wrote this book, Tailwind has become quite popular, but it's worth understanding that Tailwind *does not* provide a design system. Tailwind allows you to use a functional style of CSS to achieve almost any combination of properties and values, then performs a build step on your code to produce the CSS. You can write a class like `font-[876]` and Tailwind will create that class to set `font-weight` to 876.

This behavior, while clever, eliminates one of the main advantages of functional CSS and *is not* sustainable. You *can* configure Tailwind to have a design system by crafting your own `tailwind.config.js`. If you decide to use Tailwind, I highly suggest you do this, otherwise you will have all the mess of semantic CSS, but spread all over your view code instead of in `.css` files.

Once you have chosen a strategy, you need to use it to build the design system, and the best way to do that is to create a living style guide.

9.3 Create a Living Style Guide to Document Your Design System and CSS Strategy

A living style guide is documentation that both uses your design system and shows developers how to apply it to the view. Bootstrap's documentation[8] is an example of this. It shows both the visual appearance of the components it provides as well as the markup you need to achieve that appearance.

You need this for your app. If you don't have this, developers will not know what re-usable components exist, nor will they know how to apply the CSS strategy you have chosen. And then your CSS will be an unsustainable mess.

Let's create a style guide. We'll adopt the functional CSS strategy and use Tachyons. To specify our design system, ideally we'd use some CSS custom properties that our CSS framework knows about. Tachyons doesn't currently support this, but there is a SASS[9] port that allows customizing it.

I've created the tachyonscss-rails[10] gem that is designed to work with Tachyons, SASS, and Rails 7. We'll need to add both `sassc-rails` and this gem to our `Gemfile`:

```
# Gemfile

  # lograge changes Rails' logging to a more
  # traditional one-line-per-event format
  gem "lograge"
→
→ # Tachyons is a functional CSS framework
→ # we'll use to style our views
→ gem "tachyonscss-rails"
→
→ # tachyonscss-rails embeds a SASS version
→ # of Tachyons, so we need to include
→ # a SASS compiler
→ gem "sassc-rails"
```

---

[8]https://getbootstrap.com/docs/4.4/getting-started/introduction/
[9]https://sass-lang.com
[10]https://github.com/sustainable-rails/tachyonscss-rails

```
# View Component is used to manage
# and test complex view logic
```

Next, we'll install these two gems:

```
> bundle install
«lots of output»
```

To use this, we need to convert our `application.css` to be a SASS stylesheet. The easiest way to do that is to delete the existing file:

```
> rm app/assets/stylesheets/application.css
```

And create `application.scss` (note the file extension):

```
/* app/assets/stylesheets/application.scss */

@import "tachyons";
```

`@import` is a SASS function that brings in external SASS files. Figuring out the value to give it for an externally-required gem is not usually possible—the gem maintainer has to tell you. In this case, the gem maintainer is me, and the README indicates to use "tachyons".

As mentioned above, our design system should have at least a set of font sizes, spacings, and colors. For the sake of brevity, let's assume that our design system's spacing and colors are exactly those provided by Tachyons. Our font sizes are different. Our designer has chosen these eight sizes (specified in `rems`):

- 4.8rem
- 3.7rem
- 2.8rem
- 2.2rem
- 1.7rem
- 1.3rem
- 1.0rem
- 0.8rem

The tachyonscss-rails gem embeds the .scss files from the Tachyons SASS port. You can see what is included by looking at the gem's source on GitHub[11].

At the top are the values for font sizes, like so:

```
$font-size-headline: 6rem !default;
$font-size-subheadline: 5rem !default;
$font-size-1: 3rem !default;
$font-size-2: 2.25rem !default;
$font-size-3: 1.5rem !default;
$font-size-4: 1.25rem !default;
$font-size-5: 1rem !default;
$font-size-6: .875rem !default;
$font-size-7: .75rem !default;
```

The !default construct means that if we don't set a value for that variable, the value in _variables.scss will be used. For example, if we don't set a value for $font-size-1, the value 3rem will be used. This allows tachyons to have a default design system if we don't provide our own.

To override these, we'll set values for all nine font variables (the two smallest fonts will be the same size since we only have eight font sizes). It's important that we leave $font-size-5 as 1rem, because that is assumed by Tachyons to be the body font size, which is the size of normal text.

Note that we'll need to set these values *before* the call to @import or they won't take affect. Here's the change to app/assets/stylesheets/application.scss:

```
/* app/assets/stylesheets/application.scss */

→ $font-size-headline: 4.8rem;
→ $font-size-subheadline: 3.7rem;
→ $font-size-1: 2.8rem;
→ $font-size-2: 2.2rem;
→ $font-size-3: 1.7rem;
→ $font-size-4: 1.3rem;
→ /* font-size-5 should always be 1rem
→  * as Tachyons expects this to be the
→  * body font. */
→ $font-size-5: 1rem;
```

---

[11]https://github.com/sustainable-rails/tachyonscss-rails/blob/main/app/assets/stylesheets/scss/_variables.scss

```
→ $font-size-6: 0.8rem;
→ $font-size-7: 0.8rem;
→
  @import "tachyons";
```

With that done, we'll create our style guide, which is a demonstration of our design system. We'll create a new resource called `design_system_docs` that has an `index` action.

We'll first add the route, but only if we are in development (we don't want our users seeing the style guide):

```
# config/routes.rb

      resources :widgets, only: [ :show, :update, :destroy ]
    end

→   if Rails.env.development?
→     resources :design_system_docs, only: [ :index ]
→   end
→
    ####
    # Custom routes start here
    #
```

We still want to follow the conventions we've established about views, so that means our controller methods should expose an instance variable named `@design_system_docs`. We'll use `OpenStruct` again to create this object. It'll have three methods: `font_sizes`, `sizes`, and `colors`.

The `font_sizes` attribute will be a list of class names to use to achieve those font sizes. For `sizes`, since there are margins and padding, we'll use the numbers 1–5 and dynamically construct the class names in the view. For `colors`, we'll create a map from the color name to the CSS class that achieves it.

```
# app/controllers/design_system_docs_controller.rb

class DesignSystemDocsController < ApplicationController

  def index
    @design_system_docs = OpenStruct.new(
```

```
    font_sizes: [
      "f-headline",
      "f-subheadline",
      "f1",
      "f2",
      "f3",
      "f4",
      "f5",
      "f6",
    ],
    sizes: [ 1,2,3,4,5 ],
    colors: {
      text: "near-black",
      green: "dark-green",
      red: "dark-red",
      orange: "orange"
    }
  )
  end
end
```

The view is going to be a bit gnarly, because we have to generate markup that uses these styles but also show the code that achieved that markup. We'll have three sections and a <nav> at the top, along with a link to Tachyons' docs.

```erb
<%# app/views/design_system_docs/index.html.erb %>

<section class="pa3">
  <h1>
    Design System Docs
    <nav class="f4 di ml3">
      <a href="#font-sizes">Font Sizes</a> |
      <a href="#sizes">Sizes</a> |
      <a href="#colors">Colors</a> |
      <a href="https://tachyons.io/docs/">Tachyons Docs</a>
    </nav>
  </h1>
  <h2 id="font-sizes">Font Sizes</h2>
  <% @design_system_docs.font_sizes.
       each do |font_size_css_class| %>
    <p class="<%= font_size_css_class %> mt0 mb0">
      <%= font_size_css_class %> Font Size
    </p>
```

```
      <code><pre>
&lt;p class="<%= font_size_css_class %>"&gt;
  <%= font_size_css_class %> Font Size
&lt;/p&gt;
      </pre></code>
    <% end %>
    <h2 id="sizes">Sizes</h2>
    <% @design_system_docs.sizes.each do |size_number| %>
      <h3>Size <%= size_number %></h3>
      <div class="pa<%= size_number %> ba
                  h<%= size_number %>
                  w<%= size_number %> bg-gray">
         
      </div>
      <code><pre>
&lt;div class="pa<%= size_number %>"&gt;
  Padding all sides
&lt;/div&gt;

&lt;div class="ma<%= size_number %>"&gt;
  Margin all sides
&lt;/div&gt;
      </pre></code>
    <% end %>
    <h2 id="colors">Colors</h2>
    <% @design_system_docs.colors.each do |name, css_class| %>
      <h3><%= name.to_s.humanize %></h3>
      <div class="ma1 pv3 ph2 h4 bg-<%= css_class %> white">
        <code><pre>
&lt;div class="bg-<%= css_class %>"&gt;
  <%= name %> background
&lt;/div&gt;
        </pre></code>
      </div>
      <div class="ma1 pv3 ph2 h4 ba
                  b--<%= css_class %>
                  <%= css_class %> bg-white">
        <code><pre>
&lt;div class="<%= css_class %> b--<%= css_class %>"&gt;
  <%= name %> border and text
&lt;/div&gt;
        </pre></code>
      </div>
    <% end %>
</section>
```

Now, if you go to /design_system_docs, you should see it just like the screenshot "Font Size Documentation" on the next page, "Sizes Documentation" on page 155, and "Color Documentation" on page 156.

You may need more documentation than this, depending on what you are doing. You could also build the page statically instead of making an object like I did. In any case, this page should provide as much information as possible about your CSS strategy, the design system, any reusable components, and how to use it all.

Whenever a re-usable component is created, this page should also be updated, and you'll have to manage that with code review or pair programming.

If you can manage this, you'll stick to your CSS Strategy and leverage your design system, and while your CSS won't be amazingly perfect, it will be as sustainable as you can make it, and that's a pretty good result.

Up Next

CSS is not an easy thing to learn or manage. So it goes with JavaScript.

Font Sizes

f-headline Font Size

```
<p class="f-headline">
  f-headline Font Size
</p>
```

f-subheadline Font Size

```
<p class="f-subheadline">
  f-subheadline Font Size
</p>
```

f1 Font Size

```
<p class="f1">
  f1 Font Size
</p>
```

Figure 9.1: Font Size Documentation

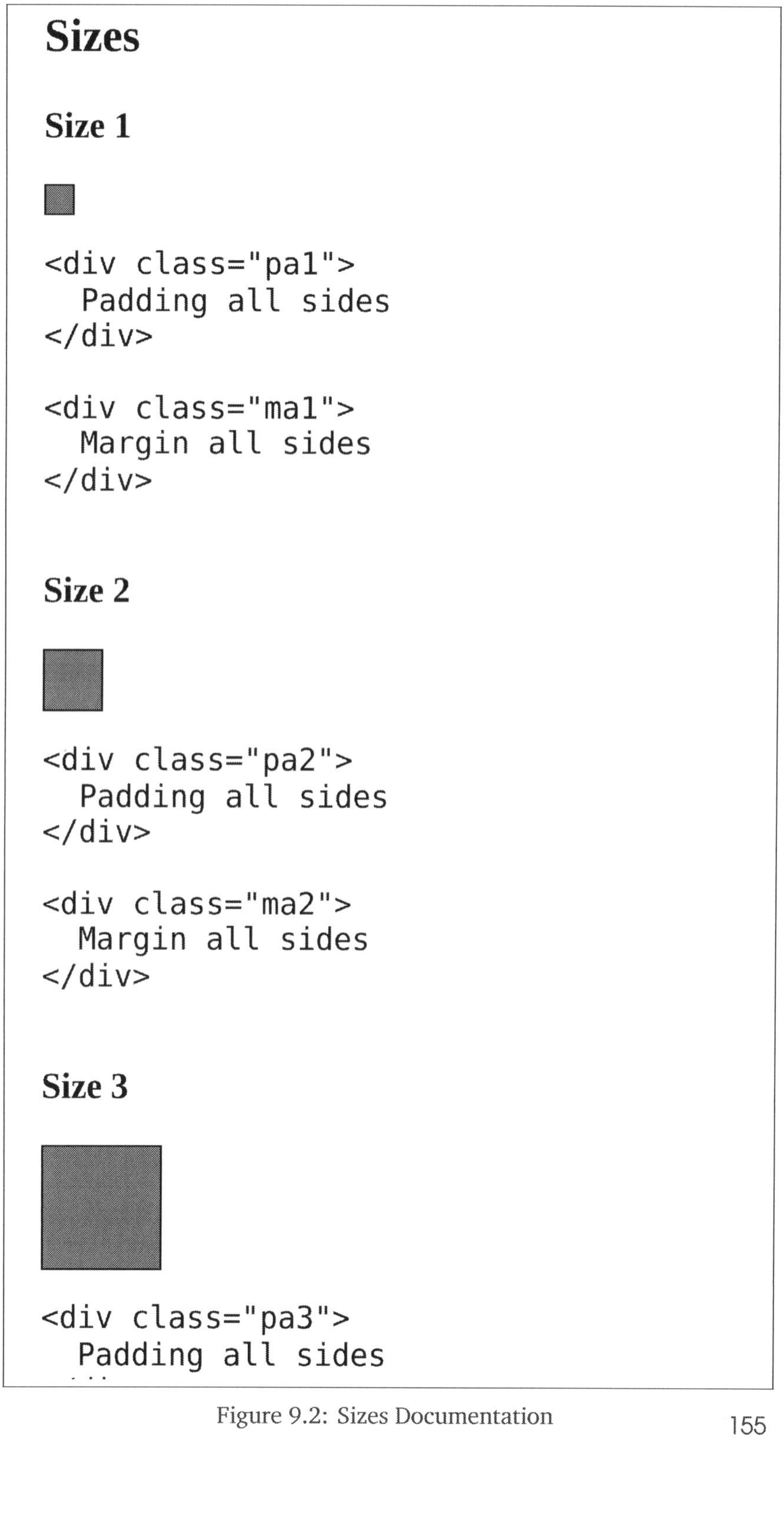

Sizes

Size 1

```
<div class="pa1">
  Padding all sides
</div>

<div class="ma1">
  Margin all sides
</div>
```

Size 2

```
<div class="pa2">
  Padding all sides
</div>

<div class="ma2">
  Margin all sides
</div>
```

Size 3

```
<div class="pa3">
  Padding all sides
```

Figure 9.2: Sizes Documentation

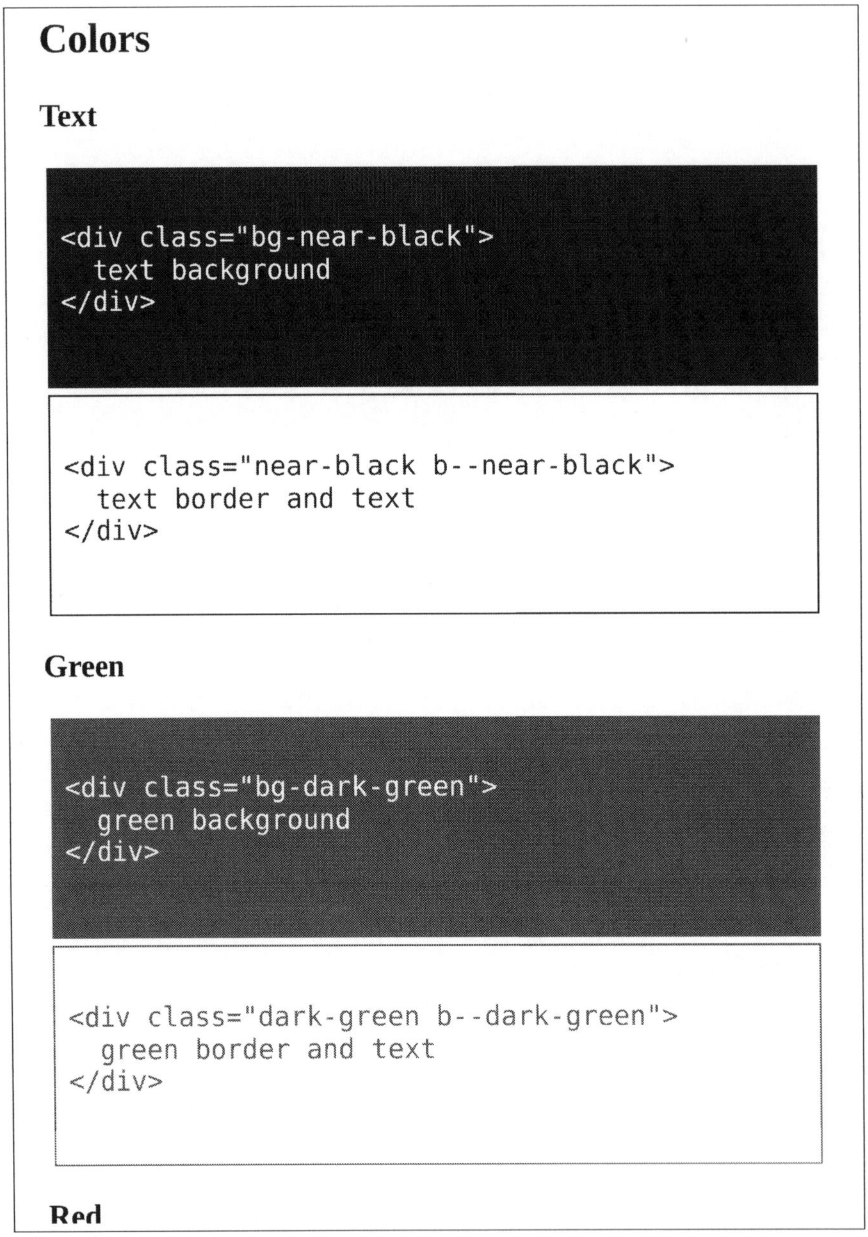

Colors

Text

```
<div class="bg-near-black">
  text background
</div>
```

```
<div class="near-black b--near-black">
  text border and text
</div>
```

Green

```
<div class="bg-dark-green">
  green background
</div>
```

```
<div class="dark-green b--dark-green">
  green border and text
</div>
```

Red

Figure 9.3: Color Documentation

10

Minimize JavaScript

JavaScript and front-end development is a *deep* topic. I won't be able to cover it all here and I definitely can't give you a guide on sustainably creating highly complex dynamic web applications that run entirely in the browser. The good news is that you almost certainly don't need your application to work that way. At best, you'll need what Zach Briggs calls "islands of interactivity"[1]: bits of dynamic behavior on some of your pages.

The single best thing you can do to keep your front-end sustainable is to use only what JavaScript you actually need to deliver value to the app's users. There are a lot of current realities about client-side JavaScript and web browsers that make it inherently more difficult to work with than back-end technologies.

In this chapter, we'll focus on JavaScript generally: how to think about it and manage it at a high level. The overall strategy here is:

- Understand why JavaScript is a more serious liability than your Ruby code.
- Embrace server-rendered views wherever client-side interactivity isn't required.
- Tweak Turbo's defaults to create a stable baseline of front-end behavior.

JavaScript solves real problems we face as developers, but it's not perfect—how could it be? The strategy here is designed to keep your app sustainable by dealing directly with the realities of JavaScript and the front-end ecosystem. It's important to make decisions based on the realities of how our tools work, not on how we wish they worked.

To understand this strategy requires being honest about how serious of a liability client-side JavaScript is to your app, so let's dive in.

10.1 How and Why JavaScript is a Serious Liability

A *liability* is something that we are responsible for. Liabilities aren't good or bad by nature, but the concept is a useful lens to understand technical decisions.

---
[1] https://modernweb.com/limit-javascript/

Your app is a liability. You are responsible for it. You are responsible for building it, maintaining it, operating it, and explaining its behavior to others. This book is about how to manage that responsibility.

But liabilities are relative. Compared to the other code in your app, client-side JavaScript (here on called simply "JavaScript") is a more serious liability. It is a large responsibility relative to the back-end, all other things being equal.

It's important to understand why this is, so that you can drive your technical architecture decisions based on realities and not dogma.

There are three contributors to JavaScript as a more serious liability:

- You have no control over the runtime environment.
- Your JavaScript's behavior is difficult or impossible to observe in production.
- The ecosystem values small decoupled libraries that tolerate breaking changes in order to progress quickly.

Let's talk about each one of these realities.

10.1.1 You Cannot Control The Runtime Environment

Your JavaScript will run on many different versions of many different brands of browsers on many different versions of many different brands of operating systems on many different versions of many different brands of computers connected to many different types of networks.

I can't think of a more difficult scenario in which to build software.

Your Ruby code, on the other hand, runs on a runtime of a single version of a single operating system on a single brand of computer using a single type of network connection. Or at least it is possible to arrange this. Certainly the use of cloud services results in some aspects of our runtime being unknown, but it's still our choice to cede that control.

The runtime environment for our JavaScript, being out of our control, means that the behavior of the code running there is hard to accurately predict. A common strategy for managing code running in unpredictable environments is to heavily monitor its behavior to find issues and fix them quickly.

But with JavaScript, this is not so easy.

10.1.2 JavaScript's Behavior is Difficult to Observe

When developing JavaScript, we can run it in a browser on our own computer, thus controlling the runtime environment during development. But even in this stable environment, actually observing the behavior of the code is surprisingly difficult.

Pretty much the only mechanisms you have in your development environment are the odd calls to `console.log` or step through the code in the browser's debugger. Browsers do provide additional tools for inspecting your code, but JavaScript's nature prevents them from being very sophisticated. When you see errors in the console, the stack traces are often wrong. Most JavaScript runtimes produce unhelpful errors such as "undefined is not a function". But at least you can do something in your own browser.

In production, JavaScript is running on the browsers of your app's users and there is no way by default for you to observe that behavior on any level. If you've ever supported applications for users at the company you work for, you've no doubt asked those users to open the browser console to help debug a problem[2].

What this means is that your code that's already running on myriad environments you cannot control also cannot be observed. The most common tool available to try to observe JavaScript's behavior is to install an error reporting system like Bugsnag. In my experience, tools like this are useful, but they produce a lot of noise and don't drive a lot of clarity (see the sidebar "A Year of JS Monitoring and Nothing to Show For It" below for an example of this). JavaScript libraries you depend on generate spurious error messages and, even with source maps on production, stack traces are almost always wrong.

> ### A Year of JS Monitoring and Nothing to Show For It
>
> When building the public website for the healthcare startup where I was CTO, I installed Bugsnag, a popular error-reporting service. Our website didn't have a lot of JavaScript, but it did have some and there were a few places where, if the JavaScript was broken, a potential customer could not proceed and sign up for the service.
>
> During the first year of its existence, this error reporting system captured and reported numerous errors, usually several a week. Without fail, they were all from marketing pixels we were using to track and analyze our paid ad performance. In a year, there were exactly two issues with our JavaScript, and these were related to users on Internet Explorer 11, which was technically below our browser baseline.
>
> We significantly dialed back our use of front-end error reporting to only those pages were it was most crucial. Those pages were the ones using our credit card processor's JavaScript to capture card information. To this day, it is those components that generate all of our front-end errors, and the errors are usually completely useless messages like "error from stripe.js".
>
> If you've ever wondered how fancy websites from big companies seem to just not work for months on end, this is probably how. They have no way to know what is truly broken.

---

[2] The associates working in Stitch Fix's warehouse called the JavaScript console "The Matrix", because it was like going behind the scenes of the real world and hacking the system.

Compare this to your back-end code. It is possible to get a very fine-grained understanding of how it behaves. By default, Rails logs requests and responses, which is more than you get with JavaScript. We set up lograge in the section "Improving Production Logging with lograge" on page 52, which makes those logs even more useful. We can write our own log messages. We can install tools like DataDog or Honeycomb to tell us how often certain parts of our app are executed and how long they took. And on and on.

This means that problems in your JavaScript code are harder to predict, harder to detect, and harder to fix once detected.

But it gets worse, because the ecosystem as it stands moves forward very fast, favoring progress over stability.

10.1.3 The Ecosystem Values Highly-Decoupled Modules that Favor Progress over Stability

We haven't set up NPM in our project, but my guess is that you have at least one project you've worked on that uses it. Take a peek into `node_modules`. On a brand new Rails 6 application there are 770 modules installed (Rails 7 does not require NodeJS). These modules are all needed for the six direct dependencies the Rails 6 app has on JavaScript modules. Our Rails app has a direct dependency on 16 Ruby Gems, which ultimately require the installation of 131 RubyGems.

The reason for this disparity is that the JavaScript ecosystem is built on many small de-coupled libraries. For example, map-obj is a library that contains a single nine-line function. That's it.

Small, de-coupled libraries aren't necessarily good or bad, but the way this affects you and your app's sustainability is that there are more packages that must interoperate with each other. When you consider that these packages are all maintained by different people with different road maps and priorities, more packages means higher risk of one thing breaking another.

If this isn't bad enough, the JavaScript ecosystem also favors progress over stability. It's not uncommon for point releases of a library to contain breaking changes. Libraries also have inter-dependencies on other libraries that are not explicit. If you've seen warnings about "peer dependencies", this means you have potentially incompatible versions of two libraries running, but you are on your own to figure out how to fix it. Usually, you can't without removing the libraries altogether from your app.

I realize Rails, too, favors progress over stability[3], but Rails goes to great pains to maintain backwards compatibility, point out deprecated APIs and provide clear upgrade paths for users. This is not common for JavaScript libraries.

---

[3] https://rubyonrails.org/doctrine

This reality results in a situation where regular updates of your dependencies can cause a cascading effect of errors that can be difficult and time-consuming to fix. While you can somewhat rely on the Rails core team to make sure the dependencies that are a part of Rails keep working with Rails, anything you bring in isn't subject to that level of care. This is your responsibility.

The single best thing you can do to manage the liabilities that come with JavaScript is to minimize its use to only where it is needed. By all means, use it when you need it, but don't use it when you don't.

A big step toward that goal is to prefer server-rendered views using ERB.

10.2 Embrace Server-Rendered Rails Views

Rails server-rendered views work very much like PHP, JSP, or ASP: the server loads an HTML template, populates that with dynamic data, renders it into HTML, and sends that HTML to the browser as part of the request/response cycle. This interaction model is easy to understand, instrument, predict, and test.

Outside of Rails, it's common for developers to send the HTML templates bundled with dynamic data to the browser and have the browser render the HTML on the client-side. With sufficiently powerful back-end APIs, developers can build the entire application to run in the browser using JavaScript and markup. This combination is known as the "JAM Stack", with "JAM" standing for JavaScript, APIs, and Markup.

Setting aside the risks with JavaScript we just discussed, JAM Stack apps are architecturally more complex. They have more moving parts that must be carefully coordinated in order to produce a working app. This means that simple changes in a JAM Stack app can be difficult to make.

The JAM Stack is not a good default choice in most cases. The power it brings is almost never worth the carrying cost—which is large. The JAM Stack approach should be treated as a surgical tool you use only when you need it, and not something to use by default.

To understand why, and thus why you should prefer server-rendered views instead, let's break down both approaches.

10.2.1 Architecture of Rails Server-Rendered Views

As mentioned above, the architecture of the default view rendering in Rails is for the server to render HTML and send that to the client as shown in the figure on the next page.

Rails allows the inclusion of JavaScript that is loaded after the page renders to provide interactive elements to the server-rendered page.

The benefits of this approach are many:

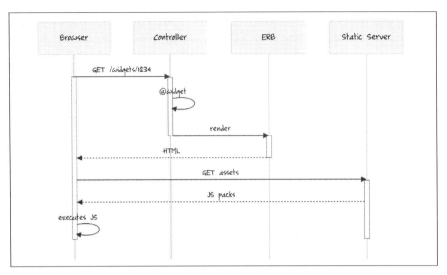

Figure 10.1: Server-Rendered Views

- It is stable and predictable, since HTML rendering happens on the server side in an environment you can control and observe.
- Because only the interactive parts of the page are using client-side JavaScript, there is minimal client-side state to manage. Most pages are stateless with no behavior on the client-side after initial rendering by the browser.
- Any features that don't manipulate the DOM on the client side can be easily and quickly tested without firing up a web browser. This makes tests of features using server-rendered views faster and less flaky.
- Click events, network errors, and loading UI are handled by the browser by default without having to do anything special.

This approach is appropriate for most common needs, such as rendering dynamic content, managing form submissions, and other basic user interactions. The main downside to this approach is that you need to manage how JavaScript interacts with the server-rendered HTML. Depending on the technology you choose, this could result in some complexity.

You may use Hotwire, which is included in Rails 7. This provides a zero-JavaScript solution for common uses cases, but leaves you on your own for anything else. Or you might choose React, which requires that some of your HTML be written in JSX, leaving you two ways to write markup. In the next chapter on page 169, we'll talk a bit about how to navigate these trade-offs.

Another perceived downside is performance. The theory goes that full page refreshes are always slower than if content is fetched with Ajax. It is true that server-rendered HTML sends more bytes over the network than an

Ajax request and it is true that re-rendering the entire page is slower than updating part of the existing DOM.

What is not true is that these differences always matter. Optimizing the performance of an application is a tricky business. Often the source of poor performance isn't what you think it might be, and it requires careful analysis to understand both where the problem lies and what the right solution is.

In my experience, most performance problems are caused by the database. If our page requires executing a database query, and that query isn't indexed, no front-end rendering optimization in the world is going to fix what a single line of SQL can.

All this to say that choosing to avoid server-rendered views because of a performance problem that you don't know you have and that you don't know matters is not a sound basis for making technical architecture decisions.

And, of course, using the JAM Stack to boost performance carries a large carrying cost. Let's see how that works.

10.2.2 Architecture of the JAM Stack

A JAM Stack app is a bundle of JavaScript that contains markup, code to render that markup, code to fetch data from a remote server, and code to manage the state driving the dynamic contents of the markup. Sometimes this code is executed on the server to pre-render the markup for a faster startup time in the browser, but the overall programming model is centered around managing DOM updates in the browser based on browser events and API calls, as shown in the figure on the next page.

State management is a significant part of a JAM Stack application, as most technologies provide a programming model where only the part of the DOM affected by state changes is updated when state does change. Thus, a JAM Stack application, in addition to having HTML templates for rendering HTML, also has a significant bit of wiring to make sure markup is connected to the correct state.

There are three benefits to this approach:

- Highly interactive UIs are easier to create by consolidating everything into a single bundle of code.
- If you do not control the back-end APIs, you can build a full-featured app with just front-end technologies.
- If the entire app uses the JAM Stack, you have a single view technology.

Carefully consider your problem space against these benefits. There are *many* downsides to this approach:

- You must carefully map JSON responses to the input of each front-end component and carefully manage the state of the app's front-end.

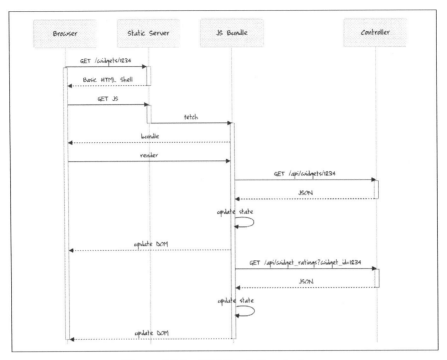

Figure 10.2: JAM Stack Rendering

There is no one accepted approach, and common tools like Redux are complex. Managing state in even small apps can be exceedingly difficult to get right.
- You must either replicate Rails' form helpers to generate the right markup or abandon them altogether, which can complicate your controller code when processing form submissions.
- You must provide a custom user experience for fault tolerance and progress, because the default for a JAM Stack application is to silently fail. If you've clicked a link in an app and nothing happens, this is why.
- You cannot adequately test this app without heavy use of browser based tests. While you can write unit tests that simulate the DOM this isn't the same as testing how the code works when fully integrated. Browser-based tests are slow and can be flaky, which makes your app's overall test suite much slower and flakier than a server-rendered equivalent.
- If you configure server-side rendering, it becomes harder to write the code, because you must account for it executing on the server *and* on a browser.
- JAM Stack apps have more code in the browser, which means more of your app is running in environments you cannot control or observe.

A JAMStack approach might feel good because it decouples the front-end from the back-end, and we are often taught that decoupling is good. But Rails is designed to couple key parts of our app together to make common needs easy to implement.

When working on a Rails app, the developers have control over the entire experience, so the back-end can be built in concert with the front-end. Decoupling them doesn't have a strong advantage. It just makes things harder to build.

That's not to say you should never use the JAM Stack in your app, but you should use it only when it's needed, and only if you are confident that the risks are outweighed by the benefits. This is not common.

10.2.3 Server-Rendered Views by Default, JAM Stack Only When Needed

I have experienced at least four different teams create sustainability problems by using the JAM Stack for features that did not require it. The strong boundary that was created between front-end and back-end meant that simple changes required orders of magnitude more work than had they used static HTML or ERB. Even basic copy changes based on dynamic data would cause a cascade of changes from the API layer to components nested several layers deep.

If you use Rails server-rendered views by default, you will create a situation in which simple things are simple. You can still use the JAM Stack in portions of your app when you determine there is a strong need to do so. See the sidebar "Single Feature JAM Stack Apps at Stitch Fix" on the next page for an example of how this can make your app successful.

> **Single Feature JAM Stack Apps at Stitch Fix**
>
> The Stitch Fix warehouse was originally managed by a run-of-the-mill Rails app that we called SPECTRE. The warehouse was comprised of different stations and the person working those stations used a custom-built screen in SPECTRE to do their job. For example, one station printed shipping labels, and another located items for a shipment.
>
> Locating items—which we called *picking*—was by far the most frequent activity in the warehouse. Users would be given five items at a time to locate. This required at least seven full-page refreshes: one to get started, one for each item, and one to tell the picker what to do after all five items were picked. The Internet connection in the warehouses was initially very slow and unreliable, so these page refreshes, driven by server requests, often timed out and caused pickers to spend too much time picking.
>
> We re-implemented this feature using the hottest front-end framework of 2014: AngularJS. The initial page load grabbed all the data, and the browser handled all interactivity during the picking process. The only network connection needed was after picking was complete. The entire picking process could be done without any network connection at all.
>
> Even though the rest of SPECTRE was driven by server-rendered views, the picking feature was a JAM Stack app that solved a real problem for users. While there was friction if you had to switch back and forth while working on SPECTRE, the result was that easy things were easy, but complex things could be built.

All this to say, you will need JavaScript. You might need very small bits of glue code between elements or full-blown interactive components, but you can't avoid it entirely. You want it predictable, stable, and small.

10.3 Tweak Turbo to Provide a Slightly Better Experience

> This section's code is in the folder 10-03/ of the sample code.

In order to effectively manage the behavior of your views, and any JavaScript that is needed, you need a solid baseline of behavior on which to build. Rails provides this, with one tiny exception: Turbo's default setting for showing a progress bar.

Turbo (formerly called Turbolinks) hijacks all clicks and form submissions and replaces them with Ajax calls. It then replaces the <body> of the page with whatever the <body> is of the returned result. This is ostensibly to make every page faster, but it often leads to your app feeling broken instead since it will only show a progress bar after 500ms of waiting.

My recommendation is to modify Turbo's progress timeout.

The reason is that Turbo can make your app feel broken any time a controller fails to respond instantly. A common rule of thumb in user experience is that if the response to a user's action takes more than 100ms to happen, the user will lose the sense of causality between their action and the result. The app will feel broken.

If your controller, along with the network time, takes more than 100ms to respond, and Turbo is enabled, your app may feel broken, because Turbo prevents the browser from showing any progress UI. Turbo will provide its own, but only if more than 500ms have elapsed. That's too long.

Fortunately, we can change the default without much code. Our app is loading Turbo from app/javascript/application.js, but we need access to the returned object in order to make configuration changes. We'll modify the import statement to assign the result to the variable Turbo, which we can then use to call setProgressBarDelay:

```
/* app/javascript/application.js */

  // Configure your import map in config/importmap.rb. Read mor...
→ import { Turbo } from "@hotwired/turbo-rails"
→
→ // The default of 500ms is too long and
→ // users can lose the causal link between clicking
→ // a link and seeing the browser respond
→ Turbo.setProgressBarDelay(100)
→
  import "controllers"
```

One thing to note about Turbo is that while the developers have gone to great lengths to make sure it plays well with the browser and any other JavaScript you may have, it *is* a layer of indirection between user actions in the browser and your code. Make sure you understand how any JavaScript that might also hook into the browser works. In particular, the use of DOMContentLoaded could cause unpredictable behavior, since it won't be triggered every time a link is clicked (you must use the turbo:load event, instead).

Up Next

These small changes will give you a more predictable base on which to build, along with a reasonable default user experience.

Of course, there's almost no way to avoid JavaScript entirely and so this leads to our next topic, which is how to manage the JavaScript you *do* have to write. You want to use whatever JavaScript you actually need to make your app succeed, but you should carefully manage it, since it is the least stable part of your app.

11
Carefully Manage the JavaScript You Need

Despite the above-average carrying cost of JavaScript in your app, you cannot avoid it, and many features of your app will require some JavaScript. You don't want to stubbornly avoid JavaScript at all costs, but you *do* want carefully manage how you use it.

This chapter will discuss three techniques to maintain control over your JavaScript, but keep in mind these are scratching the surface. The more JavaScript you have, the more closely you'll need to manage it—the same as any code in your app.

The three techniques we'll discuss here are:

- Embrace plain JavaScript for basic interactions wherever you can.
- Use at most one framework like Hotwire or React, and choose that framework for sustainability.
- Ensure your system tests break when your JavaScript is broken.

Let's jump into the first one, which is to embrace the power of plain, framework-free JavaScript.

11.1 Embrace Plain JavaScript for Basic Interactions

> This section's code is in the folder `11-01/` of the sample code.

The more dependencies your app has, the harder it's going to be to maintain. Fixing bugs, addressing security issues, and leveraging new features all require updating and managing your dependencies. Further, as we discussed way back in "Consistency" on page 14, the fewer ways of doing something in the app, the better.

Your app likely doesn't need many interactive features, especially when it's young. For any interactivity that you *do* need, it can often be simpler to build features that work without JavaScript then add interactivity on top of that. Modern browsers provide powerful APIs for interacting with your markup, and it can reduce the overall complexity of your app to use those APIs before reaching for something like React.

Let's do that in this section. Our existing widget rating system is built in a classic fashion. Although there is no back-end currently, you might imagine that it will show your rating for any widget where you've provided one. Let's suppose we want to do that without a page refresh. We want the user to submit a rating and have the page remove the widget rating form and replace it with a message like "You rated this widget 4".

Let's see how to do this with just plain JavaScript. I realize that the Hotwire[1] framework in Rails provides a zero-code solution to this exact use case. However, if you have not written plain JavaScript in a while, it's important to see just how little code is required to do this. The point I'm making in this section is that you can get quite far without taking on any dependencies.

There are a lot of ways to do it, but the way I'll show here is one that keeps the number of moving parts to a minimum. We'll render all the markup and most of the content we will need for this feature in the ERB file, using CSS to hide the markup that should not be shown.

When the user clicks on a rating, we'll run some JavaScript to modify the CSS on various parts of the markup to remove the form and show the rating, while dynamically inserting that rating into the DOM in the right place.

First, we'll add a new bit of markup that says "Thanks for rating this". Semantically, this should be inside a <p> tag. Since the rating depends on what button the user clicked on, we'll place a <span> to hold the value, and we'll use JavaScript to set it dynamically. The entire thing will need to be surrounded in a <div>.

We'll then use `data-` attributes on each bit of markup so that we can locate them using JavaScript. This is preferable to using special classes because `data-` elements aren't commonly used for styling, whereas classes are almost always used for styling.

```
<%# app/components/widget_rating_component.html.erb %>

  <section>
→   <div class="dn" data-rating-present>
→     <p>Thanks for rating this a
→       <span data-rating-label></span>
→     </p>
→   </div>
    <div class="clear-floats">
```

---

[1] https://hotwired.dev

```
          <h3 style="float: left; margin: 0; padding-right: 1rem;">
            Rate This Widget:
```

The existing `<div>` will get hidden when the user clicks a rating, so that needs a `data-` attribute as well. We'll also replace our hand-made `clear-floats` class with Tachyons' `cf` class that does the same thing.

```
<%# app/components/widget_rating_component.html.erb %>

          <span data-rating-label></span>
        </p>
      </div>
→     <div class="cf" data-no-rating-present>
        <h3 style="float: left; margin: 0; padding-right: 1rem;">
          Rate This Widget:
        </h3>
```

Next, we'll make two changes to the `button_to` call. The first is to make it a remote Ajax call to `WidgetRatingsController`. That controller currently does a redirect, but we'll remove that so that it responds with an HTTP 204. This will allow us to trigger back-end logic without a page refresh. The second change is to add a `data-` attribute to the button so that we can attach a click handler to it.

First, we'll add `remote: true` and `data-rating` to the `button_to` call:

```
# app/components/widget_rating_component.html.erb

            <li style="float: left">
              <%= button_to rating,
                      widget_ratings_path,
→                     remote: true,
→                     data: {
→                       rating: true
→                     },
                      params: {
                              widget_id: widget.id,
                              rating: rating
```

Then, we'll remove the redirect in the controller. I like to add the comment `# default render` whenever there is branching logic in a controller, since the absence of code in a Rails controller *does* imply a particular behavior is going to occur.

```
# app/controllers/widget_ratings_controller.rb

    def create
      if params[:widget_id]
        # find the widget
        # update its rating
✗ #        redirect_to widget_path(params[:widget_id]),
✗ #          notice: "Thanks for rating!"
→       # default render
      else
        head :bad_request
      end
```

Since there is no template for this controller action, the default behavior is to return an HTTP 204, which is what we want. If we wanted to render a view or take an action for a non-remote call, we can use `respond_to` to differentiate.

Next, we need to write the actual JavaScript. We'll put that in `app/javascript/widget_ratings/index.js` which we'll later reference via the main `application.js` file. The way this will work is that we'll create a function named `updateUIWithRating` that will locate all the DOM elements with `data-rating-present` and show them by adding Tachyons' `db` class, which stands for `display: block` (thus showing them).

We'll then locate all elements with `data-no-rating-present` and add `dn`, which stands for `display: none` (thus hiding them). Finally, we'll locate the `<span>` with `data-rating-label` and set its inner text to the chosen rating, which will make the user see a sentence like "You rated this widget 4".

We'll use `document.querySelectorAll`, which allows locating elements via a CSS selector and returning an array of matching elements. Even though we only have one element for each selector we're going to use, it's better to have our JavaScript not be coupled to that. Instead, it'll handle any number of those selectors. `updateUIWithRating` will accept the document and the rating as parameters.

```
/* app/javascript/widget_ratings/index.js */

const updateUIWithRating = (document, rating) => {
  document.querySelectorAll("[data-rating-present]").
```

```
    forEach( (element) => {
      element.classList.add("db")
      element.classList.remove("dn")
  })

  document.querySelectorAll("[data-no-rating-present]").
    forEach( (element) => {
      element.classList.add("dn")
  })

  document.querySelectorAll("[data-rating-label]").
    forEach( (element) => {
      element.innerText = `${rating}`
  })
}
```

Note that the way we show and hide elements is to use CSS. Because we are using functional CSS as discussed in "Functional CSS" on page 144, we can use the same techniques here that we'd use in our markup, which a is nice bit of consistency when it comes to styling the visual appearance of our app.

Now, we want this function to be run whenever a widget rating button is clicked. To do that, we need to create an onclick event handler for each button. To do *that* we have to wait until the DOM has been loaded so the buttons are there for us to hook into. Since we are using Turbo (as it is configured by default), the way to wait on the DOM to be loaded is to wait for the event turbo:load, which is the Turbo equivalent of DOMContentLoaded.

We'll wrap all of this into a function named start, and we'll export that function so it can be called in app/javascript/application.js. Note that start will require the window as a parameter. Passing in global objects like window and document keeps our functions self-contained if we should need to unit test them.

```
/* app/javascript/widget_ratings/index.js */

        element.innerText = `${rating}`
    })
  }
→
→ const start = (window) => {
→   const document = window.document
→   window.addEventListener("turbo:load", () => {
→     document.querySelectorAll(
→       "button[data-rating]"
```

```
→      ).forEach( (element) => {
→        element.onclick = (event) => {
→          const rating = element.innerText
→          updateUIWithRating(document, rating)
→        }
→      })
→    })
→ }
→
→ export const WidgetRatings = {
→   start: start,
→ }
```

The reason we exported start is so that the code in widget_rating/index.js can be separated from its actual use. This means that we need to start it up elsewhere. That location is app/javascript/application.js, which should be changed like so:

```
/* app/javascript/application.js */

  Turbo.setProgressBarDelay(100)

  import "controllers"
→
→ import { WidgetRatings } from "widget_ratings"
→ WidgetRatings.start(window)
```

Prior to Rails 7, this code would've relied on Webpacker and Webpack and been slightly different. Rails 7 introduced the concept of *import maps*, provided by importmap-rails[2]. Import maps are a modern mechanism for managing JavaScript without a pre-compiler like Webpack.

Rails won't automatically detect any new JavaScript file we create, so we must add it to the configuration in config/importmap.rb. Even though we only have one file in app/javascript/widget_ratings, we'll still use pin_all_from so that any newly-created files there in the future will be picked up without needing a configuration change.

```
# config/importmap.rb
```

---

[2]https://github.com/rails/importmap-rails

```
  pin "@hotwired/stimulus", to: "stimulus.min.js", preload: tru...
  pin "@hotwired/stimulus-loading", to: "stimulus-loading.js", ...
  pin_all_from "app/javascript/controllers", under: "controller...
→ pin_all_from "app/javascript/widget_ratings",
→              under: "widget_ratings"
```

What this does is to tell the front-end that whenever code like `import "widget_ratings"` is processed, to get the requested code from `app/javascript/widget_ratings`. The browser does all this for you. Rails will reload `config/import.rb` in theory, so if you are running your server, you should not have to restart it.

With this in place, here is the order of events on our page:

1. The page is loaded when someone navigates to the widget show page.
2. `start(window)` is called in our new JavaScript code. This registers a `turbo:load` handler.
3. The `turbo:load` event is fired.
4. Our handler is called, which attaches an `onclick` event to all five buttons we created with `button_to`.
5. The user clicks a rating
6. Because we did not call `preventDefault`, the button will submit the remote form back to the server.
7. This will trigger the `create` method of the `WidgetRatingsController`. Although this doesn't do anything now, you could imagine that it would update a rating in the database or something like that.
8. `updateUIWithRating` is called with the given rating. This hides the rating buttons and shows the "Thanks for rating" message, along with the user's specific rating.

Note that we aren't waiting for the results of our AJAX call. This may not be the right decision, depending on what the backend logic is. If there is a chance the user could make a mistake, we want to wait for the back-end to let us know if the request was successful and update the UI accordingly. In this case, we assume any invalid request is the result of someone circumventing our UI and so we won't explicitly handle it.

Putting it all together, you should be able to navigate the widget show page, click a rating and see all this working as in the screenshot on the next page.

This might have seemed like a lot of steps, but consider how little code we had to change. We needed to add some new markup, but the existing markup hardly changed at all. We had to write around 40 lines of JavaScript, and we didn't have to make any significant changes to the back-end.

This change feels commensurate with the complexity of the feature we added. If we used something like React, we would've had to rewrite the entire UI first, and then add the feature.

Widget 1234

`ID #0012.34`

Thanks for rating this a 1

Figure 11.1: Ajax-based widget rating

As I said, there are many ways to do this, but the main idea to take away is just how much you can actually do with plain JavaScript. For interactions like showing or hiding DOM elements, plain JavaScript might be a good trade-off, because we didn't need any new dependencies to do this.

As our app ages and grows, this code will remain solid and reliable. As Rails changes front-end approaches, something it has historically done frequently, plain JavaScript will continue to work.

That said, you may need more. When the interactivity you require exceeds basic Ajax calls and the showing or hiding of markup, a plain JavaScript approach could turn into a hand-rolled framework. In those cases, an off-the-shelf framework might be preferable. Adding any dependency to your app introduces a carrying cost, and a JavaScript framework is one of the largest, so you must choose carefully.

11.2 Carefully Choose One Framework When You Need It

While any dependency added to your app should be carefully considered, the front-end framework should be considered *most* carefully. As discussed in the previous chapter on page 157, JavaScript is a more serious liability, and a large framework like React or Ember exacerbates this problem. This means two things: first, you should try to have exactly one front-end framework in your app to minimize the carrying cost and second, you should carefully choose the framework for sustainability.

If you have no other constraints, Rails' default of Hotwire is a good choice, but React is also something to consider. Let's take this section to see why and how it relates to sustainability.

As your app evolves and as time goes by, versions of your dependencies—including Rails—will change. Bugs will be fixed, features will be added, and security vulnerabilities will be addressed. Your app will also gain features, change developers, change teams, and generally evolve. The more you can rely on your dependencies to weather these changes, the better.

Thus, when you make decisions for sustainability, you want to favor dependencies that are stable, widely understood, well-supported, and that easily work with Rails. These are potentially more important than features and *far* more important than personal preference.

I would urge you to make a decision aid for each framework you want to consider. Write down these criteria, along with any other that you feel are important. Here are three different versions for React, Angular, and Hotwire. I've included two subjective criteria: "Org Support", how well the overall organization supports the framework, and "Team Appetite", how excited the team would be to use the framework. We'll start with one for React.

Table 11.1: Decision Aid for React as a Front-end Framework

Criteria	Rating	Notes
Mind-share	High	Based on State of JS Survey
Stability	High	Good backwards compatibility
Rails Support	Medium	js-bundling or react-rails
Org Support	No guidance	
Team Appetite	High	

Here's how I might fill this out for Angular.

Table 11.2: Decision Aid for Angular as a Front-end Framework

Criteria	Rating	Notes
Mind-share	Medium	Trends enterprisey
Stability	Low	Frequent breaking changes
Rails Support	Medium	js-bundling
Org Support	General bad experiences	
Team Appetite	Low	

And finally, here's one for Hotwire.

Table 11.3: Decision Aid for Hotwire as a Front-end Framework

Criteria	Rating	Notes
Mind-share	Low	Subset of Rails developers at best
Stability	Medium	Used by 37Signals in production
Rails Support	High	Developed by 37Signals
Org Support	No guidance	
Team Appetite	Medium	

The point is to make an informed decision as objectively as you can. Mind-share, stability, and Rails support heavily contribute to the sustainability of your app. Do not ignore them. You'll also note that I haven't put features or any other technical considerations. These are extremely hard to quantify and even harder to value. Does the fact that Ember renders slightly faster than React actually matter? That's hard to answer.

If you have clearly defined technical requirements, *do* add them to your decision aid, but make sure you know how to measure them and how to value them. At a high level, these frameworks all tend to be equally capable of whatever it is you need to do, and none are likely to have a fatal flaw that will require excising from your codebase later.

Right now, all things being equal, React is likely the safest, best, most sustainable choice, but I don't think Hotwire is a bad choice either, mostly because it's going to be more and more integrated with Rails since the core team (and 37Signals, in particular) use and maintain it. That being said, 37Signals insist they will change things whenever and however they like, so if Hotwire stops working for them, it may be dropped from Rails in a future release or undergo radical breaking changes.

Whatever you do, don't add multiple frameworks. This will create a sustainability problem as your app matures. You will have more libraries to deal with keeping updated and will be more affected by the instability in the JavaScript ecosystem.

If your chosen framework isn't working out as well as you hoped, I recommend you scope a project to migrate to a new framework so that you can quickly transition and avoid the carrying cost of multiple frameworks.

The last technique to discuss is testing.

11.3 Ensure System Tests Fail When JavaScript is Broken

> This section's code is in the folder 11-03/ of the sample code.

In the next chapter on page 181, we'll talk about the deeper value and purpose of testing, but to briefly preview it, testing is a way to mitigate the risk of shipping broken code to production.

Because of JavaScript's unique attributes as discussed in the previous chapter on page 157, it may seem that there is greater value in unit testing JavaScript that is already covered by system tests if that JavaScript is complex.

That said, unit testing JavaScript is not easy. There is no all-in-one testing framework and setting up JavaScript-based tests requires a lot of decisions, plumbing, and dependencies. It also requires having Node installed in your development environment, which results in testing your JavaScript in an environment that is not the same as that where it runs: Node is a server-side platform, whereas your JavaScript runs in a web browser.

To make matters worse, common tools for JS testing fall out of favor quickly, as you can see in the State of JS Survey results[3].

The previous edition of this book had us set up Jest[4] and write a unit test of the code we wrote in the last section. I no longer believe it is worth doing based on the code we have and the approach we have taken thus far. This chapter of the book broke every time there was a change in the underlying tooling, and I think there is a sustainability lesson here.

Your system tests (discussed in the next chapter) should fail if your JavaScript is broken. While a unit test might be a faster way to know this, the carrying cost of Node, NPM, and the modules required for even a basic testing toolchain may be too high for the value they bring, especially if you are really minimizing JavaScript. In particular, if you are using Hotwire and related technologies, you may not even *have* that much JavaScript to test.

What I would recommend instead is to include unit testing as part of your technology decision aide. For example, Hotwire provides zero-code solutions to common use cases, thus no unit testing would be required, since there is no code. React *may* require unit tests, and setting this up is relatively supported by the community. Arbitrary testing of plain JavaScript is less-supported, though possible.

My recommendation is to add JavaScript unit testing if you truly believe the value it brings exceeds the carrying cost of the toolchain required, and to choose your toolchain based on community support and stability. I would also strongly recommend that you not rely entirely on Node-based unit tests to ensure the proper functioning of your JavaScript, because your JavaScript will be run in a browser.

Up Next

As mentioned above, your view should be tested and those tests should fail if the JavaScript is broken. That's what we'll cover next.

---

[3] https://2020.stateofjs.com/en-US/technologies/testing/
[4] https://jestjs.io

12
Testing the View

We wrote tests for our helpers way back in "Helpers Should Be Tested and Thus Testable" on page 130, but generally avoided talking about an overarching testing strategy. That's what we're going to talk about here.

Testing can be a boon to sustainability, but it can also work against you. If tests are too brittle, duplicative, slow, or focused on the wrong things, the test suite will drag the team down.

This chapter will introduce a basic testing strategy and then discuss some useful tactics for implementing that strategy around the view code we've been writing. This strategy and its tactics are based on certain values as it relates to software quality, so let's state those first.

12.1 Understand the Value and Cost of Tests

Kent Beck, who, among other things, is a major proponent of Test-Driven Design, said[1]:

> I get paid for code that works, not for tests, so my philosophy is to test as little as possible to reach a given level of confidence.

This is a great clarifying statement about the purpose of tests, in particular given who said it.

Tests give confidence that our code is working. We can get that confidence in other ways, such as manually checking the code, pair programming, code reviews, or monitoring the app in production. These mechanisms have different costs and different levels of effectiveness.

Another way to put this is that tests are a tool to mitigate risk: the risk of code failing in production. They have a cost, primarily a carrying cost. And that cost has to justify the value the tests bring, otherwise we are not using our time and resources wisely, and our app will become less and less sustainable.

To make sure tests mitigate the right risks and provide the maximum value, they must be user-focused.

---
[1] https://stackoverflow.com/questions/153234/how-deep-are-your-unit-tests/153565

A user-focused test is one that exercises a part of the software the way a user would use it. In a Rails app, that means a system test.

System tests are expensive. They have a high carrying cost, but if we approach them in the right way, they can bring immense value. The key is to avoid over-testing.

The strategy I recommend is to have a system test for every major user flow, use unit tests to get coverage of anything else that is important, and closely monitor production for failures.

A "major" flow is one that is critical to the problem the app exists to solve. It's something that, if broken, would severely impact the efficacy of the app. Authentication is a great example. An FAQ page would not be a good example (in most cases).

The point is, you have to decide what is and is not a major user flow. Most of your app's features ought to be major flows, because hopefully you are only building features that matter. But however many it is, they should have system tests.

To keep system tests manageable, we'll talk through the following tactics:

- Do not use a real browser for features that don't require JavaScript.
- Test against markup and content by default.
- If markup becomes unstable, use `data-testid` to locate elements needed for a test.
- Cultivate diagnostic tools to debug test failures.
- Fake out the back-end to get the test of the front-end passing, then use that test to drive the back-end implementation.
- Use a real browser for any feature that *does* require JavaScript.

Let's start with the basics.

12.2 Use `:rack_test` for non-JavaScript User Flows

> This section's code is in the folder 12-02/ of the sample code.

Because we're only using JavaScript where we need it, and because we are favoring Rails' server-rendered views, most of our features should work without requiring JavaScript[2]. One of the benefits to this approach is that we can test these features without using a real web browser.

Rails system tests use Chrome by default. We'll set that up later, but for now, let's codify our architectural decisions around server-rendered views by making the default test driver for system tests the `:rack_test` driver.

---

[2]This doesn't mean there isn't any JavaScript for these features, just that the features can be exercised without JavaScript executing at all.

We can do this in test/application_system_test_case.rb.

```
# test/application_system_test_case.rb

require "test_helper"

class ApplicationSystemTestCase < ActionDispatch::SystemTestC...
→   driven_by :rack_test
end
```

There is currently an issue with Rails 7 that causes system tests to run in the wrong environment when using the dotenv-rails gem, which we are using. To work around that, we're going to add some code to Rakefile, like so:

```
# Rakefile

# Add your own tasks in files placed in lib/tasks ending in ....
# for example lib/tasks/capistrano.rake, and they will automa...

→ # This works around an issue with Rails 7 and dotenv-rails where
→ # tests are run in the wrong Rails environment
→ if Rake.application.top_level_tasks.grep(
→     /^(default$|test(:|$))/
→   ).any?
→
→   ENV["RAILS_ENV"] ||= if Rake.application.options.show_tasks
→                          "development"
→                        else
→                          "test"
→                        end
→
→ end
require_relative "config/application"

Rails.application.load_tasks
```

We have a major user flow where the user sees a list of widgets, clicks one, and sees more information about that widget. It does not require JavaScript, so we can write a test for it now. We'll do that in test/system/view_widget_test.rb:

183

```
# test/system/view_widget_test.rb

require "application_system_test_case"

class ViewWidgetTest < ApplicationSystemTestCase
  test "we can see a list of widgets and view one" do
    # test goes here
  end
end
```

What we want to check here is that:

1. When we navigate to the widgets path, we see a list of widgets.
2. When we click one of those widgets, we are taken to that widget's page.
3. That widget's page shows some basic information about the widget.

This leads to some open questions:

- What does a list of widgets actually mean?
- What is being clicked on when we want to view a particular widget's page?
- What constitutes "basic information" about a widget?

Answering questions like these requires understanding why the feature exists and is important. You should *not* assert every piece of content and markup on the page. Instead, find the minimum indicators that the feature is providing the value it's supposed to provide.

For this widget flow, let's assume that if we see two widgets on the index page and the show page shows the chosen widget's name and formatted ID, we are confident the flow is working.

Because our only indicators of this are the presence of content and markup, we *will* have to assert against that, so let's do the simplest thing we can, which is to assert against the markup and content that's there.

12.3 Test Against Default Markup and Content Initially

> This section's code is in the folder 12-03/ of the sample code.

We'll use the DOM to locate content that allows us to confidently assert the page is working. As a first pass, we'll use the DOM as it is. That means we'll expect two <li>s in a <ul> that have our widget names in them. We'll click an <a> inside one, and expect to see the widget's name in an <h1> with its formatted ID in an <h2>.

We'll assert on regular expressions instead of exact content, so that trivial changes in copy won't break our test. Also note that we're using case-insensitive regular expressions (they end with /i) to further insulate our tests from trivial content changes.

```
# test/system/view_widget_test.rb


  class ViewWidgetTest < ApplicationSystemTestCase
    test "we can see a list of widgets and view one" do
→     visit widgets_path
→
→     widget_name = "stembolt"
→     widget_name_regexp = /#{widget_name}/i
→
→     assert_selector "ul li", text: /flux capacitor/i
→     assert_selector "ul li", text: widget_name_regexp
→
→     find("ul li", text: widget_name_regexp).find("a").click
→
→     # remember, 1234 is formatted as 12.34
→     formatted_widget_id_regexp = /12\.34/
→
→     assert_selector "h1", text: widget_name_regexp
→     assert_selector "h2", text: formatted_widget_id_regexp
    end
  end
```

This test is hopefully easy to understand because it maps clearly to the existing page's markup and asserts based on the content we expect to be there.

Let's run this test:

```
> bin/rails test test/system/view_widget_test.rb || echo \
  Test Failed
Running 1 tests in a single process (parallelization thresho...
Run options: --seed 43669

# Running:
```

```
F

Failure:
ViewWidgetTest#test_we_can_see_a_list_of_widgets_and_view_on...
expected to find visible css "h1" with text /stembolt/i but ...

bin/rails test test/system/view_widget_test.rb:4



Finished in 0.605165s, 1.6524 runs/s, 4.9573 assertions/s.
1 runs, 3 assertions, 1 failures, 0 errors, 0 skips
Test Failed
```

The error message is not very helpful. It tells us what assertion failed, but it doesn't tell us why. To figure this out often requires some trial and error.

A common tactic is to add something like `puts page.html` right before the failing assertion, but let's make a better version of that concept that we can use as a surgical diagnostic tool.

12.4 Cultivate Explicit Diagnostic Tools to Debug Test Failures

> This section's code is in the folder 12-04/ of the sample code.

A big part of the carrying cost of system tests is the time it takes to diagnose why they are failing when we don't believe the feature being tested is actually broken. The assertions available to Rails provide only rudimentary assistance. Your team will eventually learn to use `puts page.html` as a diagnostic tool, but let's take time now to make one that works a bit better.

Let's wrap `puts page.html` in a method called `with_clues`. `with_clues` will take a block of code and, if there is any exception, produce some diagnostic information (currently the page's HTML) then re-raise the exception. This will be a foothold for adding more useful diagnostic information later.

Let's put this in a separate file and module, then include that into `ApplicationSystemTestCase`. As we build up a library of useful diagnostic tools, we don't want our `test/application_system_test_case.rb` file getting out of control.

We'll put this in `test/support/with_clues.rb`:

```
# test/support/with_clues.rb
```

```ruby
module TestSupport
  module WithClues
    # Wrap any assertion with this method to get more
    # useful context and diagnostics when a test is
    # unexpectedly failing
    def with_clues(&block)
      block.()
    rescue Exception => ex
      puts "[ with_clues ] Test failed: #{ex.message}"
      puts "[ with_clues ] HTML {"
      puts
      puts page.html
      puts
      puts "[ with_clues ] } END HTML"
      raise ex
    end
  end
end
```

Now, we'll include this module into `ApplicationSystemTestCase` so that all of our tests have access to the method. We'll need to `require` the file first:

```ruby
# test/application_system_test_case.rb

  require "test_helper"
→ require "support/with_clues"

  class ApplicationSystemTestCase < ActionDispatch::SystemTestC. . .
    driven_by :rack_test
```

Now we can use the module:

```ruby
# test/application_system_test_case.rb

  require "support/with_clues"

  class ApplicationSystemTestCase < ActionDispatch::SystemTestC. . .
→   include TestSupport::WithClues
    driven_by :rack_test
  end
```

Note that we've prepended messages from this method with [with_clues] so it's clear what is generating these messages. There's nothing more difficult than debugging code that produces output whose source you cannot identify.

If we wrap the assertion like so:

```
# test/system/view_widget_test.rb

      # remember, 1234 is formatted as 12.34
      formatted_widget_id_regexp = /12\.34/

→     with_clues { assert_selector "h1", text: widget_name_regexp }
      assert_selector "h2", text: formatted_widget_id_regexp
    end
  end
```

When we run the test, we'll see the HTML of the page:

```
> bin/rails test test/system/view_widget_test.rb || echo \
  Test Failed
Running 1 tests in a single process (parallelization thresho...
Run options: --seed 2051

# Running:

[ with_clues ] Test failed: expected to find visible css "h1...
[ with_clues ] HTML {

<!DOCTYPE html>
<html>
  <head>
    <title>Widgets</title>
    <meta name="viewport" content="width=device-width,initia...



    <link rel="stylesheet" href="/assets/application-45c6610...
    <script type="importmap" data-turbo-track="reload">{
  "imports": {
    "application": "/assets/application-859894971255110068d2...
    "@hotwired/turbo-rails": "/assets/turbo.min-dfd93b3092d1...
    "@hotwired/stimulus": "/assets/stimulus.min-dd364f16ec95...
    "@hotwired/stimulus-loading": "/assets/stimulus-loading-...
    "controllers/application": "/assets/controllers/applicat...
```

```
        "controllers/hello_controller": "/assets/controllers/hel...
        "controllers": "/assets/controllers/index-2db729dddcc5b9...
        "widget_ratings": "/assets/widget_ratings/index-b6eb9ad1...
    }
}</script>
<link rel="modulepreload" href="/assets/application-85989497...
<link rel="modulepreload" href="/assets/turbo.min-dfd93b3092...
<link rel="modulepreload" href="/assets/stimulus.min-dd364f1...
<link rel="modulepreload" href="/assets/stimulus-loading-357...
<script src="/assets/es-module-shims.min-4ca9b3dd5e434131e3b...
<script type="module">import "application"</script>
  </head>

  <body>
    <h1>Widget 1</h1>
<h2>ID #<span style="font-family: monospace">0000001</span><...

<section>
  <div class="dn" data-rating-present>
    <p>Thanks for rating this a
      <span data-rating-label></span>
    </p>
  </div>
  <div class="cf" data-no-rating-present>
    <h3 style="float: left; margin: 0; padding-right: 1rem;"...
      Rate This Widget:
    </h3>
    <ol style="list-style: none; padding: 0; margin: 0">
        <li style="float: left">
          <form class="button_to" method="post" action="/wid...
        </li>
        <li style="float: left">
          <form class="button_to" method="post" action="/wid...
        </li>
        <li style="float: left">
          <form class="button_to" method="post" action="/wid...
        </li>
        <li style="float: left">
          <form class="button_to" method="post" action="/wid...
        </li>
        <li style="float: left">
          <form class="button_to" method="post" action="/wid...
        </li>
    </ol>
  </div>
</section>
```

```
    </body>
</html>

[ with_clues ] } END HTML
F

Failure:
ViewWidgetTest#test_we_can_see_a_list_of_widgets_and_view_on...
expected to find visible css "h1" with text /stembolt/i but ...

bin/rails test test/system/view_widget_test.rb:4



Finished in 0.261213s, 3.8283 runs/s, 11.4849 assertions/s.
1 runs, 3 assertions, 1 failures, 0 errors, 0 skips
Test Failed
```

We can see that the problem is that our faked-out data isn't consistent. The fake widgets in the index view are not the same as those in the show view. We'll fix that in a minute.

Note that `with_clues` is a form of executable documentation. `with_clues` is the answer to "How do I figure out why my system test failed?". As your team learns more about how to diagnose these problems, they can enhance `with_clues` for everyone on the team, including future team members. This reduces the carrying cost of these tests.

While this implementation is perfectly fine, it's really only a demonstration of the concept of creating a diagnostic tool. If you'd like to use `with_clues` in your app, you can use the gem with_clues[3] that was extracted from codebases where this concept was developed.

OK, to fix our test, we should make our faked-out back-end more consistent.

12.5 Fake The Back-end To Get System Tests Passing

> This section's code is in the folder 12-05/ of the sample code.

System tests are hard to write in a pure test-driven style. You often need to start with a view that actually renders the way it's intended, and then write your test to assert behavior based on that.

If you are *also* trying to make the back-end work at the same time, it can be difficult to get everything functioning at once. It's often easier to take it one

---

[3]https://github.com/sustainable-rails/with_clues

step at a time, and since we are working outside in, that means faking the back-end so we can get the view working.

Once you have the view working, you don't actually need a real back-end to write your system test. If you write your system test against a fake back-end, you can then drive your back-end work with that system test. This leaves you where you want to be: an end-to-end test of the actual functionality. It's just easier to get there by starting off with a fake back-end.

Let's do that now. We need the hard-coded Stembolt to have an ID of 1234, and we need our show page to detect item 1234 and use the name "Stembolt" instead of "Widget 1234". We can do this in WidgetsController:

```
# app/controllers/widgets_controller.rb
  end
  def index
    @widgets = [
→     OpenStruct.new(id: 1234, name: "Stembolt"),
      OpenStruct.new(id: 2, name: "Flux Capacitor"),
    ]
  end
```

Next, we need the show method to use the name "Stembolt" if the id is 1234:

We'll create a variable called widget_name:

```
# app/controllers/widgets_controller.rb
        country: "UK"
      )
    )
→   widget_name = if params[:id].to_i == 1234
→                   "Stembolt"
→                 else
→                   "Widget #{params[:id]}"
→                 end
    @widget = OpenStruct.new(id: params[:id],
                             manufacturer_id: manufacturer.id...
                             manufacturer: manufacturer,
```

And we'll use that for the name: value in our OpenStruct:

191

```
# app/controllers/widgets_controller.rb

      @widget = OpenStruct.new(id: params[:id],
                               manufacturer_id: manufacturer.id. . .
                               manufacturer: manufacturer,
→                              name: widget_name)
      def @widget.widget_id
        if self.id.to_s.length < 3
          self.id.to_s
```

Now that our faked-out back-end is more consistent with itself, our test should pass:

```
> bin/rails test test/system/view_widget_test.rb
Running 1 tests in a single process (parallelization thresho. . .
Run options: --seed 2421

# Running:

.

Finished in 0.260428s, 3.8398 runs/s, 15.3593 assertions/s.
1 runs, 4 assertions, 0 failures, 0 errors, 0 skips
```

With this test passing, we should *remove* our diagnostic call to `with_clues`, because we really don't want it littered all over the codebase.

```
# test/system/view_widget_test.rb

      # remember, 1234 is formatted as 12.34
      formatted_widget_id_regexp = /12\.34/

→     assert_selector "h1", text: widget_name_regexp
      assert_selector "h2", text: formatted_widget_id_regexp
    end
  end
```

What if our view's markup changes in a way that causes our tests to fail but doesn't affect the app's functionality? For example, we may change the <h1> to an <h2> to address an issue with accessibility. This will cause our test to fail even though its functionality is still working, since this is not a test what tags were used in the view. This sort of test failure can create drag on the team and reduce sustainability. Chasing the markup can be an unpleasant carrying cost, so let's talk about a simple technique to reduce this cost next.

12.6 Use data-testid Attributes to Combat Brittle Tests

> This section's code is in the folder 12-06/ of the sample code.

The tags used in our view are currently semantically correct, and thus our tests can safely rely on that. However, these semantics might change without affecting the way the page actually works. Suppose our designer wants a new message, "Widget Information", on the page as the most important thing on the page.

That means our widget name should no longer be an <h1>, but instead an <h2>.

Here's the change to update the view:

```
<%# app/views/widgets/show.html.erb %>

→ <h1>Widget Information</h1>
→ <h2><%= @widget.name %></h2>
  <h2>ID #<%= styled_widget_id(@widget) %></h2>
  <% if flash[:notice].present? %>
    <aside>
```

This change will break our tests even though the change didn't affect the functionality of the feature:

```
> bin/rails test test/system/view_widget_test.rb || echo Test \
  Failed
Running 1 tests in a single process (parallelization thresho...
Run options: --seed 40241

# Running:

F

Failure:
ViewWidgetTest#test_we_can_see_a_list_of_widgets_and_view_on...
expected to find visible css "h1" with text /stembolt/i but ...

bin/rails test test/system/view_widget_test.rb:4
```

```
Finished in 0.268304s, 3.7271 runs/s, 11.1813 assertions/s.
1 runs, 3 assertions, 1 failures, 0 errors, 0 skips
Test Failed
```

We can see what's broken, but it's not clear the best way to fix it. If we change the tag name used in `assert_selector` that might fix it now, but this same sort of change could break it again, and we'd have to fix this test again. This can be a serious carrying cost with system tests and we need to nip it in the bud now that it's broken the first time.

We'll assume that the widget name can be in *any* element that has the attribute `data-testid` set to `"widget-name"`:

```
# test/system/view_widget_test.rb

    # remember, 1234 is formatted as 12.34
    formatted_widget_id_regexp = /12\.34/

→   assert_selector "[data-testid='widget-name']",
→                   text: widget_name_regexp
    assert_selector "h2", text: formatted_widget_id_regexp
  end
end
```

Our tests will still fail, but now when we fix them, we can fix them for hopefully the last time. We can add the `data-testid` attribute to the `<h2>`:

```
<%# app/views/widgets/show.html.erb %>

  <h1>Widget Information</h1>
→ <h2 data-testid="widget-name"><%= @widget.name %></h2>
  <h2>ID #<%= styled_widget_id(@widget) %></h2>
  <% if flash[:notice].present? %>
    <aside>
```

And *now* our test should pass:

```
> bin/rails test test/system/view_widget_test.rb
```

```
Running 1 tests in a single process (parallelization thresho...
Run options: --seed 35741

# Running:

.

Finished in 0.258705s, 3.8654 runs/s, 15.4616 assertions/s.
1 runs, 4 assertions, 0 failures, 0 errors, 0 skips
```

If this view changes a third time, we just need to make sure `data-testid="widget-name"` is attached to whatever DOM node holds the widget's name.

Why didn't we do this from the start? Why didn't we tag everything with `data-testid`?

Having to tag every single DOM element with `data-testid` is friction. It represents an opportunity cost with each feature, and it gets harder over time because you must choose names for these tags. It means that even for parts of the view that never change, we're creating an extra burden.

So, to balance the desire to test against a semantic DOM, but also not have to constantly change tests, we adopt a simple convention: the first time a test must be changed to accommodate DOM changes, stop using the DOM for that assertion and start using `data-testid`. This is much more sustainable than having to constantly change tests or always use `data-testid`.

The reason to use `data-testid` and not, for example a more semantic CSS class like `class="widget-name"` is to make it very clear what this seemingly extraneous markup is for. There can be no doubt that `data-testid` is for a test. Something like `class="widget-name"` might seem meaningless and perhaps could be accidentally removed in the future, thus breaking tests.

Up to now, we've talked about testing a view rendered entirely server-side with no client-side interactivity. Since our app will certainly have at least *some* dynamic client-side behavior, we can't test that using `:rack_test`. Our widget rating feature, for example, can't be tested without using a real browser. Let's set that up next.

12.7 Test JavaScript Interactions with a Real Browser

> This section's code is in the folder 12-07/ of the sample code.

If we have features that require JavaScript, or that won't work if our JavaScript is broken, we need to test them in a real browser. While unit tests could help, they won't give complete confidence because we need to see the JavaScript executing in context.

Since we've set our system tests to use `:rack_test`, that means they won't use a real browser and JavaScript won't be executed. We need to allow a subset of our tests to actually use a real browser (which is what Rails' system tests do by default).

To that end, we'll create a subclass of our existing `ApplicationSystemTestCase` that will be for browser-driven tests. We'll call it `BrowserSystemTestCase` and it will configure Chrome to run the tests[4].

The default configuration for Rails is to use a real Chrome browser that pops up and runs tests while you watch. This is flaky, annoying, and difficult to get working in a continuous integration environment.

Fortunately, it's unnecessary as Chrome has a headless mode that works exactly the same way as normal Chrome, but does everything offline without actually drawing to the screen[5]. Practically speaking, Chrome won't work in our Docker-based setup anyway.

12.7.1 Setting Up Headless Chrome

It helps to know a little bit about what's going on between Rails, your OS, and Chrome. Since automated browser testing became common, the way to make it work has changed a lot over the years, and I expect it to keep changing. Ultimately, our test suite needs to make a network connection to a running browser in order to tell it to do things, as well as to make assertions about what's happening on the page.

Our tests use Capybara which communicates with the browser via Selenium[6]. Selenium has a component called *WebDriver* that provides an abstraction over many browsers to drive them. Each browser has an adapter and for Chrome, it's called Chromedriver[7]. Chromedriver manages starting up Chrome to allow Selenium's WebDriver to talk to it, which is what allows our Capybara-based tests to test in a real browser.

The way we'll do this is to register what Selenium calls a *driver*, which basically represents a web browser. Instead of calling our driver "chrome", let's call it `root_headless_chrome` to signify that it's headless (no graphical UI will run) *and* that it's set up to run as root inside a Docker container.

Here's how we do that, at the top of `application_system_test_case.rb`:

```
# test/application_system_test_case.rb
```

---

[4]If you are using RSpec, this is something you'd implement with tags, as that is a more natural fit for RSpec.
[5]This is what I've been using to create the screenshots for this book.
[6]https://www.selenium.dev
[7]https://chromedriver.chromium.org/downloads

```
  require "test_helper"

Capybara.register_driver :root_headless_chrome do |app|
  options = Selenium::WebDriver::Options.chrome(
    args: [
      "headless",
      "disable-gpu",
      "no-sandbox",
      "disable-dev-shm-usage",
      "whitelisted-ips"
    ],
    logging_prefs: { browser: "ALL" },
  )
  Capybara::Selenium::Driver.new(
    app,
    browser: :chrome,
    options: options
  )
end # register_driver

  require "support/with_clues"

  class ApplicationSystemTestCase < ActionDispatch::SystemTestC...
```

I won't claim to have a deep understanding of what all of those strings given to args actually do, but suffice it to say, they were needed to make this work inside a Docker container. Of note is the `logging_prefs` option. We'll see a bit later how we can print the messages sent to the JavaScript console, and by default, Selenium only allows access to errors and warnings. By using { browser: "ALL" }, we can get all the messages.

There's one more step I need to do that you may not. Since this book was first published, Apple has started selling computers with Apple Silicon chips. They are not compatible with the previous generation of Intel chips. Although macOS provides an emulation layer, when running an Intel-based Docker container on an Apple Silicon-based computer, not everything is properly emulated. As luck would have it, Chrome requires some of those features, so basically doesn't work inside the Docker environment used by this book.

To make matters worse, there is no version of Chrome that runs on Linux running on Apple Silicon, there is only a macOS version. But, Chromium, upon which Chrome is based, *does* run on Linux on Apple Silicon. It will need to be installed and we'll need to specify the path to the version of chromedriver installed with Chromium. Gotta love web development.

Installing Chromium highly depends on your OS and, if you are running on macOS or an Intel-based Linux or Windows computer, you don't need to do this. The Docker-based setup uses Debian linux and does this to install Chromium:

```
apt-get -y install chromium chromium-driver
```

To tell Selenium where chromedriver is, we'll need to set `driver_path` on `Selenium::WebDriver::Chrome::Service`, which we should do right at the top of our `application_system_test_case.rb` file:

```
# test/application_system_test_case.rb

  require "test_helper"

→ Selenium::WebDriver::Chrome::Service.driver_path =
→   "/usr/bin/chromedriver"

  Capybara.register_driver :root_headless_chrome do |app|
    options = Selenium::WebDriver::Options.chrome(
```

Note that the right path for your environment might be different, and if you can use Chrome, that will make this much easier. This API is not documented by Selenium, so it may change. All part of the fun.

Now, let's create `BrowserSystemTestCase` which will use the newly-registered driver and extend `ApplicationSystemTestCase`. Since our existing tests (and any new ones) will include it, we'll put it in test/application_system_test_case.rb:

```
# test/application_system_test_case.rb

    include TestSupport::WithClues
    driven_by :rack_test
  end

→ # Base test class for system tests requiring JavaScript
→ class BrowserSystemTestCase < ApplicationSystemTestCase
→   driven_by :root_headless_chrome, screen_size: [ 1400, 1400 ]
→ end
```

While we are setting up our system tests, let's configure Capybara to recognize `data-testid` (which we adopted earlier in this chapter on page 193) whenever we use helpers like `click_on`. This will go in `test/test_helper.rb`:

```
# test/test_helper.rb

  ENV["RAILS_ENV"] ||= "test"
  require_relative "../config/environment"
  require "rails/test_help"
→ Capybara.configure do |config|
→   # This allows helpers like click_on to locate
→   # any object by data-testid in addition to
→   # built-in selector-like values
→   config.test_id = "data-testid"
→ end

  module ActiveSupport
    class TestCase
```

Now, let's write our first browser-driven test case.

12.7.2 Writing a Browser-driven System Test Case

We'll write a test case of the widget rating feature, which will look very much like the one we wrote before.

To test the widget rating feature, we need to:

1. Navigate to a widget page.
2. Click a rating button.
3. Check that the DOM reflects our rating.

We'll create this test in `test/system/rate_widget_test.rb` and it will look for an element matching `[data-rating-present]` that has text content including the rating the test will choose.

Even though this content is not initially visible and some of it (the rating itself) isn't even in the DOM, Capybara will wait a small amount of time for the matching markup and content to appear:

```
# test/system/rate_widget_test.rb
```

```
require "application_system_test_case"

class RateWidgetsTest < BrowserSystemTestCase
  test "rating a widget shows our rating inline" do
    visit widget_path(1234)

    click_on "2"

    assert_selector "[data-rating-present]",
                    text: /thanks for rating.*2/i
  end
end
```

The test should pass:

```
> bin/rails test test/system/rate_widget_test.rb
Rack::Handler is deprecated and replaced by Rackup::Handler
Running 1 tests in a single process (parallelization thresho...
Run options: --seed 61296

# Running:

Capybara starting Puma...
* Version 6.4.0 , codename: The Eagle of Durango
* Min threads: 0, max threads: 4
* Listening on http://127.0.0.1:42029
.

Finished in 1.361959s, 0.7342 runs/s, 0.7342 assertions/s.
1 runs, 1 assertions, 0 failures, 0 errors, 0 skips
```

If you change the test to inherit from our `ApplicationSystemTestCase`, you will see that the test fails, because JavaScript is not executed. More importantly, if you break the JavaScript, the test will also fail. I highly recommend doing this to make sure your test is testing what you think it's testing. When doing test driven development, you typically watch for your test to fail in just the right way. For system tests, as discussed, this is not always ideal. So, it's good to undo or break your code to make sure the test also breaks.

One other thing to note about why this test works is that Capybara waits for DOM content to become available, to account for changes in the DOM that JavaScript makes. This means that you must make sure that changes you make to the DOM can be unambiguously detected. `data-testid` can be used to help do this if you can't otherwise write markup that can be relied upon.

Now that we've added browser-based tests, it may be useful to see the browser's logs whenever we use `with_clues`. Let's add that ability as a demonstration of the power of built-in diagnostics we discussed earlier in the chapter on page 186

12.7.3 Enhancing `with_clues` to Dump Browser Logs

As a diagnostic tool, `with_clues` needs to be pretty fault-tolerant. It's only ever called when a test fails, so we don't want it masking a test failure if it itself fails. Since `with_clues` will be used for both browser and non-browser tests, we need to take extra care when trying to print out the browser's logs. Prepare for some `if` statements.

```ruby
# test/support/with_clues.rb

      block.()
    rescue Exception => ex
      puts "[ with_clues ] Test failed: #{ex.message}"
→     if page.driver.respond_to?(:browser)
→       if page.driver.browser.respond_to?(:logs)
→         logs = page.driver.browser.logs
→         browser_logs = logs.get(:browser)
→         browser_logs.each do |log|
→           puts log.message
→         end
→         puts "[ with_clues ] } END Browser Logs"
→       else
→         puts "[ with_clues ] NO BROWSER LOGS: " +
→              "page.driver.browser" +
→              "#{page.driver.browser.class} " +
→              "does not respond to #logs"
→       end
→     else
→       puts "[ with_clues ] NO BROWSER LOGS: page.driver " +
→            "#{page.driver.class} does not respond to #browser"
→     end
→     puts
      puts "[ with_clues ] HTML {"
      puts
      puts page.html
```

Whew! The reason we didn't use `try` is because we want to give a specific message about why the logs aren't being output. If someone adds a third driver later—say Firefox—and it doesn't provide log access in this way, these error messages will help future developers figure out how to address it. It certainly helped me when Selenium changed this API since the last version of this book was published!

Note that if you'd like to use `with_clues`, I extracted it to a gem called with_clues[8] that provides all this and a bit more, including explicit support for RSpec.

Up Next

This covers system tests and hopefully has provided some high level strategies and lower-level tactics on how to get the most out of system tests and keep them sustainable. We'll discuss unit tests later as we delve into the back-end of Rails. In fact, that's up next since we have now completed our tour of the view layer.

---

[8]https://github.com/sustainable-rails/with_clues

13
Models, Part 1

Although Rails is a Model-View-Controller framework, the model layer in Rails is really a collection of record definitions. Models in Rails are classes that expose attributes that can be manipulated. Traditionally, those attributes come from the database and can be saved back, though you can use Active Model to create models that aren't based on database tables.

No matter what else goes into a model class, it mostly exists to expose attributes for manipulation, like a record or struct does in other languages. As outlined in "Business Logic (Does Not Go in Active Records)" on page 57, that's all the logic that should go in these classes. I find it helpful to think of Active Records as *models* of a *database table*, which is what they are (and they are darn good at it!).

When you follow that guidance, the classes in app/models—the model layer—become a library of the data that powers your app. Some of that data comes directly from a database and some doesn't, but your model layer can and should define the *data model* of your app. This data model represents all the data coming in and going out of your app. The service layer discussed in the business logic chapter deals in these models.

This chapter will cover the basics around managing that. We'll talk about Active Records and their unique place in the Rails Architecture, followed by Active Model, which is a powerful way to create Active Record-like objects that work great in your view.

There are other aspects of models that we won't get to until Models, Part 2 on page 255, since we need to learn about the database and business logic implementation first.

Let's start with accessing the data in our database using Active Record.

13.1 Active Record is for Database Access

> This section's code is in the folder 13-01/ of the sample code.

With two lines of code, an Active Record can provide sophisticated access to a database table, in the form of class methods for querying and a record-like object for data manipulation. It's one of the core features of Rails that makes developers feel so productive.

In my experience, when you place business logic elsewhere, you don't end up needing much code in your Active Records. Those few lines of code you do need are often enough to enable access to all the data your app needs.

That said, there are times when we need to add code to Active Records. The three main types of code are:

- additional configuration such as `belongs_to` or `validates`.
- class methods that query the database and are needed by multiple other classes to reduce duplication.
- instance methods that define core domain attributes whose values can be directly derived from the database, without the application of business logic.

Let's dig into each of these a bit, but first we need some Active Records to work with.

13.1.1 Creating Some Example Active Records

First, we'll create the `Manufacturer` model. A manufacturer has a name as well as an address which I'll put directly on the table for now (this might not be ideal, but we'll worry about that in a future chapter).

Note that we're using the `text` type for all of our string-based fields. There is no reason to use varchar types in Postgres. Hubert Lubaczewski wrote a blog post[1] that has a pretty good overview about why.

```
> bin/rails g model manufacturer name:text address:text \
    city:text post_code:text
      invoke    active_record
      create    db/migrate/20231204235350_create_manufacture...
      create    app/models/manufacturer.rb
      invoke    test_unit
      create      test/models/manufacturer_test.rb
      create      test/fixtures/manufacturers.yml
```

Next, we'll create the `Widget` model which has a name, a status, and a reference to a manufacturer:

```
> bin/rails g model widget name:text status:text \
    manufacturer:references
      invoke    active_record
```

---
[1] https://www.depesz.com/2010/03/02/charx-vs-varcharx-vs-varchar-vs-text/

```
create    db/migrate/20231204235351_create_widgets.rb
create    app/models/widget.rb
invoke    test_unit
create      test/models/widget_test.rb
create      test/fixtures/widgets.yml
```

This should've created two classes in app/models as well as the database migrations. Let's run those now.

```
> bin/rails db:migrate
== 20231204235350 CreateManufacturers: migrating ===========...
-- create_table(:manufacturers)
   -> 0.0071s
== 20231204235350 CreateManufacturers: migrated (0.0071s) ==...

== 20231204235351 CreateWidgets: migrating ================...
-- create_table(:widgets)
   -> 0.0051s
== 20231204235351 CreateWidgets: migrated (0.0051s) ========...
```

With these created, let's now talk about Active Record's configuration DSL.

13.1.2   Model the Database With Active Record's DSL

Because we created Widget with manufacturer:references, Rails was able to automatically set that relationship up for us:

```
> cat app/models/widget.rb
class Widget < ApplicationRecord
  belongs_to :manufacturer
end
```

Rails *could've* modified app/models/manufacturer.rb to create the inverse relationship, but it doesn't know if the relationship is a to-many or a to-one, and Rails doesn't want to presume we actually want it modeled either way. The question is: should we model it now?

You're creating Active Records when you create database tables, so this is the time to codify the meaning of the relationships in your database. By adding a call to has_many, you are explicitly documenting that this model has a to-many relationship. If it has a to-one relationship, you would use has_one. If you do nothing, no one will know the intention.

The relationship here is a to-many, so we'll add a call to has_many to app/models/manufacturer.rb:

```
# app/models/manufacturer.rb

class Manufacturer < ApplicationRecord
→   has_many :widgets
end
```

On rare occasions you don't want to allow this relationship to exist in code. If this applies to you, add a code comment explaining why, so a future developer doesn't inadvertently add it.

Regarding additional configuration such as validations, I would recommend you add only what configuration you actually need. Think about it this way: if there is no code path in your app to set the name of a widget, what purpose could a presence validation on that field possibly serve?

Next, let's talk about the class methods you might add to your Active Record.

13.1.3 Class Methods Should Be Used to Re-use Common Database Operations

If you look at the class methods that are provided by Rails (excluding the DSL methods previously discussed), they all center around providing ways of accessing the underlying database. This is a good guide for the types of methods *you* should add. But, I would recommend you only add methods to facilitate re-use.

Said another way, add class methods to your Active Record only if both of these criteria hold:

- There is a need for the method's logic in more than one place.
- The method's logic is related to database manipulation only and not coupled to business logic.

Let's see an example. Suppose widgets can have one of three statuses: "fresh", "approved", and "archived". Fresh widgets require manual approval, so we might write some code like this in a background job that emails our admin team for each fresh widget they should approve:

```
class SendWidgetApprovalEmailJob
  def perform
    Widget.where(status: "fresh").find_each do |widget|
      AdminMailer.widget_approval(widget).deliver_later
    end
```

```
    end
end
```

There's no particular reason that `where(status: "fresh")` should be wrapped in a class method on `Widget`. Widget's public API includes the method `where`, and the purpose of `Widget` is facilitate database access. Thus, calling `where` is a normal, expected, acceptable thing to do.

That said, we may need this query in more than one place. For example, manufacturers might want to see what widgets are still fresh, perhaps in a `Manufacturer::WidgetsController`:

```
def index
  @widgets = Widget.where(status: "fresh")
end
```

Using this in two places creates duplication we may want to avoid, particularly because the string `"fresh"` is a specific value from the database.

```
  class Widget < ApplicationRecord
    belongs_to :manufacturer

→   def self.fresh = self.where(status: "fresh")
  end
```

Now, anyone needing fresh widgets doesn't have to worry about what string is used in the database to represent this.

Let's see a subtly different example where this would not be the right solution.

Suppose our manufacturers need to see a list of recently approved widgets. Suppose that "recently" is defined as approved in the last 10 days. We might write this code:

```
def index
  @widgets = Widget.where(status: "approved").
                    where(updated_at: 10.days.ago..)
end
```

The 10.days.ago is certainly business logic, as is the combination of it with the "approved" status. The concept of "recently approved" might change, and it might be different depending on context. This should *not* go into the Widget class. We'll talk about the ramifications of putting business logic in controllers in "Controllers" on page 313, but if we need to re-use this logic, the place to put it is in the service layer (which we'll talk about in "Business Logic Class Design" on page 241).

Lastly, let's talk about instance methods.

13.1.4 Instance Methods Should Implement Domain Concepts Derivable Directly from the Database

Pretty much all of the same guidance I gave in the previous section applies here. Further, the chapter on business logic on page 57 outlines why you shouldn't put instance methods on Active Records that implement that logic.

Outside of business logic, the most common area of trouble for instance methods on an Active Record has to do with derived data—data whose value is based on the data in the database. Sometimes this derived data is presentational and use-case specific, but other times it represents a true domain concept that is core to the models' existence.

As discussed in the many View chapters, including "Don't Conflate Helpers with Your Domain" on page 120, you need to be careful about how you model the data inside the application. This requires a solid understanding of your domain and carefully naming your attributes.

The convention I'm suggesting here is to make instance methods on your Active Records *only* when you have a strongly-defined domain concept whose value can be directly derived from the database, without any real logic applied.

Previously, we created the method `widget_id` to hold the formatted ID of a widget, since that was part of our domain. Digging deeper, the reasoning for this is that users use this as an identifier. They write it down, paste it into emails, and discuss it verbally.

Since it's based on the actual database primary key and not a separate field, this could be a good candidate for an instance method, though the name `widget_id` leaves a lot to be desired. Let's call it `user_facing_identifier` instead, and we'll add it to the Widget class.

```
# app/models/widget.rb

class Widget < ApplicationRecord
  belongs_to :manufacturer
→
```

```
  def user_facing_identifier
    id_as_string = self.id.to_s
    if id_as_string.length < 3
      return id_as_string
    end

    "%{first}.%{last_two}" % {
      first: id_as_string[0..-3],
      last_two: id_as_string[-2..-1]
    }
  end
end
```

If the *only* methods we add to Widget are for clearly defined concepts derivable from data, we can start to understand our domain better by looking at the Active Records. Instead of seeing a mishmash of command methods that invoke logic, presentational attributes, and use-case-specific values, we see only the few additional domain concepts that we need but aren't in the database.

Note that this method deserves a test, but we're not going to talk about testing models until "Models, Part 2" on page 255.

As a contrast to user_facing_identifier, suppose we need to show the first letter of the status on the widget show page. Suppose further that this is for aesthetic reasons and that the "short form" of a status isn't part of the domain—users don't think about it.

In this case, we should *not* create a method on Widget with this logic. Instead, we should put this logic in the view, or even make a helper. If our needs were even greater, such as deriving new fields of a widget based on the application of complex logic, we should make an entirely new class.

For that, we should use Active Model.

13.2 Active Model is for Resource Modeling

> This section's code is in the folder 13-02/ of the sample code.

Suppose we need to produce a report about the shipping zone to a given user, for each widget, from its manufacturer. A shipping zone is a rough approximation about how long it takes to mail something from one place to another, and we can calculate it based on two post codes: the user's and the manufacturer's.

We discover that our users refer to this as a "user shipping estimate", and that a list of widget names, ids, and zone numbers can be fed into many downstream systems that already exist. Our job is to produce these values.

Because we use resources for our routing, we'll have a route like `/user_shipping_estimates` that, when given a destination postal code, will render a list of estimates based on our current database of widgets. Ideally, we could use objects that behave like Active Records and thus could be used with Rails form and URL helpers.

This is what Active Model does. Let's create our `UserShippingEstimate` resource. We need to include `ActiveModel::Model` and define our attributes with `attr_accessor`. Just these two bits of code will enable several handy features of our class. It will give us a constructor that accepts attributes as a `Hash`, and will enable `assign_attributes` for bulk assignment.

```
# app/models/user_shipping_estimate.rb

class UserShippingEstimate
  include ActiveModel::Model
  attr_accessor :widget_name,
                :widget_user_facing_id,
                :shipping_zone,
                :destination_post_code
end
```

To make our model work with some of Rails' form and URL helpers, we need to tell Rails what fields uniquely identify an instance of our model. For Active Records, that is simply the `id` field, and this is what Active Model will use by default. But Rails defines the method `to_key` (in `ActiveModel::Conversions`, included by `ActiveModel::Model`) to allow us to override it.

In our case, `user_facing_identifier` isn't sufficient to uniquely identify a `UserShippingEstimate` because the estimate changes based on the `destination_post_code`. By combining both `user_facing_identifier` and `destination_post_code`, we *can* uniquely identify a shipping estimate.

Thus, if we implement `to_key`, we can use our model in Rails views the same as we could an instance of an Active Record. We also need to tell Rails that our object actually has an identifier, which requires that we implement `persisted?` to return true. `to_key` should return an array of the values comprising the unique identifier, like so:

```
# app/models/user_shipping_estimate.rb

              :widget_user_facing_id,
              :shipping_zone,
```

```
          :destination_post_code

  def persisted?
    true
  end

  def to_key
    [ self.widget_user_facing_id,
      self.destination_post_code ]
  end
end
```

That's it! We now have an Active Record-like object:

```
> bin/rails c
rails> user_shipping_estimate = UserShippingEstimate.new(
        widget_name: "Stembolt",
        widget_user_facing_id: "123.45",
        shipping_zone: 4,
        destination_post_code: "90210")
rails> Rails.application.routes.draw do
rails*   resources :user_shipping_estimates
rails> end
rails> app.user_shipping_estimate_path(user_shipping_estimate)
=> "/user_shipping_estimates/123.45-90210"
```

As a class in app/models, this adds to our growing library of data definitions. While the class alone can't completely explain what a "user shipping estimate" is, the few lines of code in the class tell quite a bit: it has four attributes, two of which uniquely identify it. This is surprisingly powerful, especially when everything in app/models is designed the way we've described.

It's important to note that Rails didn't always provide Active Model. Even today, the model generator produces an Active Record. This has led to countless libraries that allow you to define record-like objects, wrap Active Records, or create delegates to simulate a class that works in Rails view helpers. You don't need them.

The Rails team has gone to great lengths to extract the parts of Active Record that don't depend on the database into modules that make up Active Model. This gives us powerful tools to create objects that work the way we want, work with Rails view helpers, and don't require a third party library. Today, you should not have much need for third party gems to create record-like classes.

Up Next

We can start to see some larger architectural principles taking shape. See the figure "Consistency Across Layers" below for how we can trace names and concepts from the URLs all the way to the model layer, and that it doesn't matter if data is stored in the database or not. This architectural consistency helps greatly with sustainability.

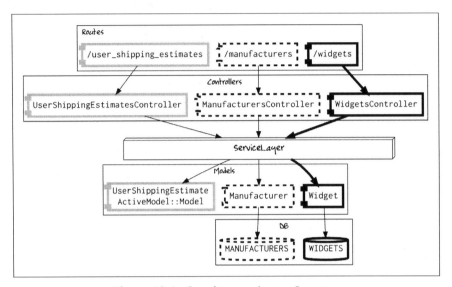

Figure 13.1: Consistency Across Layers

We haven't finished with models, yet. In particular, we still need to discuss validations, callbacks, and testing. We'll get to that, but first we need to learn about structuring our business logic and database design. The database is next.

14
The Database

For most apps, the data in its database is more important than the app itself. If a cosmic entity swooped in and removed your app's source code from all of existence, you could likely recreate it, since you'd still have the underlying data it exists to manage. If that same entity instead removed your *data*... this would be an extinction-level event for your app.

What this thought experiment tells me is that the way data is managed and stored requires a bit more care and rigor than is typically applied to code. This "care and rigor" amounts to spending more time modeling the data and using everything available in your database to keep the data correct, precise, and consistent.

This contradicts Rails' overly simplistic view of the database. By only following Rails' defaults, and designing your database when you write migrations, you will eventually have inconsistent or incorrect data, and likely a fair bit of unnecessary complexity in your code to deal with it.

That said, there are some realities about using a database we have to account for:

- Databases provide much simpler types and validations than our code.
- Large or high-traffic databases can be hard to change.
- Databases are often consumed by more than just your Rails app.

To navigate this, we'll talk about the logical model of the data—the one the users talk about and understand—as distinct from the physical model—what tables, columns, indexes, and constraints are actually in the database. With regard to the physical model, we'll break that down into two distinct steps for development. We'll learn how to decide what database structures you want first, and then how to write a proper Rails migration to create them.

First, let's define logical and physical models.

14.1 Logical and Physical Data Models

When you run `bin/rails g migration` to create a database migration, you are manipulating the *physical* data model: the actual schema in the database. The *logical* model is the data model as understood by users and other interested parties. For simple domains, these models are often very similar, but it's important to understand the differences.

The logical model is a tool to get alignment between the developers who build the app and the users or other stakeholders who know what problems the app needs to solve. Users won't usually care about physical elements such as indexes, join tables, or reference data lookup tables when discussing how the app should behave.

The logical model is in the language of the users, at the level of abstraction they understand. This is often insufficient for properly managing the data, but you can't make a database without an understanding of the domain.

For example, a user will think that a widget has a status, or a manufacturer has an address. This doesn't mean that the widget *table* must have a status *column* or that the manufacturer *table* has columns for each part of an address. You may not want to (or be able to) model it that way in the database.

See the figure "Example Logical and Physical Models" on the next page for an example of a logical and physical model for a hypothetical widget and manufacturer relationship.

It stands to reason, then, that you should create a logical model to build alignment before you start thinking about the physical model.

14.2 Create a Logical Model to Build Consensus

The logical model is a tool to build consensus with the developers who must write the software and anyone else that understands what the software must do or what problems it must solve. The logical model is where you can identify requirements for the data to be stored without worrying (yet) about how to store it.

I recommend that the developers either lead this process or have final approval, since this model is input into their work. While non-developers can do a good job of drafting logical models, there are often some fine details they miss that a developer will need to know in order to move forward.

I don't want you to think of the logical model as some grandiose document created by a formalized process. Often a single spreadsheet is sufficient. No matter how you do it, I highly recommend writing it down and being explicit. It's usually sufficient to capture:

- The names of all entities or "things" to be managed
- For each attribute of those entities:
    - The name of it
    - What type of data it is

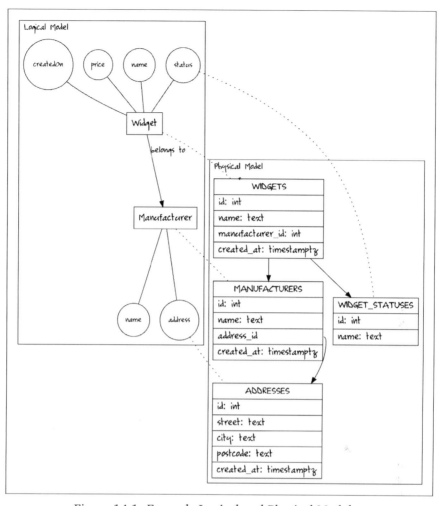

Figure 14.1: Example Logical and Physical Models

- Is it a required value?
- What other requirements are there, such as allowed values, uniqueness, etc.

• For each entity, what uniquely identifies it? Can two entities have the exact same values for all attributes and, if so, what does that mean?

For example:

Table 14.1: Example logical model as a spreadsheet

Entity	Attribute	Type	Req?	Other Requirements
Widget	name	String	Y	unique to manufacturer
Widget	status	String	Y	"Fresh", "Approved", or "Archived"
Widget	price	Money	Y	Not negative, <= than $10,000
Widget	created	Date	Y	
Manufacturer	name	String	Y	unique
Manufacturer	address	Address	Y	street and zip is fine

However you draft this logical model, make sure you have a good sense of the allowed values for each attribute. If the user uses attribute types like "Address", define a new entity called "Address" and identify its requirements. For more general types like "String" or "Date", try to get clarity on what values are allowed. There are a lot of strings in the world and probably not all of them are a valid widget status.

As to the uniqueness questions, getting these right can greatly reduce confusion in the actual data. Often there are several sets of values that represent uniqueness. For example, the widget ID we've discussed previously sounds like a unique value. But you also may want widget *names* to be unique. It's fine to have multiple unique identifiers for entities, but it's important to understand all of them.

The less familiar you are with the domain, or the newer it is, the more time you should spend exploring it before you start coding. Mistakes in data modeling are difficult to undo later and can create large carrying costs in navigating the problems created by insufficient modeling.

You don't have to know everything, but even knowing how data *might* be used is useful. You don't have to handle those "someday, maybe" requirements, but knowing how stable certain requirements are can help you properly translate them to the physical model. Stable requirements can be enforced in the database; unstable requirements might need to be enforced in code so they can be more easily changed.

Once you have alignment, you can build the physical model, which you should do in two steps: plan it, then create it.

14.3 Planning the Physical Model to Enforce Correctness

> This section's code is in the folder 14-03/ of the sample code.

Translating the logical model to the physical model requires making several design decisions, especially as the app becomes more complex and needs to manage more types of data.

This should be done in two discrete steps. This section discusses the first, which is to plan exactly how you are going to store the data in the database. The next section discusses how to write a Rails migration to implement this plan.

Whereas the logical model was for building alignment and discovering business rules, the physical model is for accurately managing data that conforms to those rules. This means that correctness, precision, and accuracy are paramount.

The design decisions you'll make amount to how and where you will enforce the correctness of the data. Your database is an incredibly powerful tool to do this, and it's where most of your constraints around correctness should go.

14.3.1 The Database Should Be Designed for Correctness

Rails' view of the database is that it's more or less a dumb store and Rails—via validations and other mechanisms—will keep the data correct. This is unrealistic, even in simple circumstances. Active Record provides a public API to bypass validations, and the reality of most systems is that Things That Aren't Rails will be accessing the database directly.

For example, it's common to connect business and financial reporting systems directly to the app's database. It's often much more economical and flexible to allow business users to query the data however they like than to get developers to build custom views for them. Tools like Looker[1] or Heroku Dataclips[2] provide ways of turning SQL into reports. Common data warehousing techniques usually involve dumping the entire operational database into another system where it can be analyzed.

If these systems have to deal with incorrect or ambiguous data, in the best case, they will be complex and difficult to maintain. More realistically, the reports will simply be wrong. If, on the other hand, these systems can rely on the data in the database being correct and unambiguous, the reports are more valuable and can lead to better decisions.

For simple to moderate requirements, you can use the database to absolutely ensure the data is correct and precise. For complex requirements, you may need to use code in addition to the database. Unstable requirements benefit from being implemented in code, because the database will become harder to change as time goes on. Stable or critical requirements, however, benefit greatly from being enforced in the database.

---
[1] https://looker.com
[2] https://devcenter.heroku.com/articles/dataclips

No matter what, we're going to use database-specific features. That requires using a SQL schema instead of a Ruby-based one.

14.3.2 Use a SQL Schema

It's rare to create an app that must connect to many different types of databases. It's also rare to migrate from one database type to another. Thus, we should not be shy about using database-specific features whenever it helps us meet our users' needs. Rails' API for managing the database doesn't provide access to all of these features, however.

This matters because Rails uses a schema file to maintain the test database, as well as to initialize a development database in a fresh environment. We need that schema to match production, so we cannot use db/schema.rb, and instead must use SQL.

Fortunately, this is a one-line configuration change in config/application.rb

```
# config/application.rb

      # per-controller helpers
      g.helper false
    end
→
→   # We want to be able to use any feature of our database,
→   # and the SQL format makes that possible
→   config.active_record.schema_format = :sql
  end
end
```

Note that we added a comment as to why we made this change. It's important that all deviations from Rails' defaults are understood by current and future team members. Comments are an easy way to make that happen. Git commit messages are not.

We should also delete db/schema.rb, since that will no longer be used. Rails will store the SQL schema in db/structure.sql.

```
> rm db/schema.rb
```

I recommend this change for all database types, because it costs nothing and provides a lot of benefit.

For Postgres specifically, we need to make another change, which is to use `TIMESTAMP WITH TIME ZONE` for timestamps.

14.3.3 Use TIMESTAMP WITH TIME ZONE For Timestamps

The SQL standard provides for the TIMESTAMP fields to store... timestamps. A timestamp is a number of milliseconds since a reference timestamp, usually midnight on January 1, 1970 in UTC.

The TIMESTAMP data type does not store a time zone, however. Most databases store timestamps in UTC and provide an automatic translation based on... well, it's complicated.

By default, the computer your database is running on is configured with a system time zone. This can be hard to inspect or control. The connection to the database itself can override this. The code that makes a connection to the database can override this as well. Rails can override this. Your code can override Rails.

This means that your timestamps will be translated using a reference time zone that might not be obvious. And if the wrong reference is used when reading those timestamps out, the reader can interpret the timestamp differently. Even though Rails defaults to using UTC, some other process might be configured differently. This is extremely confusing.

Postgres provides the data type TIMESTAMPTZ (also known as TIMESTAMP WITH TIME ZONE) that avoids this problem. It stores the reference time zone with the timestamp so it's impossible to misinterpret the value. Postgres expert Dave Wheeler wrote a blog post[3] that can provide you more details.

We can make Rails use this type by default. The class PostgreSQLAdapter (which is in the ActiveRecord::ConnectionAdapters namespace) has an attribute named datetime_type that allows overriding the default SQL type used whenever a migration has a datetime in it.

We can set this to :timestamptz and all of our migrations will use TIMESTAMPTZ instead of TIMESTAMP. This can be done anywhere as long it loads when Rails does. Best place to do that is in config/initializers/postgres.rb:

```
# config/initializers/postgres.rb

require "active_record/connection_adapters/postgresql_adapter"
ActiveRecord::ConnectionAdapters::PostgreSQLAdapter.datetime_type =
  :timestamptz
```

Now, when we write code like t.timestamps or t.datetime, Rails will use TIMESTAMP WITH TIME ZONE and all of our timestamps will be stored without ambiguity or implicit dependence on the system time zone.

---

[3] https://justatheory.com/2012/04/postgres-use-timestamptz/

With this base, we can start planning the physical model.

14.3.4 Planning the Physical Model

A formal way to model a database is called *normalization*, and it's a dense topic full of equations, confusing terms, and mathematical proofs. Instead, I'm going to outline a simpler approach that might lack the precision of theoretical computer science, but is hopefully more approachable.

Here's how to go about it:

1. Create a table for each entity in the logical model.
2. Add columns to associate related models using foreign keys.
3. For each attribute, decide how you will enforce its requirements and create the needed columns, constraints, and associated tables.
4. Create indexes to enforce all uniqueness constraints.
5. Create indexes for any queries you plan to run.

To do this, it's immensely helpful if you understand SQL. In addition to knowing how to model your data, knowing SQL allows you to understand the runtime performance of your app, which will further help you with data modeling. Of all the programming languages you will ever learn, SQL is likely to remain useful for your entire career. Execute Program[4] has a course that will help.

Outside of learning SQL, the hardest part of the planning process is step 3: deciding how to enforce the requirements of each attribute.

You will bring together some or all of the following techniques:

- Choosing the right column type
- Using database constraints
- Creating lookup tables
- Writing code in your app

Let's dive into each one of these.

Choosing the Right Column Type

Each column in the database must have a type, but databases have few types to choose from. Usually there are strings, dates, timestamps, numbers, and booleans. That said, familiarize yourself with the types of *your* database. Unless you are writing code that has to work against *any* SQL database (which is rare), you should not be bound by Rails' least-common-denominator set of types.

---

[4]https://www.executeprogram.com/courses/sql/lessons/basic-tables

The type you choose should allow you to store the exact values you need. It should also make it difficult or impossible to store incorrect values. Here are some tips for each of the common types.

Strings In the olden days, choosing the size of your string mattered. Today, this is not universally true. Consult your database's documentation and use the largest size type you can. For example, in Postgres, you can use a TEXT field, since it carries no performance or memory burden over VARCHAR. It's important to get this right because changing column types later when you need bigger strings can be difficult.

Rational Numbers Avoid FLOAT if possible. Databases store FLOAT values using the IEE 754[5] format, which *does not store precise values*. Either convert the rational to a base unit (for example, store money in cents as an integer), or use the DECIMAL type, which *does* store precise values. Note that neither type can store all rational numbers. One-third, for example, cannot be stored in either type. To store precise fractional values might require storing the numerator and denominator separately.

Booleans Use the boolean type. Do not store, for example, "y" or "n" as a string. There's no benefit to doing this and it's confusing. And yes, people do this and I don't understand why.

Dates Remember that a date is not a timestamp. A date is a day of the month in a certain year. There is no time component. The DATE datatype can store this, and allow date arithmetic on it. Don't store a timestamp set at midnight on the date in question. Time zones and daylight savings time will wreak havoc upon you, I promise.

Timestamps As opposed to a date, a timestamp is a precise moment in time, usually a number of milliseconds since a reference timestamp. As discussed above, use TIMESTAMP WITH TIME ZONE if using Postgres. If you aren't using Postgres, be *very explicit* in setting the reference timezone in all your systems. Do not rely on the operating system to provide this value. Also, *do not* store timestamps as numbers of seconds or milliseconds. The TIMESTAMP WITH TIME ZONE and TIMESTAMP types are there for a reason.

Enumerated Types Many databases allow you to create custom enumerated types, which are a set of allowed values for a text-based field. If the set of allowed values is stable and unlikely to change, an ENUM can be a good choice to enforce correctness. If the values might change, a lookup table might work better (we'll talk about that below).

No matter what other techniques you use, you will always need to choose the appropriate column type. Next, decide how to use database constraints.

---

[5] https://en.wikipedia.org/wiki/IEEE_754

Using Database Constraints

All SQL databases provide the ability to prevent NULL values. In a Rails migration, this is what `null: false` is doing. This tells the database to prevent NULL values from being inserted. Any required value should have this set, and most of your values should be required.

Many databases provide additional constraint mechanisms, usually called *check constraints*. Check constraints are extremely powerful for enforcing correctness. For example, a widget's price must be positive and less than or equal to $10,000. With a check constraint this could be enforced:

```
ALTER TABLE
  widgets
ADD CONSTRAINT
  price_positive_and_not_too_big
CHECK (
  price_cents >  0 AND
  price_cents <= 1000000
)
```

If you try to insert a widget with a price of -$100 or $300,000, the database will refuse. Thus, you can be absolutely sure the price is valid. Check constraints can do all sorts of things. If you want all widget names to be lowercase, you can do that, too:

```
CHECK (
  lower(name) = name
)
```

Modifying these constraints becomes more difficult as the database gets larger, because these sorts of changes can create locks on the table that prevent access or modification or both. This can create downtime for your app. There are strategies to deal with this that are beyond the scope of this book, but the strong migrations gem[6] is a great place to start with understanding them. Note, however, that it's entirely likely that you will *never* reach the size of database where this would be a problem.

Here are the guidelines I find most useful:

- Any stable requirement should be implemented as a check constraint.

---

[6] https://github.com/ankane/strong_migrations

- Any critical requirement should be implemented as a check constraint.
- Unstable requirements on tables expected to grow might be better implemented in code, so you can change them frequently, but it still might be better to use a check constraint and wait for the table to actually get large enough to be a problem.

The next technique for enforcing correctness is the use of lookup tables.

Using Lookup Tables

When a column's value should be one value from a static list of possible values, an ENUM can work as we discussed above. If the possible values are likely to change, or if users are modifying those values, *or* if you need additional metadata to go along with the values, an ENUM won't work. In these cases, you need a lookup table.

In the data model above on page 215, you can see an example of this for the widget's status. Suppose we had three widgets in the database, two of which have the status "Fresh" and the other "Approved". Here's how that would look in the database using a lookup table:

Table 14.2: Example widgets table referencing a lookup table

id	name	widget_status_id
10	Stembolt	1
11	Thrombic Modulator	1
12	Tachyon Generator	2

Table 14.3: Example widget_statuses lookup table

id	name
1	Fresh
2	Approved
3	Archived

Note a key difference between the physical and logical model. The logical model simply states that a widget has a status attribute. To enforce correctness and deal with a potentially unstable list of possible values, we are modeling it with a new table. In our code, a widget will belong_to a status (which will has_many widgets).

When using lookup tables, you must create a *foreign key constraint*. This tells the database that the value for widget_status_id *must* match an id in the referenced widget_statuses table. This prevents widgets from having invalid or unknown statuses, since widget_statuses contains all known valid statuses.

A lookup table also allows modeling metadata on the referenced value. For example, if only "Approved" widgets can be sold, we might model that with a boolean column on the `widget_statuses` table:

Table 14.4: Example `widget_statuses` lookup table with metadata

id	name	allows_sale
1	Fresh	false
2	Approved	true
3	Archived	false

The last tool available to enforce correctness is your app.

Enforcing Correctness in App Code

Some requirements are too difficult to enforce at the database layer, either because of necessary complexity or because of a lack of stability. In these cases, your app can enforce correctness by refusing to write data that violates the requirements.

Rails validations are quite powerful at doing this, and this is the mechanism you should use if you must validate correctness in code. Just be aware that Active Record's public API allows circumventing the validations. Anything your database can possibly store, you can put into it using Active Record, no matter what validations you have created.

That said, some requirements are so complex that using validations becomes quite difficult and you'll need to write a bunch of code to prevent bad data from getting written.

For example, if only supervisors can change a widget's status to "Approved" for manufacturers created before July 10, 1998, except for the manufacturer "Cyberdyne Systems", this is going to be a convoluted and hard-to-understand validation. It would be simpler as code (and relatively straightforward to implement if you've followed the previous guidance and avoided putting business logic in your Active Records).

Once you have decided how you are going to model everything, it's time to make your migrations.

14.4 Creating Correct Migrations

> This section's code is in the folder 14-04/ of the sample code.

Writing migrations is how we programmatically modify the database to conform to the physical schema we want to use. Because Rails' API for doing this is not SQL, it's important that we take some time to make sure the migrations we write result in the schema we need. Rails' API is powerful and will save us time and make the work easier, but it lacks a few useful defaults.

In the previous chapter, we created models so we could talk about some model basics. Rather than edit those models and the schema it created, let's start over (you can't do this in real life, but it'll make this chapter simpler if we do).

If we delete the migrations and fixtures created by bin/rails g model and re-run bin/setup, we should be good to go.

```
> rm db/migrate/* test/fixtures/*.* && bin/setup
«lots of output»
```

The figure "Example Logical and Physical Models" on page 215 outlines what we're going to do, but to re-iterate:

- A Widget has a name, price, status, and manufacturer, all of which are required.
- A Manufacturer has a name and an address, both of which are required.
- An address is a street and a zip code (both required).
- Widget names must be unique within a manufacturer.
- Manufacturer names must be unique globally.
- We'll use lookup tables for addresses and widget statuses.
- We'll use a database constraint to enforce a price's lower-bound, but code for the upper-bound.

It's important that changes that logically relate to each other go in a single migration file. Some databases, including Postgres, run migrations in a transaction, which allows us to achieve an all-or-nothing result. Either our entire change is applied successfully, or none of it is.

While we still want to end up with one migration, I find it easier to built it iteratively. Write some of the migration, apply it and check it, then rollback and continue until everything is correct.

The figure "Authoring Migrations" on the next page outlines this basic process:

1. Create your migration file.
2. Add some code to it.
3. Apply the migrations and check the database to see if it had the desired effect.
4. If anything is wrong, or you aren't yet done, roll back the changes.
5. Repeat until you have correctly modeled the physical changes.

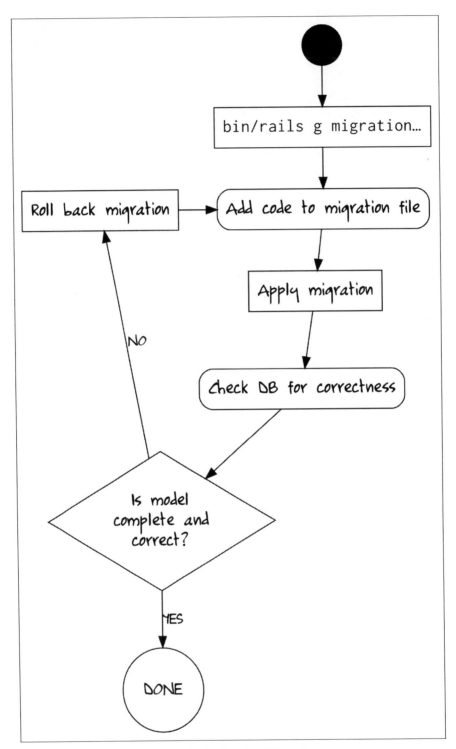

Figure 14.2: Authoring Migrations

This allows you to take each change step-by-step, but still end up with only one migration file that makes the cohesive change you're making. In our case, we want a single migration that creates the needed tables.

14.4.1 Creating the Migration File and Helper Scripts

Before we create the migration file, we need three scripts to help this process. I find that `bin/rails db:migrate` and `bin/rails db:rollback` don't consistently modify both the development and test schema. This can result in a test schema that is not the same as what's described in the migration file, which can cause some confusing test behavior. Rather than document this problem, let's make two scripts to handle applying migrations and rolling them back.

Here's the script to migrate all databases (note again the duplicated checks for -h and friends):

```sh
# bin/db-migrate

#!/bin/sh

set -e

if [ "${1}" = -h     ]    || \
   [ "${1}" = --help ] || \
   [ "${1}" = help ]; then
  echo "Usage: ${0}"
  echo
  echo "Applies outstanding migrations to dev and test databases"
  exit
else
  if [ ! -z "${1}" ]; then
    echo "Unknown argument: '${1}'"
    exit 1
  fi
fi

echo "[ bin/db-migrate ] migrating development schema"
bin/rails db:migrate

echo "[ bin/db-migrate ] migrating test schema"
bin/rails db:migrate RAILS_ENV=test
```

Here's the one we'll use to roll back all databases:

```
# bin/db-rollback

#!/bin/sh

set -e

if [ "${1}" = -h ]      || \
   [ "${1}" = --help ] || \
   [ "${1}" = help ]; then
  echo "Usage: ${0}"
  echo
  echo "Rolls back the current migration from dev and test databases"
  exit
else
  if [ ! -z "${1}" ]; then
    echo "Unknown argument: '${1}'"
    exit 1
  fi
fi

echo "[ bin/db-rollback ] rolling back development schema"
bin/rails db:rollback

echo "[ bin/db-rollback ] rolling back test schema"
bin/rails db:rollback RAILS_ENV=test
```

Let's also make a script called `bin/psql` that connects to our development database. I realize that `bin/rails dbconsole` does this, but a) it requires us to type a password each time, and b) it's incredibly slow to start up because it must load Rails first, only to delegate to the `psql` command-line client.

```
# bin/psql

#!/bin/sh

set -e

if [ "${1}" = -h ]      || \
   [ "${1}" = --help ] || \
   [ "${1}" = help ]; then
  echo "Usage: ${0}"
  echo
  echo "Uses psql to connect to dev database directly"
```

```
      exit
    else
      if [ ! -z "${1}" ]; then
        echo "Unknown argument: '${1}'"
        exit 1
      fi
    fi

    echo "[ bin/psql ] Connecting to widgets_development"
    PGPASSWORD=postgres psql -U postgres \
                             -h db \
                             -p 5432 \
                             widgets_development
```

Note that because we have consolidated all dev-environment configuration, we can safely rely on the database connection information to be consistent for all developers, and thus hard-code it into this script.

We'll need to make them executable:

```
> chmod +x bin/db-migrate bin/db-rollback bin/psql
```

It's also a good idea to add these to bin/setup help. I'll leave that as an exercise for the reader.

Now, let's create our migration file:

```
> bin/rails g migration make_widget_and_manufacturers
      invoke  active_record
      create    db/migrate/20231204235403_make_widget_and_ma...
```

For the sake of repeatability when writing this book, I'm going to rename the migration file to a name that's not based on the current date and time. You don't need to do this.

```
> mv db/migrate/*make_widget_and_manufacturers.rb \
  db/migrate/20210101000000_make_widget_and_manufacturers.rb
```

With that set up, we can now iteratively put code in this file to generate the correct schema we want.

14.4.2 Iteratively Writing Migration Code to Create the Correct Schema

We'll need to work a bit backward. We can't create `widgets` first, because it must reference `widget_statuses` and `manufacturers`. `manufacturers` must reference `addresses`. So, we'll start with `widget_statuses`.

By default, Rails creates nullable fields. We don't want that. Fields with required values should not allow null. We'll use `null: false` for these fields (even for nullable fields I like to use `null: true` to make it clear that I've thought through the nullability).

I also like to document tables and columns using `comment:`. This puts the comments in the database itself to be viewed later. Even for something that seems obvious, I will write a comment because I've learned that things are never as obvious as they might seem.

```ruby
# db/migrate/20210101000000_make_widget_and_manufacturers.rb

class MakeWidgetAndManufacturers < ActiveRecord::Migration[7....
  def change
→   create_table :widget_statuses,
→     comment: "List of definitive widget statuses" do |t|
→
→     t.text :name, null: false,
→       comment: "The name of the status"
→     t.timestamps null: false
→   end
→
→   add_index :widget_statuses, :name, unique: true,
→     comment: "No two widget statuses should have the same name"
  end
end
```

Note that I've created a unique index on the `:name` field. Although database indexes are mostly for allowing fast querying of certain fields, they are also the mechanism by which databases enforce uniqueness. Thus, to prevent having more than one status with the same name, we create this index, specifying `index: { unique: true }`.

This will create a case-sensitive constraint, meaning the statuses `"Fresh"` and `"fresh"` are both allowed in the table at the same time. Currently, the developers control the contents of this table, so a unique index is fine—we won't create a duplicate status in a different letter case. If the contents of this field were user-editable, I might create a case-insensitive constraint instead. Sean Huber wrote a short blog post[7] about how you could do this if you are interested.

Next, let's create the addresses table. Our user's documentation said "street and zip is fine", so we'll create the table with just those two fields for now.

```
# db/migrate/20210101000000_make_widget_and_manufacturers.rb

      add_index :widget_statuses, :name, unique: true,
        comment: "No two widget statuses should have the same n...
→     create_table :addresses,
→       comment: "Addresses for manufacturers" do |t|
→
→       t.text :street, null: false,
→         comment: "Street part of the address"
→       t.text :zip, null: false,
→         comment: "Postal or zip code of this address"
→
→       t.timestamps null: false
→     end
→
    end
  end
```

Again, liberal use of comment: will help future team members. At this point, I like to run the migrations to make sure everything's working before proceeding.

```
> bin/db-migrate
[ bin/db-migrate ] migrating development schema
== 20210101000000 MakeWidgetAndManufacturers: migrating ====...
-- create_table(:widget_statuses, {:comment=>"List of defini...
   -> 0.0069s
-- add_index(:widget_statuses, :name, {:unique=>true, :comme...
   -> 0.0013s
-- create_table(:addresses, {:comment=>"Addresses for manufa...
   -> 0.0024s
== 20210101000000 MakeWidgetAndManufacturers: migrated (0.01...

[ bin/db-migrate ] migrating test schema
== 20210101000000 MakeWidgetAndManufacturers: migrating ====...
```

[7] http://shuber.io/case-insensitive-unique-constraints-in-postgres/

```
-- create_table(:widget_statuses, {:comment=>"List of defini...
   -> 0.0039s
-- add_index(:widget_statuses, :name, {:unique=>true, :comme...
   -> 0.0010s
-- create_table(:addresses, {:comment=>"Addresses for manufa...
   -> 0.0021s
== 20210101000000 MakeWidgetAndManufacturers: migrated (0.00...
```

I also like to connect to the database and describe the tables to see if it looks correct. It may seem silly, but looking at the same information in a different way can often uncover mistakes.

With Postgres, you can use the `bin/psql` script we made and type `\d+ widget_statuses` or `\d+ addresses` to display the schema. If anything looks wrong—including a spelling error in a comment—use `bin/db-rollback`, fix it, and move on.

Of course, we aren't done yet, so we'll `bin/db-rollback` anyway.

```
> bin/db-rollback
[ bin/db-rollback ] rolling back development schema
== 20210101000000 MakeWidgetAndManufacturers: reverting ====...
-- drop_table(:addresses, {:comment=>"Addresses for manufact...
   -> 0.0012s
-- remove_index(:widget_statuses, :name, {:unique=>true, :co...
   -> 0.0014s
-- drop_table(:widget_statuses, {:comment=>"List of definiti...
   -> 0.0005s
== 20210101000000 MakeWidgetAndManufacturers: reverted (0.00...

[ bin/db-rollback ] rolling back test schema
== 20210101000000 MakeWidgetAndManufacturers: reverting ====...
-- drop_table(:addresses, {:comment=>"Addresses for manufact...
   -> 0.0006s
-- remove_index(:widget_statuses, :name, {:unique=>true, :co...
   -> 0.0011s
-- drop_table(:widget_statuses, {:comment=>"List of definiti...
   -> 0.0003s
== 20210101000000 MakeWidgetAndManufacturers: reverted (0.00...
```

Because widgets must refer to manufacturers, we need to make manufacturers next. We'll use `references` to create the foreign key from manufacturers to addresses. Rails' default is to skip creating a foreign key constraint. This is not a good default, because there's no benefit to skipping foreign key constraints.

We'll use `foreign_key: true` to make sure the constraint gets created. We cannot have manufacturers referencing non-existent addresses. We'll also add an index to the reference because we'll definitely be navigating these foreign keys and an index will ensure that navigation performs well.

```
# db/migrate/20210101000000_make_widget_and_manufacturers.rb

      t.timestamps null: false
    end

→   create_table :manufacturers,
→     comment: "Makers of the widgets we sell" do |t|
→
→     t.text :name, null: false,
→       comment: "Name of this manufacturer"
→
→     t.references :address, null: false,
→         index: true,
→         foreign_key: true,
→         comment: "The address of this manufacturer"
→
→     t.timestamps null: false
→   end
→
→   add_index :manufacturers, :name, unique: true
→
  end
end
```

And now, finally, we can make the widgets table:

```
# db/migrate/20210101000000_make_widget_and_manufacturers.rb

      add_index :manufacturers, :name, unique: true

→   create_table :widgets,
→     comment: "The stuff we sell" do |t|
→
→     t.text :name, null: false,
→       comment: "Name of this widget"
→
→     t.integer :price_cents, null: false,
→       comment: "Price of this widget in cents"
→
```

```
      t.references :widget_status, null: false,
        index: true,
        foreign_key: true,
        comment: "The current status of this widget"

      t.references :manufacturer, null: false,
        index: true,
        foreign_key: true,
        comment: "The maker of this widget"

      t.timestamps null: false
    end

  end
end
```

We have only two steps left. We must enforce the uniqueness of widget names amongst manufacturers, and enforce the widget's price allowed values. We'll tackle the uniqueness requirement next.

To enforce the widget name/manufacturer uniqueness requirement, we can create our own index on both fields using add_index:

```
# db/migrate/20210101000000_make_widget_and_manufacturers.rb

      t.timestamps null: false
    end

    add_index :widgets, [ :name, :manufacturer_id ],
      unique: true,
      comment: "No manufacturer can have two widgets with " +
               "the same name"

  end
end
```

This allows many widgets to have the same name, as long as they don't also have the same manufacturer.

To create the constraint on price, we can use the add_check_constraint method. Prior to Rails 6.1, you needed to use reversible and execute to put raw SQL in your migration. No longer!

We'll add this to the migration file:

```
# db/migrate/20210101000000_make_widget_and_manufacturers.rb
          comment: "No manufacturer can have two widgets with " +...
                   "the same name"
→       add_check_constraint(
→         :widgets,
→         "price_cents > 0",
→         name: "price_must_be_positive"
→       )
→
      end
   end
```

If you don't know SQL or it's still new to you, this syntax for what goes into the second argument of add_check_constraint can seem daunting and hard to derive. Your database's documentation is a great place to start and you *can* piece it together from that. A little bit of trial-and-error also helps, and since you can easily apply and rollback your migration, a combination of reading docs and trying things out will allow you to arrive at the right syntax. That's how I did it!

Also note that we used the optional :name parameter to give the constraint a name. Like adding comments to our tables and columns, giving constraints a descriptive name can be useful. If the constraint is violated, the name will appear in the error message and it can be helpful to use that to start figuring out what might have gone wrong.

Lastly, you'll notice that we didn't need to use any raw SQL, but we are still using a SQL-based schema. A SQL-based schema is always a better option from the start, because they you don't have to remember to change it later if you *do* need to use SQL in your migrations.

Let's apply it:

```
> bin/db-migrate
«lots of output»
```

We aren't *quite* done, because we have not modeled the upper-limit on price. We planned to do that in code, so we need to make sure all of our model classes are created and correct, following the guidelines we learned about in "Active Record is for Database Access" on page 203.

First up is WidgetStatus. Since there is a to-many relationship with widgets, we'll use has_many :widgets. Note that this file will not already exist and you must create it.

```
# app/models/widget_status.rb

class WidgetStatus < ApplicationRecord
  has_many :widgets
end
```

Next is `Address`. It has a to-many relationship with manufacturers, since multiple manufacturers can exist at the same address. Also note that this file won't already exist.

```
# app/models/address.rb

class Address < ApplicationRecord
  has_many :manufacturers
end
```

We'll add the other end of the relationship to `Manufacturer`:

```
# app/models/manufacturer.rb

  class Manufacturer < ApplicationRecord
    has_many :widgets
→   belongs_to :address
  end
```

Finally we'll model `Widget`. Because we did not model the price's upper-end in the database, we should add it to the code now as a validation. Even though we have no use-case that would trigger this validation, since it's part of the logical data model that we couldn't model in the database, we have to put it here.

Note that we *aren't* putting any other validations in these models. The database will enforce correctness and prevent bad data from being written. We only need redundant checks if there's a specific reason. We'll discuss this more in "Validations Don't Provide Data Integrity" on page 255.

```
# app/models/widget.rb
```

```
      last_two: id_as_string[-2..-1]
    }
  end
→ belongs_to :widget_status
→ validates :price_cents,
→   numericality: { less_than_or_equal_to: 10_000_00 }
end
```

If you aren't used to database constraints, it might feel like we've put business logic in our database. In a way, we have, and we really should consider testing some of it. The check constraint, in particular, seems hard to be confident in without a test.

Let's see what a test looks like for our database constraints.

14.5 Writing Tests for Database Constraints

> This section's code is in the folder 14-05/ of the sample code.

Like all tests, tests for the correctness of the data model have a carrying cost. I don't see a lot of value in testing `null: false`, or `unique: true`, because these tend to be easy to get right. Check constraints are more like real code and thus easier to mess up. I usually write tests for them.

Let's write a test for the constraint around the widget's price. We'll need two tests: one that successfully sets the widget's price to a correct value, and another that fails in an attempt to set it to a negative value.

Because this is testing the database and not the code in app/models, our tests will use `update_column`, which skips validations and callbacks, writing directly to the database. If we used `update!` instead, and we later added validations to the Widget class, our test would fail to write the database at all. Using `update_column` ensures we are testing the database itself.

To do that, we'll set up a valid widget in the setup method, which requires a widget status and a manufacturer (which requires an address).

```
# test/models/widget_test.rb

require "test_helper"

class WidgetTest < ActiveSupport::TestCase
  setup do
    widget_status = WidgetStatus.create!(name: "fresh")
    manufacturer = Manufacturer.create!(
```

```ruby
      name: "Cyberdyne Systems",
      address: Address.create!(
        street: "742 Evergreen Terrace",
        zip: "90210"
      )
    )
    @widget = Widget.create!(
      name: "Stembolt",
      manufacturer: manufacturer,
      widget_status: widget_status,
      price_cents: 10_00
    )
  end
  test "valid prices do not trigger the DB constraint" do
    assert_nothing_raised do
      @widget.update_column(
        :price_cents, 45_00
      )
    end
  end
  test "negative prices do trigger the DB constraint" do
    ex = assert_raises do
      @widget.update_column(
        :price_cents, -45_00
      )
    end
    assert_match(/price_must_be_positive/i,ex.message)
  end
end
```

Note the way we are checking that we violated the constraint. We check that the message in the assertion references the constraint name we used in the migration: `price_must_be_positive`. This means our test should hopefully *only* pass if we violated that constraint, but fail if we get some other exception.

Now, let's run the test.

```
> bin/rails test test/models/widget_test.rb
Running 2 tests in a single process (parallelization thresho...
Run options: --seed 53004

# Running:

..
```

```
Finished in 0.046877s, 42.6650 runs/s, 85.3301 assertions/s.
2 runs, 4 assertions, 0 failures, 0 errors, 0 skips
```

This should pass. While we could write a test for the validation, I find those sorts of tests less valuable since the code is straightforward with no real logic.

Up Next

Data modeling is not easy and it can take a lot of experience to get comfortable with it. Hopefully, I've stressed how important it is to create your database in a way that favors correctness and precision at the database layer, as well as some helpful techniques to get there.

In the chapter after next, we'll finish talking about models, but to do that, we need to revisit business logic. While our database schema implements some of our business rules, most of the logic that makes our app special will be in code, so let's talk about that next.

15

Business Logic Code is a Seam

Way back at the start of the book, I outlined a core part of sustainable Rails architecture, which is to not put business logic in the Active Records. In particular, the section "Business Logic in Active Records Puts Churn and Complexity in Critical Classes" on page 61 outlines why. The chapter was light on details about how to structure the classes that *do* contain business logic. That's what we'll discuss here.

As mentioned in that chapter, the key thing to do is isolate your business logic from your Active Records and other Rails-managed classes. How your business logic is structured is less important. But it's not unimportant.

The way to think about the API of your business logic class is as a *seam*. On one side of this seam is code managed by Rails inside a controller, job, or rake task. On the other side is logic specific to your domain and a particular use-case that might use Rails, but isn't managed by it (see the figure on the next page).

I like to refer to this as your app's *service layer*. This term appears in Martin Fowler's *Patterns of Enterprise Application Architecture*, which was the basis for creating Active Record. Fowler defines the service layer as follows:

> A Service Layer defines an application's boundary and its set of available operations from the perspective of interfacing client layers. It encapsulates the application's business logic, controlling transactions and coordinating responses in the implementation of its operations.

This is precisely what I am recommending you do, and this chapter is about that, and what it may look like.

To understand this, we need to first be clear about what's important—and not very important—about the code that implements business logic. We'll then talk about the seam itself, which has three parts: a class, a method, and a return value. The strategy I will advocate is to have a stateless class named for the specific process or use case it implements, a single method that accepts the parameters needed to perform the logic, and an optional

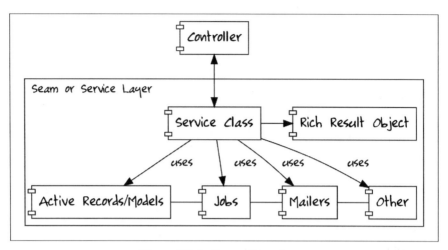

Figure 15.1: Seam Overview

richly-defined result object describing what happened. This forms a base on which future complexity can be most easily managed and requires the fewest design decisions to get a working implementation.

Let's first talk about important considerations regarding the code implementing the business logic, namely that its behavior is as transparent as possible.

15.1 Business Logic Code Must Reveal Behavior

The code implementing business logic is the most critical in your app, since it delivers the results your app exists to deliver. It is also the least stable, since it is implemented iteratively and must be responsive to change. It stands to reason that this code, apart from working, must be easy to understand, since understanding code is required to change it.

And *this* means that the code must be *behavior-revealing* (as opposed to *intention-revealing*). It must be as easy as possible to understand what the code *actually does*. Do not lose sight of this, and be wary of making changes for other reasons.

In particular, it does not matter if

- the code is "object-oriented" (whatever that means).
- you use functional programming.
- the code can be re-used.
- the implementation is "elegant" or "clean" (again, whatever they mean).
- some code metrics have been satisfied.
- you have used design patterns.

- you have used idiomatic Ruby or Rails (whatever they... well, you get the point).

I mention this because I have seen time and time again developers write code to serve one or more of the above purposes at the cost of clarity in behavior. Refactoring code to be "more OO" is a specious activity. In particular, the so-called SOLID Principles can wreak havoc on a codebase when applied broadly[1]. I've been guilty of this many times in my career. Some of the most elegant, compact, object-oriented code I've ever written was the most difficult to understand and change later[2].

This isn't to say there is no value in the list above. Design patterns, object-oriented programming, and Ruby idioms do serve a purpose, but it should be directed toward the larger goal, which is to write code that can be easily changed... by being behavior-revealing.

The technique I have had the most success with—and seen others succeed with as well—is to create a single class and method from which a given bit of business logic is initiated. That class and method (as well as the object the method returns) represent a *seam* or dividing line between the generic world of Rails-managed code, and my own. The internals of that class can then be freely structured as needed.

15.2 Services are Stateless, Explicitly-Named Classes with Explicitly-Named Methods

When implementing the business logic, there are a lot of design decisions that need to be made. The architecture of our app serves to—in part—tell us how to make some of those decisions. Not putting our business logic in an Active Record is a start. We can eliminate even more design decisions by creating conventions around this seam between our logic and the Rails-managed outside world.

What is the absolute simplest thing we can do (besides putting our code directly in `Object`)? If we had no Rails, no framework, no libraries, we'd need to make a class with a method on it, and call that method. Suppose *this* is our strategy for business logic? Suppose we always put new code in a new class and/or a new method? This would eliminate a lot of design decisions.

It turns out this strategy has further advantages beyond eliminating design decisions. First, it doesn't require changing any existing code, which reduces the chances of us breaking something. Second, it provides a ton of flexibility

---

[1] I even wrote a short book about it: https://solid-is-not-solid.com
[2] If you are thinking maybe I just wasn't doing it right, well, maybe I wasn't. But that's still the point. I don't claim to be the best developer in the world, but I'm at least average. And if, after 20 years of working in object-oriented languages, I'm not able to "do it right", I think maybe, just maybe, the problem isn't entirely me.

to respond to change in the future. It's much easier to combine disparate bits of code that turn out to be related than it is to excise unrelated code inside a large, rich class.

Classes like this are often called *services*, and I would encourage the use of this term. It's specific enough to avoid conflating with models, databases, data structures, controllers, or mailers, but general enough to allow the code to meet whatever needs it may have.

So what do we call these services?

15.2.1 A `ThingDoer` Class With a `do_thing` Method is Fine

Barring extenuating circumstances, I will choose a noun for the class name, and make it as specific and explicit as possible to what I'm implementing, in the context of the domain and app at that time. This means that early on, the names are broad, like `WidgetsCreator`. Later, when our domain and app are more complex, we may need more explicit names like `PromotionalWidgetsCreator`.

The method name is a verb representing whatever process or use-case is being implemented, which will create some redundancy. For example, `create_widget`. You might be feeling a bit uncomfortable right now, because you are no-doubt envisioning "enterprisey" code like this:

```
WidgetsCreator.new.create_widget(...)
```

What I'm suggesting will definitely result in code like this. I won't claim this code is elegant, but it does have the virtue of being pretty hard to misinterpret. It also closes the fewest doors to changes in the future.

Now, you might think "We *have* a `Widget` class and it *has* a `create` method. Isn't *that* where widget creation should go?". I understand this line of thinking, but remember, `Widget` is a class to manipulate a database table that holds one particular representation of a real-life widget. And the `create` method is one way (out of many) to insert rows into that table. This isn't my opinion—this is what Rails provides. It's the very essence of the `Widget` class. And there is no reason to conflate inserting database rows with the business process of widget creation.

And, what if we require another way to create a widget? `WidgetsCreator` can grow a new method, or we can make a whole new class to encapsulate that process. We can couple these implementations only as tightly as the underlying process in the real world is coupled. Our code can reflect reality. Wrapping it around the insertion of a row in a database divorces our code from reality.

You might be thinking we should not have to call `new` or perhaps `create_widget` should be named in a more generic way, like `call`. We'll get to that, but let's talk about input to this method first.

15.2.2 Methods Receive Context and Data on Which to Operate, *not* Services to Delegate To

There are typically three types of objects you need access to in order to implement your business logic in a Rails app:

- Rails-managed classes like your Active Record classes, Jobs, or Mailers
- Data-holding objects (Active Records or Active Models), which are typically what is being operated on or a context in which an operation must occur
- Other services needed by your service to which you delegate some responsibility

A significant design decision—after naming your class and method—is how your method's code will get access to these objects.

Rails-managed Classes In the vein of facing reality and treating things as they are—not how we might like them to be—we are writing a Rails app. Rails provides jobs, mailers, and Active Records. Using them directly—thus creating a hard dependency—is fine. We are likely not (or shouldn't be) writing code to work in any Ruby web framework. Further, unless our code needs to be agnostic of mailer, model, or job, there's no value in abstracting the actual implementation. The class needs what it needs and we should be explicit about that.

Data-holding Objects Your method exists to operate on data or perform a process in the context of data, and this data should be passed to the method directly. This information is not specific to the logic, but is an input to that logic. For example, if Pat edits a widget, the logic is the same as if Chris edited a different widget. So we'd pass an instance of `User` and an instance of `Widget` to our method.

Other Services Other services, be they services you create, or third party classes you've added to your app, should either be referred to directly—if callers should not configure them or specify them—or passed into the constructor—if the caller *must* configure or specify them. Note the distinction. If the logic requires a specific implementation, it should be strongly dependent on that. If it's not, it shouldn't be. Making all dependencies generic and injectable belies the way the logic will actually work.

When you follow these guidelines, your code will communicate clearly how it works and what its requirements are. For example:

```ruby
class WidgetsCreator
  def initialize(notifier: )
    @notifier = notifier
  end

  def create_widget(widget_params)
    widget = Widget.create(widget_params)
    if widget.valid?
      @notifier.notify(:widget, widget.id)
      sales_tax_api.charge_tax(widget)
    end

  end

private

  def sales_tax_api
    @sales_tax_api ||= ThirdParty::Tax.new
  end
end
```

This code has a:

- dependency on some sort of `notifier`.
- hard dependency on `ThirdParty::Tax` as well as `Widget`
- per-method-call dependency on `widget_params`.

That tells you a lot about the runtime behavior of this code. If `Widget` and `ThirdParty::Tax` were also passed into the constructor, you'd have more sleuthing to do in order to figure out what this routine did. *And* you'd know less about how coupled this routine is to the various objects it needs to do its work.

This code reflects reality: it wasn't built to function on a generic Active Record or a generic tax service. Thus, we can more easily understand its behavior. This means it'll be easier to change and more sustainable to maintain.

You may have thoughts about this, but let's wait one more section, because the last bit of our seam requires a return value. For that, I recommend using rich result objects.

15.2.3 Return Rich Result Objects, not Booleans or Active Records

A caller often needs to know what happened in the call they made. Not always, but often. Typical reasons are to report errors back to the user, or to feed into logic it needs to execute. As part of the seam between the outside world and our business logic, a boolean value—true if the call "succeeded", false otherwise—is not very useful and can be hard to manage[3].

If, instead, you return a richer object that exposes details the caller needs, not only will your code and tests be more readable, but your seam can now grow more easily if needs change.

A rich result doesn't have to be fancy. I like creating them as inner classes of the service's class as a pretty basic Ruby class, like so:

```ruby
class WidgetsCreator
  def create_widget(widget_params)
    if ...
      Result.new(created: true, widget: widget)
    else
      Result.new(created: false, widget: widget)
    end
  end

  class Result
    attr_reader :widget
    def initialize(created:, widget: nil)
      @created = created
      @widget = widget
    end

    def created?
      @created
    end
  end
end
```

Note how we used a specific past-tense verb—created?—and not something generic like succeeded?. Also note that we are including more than just an indicator of success. In this case, we're returning the widget we attempted to create, because the caller will need access to the validation errors. But

---

[3]If you've ever experienced a website or app giving you a generic message like "The operation could not be completed", you can be sure there is a boolean return value somewhere that has made it difficult or impossible to provide a useful error message.

we could include any other things that are relevant *and* we can enhance this class over time without having to touch any Active Records.

The caller's code will then read as more specific and explicit:

```
result = WidgetsCreator.new.create_widget(widget_params)
if result.created?
  redirect_to widget_path(result.widget)
else
  @widget = result.widget
  render "new"
end
```

Result objects should not be generic. Over time, you may see that related concepts and logic have related result classes, and you can certainly extract duplication then, but by default, don't make a generic result class library. Take the 20 seconds required to type out what initially might amount to wrapping a boolean value.

Rich results shine in two places as you later change code. First, if your needs change, you have a return object that you control and can change. Perhaps the results of widget creation aren't just "did it get created or not":

```
      result = WidgetsCreator.new.create_widget(widget_params)
      if result.created?
        redirect_to widget_path(result.widget),
          info: "Widget created"
→     elsif result.existing_widget_updated?
→       redirect_to widget_path(result.widget),
→         info: "Widget updated"
      else
        @widget = result.widget
        render "new"
      end
```

If we'd started off with a boolean return value, this change would be significant. A result object can also wrap sophisticated errors (or, more commonly, refer to relevant Active Records/Models that themselves expose validation errors).

The other benefit to rich result objects is with testing. They can make tests more clear, certainly, but they can also cause your tests to fail in an obvious way if you change the contract of the seam.

For example, here is how we might mock our service using RSpec's mocking library[4]:

```
mocked_widgets_creator = instance_double(WidgetsCreator)
allow(mocked_widgets_creator).to
  receive(:create_widget).and_return(
    WidgetsCreator::Result.new(created: false)
  )
```

Compare this to `receive(:create_widget).and_return(false)`. The rich result is more explicit. Now if we change `WidgetsCreator` and modify the `Result` to require additional constructor parameters, *this* test will fail with an error related to that new required parameter. This will be a strong indicator that the class we are testing is now mis-using `WidgetsCreator` and could break in production.

Do not use an Active Record for this purpose. Active Records are for database access and, even though they also contain a powerful validation API, the entire purpose of the rich result object is that you can control it as part of the seam you are building.

Note that you should not create any sort of return value if one isn't needed. If the caller of your service doesn't need to know what happened, don't return anything. You can always add a return value later.

Bringing it all together, the figure "Business Logic Seam with Rich Result" on page 250 shows the various pieces.

I want to talk through a few patterns I see around this topic and why you should be wary adopting them. They aren't wrong, so I'm not calling them anti-patterns, but there are trade-offs to consider.

15.3 Implementation Patterns You Might Want to Avoid

There are three patterns I have seen frequently that I don't think deliver the value developers often think they will. I'm not saying you should never use these patterns. I'm saying you need to be honest about the problem you are solving by applying them, how serious that problem is, and how well they actually do solve it. The patterns are:

- Creating class methods instead of instance methods.
- "Service Objects", which are typically classes that have a single parameterless method named `call`
- Using dependency injection.

---

[4]RSpec's mocking system *is* superior to minitest's. It's more powerful and easier to predict what it's doing if you don't already know RSpec.

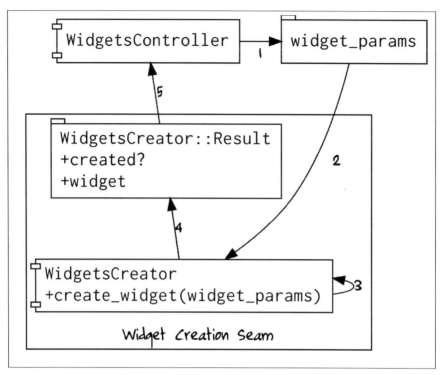

Figure 15.2: Business Logic Seam with Rich Result

15.3.1 Creating Class Methods Closes Doors

Developers often bristle at having to call .new or putting a method in a class that has no state. They think it's more clean/compact/expedient/correct to declare this lack of state by making a class method:

```
class WidgetsCreator
  def self.create_widget(widget_params)
    # ...
  end
end

## to use:

WidgetsCreator.create_widget
```

This approach might save a few keystrokes, but it prevents you from encapsulating state later, if you should need to.

Some developers will try to split the difference and use the Singleton Pattern[5]:

```
class WidgetsCreator

  def self.create_widget(widget_params)
    self.instance.create_widget
  end

  def create_widget(widget_params)
    # ...
  end

private

  def self.instance
    @instance ||= self.new
  end
end
```

This is better, but still unnecessary. It saves callers from typing four characters at the cost of maintaining a lot of code to manage the singleton instance or—worse—the use of a gem that does it for you. It will also require you to think through multi-threading issues at some point, and those are notoriously hard to get right.

15.3.2 "Service Objects" Using call Solve No Problem and Obscure Behavior

Many Rails developers are theoretically onboard with the concept of a service layer, but some implement it using the Gang of Four's command pattern[6], and call it a "service object".

These classes accept all parameters on the constructor, then have a method called call that takes no parameters and performs the operation, like so:

```
class WidgetsCreator
  def initialize(widget_params)
    @widget_params = widget_params
  end
```

---
[5]https://en.wikipedia.org/wiki/Singleton_pattern
[6]https://en.wikipedia.org/wiki/Command_pattern

```
  def call
    @widget_params....
  end
end

## to use:

WidgetsCreator.new(widget_params).call
```

There are even gems and libraries that wrap this into a DSL to, in theory, make it easier to manage these classes. There is almost no reason to create classes like this in a Rails app.

Outside of Rails, a class designed this way is used when you wish to execute some code at a different time or location than when that code's input parameters were available. This situation arises frequently in Rails apps, but in those cases you would use a background job, not a so-called "service object". Rails background jobs *are* the Rails implementation of the command pattern.

There is little benefit to adding a second set of classes that use the command pattern, however there are several downsides:

- Having all your core logic be invoked with the same method name—`call`—can be incredibly confusing, as compared to methods that say what they do.
- You cannot share code using private methods because your class may only have one public method. Code re-use through private methods is extremely powerful, and this pattern makes that difficult or impossible to do.
- Collecting parameters in one method (the constructor) and using them in another (`call`) splits up core logic for no benefit. It also can make complex routines more difficult to understand since parameters are initialized far from where they are used.

This isn't to say that creating a specialized set of classes that respond to the same interface is always bad. But, as a default way of designing your core business logic, "service objects"—AKA the command pattern—is not a good one.

15.3.3 Dependency Injection *also* Obscures Behavior

Dependency Injection involves passing *all* needed dependent objects to the class that needs them. This means that your business logic code will never call `.new` (since this creates objects, and those should be injected) and never refer to a class directly (since, even though a class is an object, the object should be injected, not pulled out of the air).

Our `WidgetsCreator` might look like this, if it were implemented using dependency injection:

```ruby
class WidgetsCreator
  def initialize(notifier:,
                 sales_tax_api:,
                 widget_repository:)

    @notifier         = notifier
    @sales_tax_api    = sales_tax_api
    @widget_repository = widget_repository

  end

  def create_widget(widget_params)
    widget = widget_repository.create(widget_params)
    if widget.valid?
      notifier.notify(:widget, widget.id)
      sales_tax_api.charge_tax(widget)
    end
  end

private

  attr_reader :notifier, :sales_tax_api, :widget_repository

end
```

This might seem nice—we've removed hard dependencies and deferred configuring this object to somewhere else, allowing this object to focus only on the logic it exists to implement. But this has obscured reality.

The reality is that this logic *is coupled* to `Widget` and `ThirdParty::Tax`. There was no requirement for alternative implementations of these classes. Thus, the class has behavior that is not required or needed. This means that all callers must now encode this truth about the system, *or* we must introduce a new set of classes to manage the construction of objects of this class.

In a language like Java, where mocking dependencies is quite difficult, you have to design your code this way to avoid complicated tests. In Ruby, there is no need—we can mock whatever we like. Dependency injection ends up creating classes that are either more flexible than they need to be, or appear to be more flexible, but actually aren't.

That said, sometimes a class *does need* to be flexible. Some classes are designed to make use of an object that conforms to some well-known interface. In that case, dependency injection is a great pattern. You just don't need to use it by default. Flexibility leads to complexity, and a key way to achieve sustainability is to avoid *unneeded* complexity.

Up Next

This chapter was a lot of theory and rhetoric and light on useful examples. If you can bear with me, the impact of the guidelines outlined here will be more apparent with an end-to-end example (which will also afford us to talk about testing). We'll get to that after the following chapter. We must return to models and see how stuff like callbacks, validations, and other model-related features fit into all this. That's what's next.

16
Models, Part 2

> This section's code is in the folder 16-01/ of the sample code.

Now that we've had an intro to models, a full discussion of business logic, and a journey through database design, I want to cap off the models discussion by talking about validations, callbacks, scopes, and testing. Then, in the next chapter, we can see an end-to-end example of how this all fits together, which I think will paint a complete picture of the sustainable approach to business logic.

I've made the point several times to keep business logic out of Active Records, but I've also heavily implied that we should be using validations, which are a form of business logic. We also talked briefly about managing queries, along with a handful of references to avoid callbacks. This chapter will cover all of these topics.

Let's start with validations, which are great at user experience management and not so great at data integrity.

16.1 Validations Don't Provide Data Integrity

When we discussed database modeling in "The Database" on page 213, we spent a fair bit of time talking about how to enforce the types of data that get stored, in particular ensuring that only valid values could be stored in the database.

This is ostensibly what Rails validations exist to do, and we even used a validation for this purpose in that chapter.

The reality is that Rails validations absolutely cannot ensure data integrity. If you design your system as if they do, you will become confused about how invalid data ends up in the database. The only tool that *can* ensure data integrity is the database itself.

Let's go over *why* Rails validations can't provide data integrity, as this is not often obvious to developers. There are three reasons.

- Any code that accesses the database outside your Rails app won't use your validations.

- Rails provides a public API on each Active Record to allow bypassing validations.
- Some validations don't actually work due to race conditions.

The biggest reason for me is the first one: someone else might access the database.

16.1.1 Outside Code Naturally Skips Validations

Although we'd like to think that the database is a private, encapsulated service only available to our Rails app, this is not often the case. Developers or system administrators occasionally need to connect to the database directly to address production issues. We may have one-off batch jobs that simply *have* to run outside our Rails app (or that we may want to). We might even allow other apps to write to our database as a means of application integration.

You might think these types of scenarios are process or system architecture failures. I assure you, they are very real and often the result of carefully-managed trade-offs to deliver value at low cost. To put it another way, if your app architecture falls apart when an external process accesses its database, you will either have to live with bad data, or pay a constant *political* carrying cost keeping those external processes away from your database. See the sidebar "Machine Learning Integration in Postgres" below for an example.

> **Machine Learning Integration in Postgres**
>
> In the early days at Stitch Fix, there was a small engineering team and a *very* small data science team: one person named Bhaskar. Bhaskar produced the Stitch Fix styling algorithm, which was the proprietary process by which our inventory was personally matched to each customer.
>
> The output of Bhaskar's algorithm was a list of every piece of clothing we sold, cross-referenced against every customer to produce a "match score" that told us how likely that customer was to buy that piece of clothing, according to the algorithm. The way this was integrated into the website was a database table. Bhaskar and the engineering team agreed that this one table would be read-only to us, and write-only to him.
>
> If we had instead insisted on some sort of architectural purity by which writing to the database was forbidden, it would've created tons of work for everyone, delay the delivery of value to the business, and result in a carrying cost we didn't need to bear. At the size Stitch Fix is now, preventing direct database integration is a great idea that helps teams manage their respective apps. At that early stage, however, it would've been a terrible decision. Integrating at the database was the right call.

Of course, it doesn't require an outside system to circumvent Rails validations. Rails will happily let *you* do it!

16.1.2 Rails' Public API Allows Bypassing Validations

All Active Records have the method `update_column`, which updates the database directly, skipping validations. The existence of this method (and others that allow it like `save(validate: false)`) implies that there are times when your validations may not apply. If that's not actually true—if your validations should always apply—there's no way to achieve that with Active Record.

And *this* means that no matter how well-factored your code is, it can end up writing data that violates the domain, either due to a misunderstanding by a developer, a bug, or a mistake made in a production Rails console.

The database, on the other hand, does not allow such circumvention, so when you encode a domain rule in the database, misunderstandings, bugs, and mistakes will generate errors, but they won't result in bad data being in the database.

Of course, even if `update_column` didn't exist, not all validations actually work.

16.1.3 Some Validations Don't Technically Work

I'm hard-pressed to meet a Rails developer that has not run afoul of `validates_uniqueness_of`, which is a validation that seeks to ensure a given value is unique. The documentation for this method[1] spends a good amount of space outlining why this validation doesn't really work:

> Using this validation method in conjunction with `ActiveRecord::Base#save` does not guarantee the absence of duplicate record insertions, because uniqueness checks on the application level are inherently prone to race conditions.

The implementation of `validates_uniqueness_of` is to query the database for the value that's about to be saved. If that value isn't found, the record is considered valid and thus saved. But, if another record with the same value is saved during that time, both records are saved, thus violating our rules about uniqueness.

This isn't to say that `validates_uniqueness_of` isn't useful, it's just not able to guarantee uniqueness. The only way to do that is what we did previously: create a database index.

This leads nicely to the next section, because while Rails validations cannot provide data integrity, they are an amazing tool for managing the user experience around data validation.

---
[1] https://api.rubyonrails.org/classes/ActiveRecord/Validations/ClassMethods.html

16.2 Validations Are Awesome For User Experience

In the previous chapter on writing migrations on page 230, we created a validation to constrain the maximum value of a widget's price. We didn't use the database because we decided this particular domain rule wasn't stable and we wanted flexibility that comes with code changes to be able to easily change it later. This won't ensure the database contains only valid values, but it was a trade-off we made.

But validations *really* shine at something else: managing the user experience. If we were to create a form to add a widget, and a user provided a blank value, they would get an exception from the app. That's not a great experience. By adding a presence validation to the widget, we can then access structured error information to present to the user in a friendly and helpful way.

This coupling of validations, errors, and views is a big reason why working with Rails feels productive. When we call `.valid?` on an Active Record (or Active Model), it will populate the `errors` attribute with a rich data structure allowing us to give the user a detailed breakdown of all the validation errors.

Of course, these kinds of validations are technically business logic, which I went through great pains to convince you *not* to put in an Active Record. When people say that programming is all trade-offs, it's true.

We can either keep all business logic out of our models, which requires throwing out the Rails validation API (and presumably building our own replacement), *or* we can let a little bit of our business rules leak into our models and get access to an extremely powerful API for managing the user experience.

I choose the latter and you should, too. Just know that you are making a trade-off.

Speaking of trade-offs, it might seem that using both validations *and* database constraints is creating a duplication of effort. If there is a `NOT NULL` on the widget name in the database and a `validates :name, presence: true` on the model, aren't we creating problematic duplication?

It's true that if the rules around widget names change, you'll have to modify the database and the model. You might have to change a whole bunch of things. That doesn't mean all of that code is duplicative. The database constraints prevent bad data from getting into our database. The validations assist the user in providing good data. Although they are related in what they do and the way they do it, they aren't the same things.

The only other point to mention about validations is that you can use them on Active Models as well. `ActiveModel::Validations` provides most of what you get with an Active Record. This means that you can use validations on your non-database-backed resources. This wasn't always the case with Rails, so it's great that the core team has made it available!

Let's talk about callbacks next.

16.3 How to (Barely) Use Callbacks

Active Record has a detailed set of callbacks[2] available that allow you to run code at various points of a model's life-cycle. The use of these callbacks is hotly debated, and their proper intended use is unclear. My suggestion is to treat them for what they actually are, which is hooks that allow code to run during the lifecycle of various database-related activities.

For example, before_save is called only if the mode passes validations, after the database transaction has been opened, but before the database has been updated. If you need to run code at that exact moment, before_save is what you want to use. Practically speaking, you almost never need to run code at this exact moment.

Prior to Rails 7.1, before_validation was a useful callback to normalize data before validating it and writing it. For example, you could coerce a blank value to `nil`:

```ruby
before_validation do
  if self.name.blank?
    self.name = nil
  end
end
```

Rails 7.1 introduced `ActiveRecord::Normalization`[3], which alleviates the need for this by using the new `normalizes` method:

```ruby
# app/models/widget.rb

  belongs_to :widget_status
  validates :price_cents,
    numericality: { less_than_or_equal_to: 10_000_00 }
→ normalizes :name, with: ->(name) { name.blank? ? nil : name }
end
```

The only other common use for callbacks I can think of is to collect statistics about the use of certain tables. For example, if you are trying to deprecate a database table, you may want to add some logging around the use of that table in your code. You could do this with the `after_commit` callback:

[2]https://guides.rubyonrails.org/active_record_callbacks.html
[3]https://api.rubyonrails.org/classes/ActiveRecord/Normalization.html

```ruby
class OldStuff < ApplicationRecord

  after_commit do
    Rails.logger "#{caller[0]} is using OldStuff"
  end
end
```

In general, however, you want to avoid putting business logic in callbacks, and you *especially* want to avoid making network calls inside callbacks. Even something seemingly simple like queuing a job after you write a record can create serious problem. Consider this code that sends an email when a widget with a high price is created:

```ruby
class Widget < ApplicationRecord
  after_create do |record|
    if (record.price_cents > 10_000)
      HighPriceMailer.notify_admins(record).deliver_later
    end
  end
end
```

Since `after_create` runs inside a database transaction, this code will hold that transaction open while `deliver_later` completes. If this is set up to queue a job, and you are using Resque or Sidekiq (the two most popular job queueing systems for Rails), this means you are making a network call to Redis while holding a database transaction open.

If there is high activity on the WIDGETS table, or on that specific row, this will create locks in the database. These locks will cause the application to block and eventually cascade into failures that will seem to have nothing to do with database transactions or Redis. I have seen this happen first hand at far below the scale you might think could cause this.

You can avoid this by treating callbacks for what they are: a means to run code during specific phasers of a database operation. Describing your logic in those terms usually points out the problem. Would anyone design a system that made network requests to a key/value store while holding open a database transaction? Not intentionally, they wouldn't.

Next, let's talk about scopes, which are another feature of Active Record you won't end up needing much of.

16.4 Scopes are Often Business Logic and Belong Elsewhere

In earlier versions of Rails, scopes were bestowed magical powers not available to regular methods. You could chain scopes together:

```
Widget.recent.unapproved.chronological
```

Nowadays, you can achieve this chaining by declaring class methods on your Active Record—there's no need to use scope at all. This is because methods like `where` return an `ActiveRecord::CollectionProxy`, which is what allows the chaining to work.

This means that you don't even have to declare methods on your Active Record in order to query the database and chain parts of a query you might be building up. For example:

```
Widget.where("created_at > ?", 4.weeks.ago).
       where("status <> 'approved'").
       order("created_at asc")
```

Because this is part of the public API on all your Active Records, you should use `where`, `order`, `limit` and friends as needed to implement your business logic.

Only when you see a pattern of duplication should you consider extracting that duplication somewhere. I prefer the "rule of three", which states that a third time you do the same thing, extract it somewhere for re-use.

Note also that you may find it better to extract the query logic to a new service. For example, if we find ourselves constantly needing "fresh" widgets, but the definition of "fresh" is based on business rules, it might make more sense to create a `FreshWidgetLocator`.

Conversely, if we are frequently needing all widgets created in the last day, that's less about business logic and more about manipulating data directly. That would be fine as a class method on `Widget` like `created_in_last_day`.

Although we've seen a few model tests already, now is a good time to talk about how to think about testing what little code ends up in your models.

16.5 Model Testing Strategy

Models tend to be inputs to (and outputs of) your business logic. In many cases, models are only bags of data, so they don't require that much testing themselves. That said, there are three considerations related to model testing:

- Tests for database constraints, like we wrote in "Writing Tests for Database Constraints" on page 237, naturally belong in the Active Record whose backing table has the constraint.
- Although simple validations might not benefit from tests, complex validations and callbacks certainly do.
- There should be an easy ability to produce reliable and realistic test instances of the model. I prefer Factory Bot over Rails' fixtures.

Let's go through each of these in a bit more detail.

16.5.1 Active Record Tests Should Test Database Constraints

We already saw an example of this in the previous chapter, but for completeness, the model is the best place to put tests of the database constraints since the model is backed by the database table.

When writing these tests, be sure to use `update_column` so you can modify the database directly. You want your test to continue to function even if the model gets more validations or callbacks.

Also be sure you assert as closely on the error as you can. I like to watch the test fail to see what error the database produces. I'll then craft a regular expression that matches as specifically as possible so that the test will only fail if the constraint is violated.

16.5.2 Tests For Complex Validations or Callbacks

Validations that are a single line of code aren't usually worth testing, since they are more like configuration than actual logic. There's not much value in testing that you typed the value `10_000_00` in your model file.

If, however, you make use of more complex validations or use custom validators, you should write a test for this. If you put *any* code in a callback beyond basic logging, you may benefit from testing that as well, because the test will allow you to be precise in which public methods you call on your Active Record are intended to trigger the callback.

16.5.3 Ensure Anyone Can Create Valid Instances of the Model using Factory Bot

Although it's not a test of your model, creating a model should also involve ensuring there is a way for others to create valid and reasonable instances of the model for other tests. Rails provides a test fixture facility, but I find fixtures difficult to manage at even moderate scale, and have not worked with a team that found them superior to the popular alternative, Factory Bot.

Factory Bot[4] is a library to create *factories*. Factories can be used to create instances of objects more expediently than using `new`. This is because a factory often sets default values for each field. So, if you want a reasonable `Widget` instance but don't care about the values for each attribute, the factory will set them for you. This allows code like so:

```
widget = FactoryBot.create(:widget)
```

If you need to specify certain values, `create` acts very much like `new` or `create` on an Active Record:

```
widget = FactoryBot.create(:widget, name: "Stembolt")
```

A factory can also create any needed associated objects, so the above invocations will create (assuming we've written our factories properly) a manufacturer with an address as well as a widget status.

To generate dummy values, I like to use Faker[5]. Faker can provide random, fake values for fields of various types. For example, to create a realistic email address on a known safe-for-testing domain like `example.com`, you can write `Faker::Internet.safe_email`.

While Faker does introduce random behavior to your tests, I view this as a feature. It makes sure your tests don't implicitly become dependent on values used for testing. You can always re-run tests using a previous random seed if you need to debug something.

Let's set it all up. We'll use the `factory_bot_rails` gem since that sets up internals for a Rails app automatically as well as brings in the `factory_bot` gem. They go in the development and test groups.

```
# Gemfile

  # gem "image_processing", "~> 1.2"
```

[4] https://github.com/thoughtbot/factory_bot
[5] https://github.com/faker-ruby/faker

```
  group :development, :test do
    # We use Factory Bot in place of fixtures
    # to generate realistic test data
    gem "factory_bot_rails"

    # We use Faker to generate values for attributes
    # in each factory
    gem "faker"

    # See https://guides.rubyonrails.org/debugging_rails_applic...
    gem "debug", platforms: %i[ mri windows ]
  end
```

```
> bundle install
«lots of output»
```

It's important that our factories produce instances that pass validations and satisfy all database constraints. To help us manage this, Factory Bot provides `FactoryBot.lint`, which will create all of the configured factories and raise an exception if any fail to create due to constraint or validation failures.

I like to wrap a call to this in a test so it runs as part of our test suite. Let's do that before we actually make any factories:

```
# test/lint_factories_test.rb

require "test_helper"

class LintFactoriesTest < ActiveSupport::TestCase
  test "all factories can be created" do
    FactoryBot.lint traits: true
  end
end
```

Now, let's create a factory for addresses, and we'll initially create it to produce invalid data (so we can see our lint test fail).

Factories traditionally go in `test/factories` (or `spec/factories` if using RSpec). The code itself is revealing of intent and does what it appears to do, but relies on meta-programming to do it. I'll explain how it works, but first, here's what it looks like:

```
# test/factories/address_factory.rb

FactoryBot.define do
  factory :address do
    street { Faker::Address.street_address }
  end
end
```

You can likely reason that this produces an `Address` whose `street` value comes from the `Faker` call being made. But I want to explain a bit about how that works. First, `factory :address` knows to create an instance of `Address`, just as `factory :widget_status` would know to create an instance of `WidgetStatus`. Factory Bot is following the various Rails conventions[6].

Second, the method calls with blocks inside the `factory :address` block are declaring test values to use for attributes of `Address`. Because `Address` has a `street` attribute, the dynamically-created method `street` is how we indicate the value to use for it when creating an `Address`.

In this case, the block being given is evaluated each time we want an instance in order to get the value. That value is `Faker::Address.street_address`, which returns a randomly generated, realistic street address like "742 Evergreen Terrace".

Any attribute we don't list will have a value of `nil`. Since we omitted zip and since zip is required by the database, running our lint test should fail:

```
> bin/rails test test/lint_factories_test.rb || echo \
  Test failed
Running 1 tests in a single process (parallelization thresho...
Run options: --seed 63490

# Running:

E

Error:
LintFactoriesTest#test_all_factories_can_be_created:
FactoryBot::InvalidFactoryError: The following factories are...

* address - PG::NotNullViolation: ERROR:  null value in colu...
DETAIL:  Failing row contains (3, 67326 Effertz Divide, null...
```

---
[6]I've long internalized this sort of thing, but I can't understand why using `:address` is better than using the class name—`Address` or `"Address"`. The latter is super clear, the same amount of typing, and doesn't require explanation.

```
          (ActiveRecord::NotNullViolation)
              test/lint_factories_test.rb:5:in `block in <class:LintFa...

  bin/rails test test/lint_factories_test.rb:4


  Finished in 0.468395s, 2.1350 runs/s, 0.0000 assertions/s.
  1 runs, 0 assertions, 0 failures, 1 errors, 0 skips
  Test failed
```

Let's fix the factory so it produces a valid Address:

```
# test/factories/address_factory.rb

  FactoryBot.define do
    factory :address do
      street { Faker::Address.street_address }
→     zip { Faker::Address.zip }
    end
  end
```

Now, our lint test should pass:

```
> bin/rails test test/lint_factories_test.rb
Running 1 tests in a single process (parallelization thresho...
Run options: --seed 12333

# Running:

.

Finished in 0.097839s, 10.2208 runs/s, 0.0000 assertions/s.
1 runs, 0 assertions, 0 failures, 0 errors, 0 skips
```

Let's make a factory for manufacturer, which requires an address. Factory Bot provides a shorthand for creating related objects:

```
# test/factories/manufacturer_factory.rb

FactoryBot.define do
```

```
  factory :manufacturer do
    name { Faker::Company.name }
    address
  end
end
```

The call to `address` on its own works because Factory Bot knows this is not a normal attribute, but a reference to a related object. Since there is a factory for that relation, Factory Bot will use that as the value for address.

One thing that can lead to flaky tests is when randomness ends up producing the same value multiple times in a row for a field that must be unique. While it doesn't happen often, it does happen. Faker can manage this by calling `unique` on any class before calling the data-generating-method. Let's use this in our widget status factory, because widget statuses must be unique (we should've used that on the Manufacturer name as well).

```
# test/factories/widget_status_factory.rb

FactoryBot.define do
  factory :widget_status do
    name { Faker::Lorem.unique.word }
  end
end
```

`Faker::Lorem` will use Lorem Ipsum[7] to come up with a fake word. Because we used `unique`, no `WidgetStatus` instance we create with this factory will ever have the same value.

Note that we did not use one of the known values for widget status. This is a bit of a trade-off. Even though widget statuses have a set of known valid values, since those values are in the database, our code should generally not be coupled to them. Thus, a test that needs any old widget status should not care what the value is.

That said, if we *do* need to create a status from one of the known valid values, we can do that like so:

```
widget = FactoryBot.create(
  :widget,
  status: FactoryBot.create(
```

---

[7]https://en.wikipedia.org/wiki/Lorem_ipsum

```
          :widget_status,
          name: "Approved")
)
```

For completeness, let's create the widget factory.

```
# test/factories/widget_factory.rb

FactoryBot.define do
  factory :widget do
    name         { Faker::Lorem.unique.word }
    price_cents  { Faker::Number.within(range: 1..10_000_00) }
    manufacturer
    widget_status
  end
end
```

Our lint test should still pass:

```
> bin/rails test test/lint_factories_test.rb
Running 1 tests in a single process (parallelization thresho...
Run options: --seed 38418

# Running:

.

Finished in 0.120416s, 8.3045 runs/s, 0.0000 assertions/s.
1 runs, 0 assertions, 0 failures, 0 errors, 0 skips
```

As a final step, let's replace the setup code in our widget test with factories instead.

```
# test/models/widget_test.rb

  require "test_helper"

  class WidgetTest < ActiveSupport::TestCase
    setup do
✗ #     widget_status = WidgetStatus.create!(name: "fresh")
```

```
x #      manufacturer = Manufacturer.create!(
x #        name: "Cyberdyne Systems",
x #        address: Address.create!(
x #          street: "742 Evergreen Terrace",
x #          zip: "90210"
x #        )
x #      )
x #      @widget = Widget.create!(
x #        name: "Stembolt",
x #        manufacturer: manufacturer,
x #        widget_status: widget_status,
x #        price_cents: 10_00
→      @widget = FactoryBot.create(
→        :widget
       )
     end
     test "valid prices do not trigger the DB constraint" do
```

That single line of code will use the widget factory to create the widget, which will in turn create a widget status and a manufacturer, which itself will in turn create an address. Note that you can call build to create in-memory versions of these objects without touching the database.

This test should pass:

```
> bin/rails test test/models/widget_test.rb
Running 2 tests in a single process (parallelization thresho...
Run options: --seed 63177

# Running:

..

Finished in 0.120262s, 16.6303 runs/s, 33.2607 assertions/s.
2 runs, 4 assertions, 0 failures, 0 errors, 0 skips
```

Factory Bot requires understanding a bit of implicit meta-programming, but I find that once you learn how it works, it's much simpler to maintain a suite of test data than Rails' fixtures.

Fixtures require editing YAML files whose dynamic behavior comes from ERB, and I find this clunkier than using Ruby code inside of Factory Bot's domain-specific language (DSL). If you disagree and really like fixtures, I would still encourage you to create valid fixture data for all your models so that you can access model instances easily in your tests.

Up Next

What a journey! It's now time to look at an end-to-end example. I realize we have not discussed controllers, jobs, mailers, and other stuff like that, but now that we understand the relationship between the view, models, the database, and business logic, it's time to see a real example. That's what we'll do next.

17
End-to-End Example

We haven't talked about controllers, mailers, jobs, or mailboxes yet, but we've gotten far enough in that I think a more involved is example will help codify what we've learned so far. It should crystallize the benefits of the approach toward managing business logic. What you'll see is that we avail ourselves of all that Rails has to offer, but our core business logic code will be much more sustainable than if we'd put everything on our Active Records.

17.1 Example Requirements

We'll build a feature to create widgets. In our hypothetical domain, creating a widget is a complex process. It's not just about putting valid data into the `widgets` table.

Here is what has to happen around creating widgets:

- Users must provide a name, manufacturer, and price. These will be validated using the domain rules we've discussed previously: the name must exist and be unique per manufacturer, and the price must be within 1 cent and $10,000.
- Additionally, a widget name must be more than five characters.
- Widgets are created with the status of "Fresh".
- Widgets for manufacturers created before 2010 may not be priced below $100, for legacy reasons that I'm sure many of you can imagine some version of from a past project.
- When a widget is created for more than $7,500, email the financial staff.
- When a widget is created for a manufacturer created in the last two months, email the admin staff.

This might seem convoluted, but I have rarely experienced real world requirements that aren't like this.

In the remainder of the chapter, we'll write the code to implement these requirements, starting with the UI. We'll follow the guidelines laid out already in the book and proceed to write a system test, then implement the business logic.

17.2 Building the UI First

> This section's code is in the folder 17-02/ of the sample code.

No matter how the UI must be styled, it needs to allow the user to select a manufacturer, enter a widget name and price, and see any validation errors related to the data entered. We'll create the UI using semantic markup that is connected to the controller, which we'll leave pretty bare. We'll freshen up the UI using our design system, then write a system test. When that system test is done, we can start on the business logic.

Before we create the UI, we'll need to set up a route and some controller methods. We should also create some development data in db/seeds.rb.

17.2.1 Setting Up To Build the UI

First, we'll modify the existing widgets resource in config/routes.rb to allow :new, and create:

```
# config/routes.rb

  Rails.application.routes.draw do
→   resources :widgets, only: [ :show, :index, :new, :create ]
    resources :widget_ratings, only: [ :create ]
```

Next, we'll create some basic controller methods so our views can be rendered. For new we'll create an empty Widget, but we'll also expose the list of manufacturers, since we need that for a drop-down. If you recall from the section on exposing instance variables on page 100, we ideally expose only one instance variable for the resource in question, but we can also expose reference data when needed. The list of manufacturers qualifies as reference data.

```
# app/controllers/widgets_controller.rb

  class WidgetsController < ApplicationController
→   def new
→     @widget = Widget.new
→     @manufacturers = Manufacturer.all
→   end
→
```

```
→    def create
→      render plain: "Thanks"
→    end
→
     def show
       manufacturer = OpenStruct.new(
         id: rand(100),
```

We should also create some data to use for development.

17.2.2 Create Useful Seed Data for Development

Rails' documentation is unclear on the purpose of seed data, but it's commonly used to seed *development* data, and that's how I view it as well. Because we have set up Factory Bot to create realistic, yet fake data for tests, we can use that for our seed data, too.

There are a few considerations for seed data. First, it should run only in development, so we'll need to check for that. Second, it should ideally be idempotent without requiring a full database reset. We might not be able to do this entirely in the seed data file when the data model gets more complex, but for now we can, so we'll use `destroy_all` to delete all the data first.

Lastly, we want data that's useful in building our UI and exercising the app manually. To that end, we want to make sure a widget exists so that we can exercise trying to use the same name for two widgets belonging to the same manufacturer.

Because we are using Faker, it could be annoying to have randomly-changing names, so for this particular case, we'll give explicit names. You could give explicit names for everything if you like. It depends on what you need from the development data.

We'll replace db/seeds.rb with the following:

```
# db/seeds.rb

if !Rails.env.development?
  puts "[ db/seeds.rb ] Seed data is for development only, " +
       "not #{Rails.env}"
  exit 0
end

require "factory_bot"

Widget.destroy_all
```

```ruby
Manufacturer.destroy_all
Address.destroy_all
WidgetStatus.destroy_all

puts "[ db/seeds.rb ] Creating development data..."
FactoryBot.create(:widget_status, name: "Fresh")
10.times do
  FactoryBot.create(:manufacturer)
end
cyberdyne = FactoryBot.create(:manufacturer,
                              name: "Cyberdyne Systems")
FactoryBot.create(:widget, name: "Stembolt",
                           manufacturer: cyberdyne)
puts "[ db/seeds.rb ] Done"
```

Let's go ahead and run it now to make sure it's working:

```
> bin/rails db:seed
[ db/seeds.rb ] Creating development data...
[ db/seeds.rb ] Done
```

Note that this will be run as part of db:reset, so there's no need to change our bin/setup script. It'll now insert this data into the database after re-creating it.

Now, let's build the UI.

17.2.3 Sketch the UI using Semantic Tags

Our UI will live in app/views/widgets/new.html.erb. We'll need a form that has fields for name and price, as well as a select for manufacturer and a submit button.

Here's the first pass:

```erb
<%# app/views/widgets/new.html.erb %>

<section>
  <h1>New Widget</h1>
  <%= form_with model: @widget do |f| %>
    <%= f.label :name %>
    <%= f.text_field :name %>

    <%= f.label :price_cents %>
```

```erb
    <%= f.text_field :price_cents %>

    <%= f.label :manufacturer_id %>
    <%=
      f.select :manufacturer_id,
        options_from_collection_for_select(
          @manufacturers, "id", "name"
        ),
        {
          include_blank: "-- Choose --",
        }
    %>
    <%= f.submit "Create" %>
  <% end %>
</section>
```

Semantically, this is what is required to make the feature work. Let's make sure this is working by navigating to /widgets/new before we embark on our styling adventure. It should look amazingly awful, as in the screenshot below.

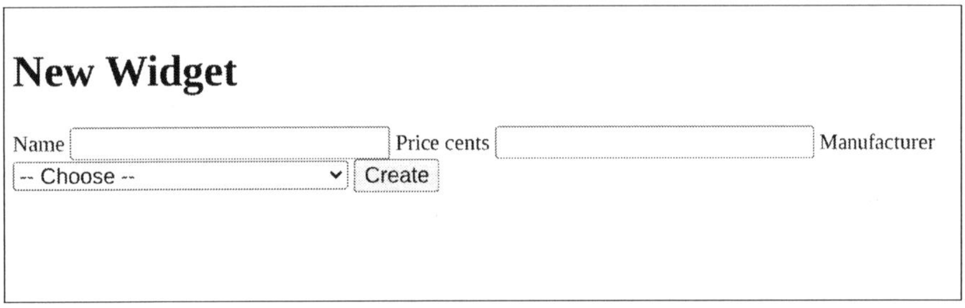

Figure 17.1: Bare-bones New Widget Page

We *could* create the system test now, but I find it easier to get at least some of the styling done first, just in case we end up needing some odd markup that could affect the test.

These are the improvements we need to make:

- The form should be better laid out and spaced.
- The manufacturers should be sorted by name.
- We need placeholders and should auto-focus the name field.
- We don't want the user to know about "cents", so that field should appear to be just "price".

Let's address those next.

17.2.4 Provide Basic Polish

First, we'll deal with the label for `price_cents`. We can do that by editing `config/locales/en.yml`, which is where Rails will look for labels to use (specifically for English).

```yaml
# config/locales/en.yml

en:
  hello: "Hello world"
→ activerecord:
→   attributes:
→     widget:
→       price_cents: "Price"
```

This incantation is not easy to find if you don't know that the problem you are solving is one about locale and internationalization (and that "internationalization" is often abbreviated as "i18n"[1]). The documentation is in the Rails Guide for Internationalization[2].

We can address the placeholders and auto-focus like so:

```erb
<%# app/views/widgets/new.html.erb %>

<h1>New Widget</h1>
<%= form_with model: @widget do |f| %>
  <%= f.label :name %>
→ <%= f.text_field :name, autofocus: true,
→       placeholder: "e.g. Stembolt" %>

  <%= f.label :price_cents %>
  <%= f.text_field :price_cents %>
```

And for the price field:

---

[1] I use an editor that was created in the 1970's and I can easily auto-complete the word "internationalization", but I guess that's just too difficult so we have to have the most ridiculous means of abbreviating technical words possible: count the number of letters in the word and subtract two. Type the first letter of the word, followed by that count (minus two, remember), followed by the last letter of the word. Sigh. This has brought us i18n, l10n, a11y, o11y, k8s, and Leto knows how many other nonsense gate-keeping terms.

[2] https://guides.rubyonrails.org/i18n.html

```
<%# app/views/widgets/new.html.erb %>

              placeholder: "e.g. Stembolt" %>

      <%= f.label :price_cents %>
→     <%= f.text_field :price_cents, placeholder: "e.g. 123.45" %>

      <%= f.label :manufacturer_id %>
      <%=
```

Note that we aren't using the placeholder as a label—that's not what placeholder text is for.

Lastly, let's sort the manufacturers. We do this in the view, because it is truly a view concern. The controller's job (as we'll discuss later) is to provide data to the view. The view's job is to make it consumable by the user.

```
<%# app/views/widgets/new.html.erb %>

      <%=
        f.select :manufacturer_id,
          options_from_collection_for_select(
→           @manufacturers.sort_by(&:name),
→           "id", "name"
          ),
          {
            include_blank: "-- Choose --",
```

That was the easy part. The hard part is making it look semi-decent. In lieu of a wireframe and spec from a designer we'll use our judgement and do our best. That will include styling validation errors.

17.2.5 Style the Form

First, let's see the form without any validation errors. A mockup is shown on the next page. Here's the code for the template:

```
<%# app/views/widgets/new.html.erb %>

<section class="center w-two-thirds helvetica pa3">
  <h1>New Widget</h1>
```

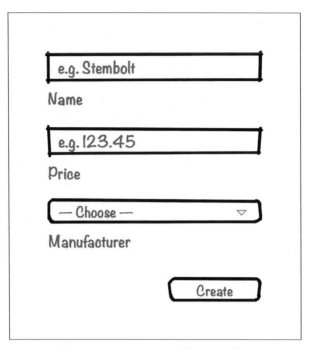

Figure 17.2: Create Widget Mockup

```erb
<%= form_with model: @widget do |f| %>
  <div class="mb3">
    <%= f.text_field :name, class: "db w-100 pa2 mb1",
        autofocus: true, placeholder: "e.g. Stembolt" %>
    <%= f.label :name, class: "fw4 i" %>
  </div>
  <div class="mb3">
    <%= f.text_field :price_cents, class: "db w-100 pa2 mb1",
        placeholder: "e.g. 123.45" %>
    <%= f.label :price_cents, class: "fw4 i" %>
  </div>
  <div class="mb3">
    <%=
      f.select :manufacturer_id,
        options_from_collection_for_select(
          @manufacturers.sort_by(&:name), "id", "name"
        ),
        {
          include_blank: "-- Choose --",
        },
        {
          class: "db w-100 pa2 mb1"
```

```
      }
    %>
    <%= f.label :manufacturer_id, class: "fw4 i" %>
  </div>
  <div class="tr">
    <%= f.submit "Create",
        class: "ba br3 ph3 pv2 white bg-dark-blue" %>
  </div>
  <% end %>
</section>
```

You can see what it looks like in the screenshot below.

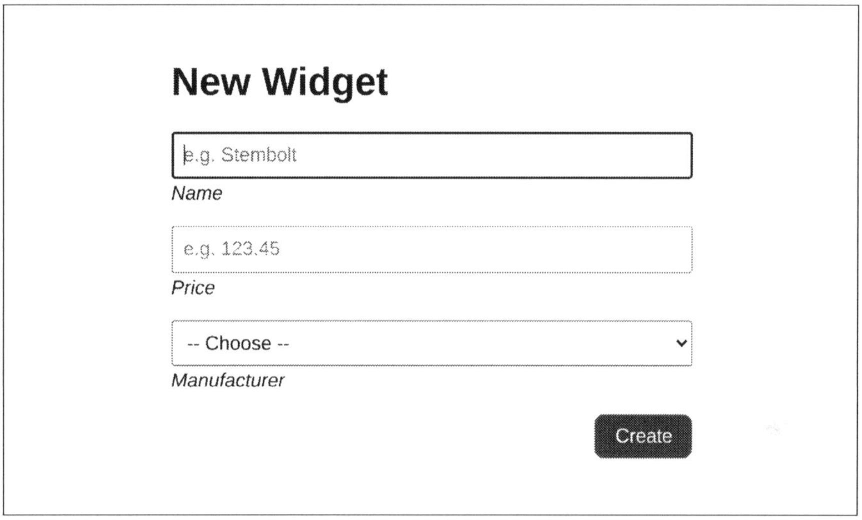

Figure 17.3: First Pass at Styling Widget Creation

A way to get comfortable with Tachyons while experiencing the value of a design system is to download this code and play with the classes. In particular, the classes for padding (classes that start with a "p") or margin (classes that start with an "m") are good to play with. Change their values to increase or decrease the spacing between components. They will all still look nice and line up. This is the power of a design system.

The last thing to do is style the errors.

17.2.6 Style Error States

There are two things to do here. First, we want a top level red box telling the user that there are errors. We then want each field to indicate the specific errors that happened.

The top level error code looks like so:

```
<%# app/views/widgets/new.html.erb %>

  <section class="center w-two-thirds helvetica pa3">
    <h1>New Widget</h1>
→   <% if @widget.errors.present? %>
→     <aside
→       class="pa3 tc ba br2 b--dark-red dark-red
→              bg-washed-red b mb3">
→       The data you provided is not valid.
→     </aside>
→   <% end %>
    <%= form_with model: @widget do |f| %>
      <div class="mb3">
        <%= f.text_field :name, class: "db w-100 pa2 mb1",
```

This might feel like a re-usable component or that the big mess of classes should be extracted to some sort of `error-dialog` class. Resist these feelings. If we need this exact markup again, we can extract it into a re-usable component by creating a partial or View Component. Since we only have this in one place, there's no value in extracting it or making it re-usable.

What we *will* want to be re-usable is the field-level error styling. Let's style the error using the label. When there's no error, we'll show the label as normal. When there *is* an error, we'll show the error messages as the label. The messages contain the field name so this should be reasonable.

Because the code will be the same for all three fields, we can extract it to a re-usable component (when I was developing this, I didn't plan on making a component, but after the third repetition of the same thing—the "rule of three"—it seemed like a good idea).

We'll use a View Component for this and call it `LabelWithErrorComponent`. It will require the Active Record, the name of the field it's labeling, and the Rails form object.

```
> bin/rails g component LabelWithError record field_name form
      create  app/components/label_with_error_component.rb
      invoke  test_unit
      create    test/components/label_with_error_component_t...
      invoke  erb
      create    app/components/label_with_error_component.ht...
```

Although a View Component's template can access instance variables, I find it better to expose them as methods. The Rails controller convention, while worth embracing in that context, is not a great object-oriented design pattern.

```ruby
# app/components/label_with_error_component.rb

# frozen_string_literal: true

class LabelWithErrorComponent < ViewComponent::Base
→  attr_reader :record, :field_name, :form
→
   def initialize(record:, field_name:, form:)
     @record = record
     @field_name = field_name
```

The ERB for the component can handle all the logic of checking for an error. It's in app/components/label_with_error_component.html.erb.

```erb
<%# app/components/label_with_error_component.html.erb %>

<% if record.errors[field_name].blank? %>
  <%= form.label field_name, class: "fw4 i" %>
<% else %>
  <%= form.label field_name,
    record.errors.full_messages_for(field_name).join(", "),
    class: "i b dark-red" %>
<% end %>
```

With this in place, we replace the label for the name field:

```erb
<%# app/views/widgets/new.html.erb %>

      <div class="mb3">
        <%= f.text_field :name, class: "db w-100 pa2 mb1",
            autofocus: true, placeholder: "e.g. Stembolt" %>
→       <%= render(
→           LabelWithErrorComponent.new(record: @widget,
→                                       field_name: :name,
→                                       form: f)
→       ) %>
      </div>
```

281

```erb
    <div class="mb3">
      <%= f.text_field :price_cents, class: "db w-100 pa2 mb1...
```

Repeat for price:

```erb
<%# app/views/widgets/new.html.erb %>

    <div class="mb3">
      <%= f.text_field :price_cents, class: "db w-100 pa2 mb1...
          placeholder: "e.g. 123.45" %>
→     <%= render(
→         LabelWithErrorComponent.new(record: @widget,
→                                     field_name: :price_cents,
→                                     form: f)
→     ) %>
    </div>
    <div class="mb3">
      <%=
```

And lastly for manufacturer:

```erb
<%# app/views/widgets/new.html.erb %>

          class: "db w-100 pa2 mb1"
        }
      %>
→     <%= render(
→         LabelWithErrorComponent.new(
→           record: @widget,
→           field_name: :manufacturer_id,
→           form: f)
→     ) %>
    </div>
    <div class="tr">
      <%= f.submit "Create",
```

To reveal this styling, we'll manually add errors to the widget in the controller:

```
# app/controllers/widgets_controller.rb

  class WidgetsController < ApplicationController
    def new
      @widget = Widget.new
→     @widget.errors.add(:name,            :blank)
→     @widget.errors.add(:manufacturer_id, :blank)
→     @widget.errors.add(:price_cents,     :not_a_number)
      @manufacturers = Manufacturer.all
    end
```

You can see the complete styling in the screenshot "New Widget Error UI" below.

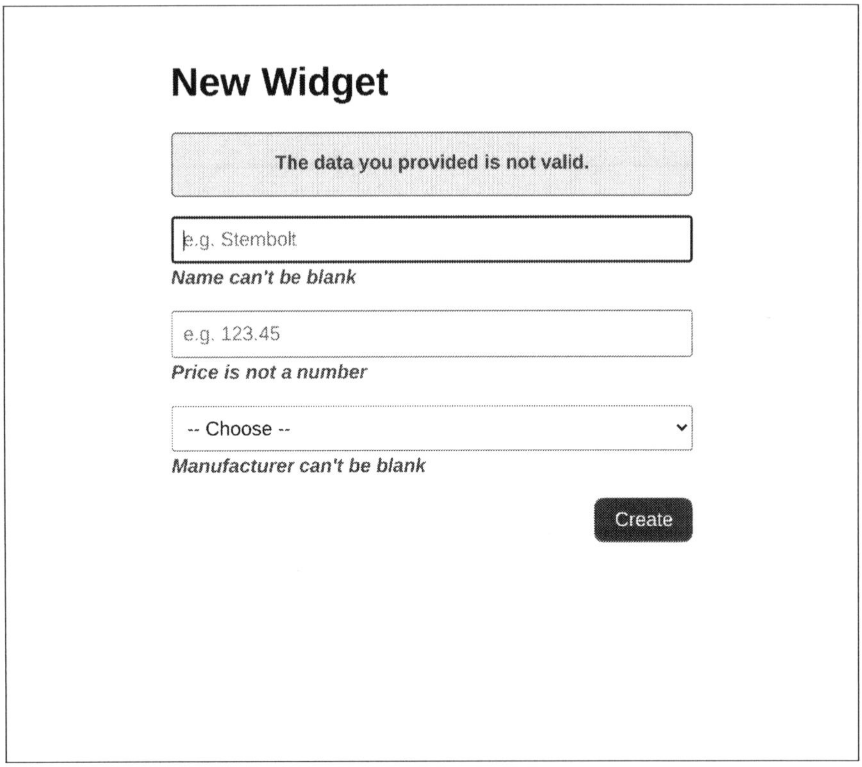

Figure 17.4: New Widget Error UI

Before writing the system test, here's a recap of how we went about this, following the guidelines discussed in previous chapters.

- We started with semantic HTML.
- We added `div` tags to afford styling.
- We extracted a re-usable component into a View Component, as opposed to extracting only the styling information as a CSS class.
- We faked out the back-end in order to do the styling we need so we aren't wrestling with both back-end logic and front-end styling at the same time.

Next, we should write a system test.

17.3 Writing a System Test

> This section's code is in the folder 17-03/ of the sample code.

In "Fake the Back-end To Get System Test Passing" on page 190, we learned about minimizing the business logic in play in order to write a system test. Let's see that in action now.

We want to test major flows, and there are two that I can see: correctly saving a widget and seeing validation errors. Our system test can't reasonably test all the back-end business logic, and it doesn't need to exhaustively test each possible error case. We really only need to make sure that all fields that could have an error will show one. Fortunately, we can create a blank widget and this will show validation errors for all three fields.

Since we don't have JavaScript, our system test can use the standard test case, `ApplicationSystemTestCase`. Let's call the test `CreateWidgetTest`:

```ruby
# test/system/create_widget_test.rb

require "application_system_test_case"

class CreateWidgetTest < ApplicationSystemTestCase
  test "we can create a widget" do
  end

  test "we can see validation errors" do
  end
end
```

Let's start with the validation errors, because the back-end is already faked-out to provide errors no matter what.

This test will go to the new widget page, skip filling in any fields, click "Create", then validate that there are errors for each field.

```
# test/system/create_widget_test.rb

    end

    test "we can see validation errors" do
→     visit new_widget_path
→
→     click_on("Create")
→
→     assert_text "The data you provided is not valid"
→     assert_text "Name can't be blank"
→     assert_text "Price is not a number"
→     assert_text "Manufacturer can't be blank"
    end
  end
```

We need something to happen when we click "Create", so let's implement create in `WidgetsController` to redirect back to widgets/new:

```
# app/controllers/widgets_controller.rb

    end

    def create
→     redirect_to new_widget_path
    end

    def show
```

The test should pass:

```
> bin/rails test test/system/create_widget_test.rb
Running 2 tests in a single process (parallelization thresho...
Run options: --seed 44550

# Running:

..

Finished in 0.371636s, 5.3816 runs/s, 10.7632 assertions/s.
2 runs, 4 assertions, 0 failures, 0 errors, 0 skips
```

We are asserting on content, and so this test could be brittle. We need to assert on something, so this is reasonable enough to get started. As we learned in "Use data-testid Attributes to Combat Brittle Tests" on page 193, we can deal with this problem when or if it shows up.

Let's write the second test for successful widget creation. We'll know this by landing on the widget show page and seeing what we entered. This will require some manufacturers to exist in the database, so that the drop-down can be used. We'll need some actual validation logic to avoid breaking the test we just wrote.

In other words, we can't *totally* fake the back-end. Fortunately, for what we're testing, we can implement something without a lot of code. We can have our controller save the widget, add validations to Widget, then implement this the old-fashioned way.

Let's write the test first. It should fill in the fields with correct values, hit "Create", then validate that we're on the widget show page.

To do that, we'll need a widget status and at least two manufacturers. The status can be created in a before block since it's needed for pretty much all the tests. For manufacturers, since they are only relevant to the test we are about to write, we'll create those at the top of the test.

```
# test/system/create_widget_test.rb

  require "application_system_test_case"

  class CreateWidgetTest < ApplicationSystemTestCase
→   setup do
→     FactoryBot.create(:widget_status, name: "Fresh")
→   end
→
→   test "we can create a widget" do
→     manufacturer       = FactoryBot.create(:manufacturer)
→     other_manufacturer = FactoryBot.create(:manufacturer)
→
→     visit new_widget_path
→
→     fill_in "widget[name]", with: "Stembolt"
→     fill_in "widget[price_cents]", with: 123
→     select manufacturer.name, from: "widget[manufacturer_id]"
→
→     click_on("Create")
→
→     assert_selector "[data-testid='widget-name']",
→       text: "Stembolt"
```

```
  end

  test "we can see validation errors" do
```

To make this pass, we have to implement `create`. We'll do that in the most basic way possible and not worry—yet—about clean code or reducing duplication or proper use of Rails. Note that when we call `render :new` we must now pass `status: :unprocessable_entity` as well, since Turbo is managing the form submission and requires an explicit HTTP status.

```
# app/controllers/widgets_controller.rb

    end

    def create
→     @widget = Widget.create(
→       name: params.require(:widget)[:name],
→       price_cents: params.require(:widget)[:price_cents],
→       manufacturer_id: params.require(:widget)[:manufacturer_id],
→       widget_status: WidgetStatus.first)
→     if @widget.valid?
→       redirect_to widget_path(@widget)
→     else
→       @manufacturers = Manufacturer.all
→       render :new, status: :unprocessable_entity
→     end
    end

    def show
```

Remember, this is just to get the system test passing. This is *not* production-ready code. If we run the test now, it'll still fail for two reasons: we aren't validating all the fields of `Widget`, and our `show` method still has all that `OpenStruct` stuff in it, meaning it's not locating the widget we just created.

First, we'll add validations to `Widget`:

```
# app/models/widget.rb

    }
  end
  belongs_to :widget_status
```

287

```
  validates :name, { presence: true }
  validates :manufacturer_id, { presence: true }
  validates :price_cents,
    numericality: { less_than_or_equal_to: 10_000_00 }
  normalizes :name, with: ->(name) { name.blank? ? nil : name...
```

Stay with me. These aren't all the validations we might want, but are enough for us to get our system tests passing. When we move onto the business logic, the system test can serve as a signal that we haven't broken any user-facing behavior.

Let's head back to `WidgetsController` and update the `show` method to look up the `Widget` from the database:

```
# app/controllers/widgets_controller.rb

      render :new, status: :unprocessable_entity
    end
  end

#   def show
#     manufacturer = OpenStruct.new(
#       id: rand(100),
#       name: "Sector 7G",
#       address: OpenStruct.new(
#         id: rand(100),
#         country: "UK"
#       )
#     )
#     widget_name = if params[:id].to_i == 1234
#                     "Stembolt"
#                   else
#                     "Widget #{params[:id]}"
#                   end
#     @widget = OpenStruct.new(id: params[:id],
#                              manufacturer_id: manufacturer.id,
#                              manufacturer: manufacturer,
#                              name: widget_name)
#     def @widget.widget_id
#       if self.id.to_s.length < 3
#         self.id.to_s
#       else
#         self.id.to_s[0..-3] + "." +
#           self.id.to_s[-2..-1]
```

```
x #        end
x #      end
→   def show
→     @widget = Widget.find(params[:id])
    end
    def index
      @widgets = [
```

Note that we removed the monkey-patched `widget_id`. We added this method to `Widget` in "Active Record is for Database Access" on page 203 and called it `user_facing_identifier`, so we need to change `styled_widget_id` in app/helpers/application_helper.erb to use that instead.

```
# app/helpers/application_helper.rb

    def styled_widget_id(widget)
      content_tag(:span,
→                 widget.user_facing_identifier.rjust(7,"0"),
                  style: "font-family: monospace")
    end
  end
```

The test of this helper is still using `OpenStruct`, so we'll need to change that to use `FactoryBot`. First, we'll change the first test:

```
# test/helpers/application_helper_test.rb

  class ApplicationHelperTest < ActionView::TestCase
    test "styled_widget_id < 6 digits, pad with 0's" do
→     widget = FactoryBot.create(:widget, id: 1234)
      rendered_markup = styled_widget_id(widget)

      assert_match /\D0012\.34\D/,rendered_markup
```

Then, the second one:

```
# test/helpers/application_helper_test.rb

  end

  test "styled_widget_id >= 6 digits, no padding" do
→   widget = FactoryBot.create(:widget, id: 987654)
    rendered_markup = styled_widget_id(widget)

    assert_match /\D9876\.54\D/, rendered_markup
```

One last thing: we should clean up the explicit error-setting we put in the new method.

```
# app/controllers/widgets_controller.rb

  class WidgetsController < ApplicationController
    def new
      @widget = Widget.new
×   #   @widget.errors.add(:name,            :blank)
×   #   @widget.errors.add(:manufacturer_id, :blank)
×   #   @widget.errors.add(:price_cents,     :not_a_number)
→
      @manufacturers = Manufacturer.all
    end
```

Now, the test should pass:

```
> bin/rails test test/system/create_widget_test.rb
Running 2 tests in a single process (parallelization thresho...
Run options: --seed 65387

# Running:

..

Finished in 0.406400s, 4.9213 runs/s, 12.3032 assertions/s.
2 runs, 5 assertions, 0 failures, 0 errors, 0 skips
```

At this point, we have the UI we want, and we have code to make it behave the way we want, at least as far as the user experience goes. We also have defined the seam between Rails and the code we have yet to write.

Our code will take a name, a price (in cents?), and a manufacturer ID. It should return, among other things, a `Widget` instance that, if there are validation errors, makes those available as an Active Record would.

Now we can implement our business logic, as well as test it for all the various edge cases we don't want to test through the UI.

17.4 Sketch Business Logic and Define the Seam

> This section's code is in the folder 17-04/ of the sample code.

Let's create the service class that will hold our business logic. This will codify the contract between our code and the controller. We should be able to do this without breaking the system test. Once that's done, we can then start to build out the real business logic.

We'll call the service `WidgetCreator`, and it'll go in `app/services/` as `widget_creator.rb`. You'll need to create the `app/services` directory. We'll give it one method, `create_widget`, and it'll accept a `Widget` instance initialized with the parameters received from the UI.

```ruby
# app/services/widget_creator.rb

class WidgetCreator
  def create_widget(widget)
    widget.widget_status = WidgetStatus.first
    widget.save

    Result.new(created: widget.valid?, widget: widget)
  end

  class Result
    attr_reader :widget
    def initialize(created:, widget:)
      @created = created
      @widget = widget
    end

    def created?
      @created
    end
  end
end
```

This may seem like a lot of code has been introduced just to call `valid?` on an Active Record, but bear with me. It will make a lot more sense when we put all the actual business logic here.

Next, we modify the controller to use this class.

```
# app/controllers/widgets_controller.rb

      @manufacturers = Manufacturer.all
    end

    def create
x #     @widget = Widget.create(
x #       name: params.require(:widget)[:name],
x #       price_cents: params.require(:widget)[:price_cents],
x #       manufacturer_id: params.require(:widget)[:manufacturer_id],
x #       widget_status: WidgetStatus.first)
x #     if @widget.valid?
x #       redirect_to widget_path(@widget)
x #     else
x #       @manufacturers = Manufacturer.all
x #       render :new, status: :unprocessable_entity
→     widget_params = params.require(:widget).permit(
→       :name, :price_cents, :manufacturer_id
→     )
→
→     result = WidgetCreator.new.create_widget(
→                Widget.new(widget_params)
→     )
→
→     if result.created?
→       redirect_to widget_path(result.widget)
→     else
→       @widget = result.widget
→       @manufacturers = Manufacturer.all
→       render :new, status: :unprocessable_entity
      end
    end
```

This looks better. The controller now has no knowledge of business logic. The only thing it knows is what the service wants, and it uses strong parameters to get that. The only logic it has is related to routing the user to the right UI, which is what controllers are for.

This means that potentially large changes in the business logic—or its implementation—won't require this controller method to change. That's a good thing.

Let's run our system test, which should still pass:

```
> bin/rails test test/system/create_widget_test.rb
Running 2 tests in a single process (parallelization thresho...
Run options: --seed 62887

# Running:

..

Finished in 0.404144s, 4.9487 runs/s, 12.3718 assertions/s.
2 runs, 5 assertions, 0 failures, 0 errors, 0 skips
```

Nice! We're almost ready to turn our attention to the business logic, but there's one thing that's a bit wrong. We are passing in `price_cents`, but we've instructed the user to enter dollars in our placeholder text. Even if we instruct the user to enter cents, they are going to enter dollars, since it's more natural.

This is a UI concern that our business logic should not have to worry about. If it wants to receive cents, it should receive cents. It could, alternately, receive dollars instead. Either way, the controller has to do something, because the value for `price_cents` is a string.

If the service wants dollars, we have to convert that string into a `BigDecimal` (since using `to_f` to make it a float will lose precision as previously discussed). If the service wants cents, the controller has to also multiply it by 100.

There are a lot of ways to solve this, but in all cases, we want the controller to handle it (we'll talk more about why this is in Controllers on page 313). The controller is receiving a string containing dollars, and the service wants cents (as an integer), so the controller should do the conversion. We'll do that right in the method:

```
# app/controllers/widgets_controller.rb

        :name, :price_cents, :manufacturer_id
      )

→     if widget_params[:price_cents].present?
→       widget_params[:price_cents] = (
→         BigDecimal(widget_params[:price_cents]) * 100
```

```
→          ).to_i
→        end
→
         result = WidgetCreator.new.create_widget(
                   Widget.new(widget_params)
         )
```

Our test isn't affected by the price, because the price is currently not shown in the UI at all. Because of this conversion, it would be a good idea to find a way to test it, so that if this conversion changed, a test somewhere would fail. Since the price is *not* in the UI, let's add an assertion about the data that gets written, so we at least have some coverage.

```
# test/system/create_widget_test.rb


         assert_selector "[data-testid='widget-name']",
           text: "Stembolt"
→        assert_equal 123_00, Widget.first.price_cents
       end

       test "we can see validation errors" do
```

This test would've failed before the conversion, and now it should pass:

```
> bin/rails test test/system/create_widget_test.rb
Running 2 tests in a single process (parallelization thresho...
Run options: --seed 64538

# Running:

..

Finished in 0.396362s, 5.0459 runs/s, 15.1377 assertions/s.
2 runs, 6 assertions, 0 failures, 0 errors, 0 skips
```

And *now* we have defined our seam: a Widget instance is passed in, and a result object is returned that tells the caller exactly what happened. The result also exposes the possibly-saved Widget.

Note that the controller no longer has to intuit that a valid active record means the process it initiated completed successfully. After all, creating a widget is more than just writing data into a database. By using the rich result object (as we discussed in "Return Rich Result Objects..." on page 247), it can be explicit about what it's checking for.

With this seam in place, we can implement the business logic, using the system test to make sure we haven't broken the user experience.

17.5 Fully Implement and Test Business Logic

> This section's code is in the folder 17-05/ of the sample code.

With our seam now defined, I find it easier to switch to a test-first workflow. The logic we have to build is pretty complex, and this will require a lot of tests.

- Create a valid widget for a manufacturer created three months ago. Check that the status is "Fresh" and that no emails were sent.
- Create a valid widget with a price of $7,500.01 and make sure the finance staff was emailed.
- Create a valid widget with a manufacturer created 59 days ago and make sure the admin staff was emailed.
- Create invalid widgets and check the errors. For these cases, you don't need to have one test for every single validation, though each *does* need testing:
    - Widgets missing a name, price, and manufacturer.
    - Widget with a four-character name.
    - Widget for an old manufacturer with a price of $99.
    - Widget with a price over $10,000.
    - Widget with a price of $0.

For the sake of brevity, we won't implement all of these right now, but we will implement a few that allow us to see the affect of Rails validations and mailers on our implementation and tests.

Let's start with the basic happy path.

```ruby
# test/services/widget_creator_test.rb

require "test_helper"

class WidgetCreatorTest < ActiveSupport::TestCase
  setup do
    @widget_creator = WidgetCreator.new
    @manufacturer = FactoryBot.create(:manufacturer,
                                      created_at: 1.year.ago)
```

```
      FactoryBot.create(:widget_status)
    end
    test "widgets have a default status of 'Fresh'" do
      result = @widget_creator.create_widget(Widget.new(
        name: "Stembolt",
        price_cents: 1_000_00,
        manufacturer_id: @manufacturer.id
      ))

      assert result.created?
      assert_equal Widget.first, result.widget
      assert_equal "Fresh", result.widget.widget_status.name
    end
end
```

This test should fail since we're using whatever status is returned by WidgetStatus.first and not looking for one named "Fresh".

```
> bin/rails test test/services/widget_creator_test.rb || echo   \
  Test Failed
Running 1 tests in a single process (parallelization thresho...
Run options: --seed 29535

# Running:

F

Failure:
WidgetCreatorTest#test_widgets_have_a_default_status_of_'Fre...
Expected: "Fresh"
  Actual: "hic"

bin/rails test test/services/widget_creator_test.rb:10



Finished in 0.122025s, 8.1951 runs/s, 24.5852 assertions/s.
1 runs, 3 assertions, 1 failures, 0 errors, 0 skips
Test Failed
```

We could fix this by naming the status we're creating in the setup block, but that won't work in production. We need to make sure that the code breaks if it doesn't choose the proper status. That means we need the "Fresh" status, but also another one that would be returned by first.

```
# test/services/widget_creator_test.rb

      @manufacturer = FactoryBot.create(:manufacturer,
                                        created_at: 1.year.ago)
      FactoryBot.create(:widget_status)
→     FactoryBot.create(:widget_status, name: "Fresh")
    end
    test "widgets have a default status of 'Fresh'" do
      result = @widget_creator.create_widget(Widget.new(
```

Let's fix the code.

```
# app/services/widget_creator.rb

  class WidgetCreator
    def create_widget(widget)
→     widget.widget_status =
→       WidgetStatus.find_by!(name: "Fresh")
      widget.save

      Result.new(created: widget.valid?, widget: widget)
```

The test should now pass:

```
> bin/rails test test/services/widget_creator_test.rb
Running 1 tests in a single process (parallelization thresho...
Run options: --seed 32174

# Running:

.

Finished in 0.137029s, 7.2977 runs/s, 21.8932 assertions/s.
1 runs, 3 assertions, 0 failures, 0 errors, 0 skips
```

Note the use of `find_by!`. Our code assumes "Fresh" is in the database, and if it's not, we want it to raise an exception, not return `nil`, since this is a condition we should not have allowed to go into production. This assumes we are monitoring for such unexpected exceptions (we'll talk more about this in Operations on page 425). Also note that we aren't thinking about refactoring. We can worry about that later (or maybe never). Right now we need to get the code working.

Next, let's write a test of a validation that doesn't yet exist. Widget names have to be five characters or longer, so let's test that.

```ruby
# test/services/widget_creator_test.rb
      assert_equal Widget.first, result.widget
      assert_equal "Fresh", result.widget.widget_status.name
    end
    test "widget names must be 5 characters or greater" do
      result = @widget_creator.create_widget(Widget.new(
        name: "widg",
        price_cents: 1_000_00,
        manufacturer_id: @manufacturer.id
      ))

      refute result.created?
      assert result.widget.invalid?

      too_short_error = result.widget.errors[:name].
        detect { |message|

          message =~ /is too short/i

        }

      refute_nil too_short_error,
        result.widget.errors.full_messages.join(",")
    end
  end
```

Note that we're checking for the specific error we expect, not just any error. Also note that second parameter to `refute_nil` is the summary of all the errors on the object, so if there *is* an error, but not the one we expect, the test failure message is actually helpful.

This test should fail at the first `refute`:

```
> bin/rails test test/services/widget_creator_test.rb || echo \
  Test Failed
Running 2 tests in a single process (parallelization thresho...
Run options: --seed 46338
```

```
# Running:

.F

Failure:
WidgetCreatorTest#test_widget_names_must_be_5_characters_or_...
Expected true to not be truthy.

bin/rails test test/services/widget_creator_test.rb:23
```

```
Finished in 0.125327s, 15.9583 runs/s, 31.9166 assertions/s.
2 runs, 4 assertions, 1 failures, 0 errors, 0 skips
Test Failed
```

To fix it, we'll add a validation to Widget that the name must be at least 5 characters long by using the length: attribute to validates.

```
# app/models/widget.rb

      }
    end
    belongs_to :widget_status
→   validates :name, {
→     presence: true,
→     length: { minimum: 5 }
→   }
    validates :manufacturer_id, { presence: true }
    validates :price_cents,
      numericality: { less_than_or_equal_to: 10_000_00 }
```

The test should now pass:

```
> bin/rails test test/services/widget_creator_test.rb
Running 2 tests in a single process (parallelization thresho...
Run options: --seed 39504

# Running:

..

Finished in 0.125747s, 15.9050 runs/s, 47.7149 assertions/s.
2 runs, 6 assertions, 0 failures, 0 errors, 0 skips
```

OK, so why is the `WidgetCreatorTest` testing code on `Widget`? The reason is that `WidgetCreatorTest` is a test of the *business process* of creating widgets. As such, it's a form of integration test. It's testing the seam between the outside world and our code. The test isn't concerned with precisely *how* the validation is implemented, just that it happens.

The only reason our `Widget` even *has* this validation is because the business process—as implemented by `WidgetCreator`—requires it. There is no other reason to have written that code. And, as you recall from the last chapter, we're putting this business logic on the Active Record because the validations API is powerful and we don't want to throw that out.

And *this* is how we can safely refactor the actual implementation of widget creation. As long as the API between our code and the controller (the seam) is stable, and as long as the contract between the UI and the controller is stable, we can do what we will inside that.

This is extremely powerful. See the sidebar "Return Processing Makeovers" below for a real world example.

> **Return Processing Makeovers**
>
> The first major feature I built at Stitch Fix was a system to process returned shipments. Stitch Fix's business model requires that un-purchased clothes get back into inventory so they can be sent out to a customer who might like what the first customer didn't.
>
> The process was complex, requiring data sanitization, purchase reconciliation, and customer service notifications. The UI was also highly experimental, since it was replacing a spreadsheet.
>
> The implementation was much like the one we've seen here. The controller exposed a complex object to render the UI, and received a different object back that was passed to a single method of a class called `ReturnProcessor`. That class returned a rich result that explained what had happened with the return.
>
> The internals of `ReturnProcessor` were enhanced and refactored as business needs changed. The UI was later completely re-imagined by our user experience team, but the seam between it and the logic—`ReturnProcessor`—was largely untouched by this process. This told me there was high value in funneling all business logic invocation through one single method.

Let's add one more test around notifying our financial staff of widgets priced higher than $7,500. This will further demonstrate the layered nature of this approach.

We can either mock a hypothetical `FinanceMailer`, or we can examine `ActionMailer::Base.deliveries` to see what was emailed. Both strategies couple us to the use of Rails mailers as the notification mechanism, but the latter avoids coupling our test to a specific mailer. Let's take that approach.

```
# test/services/widget_creator_test.rb

      refute_nil too_short_error,
        result.widget.errors.full_messages.join(",")
    end
    test "finance is notified for widgets priced over $7,500" do
      result = @widget_creator.create_widget(Widget.new(
        name: "Stembolt",
        price_cents: 7_500_01,
        manufacturer_id: @manufacturer.id
      ))

      assert result.created?
      assert_equal 1, ActionMailer::Base.deliveries.size
      mail_message = ActionMailer::Base.deliveries.first
      assert_equal "finance@example.com", mail_message["to"].to_s
      assert_match /Stembolt/, mail_message.text_part.to_s
    end
  end
```

Since `deliveries` is not well documented, it's risky to use it, but it's been in Rails for many years, so it should be stable enough to rely on. `deliveries` returns an array of `Mail::Message`, which is not part of Rails, but part of the mail[3] gem that is transitively included in all Rails apps.

The approach of examining the mail queue for just enough data to assume everything worked echoes our approach to system testing. The `WidgetCreatorTest` cares that an email was sent, but it tries to care as little as possible so that when the actual mail view is implemented, it can do what it needs to do without breaking our test. For our purposes, if an email goes to the finance team's inbox with the name of the widget, that's good enough.

When we implement the mailer for real, this test will make sure that the mail properly fits into the larger widget creation process. That mailer's test can cover all the specificities of what that email should contain.

Back to the test, we should also make sure no emails were sent in our other test, since the price there is below $7,500.

```
# test/services/widget_creator_test.rb

      assert result.created?
```

[3]https://www.rubydoc.info/github/mikel/mail/Mail

```
    assert_equal Widget.first, result.widget
    assert_equal "Fresh", result.widget.widget_status.name
→   assert_equal 0, ActionMailer::Base.deliveries.size
  end
  test "widget names must be 5 characters or greater" do
    result = @widget_creator.create_widget(Widget.new(
```

We should also make sure `deliveries` is clear before each test.

```
# test/services/widget_creator_test.rb

class WidgetCreatorTest < ActiveSupport::TestCase
  setup do
→   ActionMailer::Base.deliveries = []
    @widget_creator = WidgetCreator.new
    @manufacturer = FactoryBot.create(:manufacturer,
                                created_at: 1.year.ago)
```

To make all the tests pass, we'll need an actual mailer, so let's create it:

```
> bin/rails g mailer finance_mailer high_priced_widget
      create  app/mailers/finance_mailer.rb
      invoke  erb
      create    app/views/finance_mailer
      create    app/views/finance_mailer/high_priced_widget....
      create    app/views/finance_mailer/high_priced_widget....
      invoke  test_unit
      create    test/mailers/finance_mailer_test.rb
      create    test/mailers/previews/finance_mailer_preview...
```

We'll implement the mailer and its views to do just enough to pass our test. Here's the entire mailer:

```
# app/mailers/finance_mailer.rb

class FinanceMailer < ApplicationMailer
  def high_priced_widget(widget)
    @widget = widget
    mail to: "finance@example.com"
```

```
    end
end
```

The views can just show the widget name only for now.

```
<%# app/views/finance_mailer/high_priced_widget.text.erb %>

<%= @widget.name %>
```

```
<%# app/views/finance_mailer/high_priced_widget.html.erb %>

<%= @widget.name %>
```

The generator created a test for `FinanceMailer` that will now be broken. Let's delete that for now since we aren't actually building the real `FinanceMailer`.

```
> rm test/mailers/finance_mailer_test.rb
```

Now, we can call it in our service and get the test passing:

```
# app/services/widget_creator.rb

      widget.widget_status =
        WidgetStatus.find_by!(name: "Fresh")
      widget.save
→     if widget.price_cents > 7_500_00
→       FinanceMailer.high_priced_widget(widget).deliver_now
→     end

      Result.new(created: widget.valid?, widget: widget)
    end
```

```
> bin/rails test test/services/widget_creator_test.rb
Running 3 tests in a single process (parallelization thresho...
Run options: --seed 64930
```

303

```
# Running:

...

Finished in 0.162661s, 18.4433 runs/s, 73.7732 assertions/s.
3 runs, 12 assertions, 0 failures, 0 errors, 0 skips
```

Each of the tests we wrote should demonstrate the overall strategy to get to complete coverage. Note again, that this is a strategy, and you can apply this to RSpec-based tests if you like.

17.6 Finished Implementation

> This section's code is in the folder 17-06/ of the sample code.

I know it'll make this section even longer, but let's quickly go through the remainder of the implementation. Here are the remaining tests:

```
# test/services/widget_creator_test.rb

      assert_equal "finance@example.com", mail_message["to"].to...
      assert_match /Stembolt/, mail_message.text_part.to_s
    end
    test "name, price, and manufacturer are required" do
      result = @widget_creator.create_widget(Widget.new)

      refute result.created?

      widget = result.widget
      assert widget.invalid?

      assert widget.errors[:name].any? { |message|
        message =~ /can't be blank/i
      }, widget.errors.full_messages_for(:name)

      assert widget.errors[:price_cents].any? { |message|
        message =~ /is not a number/i
      }, widget.errors.full_messages_for(:price_cents)

      assert widget.errors[:manufacturer].any? { |message|
        message =~ /must exist/i
      }, widget.errors.full_messages_for(:manufacturer)

    end
```

```ruby
test "price cannot be 0" do
  result = @widget_creator.create_widget(Widget.new(
    name: "Stembolt",
    price_cents: 0,
    manufacturer_id: @manufacturer.id
  ))

  refute result.created?

  assert result.widget.errors[:price_cents].any? { |message|
    message =~ /greater than 0/i
  }, result.widget.errors.full_messages_for(:price_cents)

end

test "price cannot be more than $10,000" do
  result = @widget_creator.create_widget(Widget.new(
    name: "Stembolt",
    price_cents: 10_000_01,
    manufacturer_id: @manufacturer.id
  ))

  refute result.created?

  assert result.widget.errors[:price_cents].any? { |message|
    message =~ /less than or equal to 1000000/i
  }, result.widget.errors.full_messages_for(:price_cents)

end

test "legacy manufacturers cannot have a price under $100" do
  legacy_manufacturer = FactoryBot.create(:manufacturer,
    created_at: DateTime.new(2010,1,1) - 1.day)

  result = @widget_creator.create_widget(Widget.new(
    name: "Stembolt",
    price_cents: 99_00,
    manufacturer_id: legacy_manufacturer.id
  ))

  refute result.created?

  assert result.widget.errors[:price_cents].any? { |message|
    message =~ /< \$100.*legacy/i
  }, result.widget.errors.full_messages_for(:price_cents)
end
```

```
→   test "email admin staff for widgets on new manufacturers" do
→     new_manufacturer = FactoryBot.create(:manufacturer,
→       name: "Cyberdyne Systems",
→       created_at: 59.days.ago)
→
→     result = @widget_creator.create_widget(Widget.new(
→       name: "Stembolt",
→       price_cents: 100_00,
→       manufacturer_id: new_manufacturer.id
→     ))
→
→     assert result.created?
→
→     assert_equal 1, ActionMailer::Base.deliveries.size
→     mail_message = ActionMailer::Base.deliveries.first
→     assert_equal "admin@example.com", mail_message["to"].to_s
→     assert_match /Stembolt/, mail_message.text_part.to_s
→     assert_match /Cyberdyne Systems/, mail_message.text_part.to_s
→   end
  end
```

The first test—that tests for omitting all of the values—fails, but not in the right way. Our WidgetCreator has a bug, in that it assumes price_cents has a value. We can fix that by early-exiting when we see the widget is invalid:

```
# app/services/widget_creator.rb

      widget.widget_status =
        WidgetStatus.find_by!(name: "Fresh")
      widget.save
→     if widget.invalid?
→       return Result.new(created: false, widget: widget)
→     end
      if widget.price_cents > 7_500_00
        FinanceMailer.high_priced_widget(widget).deliver_now
      end
```

Next, we'll trigger the mailer to the admin team. We'll need that mailer:

```
# app/mailers/admin_mailer.rb
```

```ruby
class AdminMailer < ApplicationMailer
  def new_widget_from_new_manufacturer(widget)
    @widget = widget
    mail to: "admin@example.com"
  end
end
```

Like `FinanceMailer`, the views can be minimal for now:

```erb
<%# app/views/admin_mailer/new_widget_from_new_manufacturer.html.erb %>

<%= @widget.name %>
<%= @widget.manufacturer.name %>
```

```erb
<%# app/views/admin_mailer/new_widget_from_new_manufacturer.text.erb %>

<%= @widget.name %>
<%= @widget.manufacturer.name %>
```

Now, we use this mailer:

```ruby
# app/services/widget_creator.rb

      FinanceMailer.high_priced_widget(widget).deliver_now
    end

→   if widget.manufacturer.created_at.after?(60.days.ago)
→     AdminMailer.new_widget_from_new_manufacturer(widget).
→       deliver_now
→   end
→
    Result.new(created: widget.valid?, widget: widget)
  end
```

The rest of the changes are on the `Widget` class. We'll add a `greater_than` attribute for validating the price, but we'll also add a custom validator, `high_enough_for_legacy_manufacturers`:

```
# app/models/widget.rb

  }
  validates :manufacturer_id, { presence: true }
  validates :price_cents,
→    numericality: {
→      less_than_or_equal_to: 10_000_00,
→      greater_than: 0
→    },
→    high_enough_for_legacy_manufacturers: true
  normalizes :name, with: ->(name) { name.blank? ? nil : name...
end
```

If you haven't used custom validators before, you can implement them as a class that extends `ActiveModel::EachValidator`, like so:

```
# app/models/widget.rb

    }
  end
  belongs_to :widget_status
→
→  class HighEnoughForLegacyManufacturersValidator <
→        ActiveModel::EachValidator
→    def validate_each(record, attribute, value)
→      return if value.blank?
→      if value < 100_00 &&
→         record.manufacturer.created_at.year < 2010
→
→        record.errors.add(attribute,
→          "must be < $100 for legacy manufacturers")
→
→      end
→    end
→  end
  validates :name, {
    presence: true,
    length: { minimum: 5 }
```

This demonstrates the power of the Rails end-to-end experience and why we are using its validation system. This would've been difficult to implement another way without also having to have custom view code to manage this particular validation check.

This validation, however, will potentially break our widget factory, because it doesn't guarantee a name will be created with five or more characters. Let's change it to use `Faker::Lorem.words.join(" ")`, which will create three words and join them with a space.

```
# test/factories/widget_factory.rb

FactoryBot.define do
  factory :widget do
→   name          { Faker::Lorem.unique.words.join(" ") }
    price_cents   { Faker::Number.within(range: 1..10_000_00) }
    manufacturer
    widget_status
```

The tests should all pass.

```
> bin/rails test test/lint_factories_test.rb \
  test/services/widget_creator_test.rb \
  test/system/create_widget_test.rb
Running 11 tests in a single process (parallelization thresh...
Run options: --seed 50873

# Running:

...........

Finished in 0.459940s, 23.9161 runs/s, 78.2710 assertions/s.
11 runs, 36 assertions, 0 failures, 0 errors, 0 skips
```

Of course, we've likely broken the system tests we wrote in earlier chapters. Both `rate_widget_test.rb` and `view_widget_test.rb` expected faked-out data. Let's fix them as well, so we have a clean build by the end of all this.

First, `rate_widget_test.rb` (in `test/system`) needs to create a widget using `FactoryBot` and not assume there is one with the id 1234:

```
# test/system/rate_widget_test.rb

class RateWidgetsTest < BrowserSystemTestCase
```

```
    test "rating a widget shows our rating inline" do
→     widget = FactoryBot.create(:widget)
→     visit widget_path(widget)

      click_on "2"
```

For `test/system/view_widget_test.rb`, it's a bit trickier. The test is testing both the index and show actions, and the index action is still faked out! Let's fix that, first:

```
# app/controllers/widgets_controller.rb

    def show
      @widget = Widget.find(params[:id])
    end
    def index
✗ #     @widgets = [
✗ #       OpenStruct.new(id: 1234, name: "Stembolt"),
✗ #       OpenStruct.new(id: 2, name: "Flux Capacitor"),
✗ #     ]
→     @widgets = Widget.all
    end
  end
```

Now, our test should create some widgets to assert on. Note that we're hard-coding one of the widgets to have an ID of 1234 so that we can assert on the id-formatting logic. This could cause a problem if some other widget actually got that ID, but for now we'll assume that won't happen.

```
# test/system/view_widget_test.rb

  class ViewWidgetTest < ApplicationSystemTestCase
    test "we can see a list of widgets and view one" do
→     FactoryBot.create(:widget, name: "Flux Capacitor")
→     stembolt = FactoryBot.create(:widget, name: "Stembolt")
→     stembolt.update!(id: 1234)
      visit widgets_path

      widget_name = "stembolt"
```

Let's now check bin/ci to see if the app is still overall working:

```
> bin/ci
[ bin/ci ] Running unit tests
Running 16 tests in a single process (parallelization thresh...
Run options: --seed 48425

# Running:

................

Finished in 0.162555s, 98.4283 runs/s, 258.3743 assertions/s...
16 runs, 42 assertions, 0 failures, 0 errors, 0 skips
[ bin/ci ] Running system tests
Running 4 tests in a single process (parallelization thresho...
Run options: --seed 1153

# Running:

..Rack::Handler is deprecated and replaced by Rackup::Handle...
Capybara starting Puma...
* Version 6.4.0 , codename: The Eagle of Durango
* Min threads: 0, max threads: 4
* Listening on http://127.0.0.1:42441
..

Finished in 1.251790s, 3.1954 runs/s, 8.7874 assertions/s.
4 runs, 11 assertions, 0 failures, 0 errors, 0 skips
[ bin/ci ] Analyzing code for security vulnerabilities.
[ bin/ci ] Output will be in tmp/brakeman.html, which
[ bin/ci ] can be opened in your browser.
[ bin/ci ] Analyzing Ruby gems for
[ bin/ci ] security vulnerabilities
Updating ruby-advisory-db ...
From https://github.com/rubysec/ruby-advisory-db
 * branch            master     -> FETCH_HEAD
Already up to date.
Updated ruby-advisory-db
ruby-advisory-db:
  advisories:    827 advisories
  last updated: 2023-11-30 12:36:04 -0800
  commit:    d821bf162550302abd1fa1fe15007f3012b76f32
No vulnerabilities found
[ bin/ci ] Done
```

Everything looks great, and we're done!

Looking at `WidgetCreator` now, I'm fine with the implementation and don't see a reason to refactor it. Although the custom validator is covered by our test, I might add a more exhaustive test for it in `test/widget_test.rb` since it's fairly complex compared to the other validations. I'll leave that as an exercise for you.

Reflecting on What We've Built

Hopefully, this example has demonstrated some of the advantages of consolidating business logic behind a well-defined seam, as defined by a class, method, and rich return object.

The tests and implementation actually paint a good picture of how everything is structured, and why. We wrote code in `Widget` to make the test of `WidgetCreator` pass because that code only exists in `Widget` to satisfy `WidgetCreator`'s requirements. The `WidgetCreator` test outlines everything that's required of widget creation as we currently understand it.

If we later re-use these validations in another flow, we could certainly consider some re-work of our tests, but the requirements we have—and the code that implements them—simply don't justify it.

Also note the layering. Our system test only tests what it cares about—the user experience—and provides only cursory coverage of the widget creation process. The finer details—as well as behavior that a user cannot observe—are left to the test of our seam—`WidgetCreator`. Of course, *it* provides only cursory coverage of the behavior of `FinanceMailer`. The test for that class would iron out all the details of that email.

The strategic layering keeps our code and tests maintainable. Plus, the use of a service layer means we have a clear location where business logic is triggered. Imagine having to chase all that down across callbacks and convoluted DSLs.

Let's move onto the boundaries of our Rails app: controllers, mailers, rake tasks, and the like.

18

Controllers

If you want to respond to an HTTP request in a Rails app, you pretty much need to use a controller. That's why they exist. In this sense, only a controller can receive an HTTP request, trigger business logic based on it, then send a response, be that rendering a view or redirecting to another path.

There are four issues around controllers that can cause sustainability problems:

- Controller code is structured unlike any other code in... well... any system I've ever seen. It's not object-oriented, functional, or even procedural. Controller code can seem quite alien.
- Over-use of callbacks can create situations where code is unnecessarily spread across several methods, connected only implicitly.
- Controllers are the perfect place to insulate downstream business logic from the "hashes of strings" API Rails provides for accessing the HTTP request.
- Unit tests of controllers are often duplicative of tests in other parts of the system.

Let's start with what controllers actually are: sophisticated configuration.

18.1 Controller Code is Configuration

If I told you I was designing a system in which you'd write code that received no parameters, instead plucking them out of implicit objects available to use, and that your method's return value would be ignored, instead requiring that you manipulate implicit state by calling various methods—each of which could only be called once—you would probably not be excited about working in this system.

If I further told you that you'd not be able to instantiate the class or call the method yourself—even in a test—and that the only way to pass information to a template was to declare and assign an instance variable, you might think I was playing a very cruel trick on you.

This is how Rails controllers are designed and yet *they work great*. A Rails controller is a poster child for what is called an internal domain specific language, or "internal DSL" (*internal* because it's Ruby code and not another language made just for this purpose). Despite all of its weirdness, it works really well, as long as you treat it as what it is.

I like to think of it as a very rich configuration language. This prevents me from putting business logic in the controllers themselves, and helps me understand the purpose of the code in the controllers.

In the vein of treating Rails for what it is—not what you wish it would be—do not try to bend controller code into more traditional object-oriented structures. Embrace the controller code for what it is. Since you are making heavy use of resources (as discussed in "Don't Create Custom Actions, Create More Resources" on page 83), and since you have put your business logic behind a seam (as discussed frequently, including the previous chapter), you won't end up needing much code in your controllers.

By embracing controllers for what they are and how they work, you'll keep the code in them minimal, and thus won't need exhaustive tests for them, and this all reduces carrying costs (the key to sustainability).

That said, our controllers still do need some code in them, so let's talk about what sort of code that is and how to manage it. The biggest source of confusion in controller code is what we'll talk about next: callbacks.

18.2 Don't Over-use Callbacks

Controller callbacks (originally called *filters*) allow you to place code in other methods that run before or after code in controller methods. This is extremely useful for cross-cutting concerns that apply to many or all controller methods. Rails' cross-site request forgery (CSRF), for example, is implemented using callbacks.

Callbacks are sometimes abused by developers overzealously trying to remove duplication. Because callbacks are invoked implicitly (not explicitly like a private method) this can lead to code that, while it does remove duplication, is hard to understand since you cannot easily trace the chain of events that occur when a controller method is invoked.

For example:

```ruby
class ManufacturersController < ApplicationController
  before_action :set_manufacturer

  def edit
  end

  def update
    if @manufacturer.save
```

```ruby
      redirect_to manufacturer_path(@manufacturer)
    else
      render :edit, status: :unprocessable_entity
    end
  end

  def show
  end

private

  def set_manufacturer
    @manufacturer = Manufacturer.find(params[:id])
  end

end
```

While this code does consolidate the way in which a `Manufacturer` is loaded and exposed to the view, it has created a controller that is unnecessarily complex - the core part of what `show` and `edit` *do* has been hidden behind an implicit invocation.

As more callbacks are added, piecing together exactly what happens in these methods becomes harder, and for what gain? All to consolidate a small piece of highly stable code. If that code really *did* need to be extracted to a single source, a private method would work far better:

```ruby
class ManufacturersController << ApplicationController
  def edit
    @manufacturer = load_manufacturer
  end

  def update
    @manufacturer = load_manufacturer
    if @manufacturer.save
      redirect_to manufacturer_path(@manufacturer)
    else
      render :edit, status: :unprocessable_entity
    end
  end

  def show
    @manufacturer = load_manufacturer
  end
```

```
  private

  def load_manufacturer
    Manufacturer.find(params[:id])
  end

end
```

When callbacks are added to `ApplicationController` or any module mixed-in to the controller or `ApplicationController`, it can become quite difficult to figure out the order in which all the code executes. As a mechanism for managing duplication, callbacks just aren't the right tool: private methods will always be easier to manage and understand.

Callbacks *are* a great tool for managing duplicate code that's both not specific to any given controller method *and* is needed in many of the app's controllers. Authorization and authentication is a classic example of this.

Another example is exception handing, using the `rescue_from` callback. There are certain types of errors that can't be easily handled by the business logic and that require the same user experience when they occur. Authorization is a great example. If all of your code raises, say, a `UserNotAuthorized` exception (that I just invented for this example), you could use `rescue_from` to ensure that those users see the same page, without writing any code in any controller.

Just be wary of using callbacks too often or for code that is small is scope. They will make it harder to understand how your code will behave.

Let's talk about a more subtle type of code that ends up in controllers, which is parameter conversion.

18.3 Controllers Should Convert Parameters to Richer Types

> This section's code is in the folder 18-03/ of the sample code.

As the invokers of business logic, controllers are responsible for converting parameters into properly typed objects:

```
def show
  @widget = Widget.find(params[:id])
end
```

This code takes a string containing an identifier that we assume identifies a widget, and looks it up in the database, passing the actual widget to the view.

Because HTTP is a text-based protocol, and because Rails provides us only hashes of strings as an API into it, controllers are in the unique position to insulate the rest of the codebase from this reality.

This is complicated by the fact that Active Record handles a lot of conversions for us. For example, find knows to convert the string it was given into a number to do the database lookup. Active Record can also convert dates and booleans. For example, you can set a date to the string "2020-05-13" and Active Record will convert it when it saves to the database.

This isn't always available to us, as we saw the use of dollars in the UI for a widget's price, but the requirement by the back-end to receive cents. And, if we use custom resources based on Active Model, we can't access any of Active Record's conversions.

Nevertheless, I still believe the controller should handle getting strings into whatever types they need to be in for the business logic. Just keep in mind that for Active Records, strings *are* the type needed. In other words, there is no value in writing code like this:

```
# Not needed, since Active Record can convert the string for us
@widget = Widget.find(params[:id].to_i)
```

This will lead to inconsistency in your controllers, but it's likely worth it. You'll just need to carefully manage the conversion code. This doens't mean such code has to be inlined into the controller, however. The controller just needs to make sure the conversion happens.

For example, we might end up with a *lot* of dollars-to-cents conversions in our app. You might make a class like Price:

```
## app/models/price.rb

class Price
  attr_reader :cents
  def initialize(dollars)
    @cents = if dollars
               (BigDecimal(dollars) * 100).to_i
             end
  end
end
```

The controller would still be responsible for using this class:

```
widget_params[:price_cents] =
  Price.new(widget_params[:price_cents]).cents
```

(Note that you should *not* do this unless you need to for managing duplication. If the only dollars-to-cents conversion you ever need is in this controller, you'll be glad not to have an extra abstraction hanging around.)

In any case, this logic might not be testable from our system test. Thus, it will need a test. But to test something like this we may end up duplicating tests we already have.

18.4 Don't Over Test

> This section's code is in the folder 18-04/ of the sample code.

As mentioned in "Understand The Value and Cost of Tests" on page 181, tests aren't an end unto themselves. They have a potentially high carrying cost. Thus, we need to be careful that every test we write serves a purpose and delivers real value.

In the end-to-end example chapter on page 271, we explicitly did *not* write tests for validations in the model test because those validations were covered by the test of our service class. That was a strategic decision to reduce the carrying cost of tests without sacrificing coverage.

This applies to our controller tests, too. Ideally, we would not need controller tests at all, since our system tests would tell us if our controller code is broken. That said, the more type conversions our controllers have to do, the more likely we are to need to test them.

In the last chapter, we had to make our system test reach into the database in order to get coverage of the price conversion logic. That would be better tested in a controller test, so let's do that now.

18.4.1 Writing a Controller Test

There are two approaches we can take. One would be to mock `WidgetCreator` and assert it received converted values. The other would be to *not* mock anything and assert what ends up in the database.

One approach isn't more correct than the other—they both boil down to what you want your test to be coupled to. Because the API for creating widgets with `WidgetCreator` is relatively simple, I'm going to avoid mocking and assert on the database.

Here's what the test looks like:

```ruby
# test/controllers/widgets_controller_test.rb

require "test_helper"

class WidgetsControllerTest < ActionDispatch::IntegrationTest
  test "converts dollars to cents when creating widgets" do
    manufacturer = FactoryBot.create(:manufacturer)
    FactoryBot.create(:widget_status, name: "Fresh")
    post widgets_url, params: {
      widget: {
        name: "New Widget",
        price_cents: "123.45",
        manufacturer_id: manufacturer.id.to_s,
      }
    }

    widget = Widget.last
    refute_nil widget
    assert_redirected_to widget_path(widget)
    assert_equal 12345, widget.price_cents
  end
end
```

This test should pass:

```
> bin/rails test test/controllers/widgets_controller_test.rb
Running 1 tests in a single process (parallelization thresho...
Run options: --seed 20250

# Running:

.

Finished in 0.163104s, 6.1311 runs/s, 24.5243 assertions/s.
1 runs, 4 assertions, 0 failures, 0 errors, 0 skips
```

Note that the test ensures the parameters are strings, no matter what. This is critical, and it's a failure of Rails that it does not coerce these values to strings for you. This is because the values in production will always be strings!

I know I've made the mistake of posting a boolean to a controller in a test, only to find that while the test passed, the controller was woefully broken in production, since the string `"false"` is a truthy value.

On thing to note is that while this test exists to test the price conversion logic, we can't properly test it if widget creation is broken. Rather than duplicate all of `WidgetCreator`'s tests, we do a quick check first:

```
refute_nil widget
assert_redirected_to widget_path(widget)
```

These assertions provide no value in terms of quality assurance. We absolutely have this covered by the system test. They are a carrying cost. But they need to be there in case we run this test and widget creation is broken (even if the controller logic is still correct).

Consider the third assertion in our test, which is the only one that is providing value:

```
assert_equal 12345, widget.price_cents
```

This is the assertion that tells us if the controller is working or not. The other two assertions don't tell us that. Without those other assertions, if widget creation was broken, the test would fail in an odd way. We'd get something like `NoMethodError: no such method price_cents for NilClass`. We'd expect a failure message for this assertion to be related to the wrong value for `price_cents`, not an error.

That's why I wrote the other two assertions. If widget creation *is* broken, we'll get a failure that the `widget` was assumed to have been created. If that assertion fails, we have no confidence in our test at all, because logic it assumes is working is broken—the test itself can't technically run.

But it's hard to know that from looking at the code. We need a way to leverage the assertion library but also to indicate that some tests are just performing confidence checks before the actual test assertions execute.

18.4.2 Implementing a Basic Confidence-checking System

Sure, we could just throw `# CONFIDENCE CHECK` before these assertions, but I don't think *this* sort of code comment is nearly as useful as actual code. Let's make a method that we can use that makes it clear which assertions are checking that we can even run our test and which are the actual test.

We'll do that by assuming the existence of a method called `confidence_check` that takes a block and executes the code inside that block.

```
# test/controllers/widgets_controller_test.rb
          }
        }

        widget = Widget.last
  × #     refute_nil widget
  × #     assert_redirected_to widget_path(widget)
  →       confidence_check do
  →         refute_nil widget
  →         assert_redirected_to widget_path(widget)
  →       end
        assert_equal 12345, widget.price_cents
      end
    end
```

Now the test makes it clear that `refute_nil` and `assert_redirected_to` are only there to double-check that the basics are working before we do the *real* assertion, which follows.

In addition to demarcating the code, we need to see a helpful error in our test output letting us know that the test effectively wasn't even run because of factors outside its own control. We'll augment the exception raised by the testing framework to put a message indicating the failure is not a test failure, but a confidence check failure.

Since Ruby doesn't have a way to modify the message of a thrown exception, we'll create our own and delegate all its methods to the exception raised by the failed assertion.

We can put this in `support/confidence_check.rb` and require it inside our base test case, similar to what we did with `with_clues` in "Cultivate Explicit Diagnostic Tools to Debug Test Failures" on page 186.

```
# test/support/confidence_check.rb

module TestSupport
  module ConfidenceCheck
    class ConfidenceCheckFailed < Minitest::Assertion
      def initialize(minitest_assertion)
        super("CONFIDENCE CHECK FAILED: #{minitest_assertion.message}")
```

```ruby
      @minitest_assertion = minitest_assertion
    end

    delegate :backtrace,
      :error,
      :location,
      :result_code,
      :result_label,
      :backtrace_locations,
      :cause, to: :@minitest_assertion
  end

  # Used to indicate assertions that give confidence that
  # the test has been properly set up or that dependent
  # functionality is working
  def confidence_check(&block)
    block.()
  rescue Minitest::Assertion => ex
    raise ConfidenceCheckFailed.new(ex)
  end
  end
end
```

We'll then require this file:

```ruby
# test/test_helper.rb

    config.test_id = "data-testid"
  end

→ require "support/confidence_check"
→
  module ActiveSupport
    class TestCase
      # Run tests in parallel with specified workers
```

And then include it in the base test case:

```ruby
# test/test_helper.rb
```

```
module ActiveSupport
  class TestCase
→   include TestSupport::ConfidenceCheck
→
    # Run tests in parallel with specified workers
    parallelize(workers: :number_of_processors)
```

Now, if widget creation is broken, *this* test will show "CONFIDENCE CHECK FAILED" to indicate that it can't even perform an assertion. Note that you can follow this same approach with RSpec, but you must create your custom exception (and thus explicitly rescue), RSpec::Expectations::ExpectationNotMetError.

Since writing this book, I have extracted this to a gem called confidence-check[1] that you can use if you like. It works with RSpec as well as Rails' default test framework.

18.4.3 Avoiding Duplicative Tests

Our controller's create method has another if statement in it, related to re-rendering the new page if there is a problem creating the widget. Our instincts are that if statements require tests, but in this case, the codepath is covered. Do we really need a test?

No. These exact flows are covered by our system test, which would fail if the controller changed its logic. The only downside is that you need to figure out that the system test is failing because of the controller, not the view.

This trade-off is worth it, since isolated tests for routing and navigation don't add much value, given the existence or system tests, as described. You end up with carrying costs that don't justify their existence.

When *might* it be worth it? If the routing was based on a more complex set of logic than a simple predicate, an isolated test would be easier to use for driving changes. But, wouldn't these be major flows you'd want tested in a system test?

Up Next

When you organize code the way I'm suggesting, your controllers end up being pretty basic. That's a good thing! Where controllers process web requests, there is another construct most Rails apps need that process requests asynchronously: jobs.

---

[1] https://github.com/sustainable-rails/confidence-check

19

Jobs

One of the most powerful tools to make your app high-performing and fault-tolerant is the background job. Background jobs bring some complexity and carrying cost to the system, so you have to be careful not to swap one sustainability problem for another.

This chapter will help you navigate this part of Rails. We'll start by understanding exactly what problems background jobs exist to solve. We'll then learn why you must understand exactly how your chosen job backend (Sidekiq, Resque, etc.) works. We'll set up Sidekiq in our example app, since Sidekiq is a great choice if you don't have specific requirements otherwise.

We'll then learn how to use, build, and test jobs. After all that we'll talk about a big source of complexity around background jobs, which is making them idempotent. Jobs can and will be automatically retried and you don't usually want their effects to be repeated. Achieving idempotency is not easy or even possible in every situation.

Let's jump into it. What problems do background jobs solve?

19.1 Use Jobs To Defer Execution or Increase Fault-Tolerance

Background jobs allow you to run code outside a web request/response cycle. Sometimes you do this because you need to run some batch process on a schedule. There are two other reasons we're going to focus on, since they lead to the sort of complexity you have to carefully manage. Background jobs can allow moving non-critical code to outside the request/response cycle as well as encapsulate flaky code that may need several retries in order to succeed.

Both of these situations amount to deferring code that might take too long to a background job to run later. The reason this is important has to do with how your Rails app is set up in production.

19.1.1 Web Workers, Worker Pools, Memory, and Compute Power

In development, your Rails app uses the Puma[1] web server. This server receives requests and dispatches them to your Rails app (this is likely how it works in production as well). When a request comes in, Puma allocates a *worker* to handle that request. That worker works on only that request until a response is rendered—it can't manage more than one request at a time.

When the response is rendered, the worker can work on another request. Puma keeps these workers in a *pool*, and that pool has a finite limit. This is because each worker consumes memory and CPU (even if it's not doing anything) and, because memory and CPU are finite resources, there can only be so many workers per server.

What if all workers are handling requests? What happens to a new request that comes in when there is no worker to handle it?

It depends. In some configurations, the new request will be denied and the browser will receive an HTTP 503 (resource unavailable). In other configurations that request will be placed in a queue (itself a finite resource) to be handled whenever a worker becomes available. In this case the request will appear to be handled more slowly than usual.

While you can increase the overall number of workers through complex mechanisms such as load balancers, there is always going to be a finite amount of resources to process requests. Often this limit is financial, not technical, since more servers and more infrastructure cost more money and it may not be worth it.

Another solution to the problem of limited workers is to reduce the amount of work those workers have to do. If your controller initiates a business process that takes 500ms normally, but can be made to defer 250ms of that process into a background job, you will have doubled your worker capacity[2].

One particular type of code that leads to poor performance—and thus is a good target for moving to a background job—is code that interacts with third party APIs, such as sending email or processing payments.

19.1.2 Network Calls and Third Parties are Slow

Although our app doesn't have the ability to charge users to purchase widgets, you might imagine that it could, and that means integrating with a payment processor. And *this* means making a network call over the Internet. Although network calls within our data center can fail, network calls over the Internet are so likely to fail that you have to handle that failure as a first-order issue.

---

[1] https://puma.io
[2] Yes, this is vastly oversimplified, but the point stands.

Of course, network calls that fail don't fail immediately. They often fail after an interminable amount of time. Or not. Sometimes the network is just slow and a successful result eventually comes back.

Background jobs can help solve this problem. The figure below outlines how this works.

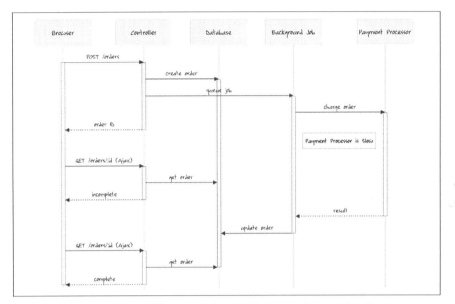

Figure 19.1: Performing Slow Code in Background Jobs

In the figure, you can see that the initial POST to create an order causes the controller to insert an order into the database then queue a background job to handle communicating with the payment processor. While that's happening, the controller returns the order ID to the browser.

The browser then uses Ajax to poll the controller's show method to check on the status of the order. The show method will fetch the order from the database to see if it's been processed. Meanwhile, the background job waits for the payment processor until it receives a response. When it does, it updates the order in the database. Eventually, the browser will ask about the order and receive a response that it's completed.

This may seem complex, but it allows the web workers (which are executing only the controller code in this example) to avoid waiting on the slow payment provider.

This design can also handle transient errors that might happen when communicating with the third party. The job can be automatically retried without having to change how the front-end works.

19.1.3 Network Calls and Third Parties are Flaky

Network calls fail. There's just no way to prevent that. The farther away another server is from *your* server, the more likely it is to fail, and even at small scale, network failures happen frequently.

In most cases, network failures are transient errors. Retrying the request usually results in a success. But retrying network requests can take a while, since network requests don't fail fast. Your background jobs can handle this.

The figure below shows how this might work.

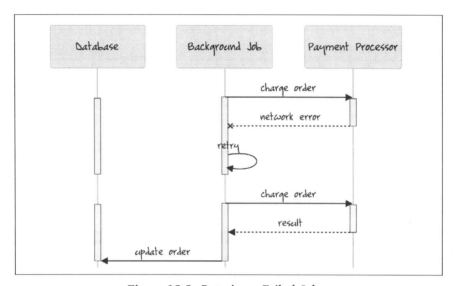

Figure 19.2: Retrying a Failed Job

When our job encounters a network error, it can retry itself. During this retry, the front-end is still diligently asking for an update. In this case it waits a bit longer, but we don't have to re-architect how the entire feature works.

This might all seem quite complex and, well, it is. The rest of this chapter will identify sources of complexity and strategies to work around them, but it's important that you use background jobs only when needed.

19.1.4 Use Background Jobs Only When Needed

At a certain scale, the benefits of background jobs outweigh their complexity, and you'd be wise to use them as much as possible. You likely aren't at that scale now, and might never be. Thus, you want to be judicious when you use background jobs.

The two main problems that happen when you do all processing in the request are over-use of resources and failures due to network timeouts.

Thus, your use of background jobs should be when you cannot tolerate these failures at whatever level you are seeing them.

This can be hard to judge. A guideline that I adopt is to always communicate with third parties in a background job, because even at tiny scale, those communications will fail.

For all other code, it's best to monitor its performance, set a limit on how poor the performance is allowed to get, and use background jobs when performance gets bad (keeping in mind that background jobs aren't the only solution to poor performance). For example, you might decide that the 90th percentile of controller action response times should always be under 500ms.

When you *are* going to use background jobs, you need to understand how the underlying system actually works to avoid surprises.

19.2 Understand How Your Job Backend Works

Rails includes a library called Active Job that provides an abstraction layer over queueing and implementing jobs. Since it is not a job queueing system itself, it unfortunately does not save you from having to understand whatever system—called a *backend*—you have chosen. Be it Sidekiq, Sucker Punch, Resque, or something else, each job backend has different behaviors that are critical to understand.

For example, Resque does not automatically retry failed jobs, but Sidekiq does. Que uses the database to store jobs, but Sidekiq uses Redis (meaning you need to have a Redis database set up to use Sidekiq and also understand what a Redis database actually is). And, of course, the default queuing system in Rails is nothing, so jobs don't run in the background without setting something up.

Here is what you need to know about the job backend you are using:

- How does queueing work?
    - How are the jobs themselves stored?
    - Where are they stored?
    - How are the arguments to the jobs encoded while jobs wait to execute?
- What happens when a job fails?
- How can you observe what's happening in the job backend?

19.2.1 Understand Where and How Jobs (and their Arguments) are Queued

When you queue a job with Sucker Punch, the job is stored in memory. Another process with access to that memory will pluck the job out of an internal queue and execute it. If you use Sidekiq, the job goes into Redis. The job class and the arguments passed to it are converted into JSON before storing, and converted back before the job runs.

It's important to know where the jobs are stored so you can accurately predict failure modes. In the case of Sucker Punch, if your app's process dies for some reason, any unprocessed job is gone without a trace.

In the case of Sidekiq (or Resque), you may lose jobs if Redis goes down, depending on how Redis is configured. If you are also using that Redis for caching, you then run the risk of using up all of the storage available on caching and will be unable to queue jobs at all.

You also need to know the mechanism by which the jobs are stored wherever they are stored. For example, when you queue a job for Sidekiq, it will store the name of the job class as a string, and all of the arguments as an array. Each argument will be converted to JSON before being stored. When the job is executed, those JSON blobs will be parsed into hashes.

This means that if you write code like this:

```
ChargeMoneyForWidgetJob.perform_async(widget)
```

The code in `ChargeMoneyForWidgetJob` will not be given a `Widget`, but instead be given a `Hash` containing whatever results from calling `to_json` on a `Widget`. Many developers find this surprising, and this is precisely why you have to understand how jobs are stored.

You also need to know what happens when jobs fail.

19.2.2 Understand What Happens When a Job Fails

When a job encounters an exception it doesn't rescue, it fails. Unlike a web request in a similar situation, which sends an HTTP 500 to the browser, the job has no client to report its failure to. Each job backend handles this situation differently by default, and has different options for modifying the default behavior.

For example, Sucker Punch does nothing by default, and failed jobs are simply discarded. Sidekiq will automatically retry them for a period of time before discarding them. Resque will place them into a special failed queue and hope you notice.

As discussed above, the ability to retry in the face of failures is one of the reasons to place code in a background job. My advice is to understand how failure is managed and then configure your jobs system and/or jobs to automatically retry a certain number of times before loudly notifying you of the job failure.

It's common for job backends to integrate with exception notification services like Bugsnag or Rollbar. You need to understand exactly how this integration works. For example, Resque will notify you once before placing the job in the failed queue. Sidekiq will notify you every time the job fails, even if that job is going to be retried.

I can't give specific advice, because it depends on what you have chosen, but you want to arrange for a situation in which you are notified when a job that should complete has failed and won't be retried. You *don't* want notification when a job fails and will be retried, nor do you need to know if a job fails whose failure doesn't matter.

Failure is a big part of the next thing you need to know, which is how to observe the behavior of the job backend.

19.2.3   Observe the Behavior of Your Job Backend

When a job fails and won't be retried, you need a way to examine that job. What class was it? What were the arguments passed to it? What was the reason for failure? You also need to know how much capacity you have used storing jobs, as well as how many and what type of jobs are waiting to be processed. You may also wish to know what jobs have failed and *will* be retried, and when they might get retried.

Many job backends come with a web UI that can tell you this. Some also include programmatic APIs you can use to inspect the job backend. Familiarize yourself with whatever is provided and make sure you use it. If there is a web UI, make sure only authorized users can access it, and make sure you understand what it's showing you.

The more you can connect your job backend's metrics to a monitoring system, the better. It can be extremely hard to diagnose problems that result from the job backend failing if you can't observe its behavior.

I have personally used Que, Resque, Sucker Punch, and Sidekiq. Of those four, Sidekiq is the best choice for most situations and if you aren't sure which job backend to use, choose Sidekiq.

We'll need to write some job code later on, so we need some sort of backend set up. Let's set up Sidekiq.

19.3   Sidekiq is The Best Job Backend for Most Teams

> This section's code is in the folder 19-03/ of the sample code.

I'm going to go quickly through this setup. Sidekiq's documentation is great and can provide you with many details about how it works. The point of this chapter is to talk about job code, not Sidekiq, but we need something set up, and I want to use something that is both realistic and substantial.

You are likely to encounter Sidekiq in the real world, and you are very likely to encounter a complex job backend configuration.

First, we'll add the Sidekiq gem to `Gemfile`:

```
# Gemfile

  # lograge changes Rails' logging to a more
  # traditional one-line-per-event format
  gem "lograge"
→
→ # Sidekiq handles background jobs
→ gem "sidekiq"

  # Tachyons is a functional CSS framework
  # we'll use to style our views
```

Then install it:

```
> bundle install
«lots of output»
```

We will also need to create the binstub so we can run it if we need to:

```
> bundle binstub sidekiq
```

Sidekiq assumes Redis is running on `localhost` by default. Assuming you are using the Docker-based setup I recommended from an early chapter of the book on page 29 , our Redis is running on port 6379 of the host `redis`, so we need to tell Sidekiq about that. Remembering what we learned in "Using The Environment for Runtime Configuration" on page 35, we want this URL configured via the environment. Let's add that to our two `.env` files.

First, is `.env.development`:

```
# .env.development

  DATABASE_URL="
    postgres://postgres:postgres@db:5432/widgets_development"
→ SIDEKIQ_REDIS_URL=redis://redis:6379/1
```

The value `redis` for the host comes from the key used in the docker-compose.yml file to set up Redis. For the test environment, we'll do something similar, but instead of /1 we'll use /2, which is a different logical database inside the Redis instance.

```
# .env.test

DATABASE_URL=postgres://postgres:postgres@db:5432/widgets_tes...
→ SIDEKIQ_REDIS_URL=redis://redis:6379/2
```

Note that we put "SIDEKIQ" in the name to indicate the purpose of this Redis. You should not use the same Redis instances for both job queueing and caching if you can help it. The reason is that it creates a single point of failure for two unrelated activities. You don't want a situation where you start aggressively caching and use up your storage preventing jobs from being queued.

Now, we'll create an initializer for Sidekiq that uses this new environment variable:

```ruby
# config/initializers/sidekiq.rb

Sidekiq.configure_server do |config|
  config.redis = {
    url: ENV.fetch("SIDEKIQ_REDIS_URL")
  }
end

Sidekiq.configure_client do |config|
  config.redis = {
    url: ENV.fetch("SIDEKIQ_REDIS_URL")
  }
end
```

Note that we used `fetch` because it will raise an error if the value `SIDEKIQ_REDIS_URL` is not found in the environment. This will alert us if we forget to set this in production.

We don't need to actually *run* Sidekiq in this chapter, but we should set it up. This is going to require that `bin/run` start two simultaneous processes: the Rails server we are already using and the Sidekiq worker process. To do *that* we'll use Foreman[3], which we'll add to the development and test sections of our `Gemfile`:

```
# Gemfile

    # We use Factory Bot in place of fixtures
    # to generate realistic test data
    gem "factory_bot_rails"

→
→   # Foreman runs all processes for local development
→   gem "foreman"

    # We use Faker to generate values for attributes
    # in each factory
```

We can install it:

```
> bundle install
«lots of output»
```

We also need to create a binstub in `bin/` for it:

```
> bundle binstub foreman
```

Foreman uses a "Procfile" to know what to run. The Procfile lists out all the processes needed to run our app. Rather than create this file, I prefer to generate it inside `bin/dev`. This centralizes the way we run our app to a single file, which is more mangeable as our app gets more complex. I also prefer to name this file `Procfile.dev` so it's clear what it's for (services like Heroku use `Procfile` to know what to run in production). Let's replace bin/run with the following:

```
# bin/dev

#!/usr/bin/env bash

set -e

echo "[ bin/dev ] Rebuilding Procfile.dev"
```

---

[3] https://ddollar.github.io/foreman/

```
echo "# This is generated by bin/dev. Do not edit" > Procfile.dev
echo "# Use this via bin/dev" >> Procfile.dev
# We must bind to 0.0.0.0 inside a
# Docker container or the port won't forward
echo "web: bin/rails server --binding=0.0.0.0" >> Procfile.dev
echo "sidekiq: bin/sidekiq" >> Procfile.dev

echo "[ bin/dev ] Starting foreman"
bin/foreman start -f Procfile.dev -p 3000
```

We'll also add `Procfile.dev` to our `.gitignore` file:

```
# .gitignore

  # and creates more problems than it solves, so
  # we never ever want to use it
  .env
→
→ # Procfile.dev is generated, so should not be checked in
→ Procfile.dev

  # .env.*.local files are where we put actual
  # secrets we need for dev and test, so
```

Now, when we run our app with `bin/dev`, Sidekiq will be started as well and any code that requires background job processing will work in development.

Let's talk about how to queue jobs and how to implement them.

19.4 Queue Jobs Directly, and Have Them Defer to Your Business Logic Code

> This section's code is in the folder 19-04/ of the sample code.

Once you know how your job backend works and when to use a background job, how do you write one and how do you invoke it?

Let's talk about invocation first.

19.4.1 Do Not Use Active Job - Use the Job Backend Directly

Active Job was added to Rails in recent years as a single abstraction over background jobs. This provides a way for library authors to interact with background jobs without having to know about the underlying backend.

335

Active Job does a great job at this, but since you *aren't* writing library code, it creates some complexities that won't provide much value in return. Since Active Job doesn't alleviate you from having to understand your job backend, there isn't a strong reason to use it.

The main source of complexity is the way in which arguments to jobs are handled. As discussed above, you need to know how those arguments are serialized into whatever data store your job system is using. Often, that means JSON.

This means that you can't pass an Active Record directly to a job since it won't serialize/de-serialize properly:

```
> bin/rails c
rails-console> require "pp"
rails-console> widget = Widget.first
rails-console> pp JSON.parse(widget.to_json) ; nil
{"id"=>1,
 "name"=>"Stembolt",
 "price_cents"=>102735,
 "widget_status_id"=>2,
 "manufacturer_id"=>11,
 "created_at"=>"2020-05-24T22:02:54.571Z",
 "updated_at"=>"2020-05-24T22:02:54.571Z"}
=> nil
```

Before Active Job, the solution to this problem was to pass the widget ID to the job, and have the job look up the `Widget` from the database. Active Job uses globalid[4] to automate this process for you. But only for Active Records and only when using Active Job.

That means that when you are writing code to queue a job, you have to think about what you are passing to that job. You need to know what type of argument is being passed, and whether or not it uses globalid. I don't like having to think about things like this while I'm coding and I don't see a lot of value in return for doing so.

Unless you are using multiple job backends—which will create a sustainability problem for you and your team—use the API of the job backend you have chosen. That means that your arguments should almost always be basic types, in particular database identifiers for Active Records.

Let's see that with our existing widget creation code. We'll move the logic around emailing finance and admin to a background job called `PostWidgetCreationJob`, which we'll write in a moment. We'll use it like so:

---

[4]https://github.com/rails/globalid

```
# app/services/widget_creator.rb

      widget.save
      if widget.invalid?
        return Result.new(created: false, widget: widget)
      end
x #     if widget.price_cents > 7_500_00
x #       FinanceMailer.high_priced_widget(widget).deliver_now
x #     end
  # XXX
x #     if widget.manufacturer.created_at.after?(60.days.ago)
x #       AdminMailer.new_widget_from_new_manufacturer(widget).
x #         deliver_now
x #     end
  # XXX
x #     Result.new(created: widget.valid?, widget: widget)
→       PostWidgetCreationJob.perform_async(widget.id)
→       Result.new(created: widget.valid?, widget: widget)
      end

      class Result
```

perform_async is Sidekiq's API, and we have to pass widget.id for reasons stated above. We'll talk about where the code we just removed goes next.

19.4.2 Job Code Should Defer to Your Service Layer

For all the reasons we don't want business logic in our controllers, we don't want business logic in our jobs. And for all the reasons we want to convert the raw data types being passed into richly-typed objects in our controllers, we want to do that in our jobs, too.

We passed in a widget ID to our job, which means our job should locate the widget. After that, it should defer to another class that implements the business logic.

Since this is still widget creation and the job is called PostWidgetCreationJob, we'll create a new method on WidgetCreator called post_widget_creation and have the job trigger that.

Let's write the job code and then fill in the new method. Since we aren't using Active Job, we can't use bin/rails g job. We also can't use ApplicationJob in its current form, but it is nice to have a base class for all jobs. Let's replace the Rails-provided ApplicationJob with one that is specific to Sidekiq.

```
# app/jobs/application_job.rb

# Do not inherit from ActiveJob. All jobs use Sidekiq
class ApplicationJob
  include Sidekiq::Worker

  sidekiq_options backtrace: true
end
```

Now, any job we create that extends `ApplicationJob` will be set up for Sidekiq and we won't have to include `Sidekiq::Worker` in every single class. We could customize the output of `bin/rails g job` by creating the file `lib/templates/rails/job/job.rb.tt`, but we aren't going to use this generator at all. The reason is that our job class will be very small and we won't write a test for it.

Here's what `PostWidgetCreationJob` looks like:

```
# app/jobs/post_widget_creation_job.rb

class PostWidgetCreationJob < ApplicationJob
  def perform(widget_id)
    widget = Widget.find(widget_id)
    WidgetCreator.new.post_widget_creation_job(widget)
  end
end
```

This means we need to create the method `post_widget_creation_job` in `WidgetCreator`, which will contain the code we removed from `create_widget`:

```
# app/services/widget_creator.rb

      Result.new(created: widget.valid?, widget: widget)
    end

→   def post_widget_creation_job(widget)
→     if widget.price_cents > 7_500_00
→       FinanceMailer.high_priced_widget(widget).deliver_now
→     end
→
```

338

```
→      if widget.manufacturer.created_at.after?(60.days.ago)
→        AdminMailer.new_widget_from_new_manufacturer(widget).
→          deliver_now
→      end
→    end
→
     class Result
       attr_reader :widget
       def initialize(created:, widget:)
```

Our app should still work, but we've lost the proof of this via our tests. Let's talk about that next.

19.5 Job Testing Strategies

> This section's code is in the folder 19-05/ of the sample code.

In the previous section, I said we wouldn't be writing a test for our Job. Given the implementation, I find a test that the job simply calls a method to have low value and high carrying cost. But, we do need coverage that whatever uses the job is working correctly.

There are three approaches to take regarding testing code that uses jobs, assuming your chosen job backend supports them. You can run jobs synchronously inline, you can store jobs in an internal data structure, executing them manually inside a test, or you can allow the jobs to actually go into a real queue to be executed by the real job system.

Which one to use depends on a few things.

Executing jobs synchronously as they are queued is a good technique when the jobs have simple arguments using types like strings or numbers *and* when the job is incidental to the code under test. Our widget creation code falls under this category. There's nothing inherent to widget creation that implies the use of jobs.

Queuing jobs to an internal data structure, examining it, and then executing the jobs manually is more appropriate if the code you are testing is inherently about jobs. In this case, the test serves as a clear set of assertions about what jobs get queued when. A complex batch process whereby you need to fetch a lot of data, then queue jobs to handle it, would be a good candidate for this sort of approach.

This approach is also good when your job arguments are somewhat complex. The reason is that queuing the jobs to an internal structure usually serializes them, so this will allow you to detect bugs in your assumptions about how arguments are serialized. It is *incredibly* common to pass in a hash with symbols for keys and then erroneously expect symbols to come out of the job backend (when, in fact, the keys will likely be strings).

The third option—using the job backend in a production-like mode—is expensive. It requires running a worker to process the jobs outside of your tests (or having your test trigger that worker somehow) and requires that the job data storage system be running *and* be reset on each new test run, just as Rails resets the database for you.

I try to avoid this option if possible unless there is something so specific about the way jobs are queued and processed that I can only detect it by running the actual job backend itself.

For our code, the first approach works, and Sidekiq provides a way to do that. We will require "sidekiq/testing" in test/test_helper.rb and then call Sidekiq::Testing.inline! around our test.

First, however, let's make sure our test is actually failing:

```
> bin/rails test test/services/widget_creator_test.rb || echo \
  Test Failed
Running 8 tests in a single process (parallelization thresho...
Run options: --seed 38421

# Running:

2023-12-04T23:55:53.753Z pid=9599 tid=803 INFO: Sidekiq 7.2....
F

Failure:
WidgetCreatorTest#test_finance_is_notified_for_widgets_price...
Expected: 1
  Actual: 0

bin/rails test test/services/widget_creator_test.rb:44

.F

Failure:
WidgetCreatorTest#test_email_admin_staff_for_widgets_on_new_...
Expected: 1
  Actual: 0

bin/rails test test/services/widget_creator_test.rb:126

.....

Finished in 0.173927s, 45.9964 runs/s, 126.4901 assertions/s...
```

```
8 runs, 22 assertions, 2 failures, 0 errors, 0 skips
Test Failed
```

Good. It's failing in the right ways. You can see that the expected effects of the code we removed aren't happening and this causes the test failures. When we set Sidekiq up to run the job we are queuing inline, the tests should start passing.

Let's start with `test/test_helper.rb`:

```
# test/test_helper.rb

  ENV["RAILS_ENV"] ||= "test"
  require_relative "../config/environment"
  require "rails/test_help"
→
→ # Set up Sidekiq testing modes. See
→ # https://github.com/mperham/sidekiq/wiki/Testing
→ require "sidekiq/testing"
  Capybara.configure do |config|
    # This allows helpers like click_on to locate
    # any object by data-testid in addition to
```

Sidekiq's default behavior is the second approach of queueing jobs to an internal data structure. To run them inline, we'll use `Sidekiq::Testing.inline!`. We'll add this to the setup block in `test/services/widget_creator_test.rb`:

```
# test/services/widget_creator_test.rb

  class WidgetCreatorTest < ActiveSupport::TestCase
    setup do
→     Sidekiq::Testing.inline!
      ActionMailer::Base.deliveries = []
      @widget_creator = WidgetCreator.new
      @manufacturer = FactoryBot.create(:manufacturer,
```

We need to undo this setting after our tests run in case other tests are relying on the default (which is fake!):

```
# test/services/widget_creator_test.rb

    FactoryBot.create(:widget_status)
    FactoryBot.create(:widget_status, name: "Fresh")
  end
→ teardown do
→   Sidekiq::Testing.fake! # the default setting
→ end
  test "widgets have a default status of 'Fresh'" do
    result = @widget_creator.create_widget(Widget.new(
      name: "Stembolt",
```

Now, our test should pass:

```
> bin/rails test test/services/widget_creator_test.rb
Running 8 tests in a single process (parallelization thresho...
Run options: --seed 35393

# Running:

2023-12-04T23:55:56.021Z pid=9674 tid=7xy INFO: Sidekiq 7.2....
........

Finished in 0.175805s, 45.5049 runs/s, 170.6434 assertions/s...
8 runs, 30 assertions, 0 failures, 0 errors, 0 skips
```

To use the second testing strategy—allowing the jobs to queue and running them manually—consult your job backend's documentation. Sidekiq provides methods to do all this for you if you should choose.

Now that we've seen how to make our code work using jobs, we have to discuss another painful reality about background jobs, which is retries and idempotence.

19.6 Jobs Will Get Retried and Must Be Idempotent

> This section's code is in the folder 19-06/ of the sample code.

One of the reasons we use background jobs is to allow them to be retried automatically when a transient error occurs. While you could build up a list of transient errors and only retry them, this turns out to be difficult, because there are a lot of errors that one would consider transient. It is easier to configure your jobs to automatically retry all errors (or at least retry them several time before finally failing).

This means that code executed from a job must be idempotent: it must not have its effect felt more than once, no matter how many times it's executed.

Consider this code that updates a widget's updated_at[5]

```
def touch(widget)
  widget.updated_at = Time.zone.now
  widget.save!
end
```

Each time this is called, the widget's updated_at will get a new value. That means this method is not idempotent. To make it idempotent, we would need to pass in the date:

```
def touch(widget, updated_at)
  widget.updated_at = updated_at
  widget.save!
end
```

Now, no matter how many times we call touch with the same arguments, the effect will be the same.

The code initiated by our jobs must work similarly. Consider a job that charges someone money for a purchase. If there were to be a transient error partway through, and we retried the entire job, the customer could be charged twice. *And* we might not even be aware of it unless the customer noticed and complained!

Making code idempotent is not easy. It's also—you guessed it—a trade-off. The touch method above probably won't cause any problems if it's not idempotent. But charging someone money will. This means that you have to understand what might fail in your job, what might happen if it's retried, how likely that is to happen, and how serious it is if it does.

This means that your job is going to be idempotent with respect to some failure modes, and not to others. This is OK if you are aware of it and make the conscious decision to allow certain scenarios to not be idempotent.

Let's examine the job we created in the last section. It's called post_widget_creation_job in WidgetCreator, which looks like so:

---

[5]I realize you would never actually write this, but idempotence is worth explaining via a trivial example as it is not a concept that comes naturally to most.

```ruby
1  def post_widget_creation_job(widget)
2    if widget.price_cents > 7_500_00
3      FinanceMailer.high_priced_widget(widget).deliver_now
4    end
5
6    if widget.manufacturer.created_at.after?(60.days.ago)
7      AdminMailer.new_widget_from_new_manufacturer(widget).
8        deliver_now
9    end
10 end
```

When thinking about idempotence, I like to go through each line of code and ask myself what would happen if the method got an error on that line and the entire thing started over. I don't worry too much initially how likely that line is to fail or why it might.

For example, if line 2 fails, there's no problem, because nothing has happened but if line 7 fails—depending on how—we could end up sending the emails twice.

Another thing I will do is ask myself what might happen if the code is retried a long time later. For example, suppose line 3 fails and the mail isn't sent to the finance team. Suppose that the widget's price is updated before the failure is retried. If the price is no longer greater than $7,500, the mail will *never* get sent to the finance team!

How we deal with this greatly depends on how serious it is if the code doesn't execute or executes many times. It also can depend on how much control we really have. See the sidebar "Idempotent Credit Card Charging" on the next page for an example where a third party doesn't make it easy to create idempotent code.

Let's turn our attention to two problems with the code. First is that we might not send the emails at all if the widget is changed between retries. Second is that a failure to send the admin email might cause us to send the finance email again.

You might think we could move the logic into the mailers and have the mailers use background jobs. I don't like having business logic in mailers as we'll discuss in "Mailers" on page 349, so let's think of another way.

Let's use two jobs instead of one. We'll have one job do the finance check based on only the price and another do the manufacturer check based on only the creation date.

> **Idempotent Credit Card Charging**
>
> The code to charge customers at Stitch Fix was originally written to run in the request cycle. It was ported from Python to Ruby by the early development team and left alone until we all realized it was the source of double-charges our customer service team identified.
>
> We moved the code to a background job, but knew it had to be idempotent. Our payment processor didn't provide any guarantees of idempotency, and would often decline a retried charge that had previously succeeded. We implemented idempotency ourselves and it was... pretty complex.
>
> Whenever we made a charge, we'd send an idempotency key along with the metadata. This key represented a single logical charge that we would not want to have happen more than once.
>
> Before making a charge, we would fetch all the charges we'd made to the customer's credit card. If any charge had our idempotency key, we'd know that the charge had previously gone through but our job code had failed before it could update our system. In that case, we'd fetch the charge's data and update our system.
>
> If we *didn't* see that idempotency key, we'd know the charge hadn't gone through and we'd initiate it. Just explaining it was difficult, and the code even more so. And the tests! This was hard to test.

First, let's remove `PostWidgetCreationJob`, since we're going to replace it with the two new jobs:

```
> rm app/jobs/post_widget_creation_job.rb
```

We'll replace our use of that job in `WidgetCreator` with the two new jobs called `HighPricedWidgetCheckJob` and `WidgetFromNewManufacturerCheckJob`.

```
# app/services/widget_creator.rb

    end
  # XXX
  # XXX
→     HighPricedWidgetCheckJob.perform_async(
→         widget.id, widget.price_cents)
→     WidgetFromNewManufacturerCheckJob.perform_async(
→         widget.id, widget.manufacturer.created_at.to_s)
      Result.new(created: widget.valid?, widget: widget)
    end
```

Note that we are calling to_s on created_at. Sidekiq cannot correctly serialize a DateTime and will emit a warning if we don't serialize it explicitly.

We'll now replace post_widget_creation with two methods that these jobs will call.

```
# app/services/widget_creator.rb
        widget.id, widget.manufacturer.created_at.to_s)
      Result.new(created: widget.valid?, widget: widget)
    end

  # def post_widget_creation_job(widget)
  #   if widget.price_cents > 7_500_00
  #     FinanceMailer.high_priced_widget(widget).deliver_now
  #   end
  # XXX
  #   if widget.manufacturer.created_at.after?(60.days.ago)
  #     AdminMailer.new_widget_from_new_manufacturer(widget).
  #       deliver_now
  #   end
  # end
  # XXX
  # class Result
    def high_priced_widget_check(widget_id, original_price_cents)
      if original_price_cents > 7_500_00
        widget = Widget.find(widget_id)
        FinanceMailer.high_priced_widget(widget).deliver_now
      end
    end

    def widget_from_new_manufacturer_check(
        widget_id, original_manufacturer_created_at)
      if original_manufacturer_created_at.after?(60.days.ago)
        widget = Widget.find(widget_id)
        AdminMailer.new_widget_from_new_manufacturer(widget).
          deliver_now
      end
    end
    class Result
      attr_reader :widget
      def initialize(created:, widget:)
        @created = created
```

And now, the jobs, starting with HighPricedWidgetCheckJob

```
# app/jobs/high_priced_widget_check_job.rb

class HighPricedWidgetCheckJob < ApplicationJob
  def perform(widget_id, original_price_cents)
    WidgetCreator.new.high_priced_widget_check(
        widget_id,
        original_price_cents)
  end
end
```

For `WidgetFromNewManufacturerCheckJob`, we have to deal with several issues we discussed above. Remember that parameters passed to jobs get serialized into JSON and back—at least when using Sidekiq. In our case, we are now passing in a `String` containing a timestamp to the job, since JSON has no data type to store a date.

Because our service layer should not be parsing strings (or hashes or whatever) into real data types, but expect to receive properly typed values, we will convert it in the job itself. Like a controller, the job code is the right place to do these sorts of conversions. Fortunately, `Date.parse` will do the right thing:

```
# app/jobs/widget_from_new_manufacturer_check_job.rb

class WidgetFromNewManufacturerCheckJob < ApplicationJob
  def perform(widget_id, original_manufacturer_created_at)
    WidgetCreator.new.widget_from_new_manufacturer_check(
        widget_id,
        Date.parse(original_manufacturer_created_at))
  end
end
```

Our tests should still pass, *and* give us coverage of the date-parsing we just had to do[6].

> bin/rails test test/services/widget_creator_test.rb

---

[6] I actually didn't catch this the first time I wrote this chapter. Later parts of the book compare the manufacturer created date to another and, even though it was really a string, the tests all seemed to pass, because I was using < to do the comparison. I changed it to use before? after some reader feedback and discovered it was a string. Even after understanding how jobs get queued in detail, and having directly supported a lot of Resque jobs (which do the same JSON-encoding as Sidekiq) for almost eight years, I still got it wrong. Write tests, people.

```
Running 8 tests in a single process (parallelization thresho...
Run options: --seed 59404

# Running:

...2023-12-04T23:56:00.306Z pid=9832 tid=8lw INFO: Sidekiq 7...
.....

Finished in 0.177779s, 44.9998 runs/s, 168.7491 assertions/s...
8 runs, 30 assertions, 0 failures, 0 errors, 0 skips
```

Wow. This is a huge amount of new complexity. What's interesting is that it revealed some domain concepts that we might not have been aware of. If it's important to know the original price of a widget, we could store that explicitly. That would save us some trouble around the finance mailer. Similarly, if it's important to know the original manufacturer of a widget, that, too, could be stored explicitly.

Perhaps you don't think that these emails are important enough to warrant this sort of paranoia. Perhaps you can think of some simpler ways to achieve what we achieved here. Perhaps you are right. Still, the point remains that if there *is* some bit of logic that you you need to execute exactly once, making that happen is going to require complexity.

Make no mistake, this is accidental complexity with a carrying cost. You absolutely have to weigh this against the carrying cost of doing it differently. I can tell you that when jobs aren't idempotent, you create a support burden for your team and customers and *this* can have a real cost on team morale. No one wants to be interrupted to deal with support.

This is why design is hard! But it helps to see what it actually looks like to deal with idempotency. I have certainly refactored code to this degree, seen that it was not the right trade-off and reverted it. Don't be afraid to revert it all back to how it was if the end result is going to be less sustainable than the original.

If you want to go deeper on Sidekiq and background jobs, I have written "Ruby on Rails Background Jobs with Sidekiq"[7] with the Pragmatic Programmers that you might find useful. It includes a more focused sample app that demonstrates the various issues you can run into with background jobs and Sidekiq, along with techniques for dealing with them.

Up Next

We're just about done with our tour of Rails. I want to spend the next chapter touching on the other *boundary* classes that we haven't discussed, such as mailers, rake tasks, and mailboxes.

---

[7] https://pragprog.com/titles/dcsidekiq/ruby-on-rails-background-jobs-with-sidekiq/

20
Other Boundary Classes

I want to touch briefly on some other parts of Rails that I had termed *boundary* classes way back in "The Rails Application Architecture" on page 19. Like controllers and jobs, rake tasks are a mechanism for triggering business logic. Mailers, like views, render output for a user. Both Rake tasks and Mailers exist at the outside of the app, interacting with the outside world, just as a controller does.

This chapter will focus on Mailers and Rake tasks. I'll mention Mailboxes, Action Cable, and Active Storage only briefly, because I have not used these parts of Rails in production. I don't want to give you advice on something I haven't actually used.

Let's start with mailers.

20.1 Mailers

> This section's code is in the folder 20-01/ of the sample code.

Mailers are a bit of an unsung hero in Rails apps. Styling and sending email is not an easy thing to do and yet Rails has a good system for handling it. It has an API almost identical to rendering web views, it can handle text and HTML emails, and connecting to any reasonable email provider is possible with a few lines of configuration. And it can all be tested.

There are three things to consider when writing mailers. First is to understand the purpose of a mailer and thus not put business logic in it. Second, understand that mailers are really jobs, so the arguments they receive must be considered carefully. Last, you need a way to actually look at your emails while styling them, as well as while using the app in development mode.

Let's start with the purpose of mailers.

20.1.1 Mailers Should Just Format Emails

Like controllers, you want your mailers to avoid having any business logic in them. The purpose of a mailer is to render an email based on data passed into it. That's it.

For example, our widget creation code has logic that sends the finance team an email if the widget's price is above $7,500. You might think it's a good idea to encapsulate the check on the widget's price in the mailer itself. There is no real advantage to doing this and it will only create sustainability problems later.

First, it requires executing the mailer to test your widget creation logic. Second, it means that if something *else* needs to happen for a high-priced widget, you have to move the check back into `WidgetCreator` anyway. It's much simpler if your mailers simply format and send mail.

Ideally, your mailers have very little logic in them at all. If you end up having complex rendering logic for an email, it could be an indicator you actually have two emails. In this case, have the business logic trigger the appropriate email instead of adding logic to the mailer itself.

The next thing to understand is that in most cases, your email is sent from a job.

20.1.2 Mailers are Usually Jobs

When you call `deliver_now` after calling a mailer, the email is sent right then and there. It's typically a better practice to call `deliver_later` so you can offload email-sending to a background job. The reasons for this are detailed in the previous chapter, "Jobs" on page 325. `deliver_later` will use Active Job to queue the mail for later delivery using whatever job backend you have chosen.

If you recall, Active Job uses something called globalid to allow you to safely serialize Active Records (and only Active Records by default) into and out of the job backend. This means that our code as it's written *will* work correctly if the email is sent via a job.

If, on the other hand, you send a non-Active Record to your mailer (including a date!), it may not be serialized and de-serialized correctly (this is why I recommended using the job backend directly for background jobs).

That said, to send emails using the job backend directly, you'd have to make your own mailer job or jobs and duplicate what Rails is already doing. My suggestion is to use Rails to send emails with Active Job, and manage the inconsistency in how arguments are handled via code review.

You could additionally require that mailer arguments are always simple values that convert to and from JSON correctly. In any case, make sure everyone understands the conventions.

Lastly, you need to understand how annoying and fussy it is to style an email.

20.1.3 Previewing, Styling, and Checking your Mail

Testing mailers works like any other class in Rails. The more difficult part is styling and checking what you've done. This is because there are *many* different email clients that all have different idiosyncrasies about how they work, how much CSS they support—if any—and what they do to render emails.

Fortunately, Rails provides the ability to preview emails in your browser. Let's style the finance email.

When we created this mailer with `bin/rails g`, it created a preview class for us in `test/mailers/previews` called `finance_mailer_preview.rb`.

If you haven't used mailer previews before, they allow you to create some test data and render an email in your browser. It's not exactly like using a real email client, but it works pretty well. Each method of the preview class causes a route to be enabled that will call that method and render the email it returns.

To create the test data, you can rely on whatever you may have put into `db/seeds.rb`, or you can use your factories. Let's use this latter approach.

We'll replace the auto-generated code with code to create a widget and pass it to the mailer. We'll use `build` instead of `create`. `build` won't save to the database. For the purposes of our mailer preview, this is fine, and, because we want to use hard-coded names, it makes things a bit easier. If we saved these records to our dev database, the first time we refreshed the page, it would try to save new records with duplicate names and cause an error.

```
# test/mailers/previews/finance_mailer_preview.rb

  # Preview this email at http://localhost:3000/rails/mailers...
  def high_priced_widget
→   manufacturer = FactoryBot.build(:manufacturer,
→                                   name: "Cyberdyne Systems")
→   widget = FactoryBot.build(:widget, id: 1234,
→                             name: "Stembolt",
→                             price_cents: 8100_00,
→                             manufacturer: manufacturer)
→   FinanceMailer.high_priced_widget(widget)
  end

end
```

We can fire up our app with `bin/dev`, and navigate to this path against your development server:

```
/rails/mailers/finance_mailer/high_priced_widget
```

You should see our very un-exciting email rendered, as in the screenshot below.

Figure 20.1: Previewing an Email

Since this is an email to our internal finance team, there's no need for it to be fancy, but it should look at least halfway decent. Let's try to create an email that looks like so:

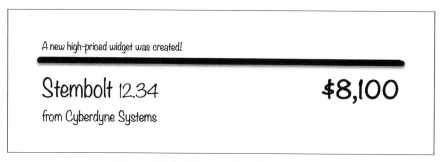

Figure 20.2: Finance Email Mockup

We want to use our design system (as discussed in "Adopt a Design System" on page 140), but we can't use CSS since few email systems support it. This is a good reminder that our design system is a *specification*, not an implementation. Our CSS strategy and related code is one possible implementation, but we can also use inline styles in our mailer views to implement the design system as well. To do that, we need to know the underlying spacing and font size values.

We know the font sizes already from when set up our style guide. For example, to get the third-largest font size, we can use a style like `font-size: 2.8rem`. For padding and other sizing, we'll need to look at how our CSS is implemented to get the specific sizes. In our case, we'll only need two of the spacings, specifically 0.25rem and 0.5rem.

And, since we can't rely on floats, flexbox, or other fancy features of CSS, we'll create the two column layout with tables...just like the olden days. Other than that, we'll still use semantic HTML where we can. This all goes in app/views/finance_mailer/high_priced_widget.html.erb:

```erb
<%# app/views/finance_mailer/high_priced_widget.html.erb %>

<article style="padding: 0.5rem;
                font-family: helvetica, sans-serif">
  <table style="width: 100%;">
    <tr>
      <td colspan="2" style="border-bottom: solid thin black;">
        <p style="padding-left: 0.25rem;">
        A new high-priced widget has been created!
        </p>
      </td>
    </tr>
    <tr>
      <td colspan="2" style="padding: 0.5rem;">
         
      </td>
    </tr>
    <tr>
      <td>
        <div style="font-size: 2.8rem; margin-bottom: 0.5rem;">
          <%= @widget.name %>
          <span style="font-size: 2.2rem">
            #<%= styled_widget_id(@widget) %>
          </span>
        </div>
        <div style="font-size: 1.3rem;">
          <%= @widget.manufacturer.name %>
        </div>
      </td>
      <td style="vertical-align: top; text-align: right">
        <div style="font-size: 2.8rem;
                    margin-bottom: 0.25rem;
                    font-weight: bold">
          <%= number_to_currency(@widget.price_cents / 100) %>
        </div>
      </td>
    </tr>
  </table>
</article>
```

In order to use `styled_widget_id` helper, we need to use the `mailer` method to bring in the methods in `ApplicationHelper`:

```
# app/mailers/finance_mailer.rb

class FinanceMailer < ApplicationMailer
→ helper :application
  def high_priced_widget(widget)
    @widget = widget
    mail to: "finance@example.com"
```

If you reload your preview, the email now looks like it should, though it certainly feels underwhelming given all the markup we just wrote. See the screenshot below.

Figure 20.3: Styled HTML Email

We should make the plain text version work, too. Let's avoid any ASCII-art and just do something basic.

```
<%# app/views/finance_mailer/high_priced_widget.text.erb %>

A new high-priced widget has been created!

<%= @widget.name %>
by <%= @widget.manufacturer.name %>

Price: <%= number_to_currency(@widget.price_cents / 100) %>
```

This can also be previewed and should look like the screenshot below.

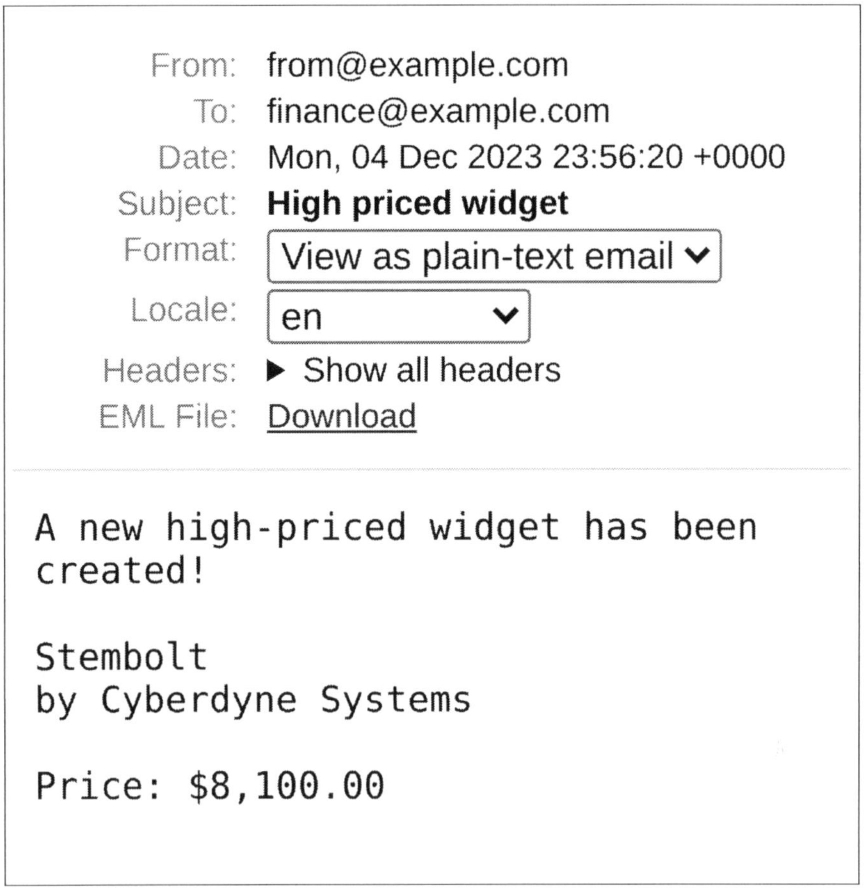

```
From:    from@example.com
  To:    finance@example.com
Date:    Mon, 04 Dec 2023 23:56:20 +0000
Subject: High priced widget
Format:  [ View as plain-text email ▾ ]
Locale:  [ en ▾ ]
Headers: ▶ Show all headers
EML File: Download

A new high-priced widget has been
created!

Stembolt
by Cyberdyne Systems

Price: $8,100.00
```

Figure 20.4: Previewing a plain text email

Note that you can use partials and View Components to create re-usable components, just as we did with web views. You may want to place partials somewhere like `app/views/mailer_components` or namespace View Components in a `mailers` directory to make it clear they are intended for mail views only.

For helpers, you can use the helpers in `ApplicationHelper` using the `helper` method, but you can make your own mail-specific helpers. I recommend again somewhere obvious like `app/helpers/mailer_helpers.rb`, so no one mistakenly uses them in web views.

Lastly, if you are going to be creating a lot of emails in your app, you should consider augmenting your style guide to show both CSS *and* inline styles so that you can easily apply the design system to your emails.

In addition to previewing emails for styling, you may want to see them delivered in development.

20.1.4 Using Mailcatcher to Allow Emails to be Sent in Development

By default, emails are not sent in development. Actually, by default they are not sent in *any* environment, but you usually end up configuring them in production only. You must set `config.delivery_method` in one of the files in `config/environments` so that Rails actually sends emails. This requires configuration from your email provider and is detailed in the Rails guides[1].

If email is a critical part of your user flows, you may want to be able to see the emails during development. For example, you might want to fire up your server, create a widget, and see that an email was actually sent to the finance team. But you probably don't want to actually email anyone for real.

To do this, you can use an app called MailCatcher[2]. MailCatcher runs an SMTP server and provides a UI similar to the Rails mailer previews we saw in the last section. It shows any email that was sent to it. The MailCatcher website outlines how to set this up in Rails.

One thing to note is that MailCatcher should *not* be installed in your `Gemfile`. It should be set up as another app entirely. If you are using the Docker-based setup, this can be achieved by using an existing Docker image that runs MailCatcher and setting that up in your `docker-compose.yml` file:

```
services:
  mailcatcher:
    image: sj26/mailcatcher
    ports:
      - "9998:1080"
```

This YAML snippet shows that MailCatcher will expose its web UI (running on port 1080) to your local machine's port 9998. Thus, you can access MailCatcher's UI at `http://localhost:9998`. Your Rails app would need to connect to an SMTP server running on port 1025 (the default) of the host `mailcatcher` (which is derived from the service name in the YAML file). MailCatcher is nice to have setup for doing end-to-end simulations or demos in your development environment.

While mailers respond to business logic by sending email, Rake tasks initiate business logic, so let's talk briefly about those.

---

[1] https://guides.rubyonrails.org/action_mailer_basics.html
[2] https://mailcatcher.me

20.2 Rake Tasks

> This section's code is in the folder 20-02/ of the sample code.

Sometimes you need to initiate some logic without having a web view to trigger it. This is where Rake tasks come in. There are two problems in managing Rake tasks: naming/organizing, and code. Before that, let's talk briefly about what should be in a Rake task.

20.2.1 Rake Tasks Are For Automation

If something needs to be automated, a Rake task is what should trigger that automation. Any time something needs to happen on a routine basis—even if the schedule is irregular—a Rake task is the simplest mechanism to trigger it.

For routine tasks that happen on a regular schedule, your job back-end may provide something (like sidekiq-scheduler[3]), but you still might have tasks that someone must manually perform on an ad-hoc basis. What you want to avoid is having a lot of documentation that tells developers what code to run in production to perform some sort of task. New team members will lack context for what they are doing and mistakes will be made. See the sidebar "When Your User ID is 1" below for an example of this.

> **When Your User ID is 1**
>
> At Stitch Fix, we used a lot of what we called *runbooks* to help perform common tasks that would be needed in response to support requests. For example, changing the internal status of some inventory to account for a mistake that couldn't be fixed by a user. These runbooks were Markdown files with instructions in them as well as code that you would copy, paste, modify, and run in a production Rails console or in a production database.
>
> A common task in these runbooks was to locate an internal user to associate with the actions being taken. This provided a rudimentary paper trail for who modified some piece of data. The runbooks would instruct you to locate your internal user via email or ID and use that when performing subsequent actions.
>
> As the creator of the internal user system, my ID was 1. My ID was also the example used in several of the runbooks. The result was that I was attributed to tons of changes in the internal systems I didn't make because an engineer was working quickly to fix a problem, copied my ID and didn't think twice (this is why I prefer automation to documentation—even the most conscientious engineers miss things when following written-out steps).
>
> Fortunately, before Stitch Fix went public, all these runbooks were replaced with auditable code that couldn't be mis-attributed.

---

[3] https://github.com/moove-it/sidekiq-scheduler

Rake tasks are also a good tool for performing one-off actions where you need some sort of auditable "paper trail". If you are in a heavily audited environment, such as one that must be Sarbanes-Oxley (SOX) compliant, you may not be able to simply change production data arbitrarily. But you *will* need to change production data sometimes to correct errors. A Rake task checked into your version control system can provide documentation of who did what, when, even if the Rake task is only ever executed once.

So, how should you organize these tasks?

20.2.2 One Task Per File, Namespaces Match Directories

To invoke a Rake task, you type `bin/rails «task_name»`. Developers often either need to figure out the task name in order to invoke it, or they may see an invocation configured and need to find the source code. These are both unnecessarily difficult if you don't keep the tasks organized.

For example, if you see that you have a task that runs periodically named `db:updates:prod:countries`, you can't just grep for that task name. You have to find `:countries` or `countries:` in a file, and then see if the namespace containing it is `db:updates:prod`. The older an app gets, the more tasks it accumulates and the harder it is to locate code.

The best way I have found to keep Rake tasks organized is as follows:

- Create a directory structure in `lib/tasks` that matches the namespaces exactly. In the example above, that means `lib/tasks/db/updates/prod/` would be where we'd find the `countries` task.
- Name the actual file using the name of the task, and place only one task in each file. That means `lib/tasks/db/updates/prod/countries.rake` would be where the task is defined.
- Name the task—the last part of the full task name—something explicit and obvious. This example of `countries` is a terrible name. Try `update_list_of_countries` instead.
- Always always always use `desc` to explain what the task does.

It might seem like overkill, but this will scale very well and no one is going to complain that they can easily figure out where a task is defined by following a convention. I'll also point out that your Rails app has no limit on the number of source files it can contain—there's plenty to go around[4].

Beyond this, you will need to think about the information architecture of your Rake tasks. This is not easy. My suggestion is the same one I've given many other times in this book, which is to look for a pattern to develop and form a convention around that.

---

[4]Yes, I know there *is* a real limit, but it's like in the billions. If you have a Rails app with billions of rake tasks, you may want to look into microservices.

As an example, here is how the `lib/tasks` directory is structured in an app I'm working on right now (I'm using the `tree`[5] command that will make ASCII art of any directory structure):

```
> tree --charset=ascii -d lib/tasks/
lib/tasks/
|-- alerting
`-- production_data
    |-- corrections
    |-- role_assignment
    `-- test_data
```

The `alerting` namespace/subdirectory holds tasks that feed into an alerting system to monitor the app. `production_data` holds tasks that manipulate data in production. `production_data/corrections` holds tasks that fix errant production data, `production_data/role_assignment` holds tasks to assign roles programmatically since there is currently no UI, and `production_data/test_data` creates data in production for the purposes of testing.

This is just an example. Observe the tasks you need and keep them organized as you see patterns.

Aside from figuring out what to name your tasks and where they should go, you also need to know how to implement them.

20.2.3 Rake Tasks Should Not Contain Business Logic

All the reasons we've discussed about why business logic doesn't go into controllers, jobs, or mailers applies to Rake tasks, too. It's just not worth it. You end up having to test the Rake tasks—not an easy prospect—and you end up with code you may need elsewhere buried in some file in `lib/tasks`.

Your Rake tasks should ideally be one line of code to trigger some business logic. If the logic is particularly esoteric to a one-off use-case, it can be hard to figure out where it should go to avoid being mistakenly re-used.

Let's make two Rake tasks to demonstrate the subtleties of this guideline. Suppose we have a new status for widgets called "Legacy", and we want any widget in "Approved" to be given the status "Legacy" if it's more than a year since creation. We'll run this task daily to automatically update the widgets.

Since this is our first task, let's not worry about namespaces—we don't have enough data about our needs to choose a good one—and put it in `lib/tasks`. We'll call the task `change_approved_widgets_to_legacy`. Because the actual code should *not* be in the Rake task, our Rake task will be pretty short:

---

[5] https://en.wikipedia.org/wiki/Tree_(command)

```
# lib/tasks/change_approved_widgets_to_legacy.rake

desc "Changes all Approved widgets to Legacy that need it"
task change_approved_widgets_to_legacy: :environment do
  LegacyWidgets.new.change_approved_widgets_to_legacy
end
```

Given the current state of the app, placing this code in `WidgetCreator` doesn't make much sense, so we'll make a new class. If our task was to perform some sort of follow-up to created widgets, it might make sense to go in `WidgetCreator`, but since this is about old widgets, we'll make a new class.

This Rake task doesn't need to be tested. We'll run it locally to make sure there are no syntax errors, and that should be sufficient. It's unlikely to ever change again and there is no value in asserting that we've written a line of code correctly by reproducing that line of code in a test.

Let's create the new class:

```
# app/services/legacy_widgets.rb

class LegacyWidgets
  def change_approved_widgets_to_legacy
    # Implementation here...
  end
end
```

This class is unremarkable. It's like any other code we'd write, and we can implement it by writing a test, watching it fail, and writing the code. Or whatever you do. The point is that the Rake task's implementation is in a normal Ruby class.

Let's consider a much different task. Suppose we have added a validation that all widget prices must end in .95, for example $14.95. We can enforce this for new widgets via validations, but all the existing ones won't necessarily have valid prices.

We need to make a one-time change to fix these. Because the way we fix them could be complicated and because we want to review and audit this change, we won't make the change in the database directly. We need some code.

Let's make the rake task. The task we just created is already in `lib/tasks`, but this new task is different. If we put our new task alongside it in lib/tasks, it could be confusing, since our new task is intended to run only one time, whereas change_approved_widgets_to_legacy is intended to run regularly.

Let's make that distinction clear by creating a namespace called one_off, meaning our task will go in lib/tasks/one_off. We'll call it fix_widget_pricing:

```
# lib/tasks/one_off/fix_widget_pricing.rake

namespace :one_off do
  desc "Fixes the widgets created before the switch to 0.95 validation"
  task fix_widget_pricing: :environment do
    # ???
  end
end
```

We need the line of code that replaces # ??? to be a single invocation of a class we can test, but since this is one-off, putting it in a class in app/services doesn't feel quite right. Just like we made it clear that the task itself is a one-off, let's create a namespace in app/services using the same name—one_off.

```
# app/services/one_off/widget_pricing.rb

module OneOff
  class WidgetPricing
    def change_to_95_cents
      Widget.find_each do |widget|
        # Whatever logic is needed to update the price
      end
    end
  end
end
```

We can use this in our Rake task:

```
# lib/tasks/one_off/fix_widget_pricing.rake

  namespace :one_off do
```

```
    desc "Fixes the widgets created before the switch to 0.95 v...
    task fix_widget_pricing: :environment do
→     OneOff::WidgetPricing.new.change_to_95_cents
    end
  end
```

Why go through the hassle of having our Rake task defer to a class in app/services that is clearly not designed to be used more than once? Doesn't this make things more complicated than they need to be?

It depends. Yes, to accomplish this particular task requires writing six additional lines of code compared to in-lining `change_to_95_cents` in the Rake task itself. The problem with in-lining is that it creates a decision-point for all Rake tasks. Should the task's code go into app/services or directly into the Rake file?

Decisions like this have a carrying cost, and the inconsistency is just not worth it. It's more sustainable to reduce this carrying cost by creating an architecture that minimizes the number of decisions that need to be made.

One common use of Rake tasks that you should be wary of, however, is for development environment automation.

20.2.4 Prefer Ruby Command Line Apps for Developer Automation

Rails includes tasks that manage the database, turn local caching on and off, and so forth. These are tasks that help you manage your development environment. When you need to create such a task, consider creating a command-line app in `bin/` instead of Rake task.

Rake tasks have only one advantage over a command-line script: access to your app's internals via Rails. A Rake task can use your Active Records, for example. But if you don't need access to your Rails app's internals, a Rake task makes for a pretty terrible developer experience.

Rake task names cannot easily be tab-completed on the command line. Passing arguments to Rake tasks is fairly difficult, since it doesn't work like any other command line app. Rake tasks also don't provide any way to document command line arguments or flags.

Instead, create a bash or Ruby script in `bin/`, much as we did in Automating Application Setup with `bin/setup` on page 40. Ruby's `OptionParser` is a well-documented class from the standard library to allow you to accept command line flags, switches, and arguments, documenting how each of them works.

Basically, if you don't need access to your Rails app's internals, and you are automating something only useful for the local development environment, create your automation in `bin/` and document its existence in `bin/setup` or your README.

Before we leave this chapter, I want to briefly touch on some of Rails' other boundary classes.

20.3 Mailboxes, Cables, and Active Storage

I have not used Action Mailbox, Action Cable, or Active Storage in production, so I am not qualified to give strong advice. That said, it might be useful to share my high level thinking about these technologies.

20.3.1 Action Mailbox

Action Mailbox, added in Rails 6, allows your app to receive emails. I have used Action Mailbox just enough to write the chapter about it in "Agile Web Development With Rails 6"[6] and that's it. It seems like a great feature, though.

Action Mailboxes are very similar to controllers, in that they are triggered by an outside request. The way I would approach writing a mailbox would be the same as writing a controller. I would handle basic type conversions and confidence-checking, and hand everything off to something in the service layer.

20.3.2 Action Cable

I have never used Action Cable, nor have I met anyone who had used it in production. That said, it's an underlying part of Turbo, which is a part of Hotwire, so I expect there to be more Action Cable in production as developers adopt Rails 7.

Action Cable requires a lot of moving parts to coordinate, including both JavaScript and Ruby code. While it certainly does work, it is much more complex than other parts of Rails.

On a few occasions when developers I know have discussed using Action Cable directly, they could usually solve their immediate problem by having the page auto-refresh. If you don't need high volumes of real-time updates on your page, you may find Action Cable has a higher carrying cost than the value it delivers.

There's no doubt in my mind that Action Cable is a great way to integrate Websockets into your app. Just know that it's complex and not widely used. That means you won't have a lot of resources available to help you if you have trouble.

---

[6] https://pragprog.com/titles/rails6/

20.3.3 Active Storage

Active Storage is a feature that abstracts access to cloud storage services like Amazon's S3. It is a technology I very much wish had existed years ago, because we wrote our own janky version of this at my last job and it was a pain to deal with.

I have not used Active Storage in production, and don't have a lot of deep thoughts about it. My guess is that it won't save you from having to understand how the backing store works. But, since it's part of Rails, it should be reliable and supported. It also serves a much more common use case than Action Cable, meaning you are likely to get better support for it if you run into trouble.

Up Next

This completes our tour of the various parts of Rails and how I believe you can work with them sustainably. The rest of the book will focus on patterns and techniques that are more broad and cross-cutting. The next chapter will talk about something that's not part of Rails but that most Rails apps need: authentication and authorization.

PART
III
———

beyond rails

21

Authentication and Authorization

One of the most common cross-cutting concerns in any app is the need to authenticate users and authorize the actions they may take in an app. Rails does not include any facility for managing this, since the way authentication is handled is far less common than, say, the way code accesses a database.

This gap requires that you do some up-front thinking and design for how you want to handle this important part of your app. For authentication, there are two common gems that handle most common cases, and we'll talk about which situations are appropriate for which. These gems—Devise and OmniAuth—allow you to avoid the difficult and error-prone task of rolling your own authentication system.

For authorization—controlling who can do what in your app—the situation is more difficult. There just aren't as many commonalities across apps related to role-based access control, so you can't pick a solution and go. We'll talk about using the popular Cancancan gem to define and manage roles, but it'll still be up to you to design a role-based system that meets your needs.

And, of course, you'll need to test your authentication and authorization systems. Remember that tests are a tool for mitigating risk, and they can work well for mitigating the risks of unauthorized access to your app. But they don't come for free.

Let's talk about *authentication* first, which is the way in which we know who a user accessing our website is. The two most common gems that provide this are Devise[1] and OmniAuth[2].

21.1 When in Doubt Use Devise or OmniAuth

Building an authentication system is not easy. There are many edge cases that allow would-be attackers to have unauthorized access to your system. Many of them are quite creative and hard to predict in advance, such as

---

[1] https://github.com/heartcombo/devise
[2] https://github.com/omniauth/omniauth

reverse-engineering the algorithm used for generating random numbers on your server and using that to guess passwords more efficiently.

Security is one of those areas where leaning heavily on expertise and experience will pay off far better than learning it from first principles. When it comes to user management, I'm almost certain that you, dear reader, are not the expert that, say, Google's entire security team is. And that's OK.

When it comes to user management, you want to ideally allow someone you trust to handle as much of the authentication as you can, be that the combined 546 contributors to Devise, or the team at Google that manages their OAuth implementation.

The simplest way that reduces risk—assuming it meets all your requirements—is to allow a third party service like Google or GitHub to manage authentication. OmniAuth can handle much of the integration for you if you go this route.

21.1.1 Use OmniAuth to Authenticate Using a Third Party

OmniAuth is a Rails API for doing OAuth[3]-style authentication. It wraps the specifics of many popular services providing you with a single API. With a few lines of code, you can allow users to log in with, say, Twitter, and not have to create an authentication system of your own.

It works by redirecting your users to the third party site, having that site do the authentication, and then redirect back to you. OmniAuth handles the specifics of integrating with each site that you choose to support (you can use as many different third parties as you want). See the figure "OmniAuth Authentication Flow" on the next page.

Note that in step 5, you will need to store some unique identifier passed from the service to associate with the user in your app. Take care with what you choose to use for this value. For example, users can change their email or username without necessarily changing their identity in your service.

The key question around using OmniAuth is about your userbase. Do they all have accounts in one or more third parties that you can trust with authentication?

If your app is used only by employees of your company, and your company requires everyone to use, say, Gmail on a company-managed account, the answer is "yes". Everyone must have a Gmail account, and you are trusting Google with your email, so you could rely on them for authentication as well.

For an app accessible to the general public, the question is harder to answer. For a service aimed at developers, it's likely a good assumption most of the userbase has GitHub accounts, but less likely they would all have Facebook accounts.

---

[3] https://oauth.net

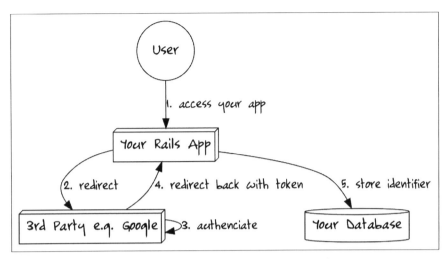

Figure 21.1: OmniAuth Authentication Flow

The main consequence of using OmniAuth is that you require your users to have an account with a trusted third-party. It's important to understand what "trusted" means in this context. A third party I trust for my app, might not be worthy of your trust for your app.

For example, if you are working on the website for the United States Internal Revenue Service (responsible for collecting taxes in the US), you probably don't want to allow a private company to even know who is logging into your service. It's not a slight on Google, but the IRS shouldn't trust Google with this information.

If you either cannot trust the third parties where your users have accounts, or your users don't have accounts with third parties you *do* trust, you'll need to build authentication into your app. For that, you should use Devise.

21.1.2 Building Authentication Into your App with Devise

Devise is a gem that provides an almost end-to-end experience for managing user accounts, logins, password resets, password rules, and user auditing. It does this by generating code to use in your app that relies on code in Devise's gem.

Devise is highly configurable and has a steep learning curve. But the documentation is great and since it's widely used, it's easy to get help for using it properly. It is worth traversing this learning curve, because authentication is so critical to most apps.

The value Devise provides is that it's battle-hardened and actively developed. Unless you are a deep expert in security, Devise will do a better job than you at managing all parts of the authentication process. Devise centers around a

User Active Record, backed by the users database table (these names are configurable).

The User model can be configured with Devise-provided modules to give your authentication process whatever features it needs. For example, you can allow users to reset their passwords using the Recoverable module. You can lock accounts after a certain number of failed attempts by using the Lockable module. There are many more.

Devise also provides a user interface for you. The views it provides are bare-bones, so you'll likely need to make use of your design system (as discussed in "Adopt a Design System" on page 140) to make them look good.

I'm not going to walk through setting up Devise as this would be duplicative of the great documentation it already has. My suggestions for using Devise are to go through the "Getting Started" part of its documentation in your app. Then, take a look at the configurable modules and bring in those that you need. You can bring others in later.

Note that you can combine both OmniAuth and Devise to allow multiple forms of authentication. This can complicate your overall authentication strategy and will reduce the security of your site, since each method of authentication is a potential attack vector. But it's an option you have if you need it.

Once you have authentication sorted out, you are likely to need some form of authorization to control which users are allowed to perform which actions in the app.

21.2 Authorization and Role-based Access Controls

In most organizations, the authentication mechanism is driven by product and business concerns, and the decision around what method to use is typically easy to make. Authorization—the mapping of what users can perform what actions—is often much more complicated.

If you are building software to be used by employees of the company, or a software-as-a-service product intended for knowledge workers, there will often be myriad features available, some of which control highly-sensitive or potentially dangerous functions. For example, you might have a feature to grant credit to users, allowing them to purchase products without using their own money. You may not want anyone at the company to be able to grant this credit.

What makes authorization tricky is that it's often difficult to clearly map users onto roles, and also difficult to know what the roles actually should be. If you make roles too general, you lose the ability to control access the way you might want. If you make roles overly-specific, you create a confusing list of permissions that can lead to errors. If you've ever worked with AWS, the list of IAM Roles is massive. You simply can't consult a list of them to decide which are the right ones for a given task.

To further complicate the task of authorization design, whatever you come up with has to be easily auditable. In other words, you need to create a system in which you can easily answer the question "What is this user allowed to do?" and prove that you have implemented this correctly to someone else.

21.2.1 Map Resources and Actions to Job Titles and Departments

If you have designed your app around many different resources that all have the same set of canonical actions (as discussed in "Don't Create Custom Actions, Create More Resources" on page 83), you can use your app's routes as a definitive list of all actions and data your app has. The ability to generate this list from code is a *gift* to your fellow security professionals and compliance team members!

You then need to map each user account to the list of routes/actions that are appropriate for that user. The best way to do *that* is to assign each user a role, based on their job title and department, and then configure access to routes and actions for each job title and department.

The reason to use job title and department is twofold. First, it's well-known, unambiguous information about each user. Second, most rules around who can do what tend to relate to job title and department anyway. The finance team can access financial records, but the marketing team probably shouldn't. The engineering team can access deployments, but the customer service team cannot, etc.

Using job title and department also means that, when your authorization code is audited, it will be far easier to understand. You are mapping a well-known concept—job title and department—to the particularities of your app.

For example, it's much easier to verify that "all senior customer service managers can create refunds" than it is to verify that "all senior customer service managers get the 'refunds' role, but sometimes other people get this role as well, but whoever has this role can create refunds". When roles can be arbitrarily assigned, you then need a system to manage *that* and *this* system must also be audited (and, of course, restricted based on role-base access controls). If you can avoid it... avoid it.

To manage the actual access restrictions, the Cancancan gem[4] gives you the plumbing you need[5]. But be warned: it includes a lot of implicit and flexible

---

[4] https://github.com/CanCanCommunity/cancancan
[5] This is a fork/continuation of the original cancan gem, which has not been maintained or transitioned to another team.

features that will complicate your application if you aren't careful in how you use them.

21.2.2 Use Cancancan to Implement Role-Based Access

Cancancan has two main parts to its API: an `Ability` class that defines what any given user is allowed to do (including unauthenticated users), and methods to use in controllers or views to check the given user's access.

For example, to allow your entire customer service team to list and view a refund (which would be the Rails actions `index` and `show`), but only allow senior managers to create them, you might write code like this:

```ruby
class Ability
  include CanCan::Ability

  def initialize(user)
    if user.present?
      if user.department == "customer_service"
        can [ :index, :show ], Refund

        if user.job_title == "senior manager"
          can [ :create, :new ] , Refund
        end
      end
    end
  end
end
```

This only defines the permissions. You still need to check them. You can use `authorize_resource` to apply a permissions check to all the standard controller actions:

```ruby
class RefundsController < ApplicationController
  authorize_resource
end
```

`authorize_resource` can determine that the resource is `Refund` based on the controller name. It will then set up its own controller callbacks to compare the user against the abilities you've defined, raising a `CanCan::AccessDenied` exception if an unauthorized user tries to access a route/action they shouldn't.

You can use rescue_from to control the user experience when that happens, for example:

```
class ApplicationController < ActionController::Base
  rescue_from CanCan::AccessDenied do
    redirect_to main_app.root_url,
      notice: "You cannot access that page"
  end
end
```

This all works based on the assumption that current_user returns an object representing who is logged in. How this is defined depends on your authentication scheme, but it's typical to store the user's ID in the session, and implement current_user in ApplicationController to examine the session and fetch the user record:

```
class ApplicationController < ActionController::Base

  def current_user
    @current_user ||= User.find_by(id: session[:user_id])
  end
end
```

Note that if you are using OmniAuth, you will need to store some record in your database when the user successfully authenticates so you can associate them with roles. This would happen in step 5 from the figure "OmniAuth Authentication Flow" on page 369.

Cancancan will also allow you to call authorize! in a controller method to authorize more explicitly, but you will find it much simpler to rely on authorize_resource and a properly-configured Ability class.

To restrict content in your views based on roles, you can use the method can?. While excessive use of this can create complicated view code, it's often handy when you want to omit links the user shouldn't see. For example, this will show the "Create Refund" link only to a user authorized to create refunds:

```
<% if can? :create, Refund %>
  <%= link_to "Create Refund", new_refund_path %>
<% end %>
```

373

Cancancan is more flexible than this, but using this flexibility will likely make your authorization system more confusing.

21.2.3 You Don't Have to Use All of Cancancan's Features

The features outlined above are sufficient to create an authorization system that will work for your needs *and* be easily auditable. The remainder of Cancancan's features will work against those goals and result in a more complicated and harder-to-understand setup.

Since you aren't using custom actions, you won't need to use that feature of Cancancan, and I suggest you avoid creating custom authorization actions if possible.

You also should avoid `load_and_authorize_resource`, which conflates an access control check with a database lookup. It will authorize a user for access to a resource, and then assign it to an instance variable after calling `find`. Intermixing authorization with data access like this will be confusing and won't provide strong benefits.

You should also resist the urge to create an internal DSL around your `Ability` class. Although an app with many actions and roles will require a large and complex `Ability` class, I would strongly recommend you manage that class using conventional means like functional decomposition.

Unlike other classes in your system, `Ability` will be modified infrequently but read very frequently, and often by people outside your team who may not be Rails developers. Thus, it's a good idea to keep your `Ability` class free of dynamic, implicit concepts. Use functional decomposition via private methods to manage the complexity of the class, but do *not* create a sophisticated abstraction layer. This will make it harder to understand.

In addition to the design work required to properly set up authentication and authorization, you should test it using system tests.

21.3 Test Access Controls In System Tests

Security incidents are expensive. They derail teams from providing business value, lead to a crisis of confidence for the company and—in many cases—expose users' personal information to bad actors. There's no way to absolutely prevent such incidents, but ensuring that your access controls are working is a huge help.

The clearest way to do this is to write system tests that exercise the system as different types of users. Depending on how complex your authorization needs are, you may need a lot of tests. Remember that tests are a mechanism for risk management. This means that you probably don't want to test every action against every possible role, but you *do* need to strategically test many roles and actions.

I would highly recommend a thorough testing of all authentication flows no matter what. This is particularly important if you are using Devise, since Devise outputs code you have to maintain yourself.

As for testing authorizations, this can be trickier. It requires a solid understanding of *why* your authorization configuration is the way it is. What problems are being solved by restricting access to various parts of the system? What is the consequence of an unauthorized person gaining access to a feature they aren't supposed to access? If that happened, would you know it had happened?

The answers to these questions can help you know where to focus. For example, if you can't tell who performed a critical action that is restricted to certain users, you should thoroughly test the access controls to that action.

You also want to make it as easy as possible for developers to test the authorizations around new features or to test changes to authorizations. There are two things you can do to help. The first is to make sure you have a wide variety of test users that you can create with a single line of code in a test. The second is to cultivate re-usable test code to setup for an authorization-related test or verify the results of one (or both).

The way to cultivate both of these is to start writing your system tests and look for patterns. If you followed my advice in "Models, Part 2" on page 262, you should have a factory to create at least one user. As you write system tests using different types of users, extract any that you use more than once into a factory. This allows future developers—yourself included—to quickly create a user with a given role.

You will also notice patterns in how you set up your test or perform assertions. Extract those when you see them. The mechanism for this depends on your testing framework. For Minitest, you can follow the pattern we established with `with_clues` and `confidence_check`, by creating modules in `test/support`:

```ruby
## test/support/authorization_system_test_support.rb
module TestSupport
  module AuthorizationSystem
    def login_as(user_factory_name)
      user = FactoryBot.create(user_factory_name)

      # Whatever else needed to log into your system as this user
    end

    def assert_no_access
      # assert whatever the UX is
      # for users being denied access
    end
```

```
    end
end

## test/system/create_manufacturer_test.rb
require "test_helper"
require "support/authorization_system_test_support"

class CreateManufacturerTest < ApplicationSystemTestCase
  include TestSupport::AuthorizationSystem

  test "only admins can create manufacturers" do
    login_as(:non_admin)

    # attempt to create a manufacturer

    assert_no_access
  end
end
```

If using Rspec, you can use this pattern for setup code, but you will likely want to make custom matchers for assertions.

If you do have security or compliance people on your team or at your company, you should use them to help think through what should and should not be tested. Most security professionals understand the concept of risk and understand the trade-offs between exhaustively testing everything and being strategic. In fact, they are better at this than most, since it's a critical part of their job. Avail yourself of their expertise.

Up Next

Continuing our discussion of sustainability issues beyond the Rails application architecture, let's talk about JSON APIs next.

22

API Endpoints

Rails is a great framework for making REST APIs, which are web services intended to be consumed not by a browser, but by another programmer. Even if your app is not explicitly an API designed for others to consume, you might end up needing to expose endpoints for your front-end or for another app at your company to consume.

The great thing about APIs in Rails is that they can be built pretty much like regular Rails code. The only difference is that your APIs render JSON (usually) instead of an HTML template. Still, developers do tend to over-complicate things when an API is involved, and often miss opportunities to keep things sustainable by leveraging what Rails gives you.

That's what this chapter is about. It's not about designing, building, and maintaining a complex web of microservices, but instead just about how to think about JSON endpoints you might use for programmatic communication between systems.

Here's what we'll cover:

- Be clear on what you need an API or JSON endpoint for.
- Approach your JSON API the same as any other Rails feature, by being resource-oriented and using canonical Rails actions.
- Use the simplest mechanisms for authentication, content negotiation, and versioning that you can.
- Use Rails' default JSON serialization as much as you can.
- Test the API with an integration test and assert on the proper encoding.

As always, we start with what problem we're trying to solve with our hypothetical API.

22.1 Be Clear About What—and Who—Your API is For

There is a big difference in building and maintaining a massive public API used by millions of developers and creating some JSON endpoints for your front-end code to consume. If you build your handful of front-end-consuming endpoints with the fit and finish of, say, the GitHub API, you will have incurred both massive opportunity costs *and* large carrying costs without benefit.

Before navigating the complex world of strategies around APIs—from authentication to data serialization—you should be honest about what your API is actually for. Write out the use cases and identify who will be using the API. It's OK to suppose some reasonable future uses and consumers, but don't let flights of fancy carry you away.

Just because you might think it would be cool to have the world's preeminent Widget API doesn't mean it will happen. And if it *did* happen, the best way to prepare for it is to minimize carrying costs around the features you *do* need to build. This is where a keen understanding of your product roadmap and overall problems your app solves are critical.

For the rest of this chapter I'm going to assume you need an API for something simple, such as consumption by your own front-end code via Ajax calls, or lightweight app-to-app integration inside your team or organization. A public-facing API that is part of your product is a different undertaking.

Keep the details about why you are building an API at the top of your mind. Developers will propose a lot of different solutions in the name of security, scalability, and maintainability. Being able to align on the actual needs of the API can help drive those conversations productively. For example, Ajax calls within your Rails app really don't require JWTs vended by a separate OAuth flow, even if such an architecture might be more scalable.

Once you understand what your API is for, you next need a general strategy for implementing it. The basis of that strategy is to adopt the same conventions we've discussed in this book: working resource-oriented, following Rails conventions, and embracing Rails for what it is—not what you wish it might be.

22.2 Write APIs the Same Way You Write Other Code

> This section's code is in the folder 22-02/ of the sample code.

Ideally, a controller that powers an API should look just as plain as any other controller:

```ruby
class WidgetsController < ApplicationController
  def index
    widgets = Widget.all
    render json: { widgets: widgets }
  end

  def create
```

```ruby
    widget = Widget.create(widget_params)
    if widget.valid?
      render json: { widget: widget }, status: 201
    else
      render json: { errors: widget.errors }, status: 422
    end
  end
end
```

You may not want *exactly* this sort of error-handling, but you get the idea. There's rarely a reason to do anything different in your API controller methods than in your non-API methods.

You would be well-served to create a separate routing namespace and thus controller namespace for your API calls. This means that while a browser might navigate to /widgets/1234 to get the view for widget 1234, an API client would access /api/widgets/1234.json to access the JSON endpoint.

The reason for this is to build in from the start a notion of separation that you might need later. For example, if you eventually need to serve your API from another app, your front-end infrastructure can route /api to a different back-end app. If both a browser and an API client used /widgets/1234, this will be harder to pull apart.

There's also little advantage in mixing the browser and API code in the same controller. Often there are little differences, and you don't always have an API endpoint for each browser-facing feature (or vice-versa). If you have duplicated code, you can share it with modules or classes.

You should also create a base controller for all your API endpoints. This allows you to centralize configuration like authentication or content-negotiation without worrying about your web-based endpoints.

Let's see both of these in action by creating an endpoint for widgets. We'll skip authentication and versioning for now—we'll talk about those in a bit.

First, we'll create the base controller, called `ApiController` and place it in app/controllers/api_controller.rb:

```ruby
# app/controllers/api_controller.rb

class ApiController < ApplicationController
end
```

Next, we'll create a route for our API endpoint, and use the `api` namespace:

```
# config/routes.rb

    resources :design_system_docs, only: [ :index ]
  end

  # All API endpoints should go in this namespace.
  # If you need a custom route to an API endpoint,
  # add it in the custom routes section, but make
  # sure the resource-based route is here.
  namespace :api do
    resources :widgets, only: [ :show ]
  end

  ####
  # Custom routes start here
  #
```

This has the nice side-effect of creating a readable route helper: api_widget_path.

Now we'll create our controller in api/widgets_controller.rb:

```
# app/controllers/api/widgets_controller.rb

class Api::WidgetsController < ApiController
  def show
    widget = Widget.find(params[:id])
    render json: { widget: widget }
  end
end
```

We'll write a test for this later, but hopefully you can see that your API controllers can—and should—be written just like any other. You will still defer business logic to the service layer, and still approach your design by identifying resources. Concerns like authentication, versioning, and serialization formats can all be handled as controller callbacks or middleware. Let's talk about those next, because you have to sort these issues out before building your API. First, we'll talk about authentication.

22.3 Use the Simplest Authentication System You Can

> This section's code is in the folder 22-03/ of the sample code.

Many developers, upon hearing "API" and "Authentication" will jump to JSON Web Tokens, or *JWT*. Or they might think "OAuth". Be careful here. If your API is simply a JSON endpoint for consumption by your front-end, you can transparently use the existing cookie-based authentication you already have. Remember, the more authentication mechanisms you support, the more vulnerable your app is to security issues, because each mechanism is an attack vector.

If your API is being consumed internally, there are two other mechanisms you should consider before adopting something complex like JWT or OAuth, especially if your API does not require a sophisticated set of authorizations. The first is good ole HTTP Basic Auth, which is a name and a password.

Rails provides a method `http_basic_authenticate_with` that you can call in your controllers to use basic auth. Every HTTP client in the known universe supports basic auth, and you can embed your credentials in a url for easy debugging and local development like so:

```
https://username:password@api.example.com/api/widgets.json
```

For example, in our base `ApiController`, you could do something like this:

```
class ApiController < ApplicationController
  skip_before_action :require_login # or whatever callback was
                                    # set up to require login
  http_basic_authenticate_with name: ENV["API_USERNAME"],
                               password: ENV["API_PASSWORD"]
end
```

You don't have to use a single set of hard-coded set of credentials, either. See the Rails documentation[1] for examples of more sophisticated setups that allow multiple credentials.

A second almost-as-simple mechanism is to use the HTTP Authorization header[2]. Despite its name, this header is used for authentication and can encode an API key. Setting HTTP headers is, like Basic Auth, something any HTTP client library can do, and can be done with any command-line HTTP client, such as `curl`. This, too, is something Rails provides support for[3].

---

[1] https://api.rubyonrails.org/classes/ActionController/HttpAuthentication/Basic.html
[2] https://developer.mozilla.org/en-US/docs/Web/HTTP/Headers/Authorization
[3] https://api.rubyonrails.org/classes/ActionController/HttpAuthentication/Token.html

I would recommend these mechanisms if you don't have specific requirements that preclude their use. *Many* high-traffic, public APIs use these mechanisms and have for years, so there is no inherent issue with scalability. They also have the virtue of being easy for any developer of any level of experience to understand quickly.

Let's set up token-based authentication for our API. Rather than hard-code a single key, let's create a database table of keys instead. This way, we can give each known client their own key, which helps with auditing. We'll also allow for keys to be de-activated without being deleted.

```
> bin/rails g migration create_api_keys
    invoke  active_record
    create    db/migrate/20231204235629_create_api_keys.rb
```

For the stability of this book, I'm going to rename the migration file. You don't have to do this.

```
> mv db/migrate/*create_api_keys.rb \
  db/migrate/20210102000000_create_api_keys.rb
```

Now, we'll create the table. It will have a key, a created date, a client name, and a deactivation date.

```
# db/migrate/20210102000000_create_api_keys.rb

  class CreateApiKeys < ActiveRecord::Migration[7.1]
    def change
→     create_table :api_keys,
→       comment: "Holds all API keys for access to the API" do |t|
→
→       t.text :key, null: false,
→         comment: "The actual key clients should use"
→
→       t.text :client_name, null: false,
→         comment: "Name of the client who was assigned this key"
→
→       t.datetime :created_at, null: false,
→         comment: "When this key was created"
→
→       t.datetime :deactivated_at, null: true,
→         comment: "When the key was deactivated. " +
→                  "When present, this key is not valid."
→
```

```
      t.timestamps
    end
```

We also don't need `updated_at` because there should never be an arbitrary update to this table—just a deactivation by setting `deactivated_at`. This is somewhat unusual, so I will deal with this with... comments!

```
# db/migrate/20210102000000_create_api_keys.rb

                "When present, this key is not valid."


→       # Note: No updated_at because there should be no updates
→       #       to rows here other than to deactivate
      end
    end
  end
```

There are a few other things we need, too. First, the API keys should be unique, so we'll need an index to enforce that constraint. Second, we don't want any client to have more than one active API key. We can achieve this with a Postgres *conditional* index. This is an index that only applies when the data matches a given WHERE clause, which we can specify to rails using the `where:` option of `add_index`.

```
# db/migrate/20210102000000_create_api_keys.rb

        # Note: No updated_at because there should be no update...
        #       to rows here other than to deactivate
      end
→     add_index :api_keys, :key, unique: true,
→       comment: "API keys have to be unique or we " +
→                "don't know who is accessing us"
→
→     add_index :api_keys, :client_name,
→               unique: true,
→               where: "deactivated_at IS NULL"
    end
  end
```

We'll run the migration:

```
> bin/db-migrate
[ bin/db-migrate ] migrating development schema
== 20210102000000 CreateApiKeys: migrating ================...
-- create_table(:api_keys, {:comment=>"Holds all API keys fo...
   -> 0.0081s
-- add_index(:api_keys, :key, {:unique=>true, :comment=>"API...
   -> 0.0051s
-- add_index(:api_keys, :client_name, {:unique=>true, :where...
   -> 0.0018s
== 20210102000000 CreateApiKeys: migrated (0.0151s) ========...

[ bin/db-migrate ] migrating test schema
== 20210102000000 CreateApiKeys: migrating ================...
-- create_table(:api_keys, {:comment=>"Holds all API keys fo...
   -> 0.0042s
-- add_index(:api_keys, :key, {:unique=>true, :comment=>"API...
   -> 0.0008s
-- add_index(:api_keys, :client_name, {:unique=>true, :where...
   -> 0.0014s
== 20210102000000 CreateApiKeys: migrated (0.0065s) ========...
```

Let's create the model and a test for that partial index, since this is somewhat complex and could be a surprising implementation to developers unfamiliar with Postgres.

First, the model, which is just two lines of code:

```
# app/models/api_key.rb

class ApiKey < ApplicationRecord
end
```

Let's create a factory for it.

```
# test/factories/api_key_factory.rb

FactoryBot.define do
  factory :api_key do
    key         { SecureRandom.uuid }
    client_name { Faker::Company.unique.name }
```

```
    end
end
```

We can now create the test of the model, which will exercise the partial index.

```
# test/models/api_key_test.rb

require "test_helper"

class ApiKeyTest < ActiveSupport::TestCase
  test "client cannot have more than one active key" do
    api_key = ApiKey.create!(
      key: SecureRandom.uuid,
      client_name: "Cyberdyne"
    )

    exception = assert_raises do
      ApiKey.create!(
        key: SecureRandom.uuid,
        client_name: "Cyberdyne"
      )
    end

    assert_match /duplicate key.*violates unique constraint/i,
                 exception.message
  end
  test "client can have more than one key if all " +
       "but one is deactivated" do
    api_key = ApiKey.create!(
      key: SecureRandom.uuid,
      client_name: "Cyberdyne",
      deactivated_at: 4.days.ago
    )

    assert_nothing_raised do
      ApiKey.create!(
        key: SecureRandom.uuid,
        client_name: "Cyberdyne"
      )
    end
  end
end
```

This test should pass:

```
> bin/rails test test/models/api_key_test.rb
Running 2 tests in a single process (parallelization thresho...
Run options: --seed 56027

# Running:

..

Finished in 0.024890s, 80.3550 runs/s, 160.7101 assertions/s...
2 runs, 4 assertions, 0 failures, 0 errors, 0 skips
```

With that in place, we can now use this table to locate API keys for authentication.

In our `ApiController`, we'll create a callback:

```
# app/controllers/api_controller.rb
  class ApiController < ApplicationController
→   before_action :authenticate
→
→   private
→
→   def authenticate
→     authenticate_or_request_with_http_token do |token, options|
→       ApiKey.find_by(key: token, deactivated_at: nil).present?
→     end
→   end
  end
```

We'll see this in action when we write our test, but you can try it locally by using `curl` to access your endpoint and see that you get an HTTP 401. If you create a record in the api_keys table, then use that key with `curl`, it should work. For example:

```
curl -V -H "Authorization: Token token=\"«api_keys.key you used»\"" \
    http://localhost:9999/api/v1/widgets/1234
```

Once you have authentication set up, you'll need some sort of content negotiation.

22.4 Use the Simplest Content Type You Can

> This section's code is in the folder 22-04/ of the sample code.

The HTTP Accept header allows for a wide variety of configurations for how a client can tell the API what sort of content type it wants back (the Content-Type header is for the server to specify what it's sending). You can ignore it altogether and always serve JSON, or you could require the content type to be application/json, or you could create your own custom content type for all your resources, or even make a content type for each resource. The possibilities—and associated carrying costs—are endless.

I would not recommend ignoring the Accept header. It's not unreasonable to ask clients to set it, it's not hard for them to do so, and it allows you to serve other types of content than JSON from your API if you should need it.

I would discourage you from using custom content types unless there is a very specific problem you have that it solves. When we discuss JSON serialization, I'm going to recommend using to_json and I'm not going to recommend stuff like JSON Schema, as it is highly complex. Thus, a content type of application/json would be sufficient.

That said, if you decide you need to use more advanced tooling like JSON Schema, a custom content type could be beneficial, especially if you have sophisticated tooling to manage it. If you have to hand-enter a lot of custom types and write custom code to parse out the types, you are probably over-investing.

While you should examine the Accept header, there's no reason to litter your API code with respond_to calls that will only ever respond to JSON. Thus, you can have a single check in ApiController for the right content type. Rails provides the request method that encapsulates the current request. It has a method format that returns a representation of what was in the Accept header. That representation can respond to json? to tell us if the request was a JSON request.

We can use this and, if the request is not JSON, return an HTTP 406 (which indicates that the app doesn't support the requested format). First, we'll specify a callback. We want it after the authentication callback since there's no sense checking the content of an unauthorized request.

```
# app/controllers/api_controller.rb

  class ApiController < ApplicationController
    before_action :authenticate
→   before_action :require_json
```

```
      private
```

Now, we'll implement `require_json`:

```
# app/controllers/api_controller.rb
        ApiKey.find_by(key: token, deactivated_at: nil).present...
      end
    end
→   def require_json
→     if !request.format.json?
→       head 406
→     end
→   end
  end
```

By implementing this as a callback (instead of a middleware), controllers can override this callback if they need to respond to some other content type. For example, if we need to allow API access to a widget's datasheet, which might be in PDF, we could customize just that endpoint:

```
class Api::WidgetDatasheetsController < ApiController
  skip_before_action :require_json
  before_action :require_json_or_pdf

  def show
    respond_to do |format|
      format.json do
        # ...
      end
      format.pdf do
        # ...
      end
    end
  end

  private

  def require_json_or_pdf
    if !request.format.json? &&
```

```
      !request.format.pdf?
        head 406
      end
    end
  end
end
```

Note that to make code like this work, you'll need to register the PDF mime type. See the documentation on `Mime::Type`[4] for more details.

Once you've added code for content types, you next need to decide how you will handle versioning, even though you might never need it.

22.5 Just Put The Version in the URL

> This section's code is in the folder `22-05/` of the sample code.

Nothing gets a debate going around API design quite like versioning. Versioning is when you decide that you need to change an existing endpoint, but maintain both the original and the changed implementations.

There are two decisions you have to make around versioning. First is to decide what constitutes a new version. Second is how to model that in your API.

I would *highly* recommend you adopt a simplified semantic versioning policy for your APIs. Semantic Versioning[5] states that a version is three numbers separated by dots, for example 1.4.5. The first is the *major* version and when this changes, it indicates breaking changes to the underlying API. Code that worked with version 1 should expect to not work with version 2. Changes to the other two numbers (called *minor* and *patch*) indicate backwards compatible changes. Code that works with version 1.3.4 should work with 1.4.5.

For your API, don't track or worry about minor versions and patches—only track major versions. If you make backwards-compatible changes to an endpoint, leave the current version as it is. *Only* when you need to make a backwards-incompatible change should you bump the version number of the API.

I would make a few additional recommendations:

- Try to avoid making breaking changes if you can. Be *really* clear on what problem you are solving by changing your API in this way. Try to think through your API design to avoid having to do this.

---
[4]https://api.rubyonrails.org/classes/Mime/Type.html
[5]https://semver.org

- Version your endpoints, not your entire API. For example, if you decide you need a new version of the widgets API, do not also make your manufacturers API version 2. Doing this will create a version explosion in your API that will be hard to manage.
- Adopt a deprecation policy as well, so you can remove old versions.

Once you've adopted a versioning policy, you next need to decide how this gets implemented in your API. There are three common mechanisms for this:

- Put the version in the URL, for example /api/v1/widgets.
- Require a version in the `Accept:` header, for example `Accept: application/json; version=1`.
- Use a custom header that has the version, for example `X-API-Version: 1`.

The simplest thing to do is to put the version in the URL. Everyone on your team will understand this and it will make the most sense overall. Non-engineers will be able to understand it as well, because it's explicit.

I know that this may not feel correct, because the version should not be considered as part of a resource locator. While adhering to idealized standards is nice, if it conflicts with sustainability, we have to look out for ourselves and do what makes our lives easier. See the sidebar "Versioning Confusion at Stitch Fix" on the next page for an example of how using headers doesn't create a sustainable environment.

Let's change our fledgling API code to use the version in the URL. First, we'll change the `config/routes.rb` file:

```
# config/routes.rb

    # add it in the custom routes section, but make
    # sure the resource-based route is here.
    namespace :api do
→     namespace :v1 do
→       resources :widgets, only: [ :show ]
→     end
    end

    ####
```

Next, we'll move our widgets controller to the V1 namespace:

```
> mkdir app/controllers/api/v1 ; mv \
  app/controllers/api/widgets_controller.rb \
  app/controllers/api/v1
```

And then we'll change the name of the controller's class:

```
# app/controllers/api/v1/widgets_controller.rb

→ class Api::V1::WidgetsController < ApiController
    def show
      widget = Widget.find(params[:id])
      render json: { widget: widget }
```

Now, our URLs and classes match precisely, and the way versioning works is pretty obvious. These are good things!

Let's talk about JSON next.

> **Versioning Confusion at Stitch Fix**
>
> At Stitch Fix, we put the version of our API in the Accept header, and created some custom code to parse that version out. That code would then route requests to a controller that had the version number in it.
>
> For example, if you requested /api/shipments and set the Accept: header to "application/json; version=2", code in our routes file would direct that request to Api::V2::ShipmentsController. If you used "application/json; version=1", it would route to Api::V1::ShipmentsController. This felt very clean at the time.
>
> After several years of reflection and real-world use, I don't think it solved an actual problem. In fact, it created confusion. First, seeing a controller like Api::V2::ShipmentsController will cause most Rails developers to assume a URL of api/v2/shipments. But that's not how this worked.
>
> Developers also had to wrestle with setting the version in the Accept header. Granted, this is not that difficult to do, but it's unusual enough that it was just confusing.
>
> And, of course, when debugging, you couldn't just look at a URL and know what code was going to be executed. You had to examine the headers, and those are not logged automatically by Rails or most HTTP clients. Overall, this "more correct" approach made life difficult for everyone and didn't provide any real benefit.

22.6 Use .to_json to Create JSON

> This section's code is in the folder 22-06/ of the sample code.

Your data model has been (presumably) carefully designed to ensure correctness, reduce ambiguity, and model the data that's important to your business. Your app's various endpoints are all resourceful, using Active Model to create any other domain concepts you need that aren't covered by the Active Records.

It therefore stands to reason that your API's JSON should mimic these carefully-designed data structures. If your API must be so different from your domain model or database model that you need a separate set of classes to create the needed JSON, something may be wrong with your modeling.

This isn't to say that your JSON payloads won't need additional metadata, but if a widget in the database has a name, it will make the most sense to everyone if the JSON representation contains a key called "name" that maps to the widget's name, just like it does in the database and code.

Of course, it's possible as time goes by that there is some drift, but in my experience this is unlikely. Thus, the way you should form JSON should be to call to_json on an Active Record or Active Model, like so:

```ruby
class Api::WidgetsController < ApiController

  def show
    widget = Widget.find(params[:id])
    # Note that Rails automatically calls to_json for you
    render json: { widget: widget }
  end

end
```

If you find yourself building a custom hash, or creating an object specifically to render JSON in your API, you should stop and reconsider if what you are doing makes sense. Perhaps you are really in need of a new resource instead?

That said, you may need your API to add or omit certain fields. For example, you might want to inline a widget's manufacturer so that clients don't have to make another call. You may also wish to omit database keys or sensitive values.

You can accomplish all of this by using a few methods that Rails uses to render JSON.

22.6.1 How Rails Renders JSON

The standard library's JSON package adds the method `to_json` to pretty much every class, but it doesn't work quite the way Rails wants, nor the way we want for making an API. Rails changes this in Active Support[6].

Rails does this by creating a protocol for objects to turn themselves into hashes, which Rails then turns into actual JSON. The method that does this is `as_json`. All objects return a reasonable value for `as_json`. For example:

```
> bin/rails c
console> puts Widget.first.as_json
=> {
  "id"=>1,
  "name"=>"Stembolt",
  "price_cents"=>747894,
  "widget_status_id"=>2,
  "manufacturer_id"=>11,
  "created_at"=>"2020-06-20T20:01:22.687Z",
  "updated_at"=>"2020-06-20T20:01:22.687Z"
}
```

This even works for non-Active Records in the way you'd expect:

```
console> estimate = UserShippingEstimate.new(
    widget_name: "Stembolt", shipping_zone: 2
  )
console> puts estimate.as_json
=> {
  "widget_name"=>"Stembolt",
  "shipping_zone"=>2
}
```

When you call `render` in a controller like so:

```
render json: { widget: widget }
```

You are asking Rails to turn the hash `{ widget: widget }` into JSON. It will recursively turn the contents into JSON as well, meaning `to_json` is called on `widget`, and the implementation of `to_json` calls `as_json`.

Of course, the JSON Rails produces might not be *exactly* what you want. Because of the `as_json` protocol, you can customize what happens.

---

[6]https://github.com/rails/rails/blob/7-1-stable/activesupport/lib/active_support/core_ext/object/json.rb

22.6.2 Customizing JSON Serialization

The as_json method takes an optional argument called options. Every object in your Rails' app will respect two options passed to as_json, which are mutually exclusive:

- :except takes an array of attribute names (as strings) for attributes to exclude from the JSON.
- :only takes an array of attribute names (as strings) for the only attributes to include in the JSON.

For example:

```
console> estimate = UserShippingEstimate.new(
    widget_name: "Stembolt", shipping_zone: 2
)
console> puts estimate.as_json(only: "widget_name")
=> {"widget_name"=>"Stembolt"}

console> Widget.first.as_json(except: [ "id", "manufacturer_id" ])
=> {
  "name"=>"Stembolt",
  "price_cents"=>747894,
  "widget_status_id"=>2,
  "created_at"=>"2020-06-20T20:01:22.687Z",
  "updated_at"=>"2020-06-20T20:01:22.687Z"
}
```

Active Records accept additional options:

- :include is an array of attributes of related models to inline. You'll notice above that by default we only see the widget_status_id and not the status object. :include allows you to change that behavior.
- :methods is an array of symbols representing method names that should be called and included in the JSON output.

For example:

```
console> Widget.first.as_json(
    methods: [ :user_facing_identifier ],
    except: [ :widget_status_id ],
    include: [ :widget_status ]
)
=> {
  "id"=>1,
```

394

```
  "name"=>"Stembolt",
  "price_cents"=>747894,
  "manufacturer_id"=>11,
  "created_at"=>"2020-06-20T20:01:22.687Z",
  "updated_at"=>"2020-06-20T20:01:22.687Z",
  "user_facing_identifier"=>"1",
  "widget_status"=>{
    "id"=>2,
    "name"=>"facere",
    "created_at"=>"2020-06-20T20:01:22.677Z",
    "updated_at"=>"2020-06-20T20:01:22.677Z"
  }
}
```

Active Models don't get these extra options by default. To grant them such powers requires mixing in ActiveModel::Serializers::JSON and implementing the method attributes to return a hash of all the model's attributes and values.

Now that we know how JSON serialization can be customized how *should* we customize it?

22.6.3 Customize JSON in the Models Themselves

Suppose we wanted our widgets API to use the JSON encoding we showed above. We could certainly achieve this in our controller like so:

```ruby
def show
  widget = Widget.find(params[:id])

  render json: {
    widget: widget.as_json(
      methods: [ :user_facing_identifier ],
      except: [ :widget_status_id ],
      include: [ :widget_status ]
    )
  }
end
```

Of course, if we need to implement the index method, that code would want to use the same options. We could create a private method in Api::V1::WidgetsController called widget_json_options, but what if there is a third place to serialize a widget? For example, if you are using a messaging system, you might encode data in JSON to send into that system. There's no reason to use a different encoding, so how do you centralize the way widgets are encoded in JSON?

The simplest way is to override as_json in the Widget class itself. Doing that would ensure that anyone who called to_json on a widget would get the single serialization format you've designed.

This might feel uncomfortable. Why are we giving our models yet another responsibility? What if we really do want a different encoding sometimes? Shouldn't we separate concerns and have serialization live somewhere else?

These are valid questions, but we must again return to what Rails and Ruby actually are and how they actually work. Rails provides a to_json method on all objects. There are several places in Rails where an object is implicitly turned into JSON using that method. That method is implemented using as_json, which is also on every single object.

Given these truths, it makes the most sense to override as_json to explicitly define the default encoding of an object to JSON. If you *do* have need for a second way of encoding—and you should be very careful if you think you do—you can always call as_json with the right options.

Let's see how to write an as_json implementation to address all of our needs. We'll make options an optional argument, and for each option *we* want to set, we'll only set it if the caller has not.

```
# app/models/widget.rb

        },
        high_enough_for_legacy_manufacturers: true
      normalizes :name, with: ->(name) { name.blank? ? nil : name...
→     def as_json(options={})
→       options[:methods] ||= [ :user_facing_identifier ]
→       options[:except]  ||= [ :widget_status_id ]
→       options[:include] ||= [ :widget_status ]
→
→       super(options)
→     end
    end
```

You could also only set default options if options is empty. Either way, adopt one policy and follow that whenever you override as_json. I would also recommend a test for this behavior. I do want to stress the point about centralizing this in the model itself. This is, like many parts of Rails, a good default. You can override this when needed, but a good default makes things easier for everyone. It's easier for the team to get right, easier for others doing code review, and it matches the way Rails and Ruby actually *are*.

One last thing about JSON encoding is the use of top-level keys.

22.6.4 Always Use a Top Level Key

The example code we've seen thus far looks like this:

```
render json: { widget: widget }
```

Why didn't we write only `render json: widget`?

Doing that would result in a JSON object like so:

```
{
  "id": 1234,
  "name": "Stembolt",
  "price_cents": 12345
}
```

There are two minor problems with this as the way your API renders JSON. The first is that you cannot look at this JSON and know what it is without knowing what produced it. That's not a major issue, but when debugging it's *really* nice to have more explicit context if it's not too much hassle to provide.

The second problem is the potential need to include metadata like page numbers, related links, or other stuff that's particular to your app and not something that should go into an HTTP header. In that case, you'd need to merge the object's keys and values with those of your metadata. This will be confusing and potentially have conflicts.

A better solution is to include a top-level key for the object that contains the object's data. Our code does that by rendering `{ widget: widget }`, which produces this:

```
{
  "widget": {
    "id": 1234,
    "name": "Stembolt",
    "price_cents": 12345
```

        }
}

Now, if you have this JSON you have a good idea what it is. If you also need to include metadata, you can include that as a sibling to `"widget":` and keep it separated.

The problem that this solution creates is that you have to remember to set the top level key in your controllers.

I would *not* recommend doing this in `as_json`, because you wouldn't do this for an array. If you had an array of widgets, you'd want something like this:

```
{
  "widgets": [
    {
      "id": 1234,
      "name": "Stembolt",
      "price_cents": 12345
    },
    {
      "id": 2345,
      "name": "Thrombic Modulator",
      "price_cents": 9876
    }
  ]
}
```

Active Records can do this automatically by setting `include_root_in_json`, but this doesn't apply to any other objects, so I would recommend against using it. Doing so requires everyone to have to think about what sort of object they are serializing and whether or not the top-level key will be there. As we've seen in the past, architectural decisions that are of the form "always do X" are easier to remember and enforce. So, always put a top-level key in your controller `render` method.

That last thing to consider about APIs is tests.

22.7 Test API Endpoints

> This section's code is in the folder 22-07/ of the sample code.

Just as you'd test a major user flow (discussed in "Understand the Value and Cost of Tests" on page 181), you should test major flows around your

API. At the very least, each endpoint should have one test to make some assertions about the format of the response. While inadvertent changes to a UI can be annoying for users, such changes could be catastrophic for APIs. A test can help prevent this.

Your test should also use the authentication mechanism and content negotiation headers. Let's write a complete set of tests for all this against our widgets endpoint.

The tests of the API should be integration tests, which means they should be in test/integration. To keep them separated from any normal integration tests we might write, we'll use the same namespaces we used for the routes and controllers, and place our test in test/integration/api/v1/widgets_test.rb.

```ruby
# test/integration/api/v1/widgets_test.rb

require "test_helper"

class Api::V1::WidgetsTest < ActionDispatch::IntegrationTest
  # tests go here
end
```

We'll need to insert an API key into the database, then perform a get passing that key in the appropriate header, along with setting the Accept: header. Here's how that looks.

```ruby
# test/integration/api/v1/widgets_test.rb

  require "test_helper"

  class Api::V1::WidgetsTest < ActionDispatch::IntegrationTest
→   test "get a widget" do
→     api_key = FactoryBot.create(:api_key)
→     authorization = ActionController::
→                       HttpAuthentication::
→                         Token.encode_credentials(api_key.key)
→
→     widget = FactoryBot.create(:widget)
→
→     get api_v1_widget_path(widget),
→       headers: {
→         "Accept" => "application/json",
→         "Authorization" => authorization
```

```
          }

          assert_response :success

          parsed_response = JSON.parse(response.body)

          refute_nil parsed_response["widget"]

          assert_equal widget.name, parsed_response.dig("widget",
                                                       "name")
          assert_equal widget.price_cents,
                       parsed_response.dig("widget", "price_cents")
          assert_equal widget.user_facing_identifier,
                       parsed_response.dig("widget",
                                           "user_facing_identifier")
          assert_equal widget.widget_status.name,
                       parsed_response.dig("widget",
                                           "widget_status",
                                           "name")
     end
end
```

Whew! One thing to note is that we aren't testing all the fields that would be in the response as implemented. I would likely build this API by writing this test first, and then implement as_json to match the output.

It also depends on how strict you want to be. For JSON endpoints consumed by a JavaScript front-end in the app itself, it's probably OK if the payload has extra stuff in it. The more widely used the endpoint, the more beneficial it is to have exactly and only what is needed. You need to consider the carrying and opportunity costs to make sure you aren't over-investing.

We also need four more tests:

- A request without an API key gets a 401.
- A request with a non-existent API key gets a 401.
- A request with a real API key that's deactivated gets a 401.
- A request without a content-type gets a 406.

We could put them in the existing widgets_test.rb, but this would imply that each endpoint would require these four tests of what is essentially configuration inside ApiController. Let's instead create two more tests, one for authentication and one for content negotiation.

First, let's create test/integration/api/content_negotiation_test.rb:

```ruby
# test/integration/api/content_negotiation_test.rb

require "test_helper.rb"

class Api::ContentNegotiationTest < ActionDispatch::IntegrationTest
  test "a non-JSON Accept header gets a 406" do
    api_key = FactoryBot.create(:api_key)
    authorization = ActionController::
                      HttpAuthentication::
                        Token.encode_credentials(api_key.key)

    widget = FactoryBot.create(:widget)

    get api_v1_widget_path(widget),
      headers: {
        "Accept" => "text/plain",
        "Authorization" => authorization
      }

    assert_response 406
  end
  test "missing Accept header gets a 406" do
    api_key = FactoryBot.create(:api_key)
    authorization = ActionController::
                      HttpAuthentication::
                        Token.encode_credentials(api_key.key)

    widget = FactoryBot.create(:widget)

    get api_v1_widget_path(widget),
      headers: {
        "Authorization" => authorization
      }

    assert_response 406
  end
end
```

If we end up with more nuanced content negotiation, tests for it can go here. Next, we'll test authentication in api/authentication_test.rb:

```ruby
# test/integration/api/authentication_test.rb
```

```ruby
require "test_helper.rb"

class Api::AuthenticationTest < ActionDispatch::IntegrationTest
  test "without an API key, we get a 401" do
    widget = FactoryBot.create(:widget)

    get api_v1_widget_path(widget),
      headers: {
        "Accept" => "application/json",
      }

    assert_response 401
  end

  test "with a non-existent API key, we get a 401" do
    authorization = ActionController::
                      HttpAuthentication::
                        Token.encode_credentials("not real")

    widget = FactoryBot.create(:widget)

    get api_v1_widget_path(widget),
      headers: {
        "Accept" => "application/json",
        "Authorization" => authorization
      }

    assert_response 401
  end

  test "with a deactivated API key, we get a 401" do
    api_key = FactoryBot.create(:api_key,
                                  deactivated_at: Time.zone.now)
    authorization = ActionController::
                      HttpAuthentication::
                        Token.encode_credentials(api_key.key)

    widget = FactoryBot.create(:widget)

    get api_v1_widget_path(widget),
      headers: {
        "Accept" => "application/json",
        "Authorization" => authorization
      }

    assert_response 401
  end
```

```
end
```

Again, if we had more complex requirements or use-cases around authentication, it can go there. Note that we're using the widgets endpoint in these tests. That's a convenience since we have the endpoint built. You could create a special one just for testing, but it's always better to test code that actually needs to exist for real reasons and not code that exists only artificially.

These tests should all pass:

```
> bin/rails test test/integration/api/authentication_test.rb \
    test/integration/api/content_negotiation_test.rb \
    test/integration/api/v1/widgets_test.rb
Running 6 tests in a single process (parallelization thresho...
Run options: --seed 40882

# Running:

......

Finished in 0.177152s, 33.8692 runs/s, 62.0935 assertions/s.
6 runs, 11 assertions, 0 failures, 0 errors, 0 skips
```

One issue that will come up if we add more API endpoints is duplication around setting up an API key and setting all the headers when calling the API from a test. As I've suggested in several other places, watch for a pattern and extract some better tooling. It's likely you'll want a base `ApiTest` that extends `ActionDispatch::IntegrationTest` that all your API tests then extend, but don't get too eager making abstractions until you see the need.

Up Next

Next, we'll move even farther outside your Rails app to talk about some workflows and techniques to help with sustainability, such as continuous integration and generators.

23
Sustainable Process and Workflows

Up to this point, we've mostly talked about the code in your Rails app. Way back in "Start Your App Off Right" on page 33, we created some scripts in bin, like bin/dev and bin/ci, which help with working on the app itself. In this chapter, I want to talk about a few other techniques that can help with sustainability of the team overall.

The techniques here are some I've used in earnest on both small and large teams and they should provide you value as well. Of course, there are many other techniques, workflows, and processes to make your team productive and development sustainable. Hopefully, learning about these processes can inspire you to prioritize team and process sustainability.

Let's start off with one that you might already be doing: continuous integration.

23.1 Use Continuous Integration To Deploy

> This section's code is in the folder 23-01/ of the sample code.

The risks mitigated by tests only happen if we are paying attention to our tests and fixing the code that's broken. Similarly, the checks we put into bin/ci for vulnerabilities in dependent libraries and analysis of the code we wrote only provide value if we do something about them.

The best way to do all that is to use a system for deployment that won't deploy code if any of our quality checks are failing. This creates a virtuous cycle of incentives for us developers. We want our code in production doing what it was meant to do. If the only way to do that is to make sure the tests are passing and there are no obvious security vulnerabilities, we'll address that.

The most common way to set all this up is to set up *continuous integration*, or *CI*.

23.1.1 What is CI?

The conventional meaning of CI is a system that runs all tests and checks of every branch pushed to a central repository[1]. When the tests and checks pass on some designated main branch, that branch is deployed to production.

This enables a common workflow as outlined in the figure "Basic CI Workflow" on the next page. This workflow allows developers to create branches with proposed changes and have bin/ci execute on the CI server to make sure all tests and checks pass. The team can do code reviews as necessary. When both bin/ci and code reviews are good, the change can be merged onto the main branch for deployment. bin/ci is run yet again to make sure the merged codebase passes all tests and checks and, if it does, the change is deployed to production.

This is a sustainable workflow, and I daresay it's not terribly new or controversial. What I want to talk about is how to make sure this process continues to be sustainable.

23.1.2 CI Configuration Should be Explicit and Managed

There are two main problems that happen with using CI. The first is that the test suite becomes so long that developers start skipping it in order to deploy. The second is that when CI fails even though the code is actually working properly, it can require an unwelcome diversion to fix the CI configuration to make the tests pass.

Both of these problems can be fixed by having an explicit CI configuration, and a commitment to manage it like any other part of the app.

Many services that provide continuous integration for developers have slick, zero-configuration on-boarding. Particularly if you are using Rails, services like Circle CI and CodeShip can automagically set everything up for you and run your tests without any configuration.

This is not sustainable. Eventually, you will run into a problem with the implicit configuration and have to debug it. This will be difficult and will happen when you aren't planning for it. My experience in this situation is that teams provide a quick-fix solution to unblock themselves and never go back to think deeply about how CI is configured and set up. This ensures the cycle repeats itself whenever it is least convenient for you and your team.

Fortunately, most CI services allow you to configure exactly what you want to happen, including the version of your database, the port it's running on, and anything else you might need. The CI service providers don't tell you

---

[1] The original meaning of CI was that all code was frequently integrated into some sort of main trunk of development to avoid too many diversions and conflicts within the code. The phrase "continuous integration" has somewhat lost this original meaning, with some teams using the term *trunk-based development* instead. When I talk about CI, I'm talking about using a central repository to run tests and deploy. *This* is the value I'm discussing. I can't speak to trunk-based development as I've never done that in a team-based environment.

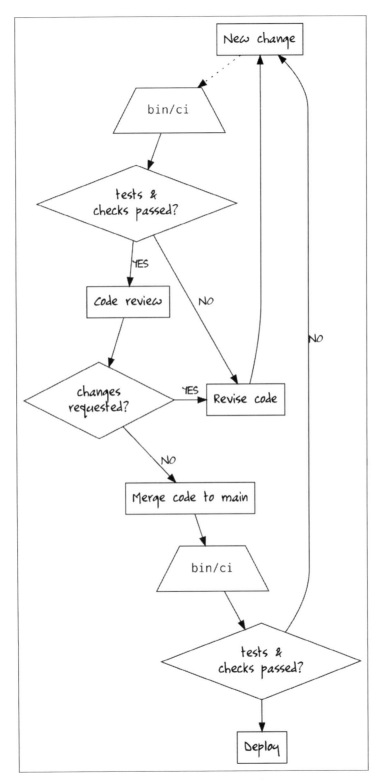

Figure 23.1: Basic CI Workflow

about this up front as it can feel daunting. But explicit configuration is sustainable.

CI is something you don't want to have to constantly manage, so it makes sense to spend as much time as you need up front creating a sustainable, explicit configuration. The reason is that the configuration inevitably breaks, meaning your app is working properly, but you can't prove it on CI because of a problem with the CI configuration itself.

When this happens, one or more developers will have to debug the configuration. If that configuration is verbose, clear, explicit, and well-documented, developers can quickly get up to speed on learning what might be a completely new set of tools for the first time.

Said another way, an explicit configuration means that more team members will be able to modify it when needed, and this contributes to an overall cultural value that maintaining this configuration is important. Make it clear to the team that this configuration, since it is the automation for production deploys, is just as critical as any feature of the app. Any work needed around CI should be prioritized and completed quickly.

A great way to address all of this is to use your development environment scripts in bin/ as part of the CI configuration.

23.1.3 CI Should be Based on bin/setup and bin/ci

Your initial CI configuration should basically run bin/setup followed by bin/ci. When this is run on some sort of designated main branch, the CI system should additionally deploy the code to production. By using your development environment scripts to power your CI configuration, you ensure that they are working, even if developers aren't running them frequently. Keeping bin/setup working is a boon to productivity and this is exactly how you make sure that happens.

Of course, it's not always possible for the exact bin/setup script to work in the CI environment. Sometimes, you can modify your CI environment so that it matches development, even if the defaults for your CI system don't initially match. For example, you could configure your CI system's Postgres to use the same username and password you use locally. This is ideal, because it means you don't have to change bin/setup.

If you can't change CI directly, another way to manage this is to leverage .env.development.local and .env.test.local. Those files aren't checked in, but they will override the values in .env.development and .env.test, respectively, if they exist. Thus, you can modify bin/setup to detect if it's running in CI and, if it is, dynamically generate those two files with CI-specific settings. Those files will only exist on the CI servers and won't necessitate further changes to your setup or test scripts.

For example, suppose that Redis in your CI environment is running on a host named ci-redis and on port 3456. That's not how your development environment works, so you can manage this by creating .env.development.local and .env.test.local in bin/setup. To detect if your script is running locally or on the CI server, most CI servers set an environment variable called CI. We'll assume that is the case here.

Here's an example of how to make bin/setup work on both local development and on the CI server:

```
# bin/setup

require "optparse"

def setup
→  if ENV["CI"] == "true"
→    log "Running in CI environment"
→
→    log "Creating .env.development.local"
→    File.open(".env.development.local","w") do |file|
→      file.puts "REDIS_URL=redis://ci-redis:3456/1"
→    end
→
→    log "Creating .env.test.local"
→    File.open(".env.test.local","w") do |file|
→      file.puts "REDIS_URL=redis://ci-redis:3456/2"
→    end
→  elsif ENV["CI"] != nil
→    # Detect if what we believe to be true about the CI env var
→    # is, in fact, still the case.
→    fail "Problem: CI is set to #{ENV['CI']}, but we expect " +
→         "either 'true' or nil"
→  else
→    log "Assuming we are running in a local development environment"
→  end
   log "Installing gems"
   # Only do bundle install if the much-faster
   # bundle check indicates we need to
```

Because you've configured your app with environment variables, this technique can handle most needs to customize behavior in CI. That said, you are going to be much better off if you can directly configure CI to use your settings.

If changing the environment doesn't fix an issue with inconsistent behavior, you can always use the environment variable check in bin/setup to do further customizations. Be careful with this as it means that any code you *aren't* running in CI won't get executed frequently.

Another issue with CI that can happen as your app ages is that the test suite becomes longer and it takes longer to do deploys. *Throughput* is a key metric for many teams that illustrates how effective they are in delivering value. In times of stress, teams can "solve" this problem by disabling tests in CI or simply skipping tests entirely. This will absolutely destroy team morale over time *and* lead to lower productivity. It can be extremely hard to recover from. Never do this.

You can certainly try to make your tests faster, but this can be time consuming and not terribly fruitful. Most CI services allow you to split your tests and checks and run them in parallel. One way to do this is to run system tests—which are typically quite slow—in parallel to your other tests. In our app, we might want to run system tests and unit tests in parallel and, in a third workstream, run our JS tests followed by all the security audits (Brakeman and bundle audit).

To do that without duplicating any code, we could break up our bin/ci script into sub-scripts. For example, bin/ci might look like this:

```
##!/usr/bin/env bash

set -e

bin/unit-tests
bin/system-tests
bin/security-audits
```

Each of these new scripts would contain the commands previously in bin/ci:

```
> cat bin/unit-tests
##!/usr/bin/env bash

set -e

echo "[ bin/ci ] Running unit tests"
bin/rails test

> cat bin/system-tests
##!/usr/bin/env bash

set -e
```

```
echo "[ bin/ci ] Running system tests"
bin/rails test:system

> cat bin/security-audits
##!/usr/bin/env bash

set -e

echo "[ bin/ci ] Analyzing code for security vulnerabilities."
echo "[ bin/ci ] Output will be in tmp/brakeman.html, which"
echo "[ bin/ci ] can be opened in your browser."
bundle exec brakeman -q -o tmp/brakeman.html

echo "[ bin/ci ] Analyzing Ruby gems for"
echo "[ bin/ci ] security vulnerabilities"
bundle exec bundle audit check --update
```

Even though a script like bin/system-tests is one line of code, it functions as a protocol we can enhance, just like all of our bin/ scripts. We can then use these scripts in our CI configuration so that if, say, what is required to run JavaScript tests changes over time, we only need to change it in one place.

With these scripts broken out, you can then configure your CI system to run them in parallel as described above and as shown in the figure "Parallel Testing With Scripts" on the next page.

When your CI system runs security audits regularly, you will find that many of your dependencies have security vulnerabilities and you'll be updating them frequently. This leads to the next technique, which is to update your dependencies on a regular basis, regardless of existing security vulnerabilities.

23.2 Frequent Dependency Updates

> This section's code is in the folder 23-02/ of the sample code.

In September 2018, GitHub posted a blog entry[2] about their 18-month journey to upgrade Rails from a very out-of-date version to the latest version at the time (5.2). I have observed a similar project on a slightly smaller scale, and it required the most talented and experienced engineers at the company to be successful.

But I can't help feeling that GitHub should've never been in this position in the first place. If it were me, I would've much rather had the members of that

---

[2] https://github.blog/2018-09-28-upgrading-github-from-rails-3-2-to-5-2/

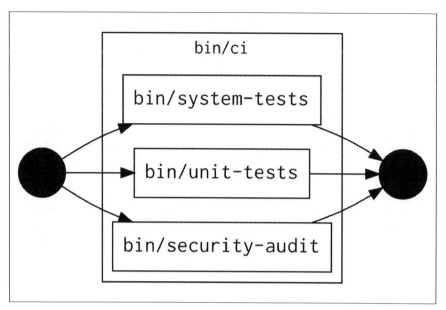

Figure 23.2: Parallel Testing With Scripts

team driving customer value directly than spending *over a year* upgrading a piece of technology. While the team did a lot of hard and amazing work, the decisions that lead to needing that work at all weren't made in the interest of sustainability.

One way to avoid this is to update dependencies frequently and try to stay up-to-date.

23.2.1 Update Dependencies Early and Often

At Stitch Fix, we decided early on that we would not have this problem. Our solution was to schedule monthly dependency updates. This meant that one day each month, we'd run `bundle update` in our Rails apps, run the tests, fix what was broken, and then be up to date. This didn't come for free, but we wanted to be on the latest stable versions of everything as frequently as we could.

This worked. We never had a team dedicated to upgrading Ruby or Rails. We never had to spend months and months on a Rails upgrade. Sure, the upgrade to Rails 4.2 wasn't pleasant, and it certainly took more than a few days, but I would say it went more or less without incident.

I highly suggest you make this part of your team culture. If you *don't* have a culture of always being on the latest version of the code you use, you will one day be required to stop everything you are doing and perform an update due to a critical security bug. This will be unpleasant. I had to do this once, and it required rewriting a gem we used from scratch because it had not been updated for the version of Rails we had to upgrade to.

Being on the latest version of your tools has many other benefits. Potential team members are much more excited to use the latest versions of tools than have to deal with out-of-date versions. If you have a security team, their job becomes much easier and you'll have a much better relationship with them. And, of course, you get access to new features of the tools you are using relatively quickly.

The hardest part of this process is managing it as the size of the team grows. The reason is that it's hard to put incentives in place to prevent teams from skipping these updates. Part of this is because the updates—and fixes they often require—aren't free and aren't always enjoyable work. There's not a natural short-term incentive for engineers to do this or for their managers to prioritize it (which is why having it as part of the culture can help).

You can ensconce this cultural value in your tools. Depending on the sophistication of your deployment toolchain, you can bake minimum required versions into it. For example, at Stitch Fix, our deployment tools would not work with any version of Ruby other than the most recent two versions. If you fell behind on updates, you couldn't deploy. It's not the most pleasant motivator, but it did work.

Outside of this, it really is a cultural value you have to bake into the team. Frequently explaining the need for it helps. Empathizing with how unpleasant it can be helps, too, and equitably rotating who's responsible each month can create some camaraderie on the team while avoiding the work always falling to the same person.

To help codify this value, you should create a basic versioning policy. Here is one that I recommend and that will serve you well.

23.2.2 A Versioning Policy

A *policy* might sound draconian, but trust me, it helps to have agreed-upon conventions written down when they can't be baked into code. It also helps to put, in writing, exactly why the team does certain things.

This is what I recommend:

- Use only the latest two minor versions of Ruby. Each December, when Ruby is updated, schedule time in January to update any apps on what is the third most-recent version. For example, in December of 2021, Ruby 3.1 was released, and so all apps using 2.7 would've been updated to at least 3.0.
- Use this exact same policy for Rails. All apps should be on the latest or second-latest version. Rails releases are less regular, but teams should budget some time each year to doing an upgrade of a minor version of Rails.

- Use this exact same policy for NodeJS, if you are using it.
- In your `Gemfile`, specify a pessimistic version constraint for Rails to keep it on the current minor version. Running a `bundle update` and getting a new minor version of Rails is not a great surprise. You want to control when the Rails version is updated.
- For as many other dependencies as you can, set no version constraint whatsoever. Let Bundler sort out the version that goes with your version of Rails.
- Note that if you are using NodeJS, there may be dependencies between some gems and some modules in `package.json`. Because JSON does not allow for comments, write comments in `Gemfile` that indicate dependencies between gems and Node modules.
- For any gem you must pin to a particular version, *write a code comment in the* `Gemfile` about why you have done this, and under what circumstances you should remove the pin. Don't let Agile Thought Leaders tell you that comments are bad. Write a novel if you have to to explain what's going on and how to tell if the reason for pinning the version still exists.

Once you have your policy, and you've set expectations with teams to do updates, there's just no getting around the difficulty of doing the actual updates and fixing whatever the break. You can make the process a bit easier by providing some automation.

23.2.3 Automate Dependency Updates

GitHub provides a feature called *Dependabot*, which will update your dependencies frequently, then open a pull request with those changes. This will trigger your CI build to let you know that everything is—or is not—working. You can even configure things so that these pull requests are automatically merged and deployed if the tests pass. This is probably a good thing to set up early on, though it can be hard to migrate to for an older app.

Another option is to at least automate how you'd update dependencies in your app, and then commit to running that automation on a regular basis.

Let's do that, by creating `bin/update`. This will do a few things. First, it will run `bundle update`. This command instructs Bundler to find the latest version of all dependencies that satisfy what is in `Gemfile`.

If you've followed the policy above, that should give you the latest point release of the minor version of Rails you are using, and the latest version of all gems that are compatible with that version of Rails.

As a reminder and check that you may still be behind the latest, we'll then execute `bundle outdated`. This will tell you if there are newer versions available of any gems you are using, regardless of what versions are in your `Gemfile`. This can help if you've temporarily pinned gems to get around an issue and could unpin them. The script will then run bin/ci to see if the updates have broken anything.

```sh
# bin/update

#!/bin/sh

set -e

echo "[ bin/update ] Updating Ruby gems"
bundle update

# Turning off exit-on-error because the outdated commands
# will usually exit nonzero and we don't want them
# to abort this script
set +e

echo "[ bin/update ] Checking for outdated gems"
bundle outdated

echo "[ bin/update ] If anything is outdated, you may have"
echo "[ bin/update ] overly conservative versions pinned"
echo "[ bin/update ] in your Gemfile"
echo "[ bin/update ] You should remove these pins if possible"
echo "[ bin/update ] and see if the app works with the "
echo "[ bin/update ] latest versions"

echo "[ bin/update ] Running bin/ci"
bin/ci
```

We'll make it executable:

```
> chmod +x bin/update
```

Let's run it. I'm going to include the massive output for this run so you can see what it looks like. All the tools that are brought together create a real hodge-podge of messy output. bundle outdated will say something like "No vulnerabilities detected" to indicate success. There may also be some odd git-related messages due to how I'm running this for the book. You may not see those, but if you do, they can be ignored.

```
> bin/update
[ bin/update ] Updating Ruby gems
```

```
Fetching gem metadata from https://rubygems.org/..........
Resolving dependencies...
Bundle updated!
[ bin/update ] Checking for outdated gems
Fetching gem metadata from https://rubygems.org/..........
Resolving dependencies...

Bundle up to date!
[ bin/update ] If anything is outdated, you may have
[ bin/update ] overly conservative versions pinned
[ bin/update ] in your Gemfile
[ bin/update ] You should remove these pins if possible
[ bin/update ] and see if the app works with the
[ bin/update ] latest versions
[ bin/update ] Running bin/ci
[ bin/ci ] Running unit tests
Running 25 tests in a single process (parallelization thresh...
Run options: --seed 40731

# Running:

...............2023-12-04T23:56:52.495Z pid=11210 tid=bqm IN...
..........

Finished in 0.222227s, 112.4978 runs/s, 274.4947 assertions/...
25 runs, 61 assertions, 0 failures, 0 errors, 0 skips
[ bin/ci ] Running system tests
Running 4 tests in a single process (parallelization thresho...
Run options: --seed 64495

# Running:

.2023-12-04T23:56:53.516Z pid=11213 tid=bqh INFO: Sidekiq 7....
.Rack::Handler is deprecated and replaced by Rackup::Handler
Capybara starting Puma...
* Version 6.4.0 , codename: The Eagle of Durango
* Min threads: 0, max threads: 4
* Listening on http://127.0.0.1:33133
..

Finished in 1.248793s, 3.2031 runs/s, 8.8085 assertions/s.
4 runs, 11 assertions, 0 failures, 0 errors, 0 skips
[ bin/ci ] Analyzing code for security vulnerabilities.
[ bin/ci ] Output will be in tmp/brakeman.html, which
[ bin/ci ] can be opened in your browser.
[ bin/ci ] Analyzing Ruby gems for
[ bin/ci ] security vulnerabilities
```

```
Updating ruby-advisory-db ...
From https://github.com/rubysec/ruby-advisory-db
 * branch            master     -> FETCH_HEAD
Already up to date.
Updated ruby-advisory-db
ruby-advisory-db:
  advisories:   827 advisories
  last updated: 2023-11-30 12:36:04 -0800
  commit:    d821bf162550302abd1fa1fe15007f3012b76f32
No vulnerabilities found
[ bin/ci ] Done
```

In addition to shell scripts that automate common tasks, there are some other techniques around automation that I want to talk about next. The first is using templates and generators to create boilerplate code.

23.3 Leverage Generators and Sample Repositories over Documentation

The first step to establishing a convention is to write it down. For example, putting business logic in app/services might be something a team would document in a README. A team might also write down examples of how to write a job or a controller.

In addition to basic automation like we did with bin/setup and bin/dev, or automatically generated documentation like we did with our style guide, automatically generating code for common use-cases can be far more compelling than documentation, especially when the boilerplate is somewhat complicated.

There are three types of code generation you may encounter:

- Creating new files in your Rails app, like we did with View Components
- Creating RubyGems to manage shared code across apps
- Creating entirely new Rails apps

23.3.1 Create and Configure Rails Generators

Many third party Rails gems come with generators. The Rails Guide[3] walks you through how to make one, and I would highly recommend you use this to codify any architecture decisions you make. On a recent project, I created a generator for creating a service.

Rails generators work well and can be tested, but exhibit undesirable behavior under certain failure modes. The primary cause is due to their core

---
[3] https://guides.rubyonrails.org/generators.html

API, which is based on Thor[4]. The API used by generators is based around searching and replacing strings in files, either by regular expression or exact matches.

For example, you might write code like so to add a `require` statement to `config/routes.rb`. This code says to search the file `config/routes.rb` for the string `"Rails.application.routes.draw do"` and insert the string `"require \"sidekiq/web\"\n\n"` before it.

```ruby
insert_into_file "config/routes.rb",
  "require \"sidekiq/web\"\n\n",
  before: "Rails.application.routes.draw do"
```

The problem is if the string isn't found in the file, Thor does not consider this an error. The generator will not report any problem and continue with its operation, leaving you with the impression that the generator worked when, in reality, it absolutely did not.

You can monkey-patch Thor to get around this issue, and if you make heavy use of generators, I suggest you do this. You can add this code anywhere before your generators run:

```ruby
require "thor"
class Thor::Actions::InjectIntoFile

  protected

  # Copied from lib/thor/actions/inject_into_file.rb so I can
  # raise if the regexp fails
  def replace!(regexp, string, force)
    return if pretend?
    content = File.read(destination)
    if force || !content.include?(replacement)
      # BEGIN CHANGE
      result = content.gsub!(regexp, string)
      if result.nil?
        raise "Regexp didn't match: #{regexp}:\n#{string}"
      end
      # END CHANGE
      # ORIGINAL CODE
      # content.gsub!(regexp, string)
      # END ORIGINAL CODE
```

[4]https://github.com/erikhuda/thor

```ruby
      File.open(destination, "wb") { |file| file.write(content) }
    end
  end
end

module Thor::Actions
  # Copied from lib/thor/actions/file_manipulation.rb
  def gsub_file(path, flag, *args, &block)
    return unless behavior == :invoke
    config = args.last.is_a?(Hash) ? args.pop : {}

    path = File.expand_path(path, destination_root)
    say_status :gsub,
               relative_to_original_destination_root(path),
               config.fetch(:verbose, true)

    unless options[:pretend]
      content = File.binread(path)
      # BEGIN CHANGE
      result = content.gsub!(flag, *args, &block)
      if result.nil?
        raise "Regexp didn't match #{flag}:\n#{content}"
      end
      # END CHANGE
      # ORIGINAL CODE: content.gsub!(flag, *args, &block)
      File.open(path, "wb") { |file| file.write(content) }
    end
  end
end
```

With this change, any time an attempt to replace code in a file using a regular expression fails, Thor will raise an error instead of doing nothing.

Despite this issue, generators are superior to documentation, since the execute your architectural and design decisions.

For Ruby Gems or entirely new Rails apps, you could also use generators, but I would recommend template repositories instead.

23.3.2 Use Template Repositories for Ruby Gems and Rails Apps

Bundler includes the `bundle gem` command to create a new Ruby Gem. `bundle gem` is a nice idea, but it doesn't provide very much beyond creating a few files for you. On your team, you'll want gems created in a particular way, perhaps with your own ancillary gems, version of Ruby, CI scripts, or gemspec.

While `bundle gem` has improved over the years, and does provide some flexibility, you'll still need to document which command line flags your team should use and this tends to eliminate many of the gains you get from code generation.

Rails provides "app templates" that work similarly to create a new Rails app. You can give `rails` the `--template` flag that will expect to contain many calls to Thor's API to create a Rails app. This suffers all the problems of using Thor we discussed above, but is exceedingly hard to test, with behavior that's hard to predict and control.

The solution to both of these issues is to use *template repositories*. This means that you'd use `bundle gem` or `rails new --template` to create an example gem or app, then manually tweak it how you like it. When a developer needs to create a new gem or Rails app, they clone that template as a starting point.

Template repositories aren't an amazing solution, but they offer you more predictability and control than using `bundle gem` or Rails app templates. At Stitch Fix, we used a Rails app template for all Rails apps and it was perpetually in a state of being only kindof working. A template repository would've been easier to use and maintain.

This section is a bit of a warning, but *any* automation is better than documentation. Documentation gets out of date quickly and can be extremely hard to follow, even for the most conscientious developer.

Speaking of Ruby Gems and Rails apps, if you do end up using multiple Rails apps (which we'll discuss in more detail in "Monoliths, Microservices, and Shared Databases" on page 453), it will be advantageous to share configuration across those apps. You can do this via RubyGems and Railties.

23.4 RubyGems and Railties Can Distribute Configuration

When you have more than one Rails application, there are often libraries you want to share between apps and those libraries require a common setup. For example, you might use a message bus like RabbitMQ or Apache Kafka for asynchronous communication. You might have a library that provides simplified access to the system, along with configuration settings such as network timeouts or error handling behavior.

Or, you might have a convention around using, say, Bugsnag as your exception-handling service, and want to have a single set of configuration settings for all apps.

A common way to manage this is to provide documentation about what to do. Or, if you've been inspired by the previous section, you could use code generation via a generator or template.

A better solution to this particular problem is to use Railties embedded in Ruby gems. Railties is a core component of how Rails works and is the API for customizing Rails' initialization procedure. By putting a Railtie inside a Ruby gem, we can automatically insert configuration into any Rails app that bundles that gem.

Let's see how it works by creating an exception-handling gem that configures and sets up Bugsnag, a common exception-handling service. Exception-handling services like Bugsnag receive reports about any exception that your app doesn't explicitly handle. These reports can alert an on-call engineer to investigate what could be a problem with the app (Airbrake and Rollbar are two other examples you may have heard of).

This example is going to be a bit contrived, because we only have one Rails app in our running example, and in the real world you would configure Bugsnag in the one and only app you have. But, to demonstrate the point, we'll imagine that we have several Rails apps that all use Bugsnag and that we want to have a common configuration.

First, let's see what this configuration is that we want to share. Let's suppose in our case, we want to configure:

- the API Key used with the service.
- the Rails environments in which errors are actually reported.
- the Git SHA-1 of the application in which an error occurs.
- some common exceptions we *don't* want reported.

Without using our to-be-implemented gem that uses Railties, the configuration would live in `config/initializers/bugsnag.rb` and look like so (assuming we are hosted on Heroku):

```ruby
## config/initializers/bugsnag.rb
Bugsnag.configure do |config|
  config.api_key = ENV.fetch("BUGSNAG_API_KEY")
  config.app_version = ENV.fetch("HEROKU_RELEASE_VERSION")
  config.notify_release_stages = ["production"]

  config.ignore_classes << ActiveRecord::RecordNotFound
end
```

This is the configuration we want to share. Don't worry too much if you don't know what's going on here. The point is that we don't want each application to have to duplicate this information or, worse, do something different. See the sidebar "Every Environment Variable is Precious" below for an example of what happens if you don't manage environment variable names.

> **Every Environment Variable Name is Precious**
>
> At Stitch Fix, there was a point where the team was around 50 developers and we had around 30 Rails apps in production as part of a microservices architecture. We had a gem that was used for consuming microservices, but the gem failed to bake in a convention about how to name the environment variable that held the API key.
>
> The result was that some apps would use SHIPPING_SERVICE_PASSWORD, some SHIPPING_API_KEY, some SHIPPING_SERVICE_KEY, and others SHIP_SVC_APIKEY. It was a mess. But, microservices *did* allow this mess to not affect the team as a whole. Until we needed to rotate all of these keys.
>
> A third party we used had a major security breach and there was a possibility that our keys could've been leaked. Rather than wait around to find out, we decided to rotate every single internal API key. If the environment variables for these keys were all the same, it would've taken a single engineer a few hours to write a script to do the rotation.
>
> Instead, it took six engineers an entire week to first make the variables consistent and *then* do the rotation. According to Glassdoor, an entry-level software engineer makes $75,000 a year, which meant this inconsistency cost us at least $9,000. The six engineers that did this were not entry-level, so you can imagine the true cost.
>
> Inconsistency is not a good thing. The consistency we paid for that week did, at least, have a wonderful return when we had to tighten our security posture before going public. The platform team was able to leverage our new-found consistent variable names to script a daily key rotation of all keys in less time and fewer engineers than it took to make the variable names consistent.

I'm not going to show all the steps for making a Ruby gem, but let's look at the gemspec we would have, as well as the main source code for the gem to see how it fits together.

First we have the gemspec, which brings in the Bugsnag gem:

```ruby
## example_com_bugsnag.gemspec
## NOTE: this file is not in a rails app!

spec = Gem::Specification.new do |s|
  s.name = 'example_com_bugsnag'
  s.version = "1.0.0"
  s.platform = Gem::Platform::RUBY
  s.summary = "Provides access and configuration to Bugsnag " +
              "for Example.Com apps"
  s.description = "Include this in your Gemfile and you will " +
                  "now have Bugsnag configured"
```

```
  # This assumes you are using Git for version control
  s.files         = `git ls-files`.split("\n")
  s.test_files    =
    `git ls-files -- {test,spec,features}/*`.split("\n")
  s.require_paths = ["lib"]

  s.add_dependency("bugsnag")
end
```

Since we used add_dependency for the Bugsnag gem, that means when an app installs *this* gem, the Bugsnag gem will be brought in as a transitive dependency. In a sense, this gem we are creating owns the relationship between our apps and Bugsnag—our apps don't own that relationship directly.

What we want is to have the above configuration executed automatically just by including the example_com_bugsnag gem. We can do this using two different behaviors of a Rails codebase. The first is Bundler, which will auto-require files for us.

When we put this into our Gemfile:

```
## Gemfile

gem "example_com_bugsnag"
```

Bundler will require the file in our gem located at lib/example_com_bugsnag.rb. This is because in config/application.rb of all Rails apps is this line of code:

```
## config/application.rb

Bundler.require(*Rails.groups)
```

Bundler.require will use require to bring in all RubyGems in our Gemfile (unless you specify require: false for that gem in the Gemfile).

We could dump all of the above code into lib/example_com_bugsnag.rb, but executing code just by requiring a file can lead to confusing problems later. We also can't exactly control when the require happens. This leads to the second piece of the puzzle: Railties.

If we put the following code in `lib/example_com_bugsnag.rb`, it will tell Rails to run this code as if it were in `config/initailizers.rb`:

```
## lib/example_com_bugsnag.rb
class ExampleComBugsnag < Rails::Railtie
  initializer "example_com_bugsnag" do |app|
    Bugsnag.configure do |config|
      config.api_key = ENV.fetch("BUGSNAG_API_KEY")
      config.app_version = ENV.fetch("HEROKU_RELEASE_VERSION")
      config.notify_release_stages = ["production"]

      config.ignore_classes << ActiveRecord::RecordNotFound
    end
  end
end
```

This will register the block of code passed to `initializer` with Rails and, whenever Rails loads the files in `config/initializers`, it will also execute this block of code, thus configuring Bugsnag. This means that with a single line of code in the `Gemfile`, any Rails app will have the canonical configuration for using Bugsnag.

And, if this configuration should ever change, you can change it, release a new version of the gem, and then, because teams are doing frequent dependency updates as discussed on page 411, the configuration update will naturally be applied to each app as the team does their updates.

This technique allows you to centralize a lot of configuration options across many apps without complex infrastructure and without a lot of documentation or other manual work. We used this technique at Stitch Fix to manage shared configuration for over 50 different Rails apps, including rolling out a highly critical database connection update in a matter of hours.

Up Next

There are likely many more workflows and techniques for sustainable development than the ones I've shared here. While these specific techniques *do* work well, your team should explicitly prioritize looking for new techniques and workflows to automate. The opportunity cost of creating shared gems, scripts, or other automation can really reduce carrying costs over time. It's a worthwhile investment.

The next chapter will be about considerations for actually operating your app in production, namely how to consider things like monitoring, logging, and secrets management.

24

Operations

I've alluded to the notion that code in production is what's important, but I want to say that explicitly right now: if your code is not in production it creates a carrying cost with nothing to offset it—an unsustainable situation.

However, being responsible for code running in production is a much different proposition than writing code whose tests pass and that you can use in your development environment. Seeing your code actually solve real users' problems and actually provide the value it's meant to provide can be a sometimes harrowing learning experience about what it means to develop software. Of course, it's also extremely rewarding.

That's what this chapter is about. Well, it's really a paltry overview of what is a deep topic, but it should give you some areas to think about and dig deeper into, along with a few basic tips for getting started.

Like may aspects of software development, production operations is a matter of a people and priorities: do you have the right people given the right priorities to make sure the app is operating in production in all the ways you need? For a small team just starting out, the answer is "no". Surprisingly, for larger teams, the answer might still be still "no"! I can't help you solve that.

What I'm going to try to help with in this chapter is understanding what aspects are important and what techniques are simplest or cheapest to do to get started. These techniques—like logging and exception management—will still be needed on even the most sophisticated team, so they'll serve you well no matter what.

As context, production operations should be driven by *observability*, which is your ability to understand the behavior of the system

24.1 Why Observability Matters

In "How and Why JavaScript is a Serious Liability" on page 157, I said, among other things, that JavaScript is difficult or impossible to observe in production, especially as compared to the back-end Rails code. What does that mean, exactly?

The term *observability* (as it applies to this conversation) originates in control theory, as explained in the Wikipedia entry[1]:

> In control theory, *observability* is a measure of how well internal states of a system can be inferred from knowledge of its external outputs.

Based on this definition, what I'm saying about JavaScript is that it's hard to understand what it actually did or is doing based just on what information gets sent back to our server (or can be examined in our browser). Even for backend code, it's not clear how to do this. Can you *really* look at your database and figure out how it got into that state?

Charity Majors has been largely responsible for applying the term "observability" to software development and I highly suggest reading in detail how she defines observability in software[2]. Her definition sets a very high bar that few teams—even highly sophisticated ones—operate the way she defines it. That's OK. As long as you start somewhere and keep improving, you'll get value out of your operations efforts.

The way I might summarize observability, such that it can drive our decision-making, is that observability is the degree to which you can explain what the software did in production and why it did that. For example, in "Understand What Happens When a Job Fails" on page 330, we discussed the notion of background jobs being automatically retried when they fail. If you notice an hourly job has not updated the database, how will you know if that job is going to be retried or simply failed?

The more aspects of the system you can directly examine and confirm, the more observable your system is, and this applies from low levels such as job control to high levels such as user transactions and business metrics. The more you can observe about your app's behavior, the better.

The reason is that if there is a problem (even if it's not with your app), someone will notice and eventually come calling wanting an explanation. From "the website is slow" to "sales are down 5% this month", problems *will* get noticed and, even if your app is running perfectly, you need to be able to actually *know* that.

For example, if the marketing team sees a dip in signups, and you can say, with certainty, that every single sign up attempt in the last month was successful, that helps marketing know where to look to explain the problem. If, on the other hand, you have no idea if your sign up code is working at all, you now have to go through the process of trying to prove it has been working... or not!

What all this says to me is that production operations and the ability to observe your app in production is as important—if not more important—than test coverage, perfect software architecture, or good database design.

---

[1] https://en.wikipedia.org/wiki/Observability
[2] https://charity.wtf/2020/03/03/observability-is-a-many-splendored-thing/

If you have done the best job anyone could ever do at those things yet be unable to explain the app's behavior in production, you are in a very bad place.

Remember, techniques like software design, testing, and observability are tools to reduce risk. A lack of observability carries a great risk, just like shipping untested code to production does.

Fortunately, there are a few low-cost, low-effort techniques that can provide a lot of observability for you that just about any engineer on your team can understand and apply. Before we talk about them, we need to understand what we need to monitor to know if the app is experiencing a problem. What we need to monitor is not usually technical. Instead, we want to monitor business outcomes.

24.2 Monitor Business Outcomes

Before considering how to observe the specific behavior of your app, you need to take a moment to not lose sight of the purpose of your app. Presumably, your app exists to deliver some sort of business value, and if it stops doing that, it's a problem—no matter what the CPU load might be. You need to monitor the expected *business outcomes*.

Suppose our app allows users to sign up for our service. You might think you can keep tabs on this feature by monitoring the number of HTTP 500 errors from the `SessionsController#create` action. This is how new customers sign up, so if it's failing, there is a problem with sign up.

Controller actions completing successfully is not a business outcome. No marketing person, executive, investor, or customer cares about what a controller is or if it's working. They only care if sign up is functional.

The reality is that there are a lot of reasons that people might not be able to sign-up for your app, and an errant controller is only one of them. In fact, there could be non-technical reasons you can't control or observe at all. At Stitch Fix, a marketing email went out once that pointed to our staging environment. Sign-ups were down because of a typo in an email—the sign up code was working perfectly.

This is why you should monitor business outcomes and not technical behavior. Technical behavior could help explain why business outcomes aren't being achieved, but it's those outcomes that are what matter and thus what should be monitored.

Figuring out what these are is a deep topic, and it requires you to understand the core business problems your app solves and to pick apart the various measurements that indicate to a business owner, executive, or other non-engineer if the app is serving its ultimate purpose.

Once you know *what* you need to monitor, the specifics of *how* to do it depend on the tools you have. And once you *do* have monitoring in place, you then will need to know how the parts of the system behave (or behaved) in order to explain why business outcomes aren't being achieved.

What all this means is that your perfectly crafted, beautiful, elegant, programmer-happy codebase is going to become littered with droppings to allow you to properly monitor your app in production. Ruby and Rails allow you to manage this sort of code in a mostly clean[3] way, but there's no avoiding it entirely.

To make matters even more complicated, achieving the level of observability that Charity Majors describes in the blog post linked above requires a significant investment in culture and tooling. You might not be able to go from zero to a fully-observable system overnight, especially if you have a small team just starting to grow.

Fortunately, there are a few cheap and easy techniques that can get you pretty far. The first one is the venerable Rails logger.

24.3 Logging is Powerful

> This section's code is in the folder 24-03/ of the sample code.

Way back at the start of the book, in "Improving Production Logging with lograge" on page 52, we set up lograge to change the format of our logs. The reason is that almost every tool for examining logs assumes one message per line, and that's not how Rails logs by default.

This matters because even the most under-funded production operations system tends to include a way to look at application logs. It might require using `ssh` to connect to the production server, then using `tail`, `grep`, `sed`, and `awk` to filter the log file, but usually there is a way to look at the logs.

Often, when there is a problem in production that no one can explain, the solution is to add more logging, deploy the app, and wait for the problem to happen again so you can get more data. This might be rudimentary, but it's still powerful!

Logging is also an extremely simple way to provide information about what the app is doing and why, and it's a concept that almost any developer of any level of experience can understand and use effectively. If only *everything* in software were like this!

---

[3] I struggled with what word to use here, because to many, "clean code" is some moralistic nonsense proselytized by members of the agile software community. That is not what I mean here. What I mean is that when code contains only what it needs to function, it's clean—free of dirt, marks, or stains. When we add log statements, metrics tracing, or performance spans, we add code that's not needed to make the app work and it gunks up our code. Thus, it's a bit dirtier than before. Nothing moral about it.

That said, not all log messages are equally effective, so you want to make sure that you and your team are writing good log messages. Consider this code:

```
## app/services/widget_creator.rb
  class WidgetCreator
    def create_widget(widget)
      widget.widget_status =
        WidgetStatus.find_by!(name: "Fresh")
      widget.save
      if widget.invalid?
        return Result.new(created: false, widget: widget)
      end
→     Rails.logger.info "Saved #{widget.id}"
```

The code might look obvious, but the log message will look like so:

```
Wed Jun 24 09:02:01 EDT 2020 - Saved 1234
```

If you came across this log statement, you would have no idea what was saved. If you were searching for confirmation that widget 1234 was saved, could you be absolutely certain that this log message confirmed that? What if the code to save manufacturers used a similar log message?

Consider the two primary use-cases of logs.

- Search the logs to figure out what happened during a certain request or operation.
- Figure out what code produced a log message you noticed but weren't searching for.

There are four techniques you should apply to your log messages to make these two use-cases easy:

- Include a request ID in every single message if you can.
- When logging identifiers, disambiguate them so it's obvious what they identify.
- Include some indicator of where the log message originated in the code.
- If there is a current authenticated user, include their identifier in the log message.

24.3.1 Include a Request ID in All Logs

Many hosting providers or web servers generate a unique value for each request and set that value in the HTTP header X-Request-Id. If that happens, Rails can provide you with that value. Each controller in a Rails app exposes the method request, which provides access to the HTTP headers. Even better, you can call the method request_id on request to get the value of the X-Request-Id header or, if there is no value, have Rails generate a unique request ID for you.

If you include this value in all your log statements, you can use the request ID to correlate all activity around a given request. For example, if you see that widget 1234 was saved as part of request ID 1caebeaf, you can search the log for that request ID and see all log statements from all code called as part of saving widget 1234. This is extremely powerful!

The problem is that Rails doesn't automatically include this value when you call Rails.logger.info. The default logging from Rails controllers *does* include this value, but lograge removes it, for whatever reason. Let's add that back and then discuss how to include the request ID in log messages that aren't written from your controllers.

First, we'll modify ApplicationController to include the request ID in a hash that lograge will have access to. We can do that by overriding the method append_info_to_payload, which Rails calls to allow inserting custom information into a special object used for each request.

```
# app/controllers/application_controller.rb

  class ApplicationController < ActionController::Base
→   def append_info_to_payload(payload)
→     super
→     payload[:request_id] = request.request_id
→   end
  end
```

This payload is available to lograge for logging. We can configure this in config/initializers/lograge.rb:

```
# config/initializers/lograge.rb

    else
      config.lograge.enabled = false
    end
→   config.lograge.custom_options = lambda do |event|
```

```
→     {
→        request_id: event.payload[:request_id]
→     }
→   end
  end
```

With this in place, all logs originating from the controller layer will include this request ID. You can fire up the app yourself and try it out. Don't forget to use `LOGRAGE_IN_DEVELOPMENT`, as instructed by `bin/setup help`.

Logging from anywhere else in the app won't have access to this value. This is because the request is not available to, for example, your service layer or Active Records. To make it available, we'll use a feature of Rails called *current attributes*. This is wrapper around *thread local storage*, which is an in-memory hash that can store data global to the current thread (but, unlike a true global variable, isolated from other threads).

To use current attributes, you define a class, usually in `app/models`, that extends `ActiveSupport::CurrentAttributes`. We'll follow the Rails API docs[4] and call it `Current`.

```
# app/models/current.rb

class Current < ActiveSupport::CurrentAttributes
  attribute :request_id
end
```

This will allow us to call `Current.request_id = «some id»` and fetch that value back out via `Current.request_id`. The value provided will be the same within the scope of a Thread, which is in the same scope as a request. Setting `request_id` is the perfect use case for a controller callback in `ApplicationController`:

```
# app/controllers/application_controller.rb

  class ApplicationController < ActionController::Base
→   before_action :set_current_request_id
→
→   def set_current_request_id
→     Current.request_id = request.request_id
→   end
```

[4] https://api.rubyonrails.org/classes/ActiveSupport/CurrentAttributes.html

```
→   def append_info_to_payload(payload)
      super
      payload[:request_id] = request.request_id
```

To put this in our logs is… a bit complicated. There is not a handy gem to do this that I have found, and the Rails logger is not sophisticated enough to allow some configuration to be set that automatically includes it. Instead, let's create a small wrapper around `Rails.logger` that our code will use. This wrapper will assemble a log message by accessing `Current` to get the request ID and prepending it to our actual log message.

It works like so:

```
log "Saved Widget #{widget.id}"
## => 2020-07-05 11:23:11.123 - request_id:1caebeaf Saved Widget 1234
```

First, we'll create a module in `lib` that will wrap calls to `Rails.logger.info` and fetch the request ID:

```
# lib/logging/logs.rb

module Logging
  module Logs
    def log(message)
      request_id = Current.request_id
      Rails.logger.info("request_id:#{request_id} #{message}")
    end
  end
end
```

Because it's in `lib/`, we have to `require` it explicitly, so, for example, in our WidgetCreator:

```
# app/services/widget_creator.rb

→ require "logging/logs"
→
→ class WidgetCreator
```

```
→   include Logging::Logs
    def create_widget(widget)
      widget.widget_status =
        WidgetStatus.find_by!(name: "Fresh")
```

Now we can add a log message:

```
# app/services/widget_creator.rb

      end
  # XXX
  # XXX
→     log "Widget #{widget.id} is valid. Queueing jobs"
      HighPricedWidgetCheckJob.perform_async(
          widget.id, widget.price_cents)
      WidgetFromNewManufacturerCheckJob.perform_async(
```

If you fire up your app now and create a widget, you should see that the Rails controller logs include a request id, but that same ID is prepended to the log message you just added.

That you have to go through these hoops isn't ideal. Rails logging is a pretty big mess and I have not found a good solution. At Stitch Fix we had a custom logging system that handled this, but it was highly dependent on undocumented Rails internals and tended to break with each new version of Rails. It was also extremely difficult for most developers to understand and modify, so it created a carrying cost that I wouldn't incur again.

To make it easy to use this new module in our non-controller code, we could include it in `ApplicationModel`, `ApplicationJob`, and other base classes. We might even create `ApplicationService` for our service-layer classes to extend and include this module there. Once we start using it ubiquitously, we can get the end-to-end request tracing discussed above.

Of course, if you are looking at logs but don't have a request ID, you will often want to know what code produced the log message you are seeing. Further, if a log message references a specific object or database row, you need more than just an ID to know what it means.

24.3.2 Log What Something is and Where it Came From

Logs are often relevant to a specific Active Record. Logging the ID is a great way to know *which* Active Record or row in the database, but you need to know what type of thing that ID refers to. Further, you might want to know *where* the log message originated so you can dial into what code was acting on what piece of data.

It would be nice if you could get this for free by calling `inspect` and having the Rails logger figure out what class called the log method:

```
log "#{widget.inspect} updated"
## => 2020-07-09 11:34:12 [WidgetCreator] <#Widget id=1234> updated
```

Unfortunately, this doesn't work the way we want. First, deriving the class name of the caller isn't a feature of the logger. Second, calling `inspect` on an Active Record will output *all* of its internal values. This can be overwhelming when trying to debug, and can expose potentially sensitive data to the log. Most of the time, you really just need the class name and its ID.

You could have the team try to remember to include all this context, like so:

```
log "#{self.class.name}: Widget #{widget.id} updated"
```

The team will not remember to do this consistently and it will be tedious to try to manage with code review.

Instead, let's enhance our abstraction that wraps the Rails logger. We can make it more useful by printing out the class name it was included into as well as accepting an optional argument of a record as context.

Let's modify `Logging::Logs` so that `log` accepts either one or two parameters. If we pass one, it behaves like it currently does—prepending the request ID to the parameter, which is assumed to be a message. If we pass *two* parameters, we'll assume the first is some object whose class and ID we want to include in the message and the second parameter is the message.

Further, because `Logging::Logs` is a module, we can include the class name of whatever class is including it in the log message as well.

This means that code like this:

```
log widget, "updated"
```

Will produce a message like this:

```
request_id: 1caebeaf [WidgetCreator] (Widget/1234) updated
```

Here's how we can do that. First, we'll allow two parameters to log:

```
# lib/logging/logs.rb

module Logging
  module Logs
→   def log(message_or_object,message=nil)
      request_id = Current.request_id
      Rails.logger.info("request_id:#{request_id} #{message}"...
    end
```

Next, we'll create the log message with both the class name where Logs was included as well as the class and ID of the message_or_object if message is present. Note that we need to be a bit defensive around the type of message_or_object in case it doesn't respond to id. If it doesn't, we'll include its class and its string representation.

```
# lib/logging/logs.rb

    module Logs
      def log(message_or_object,message=nil)
        request_id = Current.request_id
→       message = if message.nil?
→         message_or_object
→       else
→         object = message_or_object
→         if object.respond_to?(:id)
→           "(#{object.class}/#{object.id} #{message}"
→         else
→           "(#{object.class}/#{object} #{message}"
→         end
→       end
→       Rails.logger.info("[#{self.class}] " \
→                         "request_id:#{request_id} " \
→                         "#{message}")
      end
    end
  end
```

435

Now, developers can log a ton of context with not very much code. Granted, they have to provide an object as context and remember to do that, but this will be much easier to both remember and catch in a code review. Because Ruby is such a dynamic language, you can do *much* more here to magically include context without requiring it in the API.

If you like this approach, the log_method gem[5] was extracted from this book as well as several running codebases and provides even more useful logging features from the same basic log method.

Another bit of context that can be extremely helpful—and sometimes required by company policy—is the user who is performing or initiating actions in the app.

24.3.3 Use Current to Include User IDs

Just as we included the request ID in the Current model so that we could log it everywhere, we can do the same with the currently logged-in user's ID. This allows us to know *who* initiated an action. Often, in environments subject to strict compliance (like the aforementioned SOX), being able to see who did what is crucial.

No matter what mechanism you used in "Authentication and Authorization" on page 367 to add authentication, you will likely have a method in ApplicationController called current_user. To include the ID of this user in all log messages, you can do exactly what we did in "Include a Request ID in All Logs" on page 430. The only difference is that current_user may return nil, so the code in ApplicationController will need to account for this, as well as the code in Logging::Logs that pulls it out of Current.

I'll leave the specifics of the implementation to you.

Another powerful source of information about the behavior—or misbehavior—of your app is unhandled exceptions.

24.4 Manage Unhandled Exceptions

When an exception happens that is not rescued explicitly by your code, it bubbles up a large call stack inside Rails for some sort of handling. If the code was initiated by a controller, Rails will render a default HTTP 500 error. If the code was started by a Rake task, nothing special will happen. If run from a background job, it might be retried, or it might not—it depends. In any case, you need to be able to view and examine these unhandled exceptions because they indicate a problem with your app.

Certainly, unhandled exceptions aren't business outcomes, but they *are* a useful bit of telemetry to explain what's happening with your app. Often, unhandled exceptions indicate bugs in the app that need to be fixed to

---

[5]https://github.com/sustainable-rails/log_method

avoid creating confusion later when you have to diagnose a real failure. For example, if you communicate with a third party API, you will certainly get a handful of network timeouts. As mentioned in "Network Calls and Third Parties are Flaky" on page 328, your jobs will retry themselves to recover from these transient network errors. You don't need to be alerted when this happens.

Tracking unhandled exceptions isn't something your Rails app can do on its own. While the log will show exceptions and stacktraces, the log isn't a great mechanism for notifying you when exceptions occur, or allowing you to analyze the exceptions that are happening over time. You need an exception handling service.

There are many such services, such as Airbrake, Bugsnag, or Rollbar. They are all more or less equivalent, though there are subtle differences that might matter to you, so please do your research before choosing one (though the only wrong choice is not to use one). Most of these services require adding a RubyGem to your app, adding some configuration, and placing an API key in the UNIX environment.

They tend to work by registering a Rails Middleware that catches all unhandled exceptions and notifies the service with relevant information. This information can be invaluable, since it can include browser user agents, request parameters, request IDs, or custom metadata you provide. Often, you can view a specific exception in the service you've configured, find the request ID, then look at all the logs related to the request that lead to the exception.

I can't give specific guidance, since it will depend on the service you've chosen, but here are some tips for getting the most out of your exception handling service:

- Learn how the service you've chosen works. Learn how they intend their service to be used and use it that way. While the various services are all mostly the same, they differ in subtle ways, and if you try to fight them, you won't get a lot of value out of the service.
- Try very hard to not let the "inbox" of unhandled exceptions build up. You want each new exception to be something you both notice *and* take action on. This will require an initial period of tuning your configuration and the service's settings to get it right, but ideally you want a situation where any new notification from the service is actionable and important.
- If the service allows it, try to include additional metadata with unhandled exceptions. Often, you can include the current user's ID, the request ID we discussed above, or other information that the exception-handling service can show you to help figure out why the exception happened.
- Intermittent exceptions are particularly annoying because you don't necessarily need to know about each one, but if there are "too many",

you do. Consult your service's documentation for how to best handle this. You need to be *very* careful to not create alert fatigue by creating a situation where you are alerted frequently by exceptions that you can ignore.

In addition to having access to view and manage unhandled exceptions, it's helpful to be able to measure the performance of your app.

24.5 Measure Performance

Donald Knuth, Turing Award winner and author of the never-ending "Art of Computer Programming" book series, is famous for this quote about performance:

> The real problem is that programmers have spent far too much time worrying about efficiency in the wrong places and at the wrong times; premature optimization is the root of all evil (or at least most of it) in programming.

This is often quoted when developers modify code to perform better but have not taken the necessary step of understanding the current performance and demonstrating why the current level of performance is insufficient. This implies that you must measure performance before you can improve it.

Measuring the performance of your app can also help direct any conversation or complaint about the app being slow. This is because the cause of app slowness is not always what you think, and if you aren't measuring *every* aspect of the apps' behavior, you may end up optimizing the wrong parts of the app without making it perform better. See the sidebar "The App is Only as Fast as Wi-Fi" on the next page for an example of how performance measurement can lead to the right area of focus.

You need to be careful not to over-measure at first, because the code you must write to measure certain performance details has a carrying cost. For example, here is how you would measure the performance of an arbitrary block of code using Open Telemetry (which is a standard for application performance monitoring supported by several vendors):

> **The App is Only as Fast as Wi-Fi**
>
> One of the apps we built at Stitch Fix—called SPECTRE—provided tools for associates in our warehouse to do their jobs. This app wasn't part of stitchfix.com and was only used from specific physical locations with Internet connections we controlled.
>
> Over time, we'd get an increasing number of complaints that the app was slow. We had set up New Relic, which allowed us to understand the performance of every controller action in the app. Even the 95th percentile performance was good, with the average performance being great.
>
> Since we controlled the Internet connection to the warehouse, we were able to access performance monitoring of the network in the warehouse itself. While the connection to the warehouse was great—fast, tons of bandwidth, tons of uptime—the computers connecting via wi-fi were experiencing inconsistent performance.
>
> It was *these* users that were experiencing slowness, and it was because of the wi-fi network, *not* the app itself. Of course, to the users, the wi-fi connection was part of the app, and it didn't matter if the controllers were returning results quickly.
>
> We didn't have the capital or expertise to update the network hardware to provide consistent wi-fi performance throughout the warehouse, so we modified the front-end of the feature that required wi-fi to not require as much bandwidth, as described in "Single Feature JAM Stack Apps at Stitch Fix" on page 166.
>
> If we hadn't been measuring the whole system's performance, we could've spent time creating caching or other performance improvements that would've both created a carrying cost for the team and also not solved the actual performance problem.

```
  class WidgetCreator
    def create_widget(widget)
→     OpenTelemetry.tracer_provider.
→       tracer('tracer').
→       in_span("WidgetCreator/create_widget/db_operations") do

        widget.widget_status =
          WidgetStatus.find_by!(name: "Fresh")
        widget.save
        if widget.invalid?
          return Result.new(created: false, widget: widget)
        end

→     end
      HighPricedWidgetCheckJob.perform_async(
```

```
      widget.id, widget.price_cents)
    WidgetFromNewManufacturerCheckJob.perform_async(
      widget.id, widget.manufacturer.created_at)
    Result.new(created: widget.valid?, widget: widget)
  end
end
```

At a larger scale, this sort of code can be mentally exhausting to write, read, and manage.

Instead, choose a technique or tool that can automatically instrument parts of your app. For example OpenTelemetry will automatically track and measure the performance of every controller action, URL, and background job without you having to write any code at all.

This default set of measurements gives you a baseline to help diagnose a slow app. If the defaults don't show you what is performing poorly, *then* you can add code to measure different parts of your codebase.

If you need to add code to enable custom measurements, do so judiciously and don't be afraid to remove that code later if it isn't needed or didn't provide the information you wanted. Look for patterns in how you write this code and try to create conventions around it to allow the team to quickly measure code blocks as needed.

Before we leave this chapter, I want to step back from observability and talk about a more tactical issue which is how to manage secret values like API keys.

24.6 Managing Secrets, Keys, and Passwords

Way back in "Using the Environment for Runtime Configuration" on page 35, I hand-waved over managing sensitive values that must be stored in the app's UNIX environment in production. Let's talk about that now.

The short answer is, of course, that it depends. The other thing to understand is that you cannot absolutely prevent unauthorized access to your secrets. No system can absolutely prevent the exfiltration of sensitive data.

All security concerns, including managing API keys and secrets, are about reducing risk and managing the opportunity and carrying cost of doing so. Sure, you could set up your own SIPRNet[6] to keep your marketing email list safe from hackers, but that expense likely isn't worth it to mitigate the relatively smaller risk of someone stealing email addresses.

Thus, you need to weigh the risks of leaking your secrets and keys against the cost you are willing to pay to secure them. For a small team at a small

---

[6]https://en.wikipedia.org/wiki/SIPRNet

company, the risks are low, so a low-cost solution will work. For a huge public company, the calculus is different. Either way, you should constantly re-evaluate your strategy to make sure it's appropriate and the trade-offs are correct.

Evaluating the trade-offs is critical. It might seem easy to install something like Hashicorp's Vault[7], which is highly secure and packed with useful features. Operating Vault is another story. It's extremely complicated and time-consuming, especially for a team without the experience of operating systems like Vault in production. A poorly-managed Vault installation will be a far worse solution than storing your secrets in 1Password and manually rotating them once a quarter.

Don't be afraid to adopt a simple solution that your team can absolutely manage, even if it's not perfect (no solution will be, anyway). If someone brings up an attack vector that's possible with your proposed solution, quantify the risk before you seriously consider mitigating that vector. Engineers are great at imagining edge cases, but it's the level of risk and likelihood that matters most.

The End!

And that's it! We've covered a lot of ground in this book. Each technique we've discussed should provide value on its own, but hopefully you've come to appreciate how these techniques can reinforce each other and build on each other when used in combination.

I should also point out that, no matter how hard you try, you won't be able to hold onto each technique in this book—or any book—throughout the life of your app. You'll model something wrong, use the wrong name, miss a tiny detail, or have an assumption invalidated by the business at just the wrong time. Or, you'll find that at some scale, the basic techniques here don't work and you have to do something fancier. It happens. That's why we tend to work iteratively.

The most sustainable way to build software is to embrace change, minimize carrying costs, tame opportunity costs, and generally focus on problems you have, treating your tools for what they are. Try not to predict the future, but also don't be blind to it.

---

[7] https://www.vaultproject.io

PART IV

appendices

A

Setting Up Docker for Local Development

All the code written in this book, and all commands executed, are run inside a Docker container. Docker provides a virtual machine of sorts and allows you to replicate, almost exactly, the environment in which I wrote the code (see the sidebar "Why Docker?" on the next page). If you don't know anything about Docker, that's OK. You should learn what you need to know here.

Docker is traditionally used for deploying applications and services to a production environment like AWS, but it can also be used for local development. You'll need to install Docker, after which we'll create a series of configuration files that will set up your local Docker container where all the rest of the coding in this book will take place.

A.1 Installing Docker

While the main point of Docker is to create a consistent place for us to work, it does require installing it on whatever computer you are using, and *that* is highly dependent on what that computer is!

Rather than try to capture the specific instructions now, you should head to the Docker Desktop page[1] which should walk you through how to download, install, and run Docker on your computer.

---

[1] https://www.docker.com/products/docker-desktop

> **Why Docker?**
>
> I'm the co-author of Agile Web Development With Rails 6[a] and have worked on two editions of that book. Each new revision usually wreaks havoc with the part of the book that walks you through setting up your development environment. Between Windows, macOS, and Linux, things are different *and* they change frequently.
>
> While a virtual machine like Virtual Box[b] can address this issue, Docker is a bit easier to set up, and I find it useful to understand how Docker works, because more and more applications are deployed using Docker.
>
> Docker also has an ecosystem of configurations for other services you may need to run in development, such as Postgres or Redis. Using Docker to do this is much simpler than trying to install such software on your personal computer.
>
> ---
> [a] https://pragprog.com/book/rails6/agile-web-development-with-rails-6
> [b] https://www.virtualbox.org

A.2 What *is* Docker?

You can think of Docker as a tool to build and run virtual machines. It's not *exactly* that, but the mental model is close enough. There are some terms with Docker that are confusing, but they are critical to understand, especially if you experience problems and need help.

Image A Docker *image* can be thought of as the computer you might boot. It's akin to a disk image, and is the set of bytes that has everything you need to run a virtual computer. An image can be started or run with `docker start` or `docker run`.

Container A Docker *container* is an image that's being executed. It's a computer that's running. You can have multiple containers running from a single image. To use an object-oriented metaphor, if an image is a class, then a container is an instance of that class. You can run commands in a container with `docker exec`.

Dockerfile A Dockerfile (often named `Dockerfile`, but can be named anything) contains instructions on how to build an image. It is not sophisticated. Most Dockerfiles are a series of shell invocations to install software packages. If an image is an object-oriented class, the Dockerfile is that class' source code. An image is built with `docker build`.

Host You'll often see Docker documentation refer to "the host". This is *your* computer. Wherever you are running Docker, *that* is the host.

To tie all this together (as in the figure "Docker Concepts" below), a
Dockerfile is used to *build* an image, which is then *started* to become
a container *running* on your host.

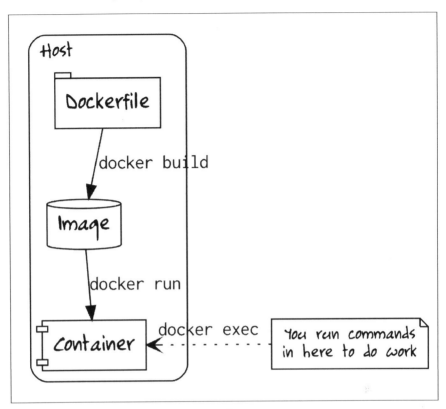

Figure A.1: Docker Concepts

A.3 Overview of the Environment

Rather than reproduce a lengthy Dockerfile, helper shell scripts and all
that, I'm going to point you to a Github repository called sustainable-
rails/sustainable-rails-dev[2], which has what you need.

I recommend you clone that and use it, like so (these commands are executed
on your computer):

```
> git clone https://github.com/sustainable-rails/sustainable-rails-dev
> cd sustainable-rails-dev
```

There is a README there you can use as a reference, but here is how the
system works:

---

[2]https://github.com/sustainable-rails/sustainable-rails-dev

1. You'll build an image that contains the basic software you need to do Ruby on Rails development. You'll use this image in a later step to create a container in which to work.
2. You'll start up three container using *Docker Compose*: the container using the image mentioned above, a container running Postgres, and a container running Redis (which is used for Sidekiq).
3. You can use a script to execute commands inside your dev container. The simplest command is bash, which will give the appearance of having logged into your dev container.

A.4 Creating the Image

Run the script `dx/build` to build the image. This will use `Dockerfile.dx` to produce an image named `davetron5000/sustainable-rails/rails-7.1`.

The first time this runs, it may take a long time, since it must download the base image for Ruby, then execute several shell scripts that may also download other files to save into the image. The output of `dx/build` contains the output of `docker build` and it has a lot of command line animations to it, but when it's done, it should have looked something like the following (keeping in mind I have truncated most of the lines as they are very long):

```
> dx/build
[+] Building 70.8s (19/19) FINISHED
 => [internal] load build definition from Dockerfile.dx        ...
 => => transferring dockerfile: 4.84kB                         ...
 => [internal] load .dockerignore                              ...
 => => transferring context: 58B                               ...
 => [internal] load metadata for docker.io/library/ruby:3.2    ...
 => CACHED [ 1/14] FROM docker.io/library/ruby:3.2             ...
 => [internal] load build context                              ...
 => => transferring context: 121B                              ...
 => [ 2/14] RUN apt-get update -yq &&      apt-get install -y  ...
 => [ 3/14] RUN apt-get update -qy && apt-get install -qy lsb  ...
 => [ 4/14] RUN sh -c 'echo "deb http://apt.postgresql.org/pu  ...
 => [ 5/14] RUN apt-get -y install chromium chromium-driver    ...
 => [ 6/14] RUN echo "gem: --no-document" >> ~/.gemrc &&       ...
 => [ 7/14] RUN apt-get update -q &&      apt-get install -qy  ...
 => [ 8/14] COPY dx/show-help-in-app-container-then-wait.sh /  ...
 => [ 9/14] RUN apt-get install -y openssh-server              ...
 => [10/14] RUN mkdir /var/run/sshd &&      echo 'root:passwor ...
 => [11/14] RUN echo "# Set here from Dockerfile so that ssh'  ...
 => [12/14] RUN mkdir -p /root/.ssh && chmod 755 /root/.ssh    ...
 => [13/14] COPY authorized_keys /root/.ssh/                   ...
 => [14/14] RUN chmod 644 ~/.ssh/authorized_keys               ...
 => exporting to image
 => => exporting layers
```

```
=> => writing image sha256:21c9f171e3eaec00bae0d0f24d8fe73b7 . . .
=> => naming to docker.io/davetron5000/sustainable-rails-dev . . .
[ dx/build ] Your Docker image has been built tagged 'davetro . . .
[ dx/build ] You can now run dx/start to start it up, though  . . .
```

Your output may be slightly different, but the final two messages prefixed with [dx/build] should indicate that everything worked. You can also verify this by running docker image ls like so:

```
> docker image ls davetron5000/sustainable-rails-dev:rails-7.1
REPOSITORY                              TAG        IMAGE ID
davetron5000/sustainable-rails-dev      rails-7.1  21c9f171e3ea
```

A.5 Starting Up the Environment

Once your image is built, you can start up the dev environment via dx/start. This may take a few seconds the first time, depending on how much Internet bandwidth you have. It will download prebuilt images for Postgres and Redis. Like dx/build, dx/start wraps Docker commands that involve a lot of command-line animations.

The output will intermix log messages from the image you built in the last section, Postgres, and Redis. The script will *exit* if anything goes wrong, so if it does not exit, that should indicate everything is working.

You can verify this by running commands inside your container.

A.6 Executing Commands and Doing Development

In another terminal window on your computer from where you ran dx/start, run dx/exec ls -l, and you should see the contents of your dev environment local directory as viewed from inside the container:

```
> dx/exec ls -l
[ dx/exec ] Running 'ls -l' inside container with service name 'sust. . .
total 264
-rw-r--r--  1 root root    4798 Oct 31 21:37 Dockerfile.dx
-rw-r--r--  1 root root    5585 Nov  1 14:31 README.md
-rw-r--r--  1 root root  230956 Nov  1 14:25 SocialImage.jpg
-rw-r--r--  1 root root    1032 Oct 31 21:39 docker-compose.dx.yml
drwxr-xr-x 10 root root     320 Nov  1 17:03 dx
```

dx/exec uses dx/docker-compose.env to know which container to connect to and run the command you gave it (ls -l in this case) inside the container where you can do development. The container can access your local files by virtue of a *bind mount* set up inside docker-compose.dx.yml (there is a comment inside there that can provide more info).

This means that you can edit files locally, using whatever editor you like, and anything you run via dx/exec will see those changes. For example, if you added a new test in test/models/widgets_test.rb, you can run that test like so:

```
> dx/exec bin/rails test test/models/widgets_test.rb
```

This will run a test inside the container against the test file you changed. You could also use bash as the command to run inside the container, which would provide a persistent command-line to run commands without needing dx/exec each time:

```
your-computer> dx/exec bash
inside-the-container> bin/rails test test/models/widgets_test.rb
inside-the-container> bin/rails test test/models/manufacturs_test.rb
```

A.7 Customizing the Dev Environment

If you use the command line frequently, you likely have some *dotfiles* or other command-line configuration. If you are like me, you may feel strangely dis-empowered when you have to use the command line without them!

You can modify Dockerfile.dx to make your configuration available, but it may take some doing. There are two steps: installation additional software, and copying configuration.

Let's take a simple example of aliasing ls to use exa[3], a fancier version of ls. Your machine likely has exa installed, but you also have some sort of alias like so:

```
alias ls=exa
```

Let's assume you have this in your home directory as the file .bashrc.

A.7.1 Installing Software

To install software, you'll use a RUN directive followed by the exact commands to install software on Debian Linux (which is what the base image uses). Most software packages provide a way to do this, and you will need to research the correct way for each tool you have. I strongly recommend you

---

[3]https://the.exa.website

include a link to where you found the installation instructions as a comment before the RUN directive.

In the case of exa, we'll add this to the end of Dockerfile.dx

```
# Based on https://the.exa.website/install/linux
RUN apt-get install -qy exa
```

The -qy tells apt-get to answer "yes" to any question, and to reduce extraneous output.

A.7.2 Copying Your Dotfiles Into the Image

Next, you'll need to add your .bashrc onto the end of /root/.bashrc inside the image. /root/.bashrc is where the user that executes commands (in this case, "root") will have their bash configuration. You can copy files into a Docker image via the COPY directive, however the files you copy into the image *must* be local to where you are running dx/build. And, the files cannot be symbolic links—they must be real files.

If you keep your dotfiles in GitHub, the simplest solution may be to clone that repo inside your dev environment. As a demonstration, I'll just create the files directly:

```
> mkdir dotfiles
> echo "alias ls=ex" > dotfiles/.bashrc
```

However the files get there, they should be inside your dev environment. You can then use COPY to get them into the image. Since you want to append dotfiles/.bashrc to whatever's there, we'll copy the files somewhere, then append them using a RUN directive. The WORKDIR directive creates and changes to a directory inside the container, so we'll use that to come up with this addition to the Dockerfile.dx:

```
# Set up a directory where our dotfiles
# can be copied
WORKDIR /root/dotfiles
# Now, copy our dotfiles to that directory
COPY dotfiles/.bashrc .
# Lastly, append our .bashrc to the canonical one
RUN cat .bashrc >> /root/.bashrc
```

Because of the use of WORKDIR, the subsequent COPY and RUN directives execute from /root/dotfiles.

Once you do this, run dx/build, hit Ctrl-C wherever you run dx/start, re-run dx/start, and finally run dx/exec bash, then use ls to see that it's respecting your alias:

```
> dx/exec bash
root@a4a92c1ce1ca:~/work# ls -lFh
Permissions Size User Date Modified Name
.rw-r--r--  4.9k root 1 Nov 17:44  Dockerfile.dx
drwxr-xr-x     - root 1 Nov 17:43  dotfiles/
drwxr-xr-x     - root 1 Nov 17:03  dx/
.rw-r--r--  5.6k root 1 Nov 14:31  README.md
.rw-r--r--  230k root 1 Nov 14:25  SocialImage.jpg
```

If you have any issues using these scripts, please reach out or open an issue on the repo.

B
Monoliths, Microservices, and Shared Databases

There wasn't an easy way to put this into the book, but since we discussed APIs in "API Endpoints" on page 377, there is an implicit assumption you might have more than one Rails app someday, so I want to spend this appendix talking about that briefly.

When a team is small, and you have only one app, whether you know it or not, you have a monolithic architecture. A monolithic architecture has a lot of advantages. Starting a new app this way has a very low opportunity cost, and the carrying cost of a monolithic architecture is quite low for quite a while.

The problems start when the team grows to an inflection point. It's hard to know what this point is, as it depends highly on the team members, the scope of work, the change in the business and team, and what everyone is working on. Most teams notice this inflection point months—sometimes years—after they cross it. Even if you know the day you hit it, you still have some decisions to make. Namely, do you carry on with a monolithic architecture? If not, what are the alternatives and how do you implement them?

In this section, I want to try to break down the opportunity and carrying costs of:

- staying with a monolithic architecture.
- deploying a microservices architecture.
- using a shared database amongst multiple user-facing apps.

The third option—sharing the database—is usually discussed as an anti-pattern, but as we'll see, it's anything but. It's important to understand that your system architecture—even if it's just one app—is never done. You never achieve a state of completeness where you can then stop thinking about architecture. Rather, the architecture changes and evolves as time goes by. It must respond to the realities you are facing, and not drive toward some idealistic end state.

So, I would strongly encourage you to understand monolithic architectures, microservices, and shared databases as techniques to apply if the situation calls for it. It's also worth understanding that any discussion of what a system's architecture is has to be discussed in a context. It's entirely possible to have 100 developers working on 30 apps and, some of which are monolithic... within a given context.

Let's start with monolithic architectures.

B.1 Monoliths Get a Bad Rap

If you have a single app, you have a monolithic architecture. In other words, a monolithic architecture is one where all functions reside in one app that's built, tested, and deployed together.

When a team is small and when an app is new, a monolith has an extremely low opportunity cost for new features as well as low carrying cost. The reason is that you can add entire features in one place, and everything you need access to for most features—the UI, the database, emails, caches—are all directly available.

The larger the team and the more features are needed, the harder a monolith can be to sustain. The carrying cost of a monolith starts rising due to a few factors.

First, it becomes harder to keep the code properly organized. New domain concepts get uncovered or refined and this can conflict with how the app is designed. For example, suppose we need to track shipping information and status per widget. Is that a set of new widget statuses, or is it a new concept? And, if we add this concept, how will it confuse the existing widget status concept?

This domain refinement will happen no matter what. The way it becomes a problem with a monolith is that the monolith has everything—all concepts must be present in the same codebase and be universally consistent. This can be extremely hard to achieve as time goes by. The only way to achieve it is through review, feedback, and revision. Whether that's an up front design process or an after-the-fact refactoring, this has an opportunity cost.

A carrying cost is the time to perform quality checks like running the test suite. The more stuff your app does, the more tests you have and the longer the test suite takes to run. If you run the test before deploys, this means you are limiting the number and speed of deploys. A single-line copy change could take many minutes (or hours!) to deploy.

Solving *this* requires either accepting the slowdown, or creating new tools and techniques to deploy changes without running the full test suite. This is an obvious opportunity cost, but it also creates a carrying cost that—hopefully—is less than the carrying cost of running the entire test suite.

Related, a monolith can present particular challenges staying up to date and applying security updates, because the monolith is going to have a lot of third-party dependencies. You will need to ensure that any updates all work together and don't create inter-related problems. This can be hard to predict.

An oft-cited solution to these problems is to create a microservices architecture. This trades some problems for new ones.

B.2 Microservices Are Not a Panacea.

Previously known as a *service-oriented architecture* (SOA), a microservices architecture is one in which functionality and data is encapsulated behind an API (usually based on HTTP), built, maintained, and deployed as a totally separate app.

The reason to do this is to solve the issues of the monolith. The internal naming, concepts, and architecture of a service don't have to worry about conflicting with other services, because they are completely separate. A microservice creates a context in which all of its internals can be understood. Taking the status example above, you might create a widget shipping service that stores a status for each widget. That status is in the context of shipping, so there's no conceptual conflict with some other service maintaining some other type of status.

Microservices also naturally solve the issue of deployment. Because each service is completely separate, to deploy a change in, say, the code around widget shipping, only requires running the tests for the widget shipping service. These tests will certainly be faster than running all the tests in an analogous monolith.

Microservices are particularly effective when the team gets large and there are clearly-defined boundaries around which sub-teams can form. This isolation allows teams to work independently and avoid conflicts when inter-team coordination is not required.

This sounds great, right? Well, microservices have a pretty large opportunity cost and a not-insignificant carrying cost. In my experience, the carrying cost is relatively stable despite the size of the team (unlike a monolith, where the cost increases forever). The opportunity cost—the amount of effort to establish a microservices architecture on any level—is large.

The reason is that you change the problem of your operations team from maintaining one app to maintaining N apps. As I'm sure you are aware, there are only really three numbers in programming: zero, one, and greater-than-one. Microservices are, by definition, greater-than-one.

First, you must have clearly-defined boundaries between services. If services are too dependent, or not properly isolated, you end up with a "distributed monolith", where you do not reap the benefits of separation. For example, what if we made a widget data service that stored all data about a widget. When our widget shipping team added its new status, that would have to be added to the widget data service. These two services are now too tightly coupled to be managed independently.

Second, you must have more sophisticated tooling to make all the services run and operate. As we discussed in "Use the Simplest Authentication System You Can" on page 381, your microservices need authentication. That means something, somewhere, has to manage the API keys for each app to talk to each other. That means that something somewhere has to know how one app locates the other to make API calls.

This implies the need for more sophisticated monitoring. Suppose a customer order page is not working. Suppose the reason is because of a failure in the widget shipping service. Let's suppose further that the website uses an order service to render its view and that order service uses the widget shipping service to get some data it needs to produce an order for the website. This transitive chain of dependencies can be hard to understand when diagnosing errors.

If you *don't* have the ability to truly observe your microservices architecture, your team will experience incident fatigue. This will become an exponentially increasing carrying cost as time is wasted, morale lowers, and staff turnover ensues.

You should almost never start with microservices on day one. But you should be aware of the carrying costs of your monolith and consider a transition if you believe they are getting too high. You need to think about an inflection point at which your monolith is costlier to maintain than an equivalent microservices architecture, as shown in the figure "Graph Showing the Costs of a Monolith Versus Microservices Over Time" on the next page.

The transition to microservices can be hard. As the necessary tooling and processes are developed, it can be disruptive to the team, as shown in "Graph Showing the Costs of a Microservices Transition", also on the next page.

One way to address the problems of the monolith without incurring the costs—at least initially—of microservices is to use a shared database.

B.3 Sharing a Database Is Viable

When the carrying cost of a monolith starts to become burdensome, there are often obvious domain boundaries that exist across the team. It is not uncommon for these boundaries to be related to user features. For example, you may have a team focused on the website and customer experience, but you might also have a team focused on back-office administrative duties, such as customer support.

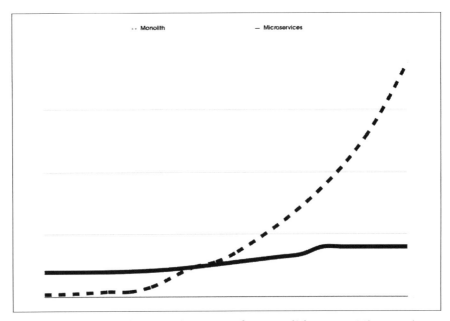

Figure B.1: Graph Showing the Costs of a Monolith Versus Microservices Over Time

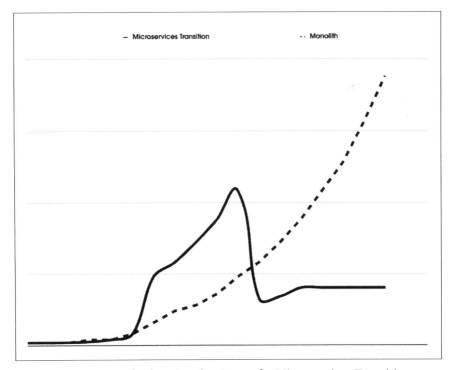

Figure B.2: Graph Showing the Costs of a Microservices Transition

Instead of putting both of these features in one app, and *also* instead of extracting shared services to allow them to be developed independently, a third strategy is to create a second system for customer support and have it share the database with the website, as shown in the figure "Sharing a Database" below.

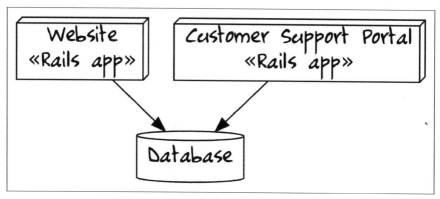

Figure B.3: Sharing a Database

As long as your domain boundaries can work simply be communicating via changes to the database, this can keep opportunity cost low, since everyone will know how to work on a database-backed Rails app. It keeps carrying costs low, too, since you don't have to invest in shared tooling or manage a large complex codebase.

As you discover more isolated needs, either from user groups needing their own user interface or isolated system requirements, you can add more apps and point them to the shared database as in the figure "Sharing a Database with More Apps" on the next page.

The most immediate carrying cost with this approach is maintaining the database migrations and the requisite Active Record models. Because of how we are writing our code—not putting business logic in the Active Records—these can be put into a gem that each app uses and that gem should not change often.

Database migrations, however, are not easy to manage when placed in a gem. You also don't want every app to be able to change the database that all apps share. You *should* centrally manage changes to the database since all apps depend on it. You can do this with a Rails app whose sole job is to manage the database schema. You can then establish a convention on the team that each proposed change to this app—which implies it is a database change—must be reviewed by all teams to ensure nothing will break.

See the figure "Managing the Shared Database" on the next page for how this might look.

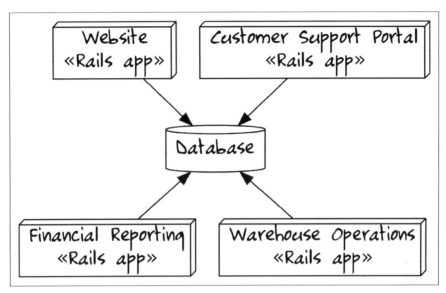

Figure B.4: Sharing a Database with More Apps

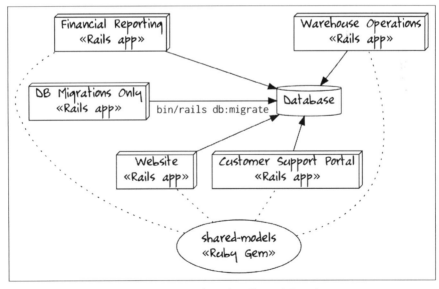

Figure B.5: Managing the Shared Database

Sharing the database doesn't abdicate your responsibility for managing code across boundaries, but it does reduce what must be managed to the database schema only. And since you are putting constraints and other data integrity controls directly into the database (as outlined in "The Database" on page 213), you won't have much risk of one app polluting the data needed by other apps.

If you are careful with changes, the overall carrying costs of this architecture can be quite low and can surpass a monolithic architecture, as shown in the figure "Graph Showing the Costs of Sharing the Database" below.

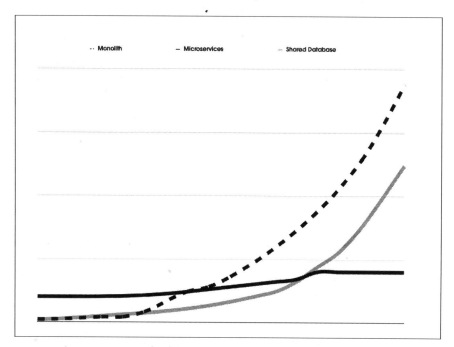

Figure B.6: Graph Showing the Costs Sharing the Database

Of course, this architecture will eventually cause problems. When you have a lot of apps sharing a database, you can certainly cause contention and locking that can be hard to predict or observe. That's what happened in the anecdote in the sidebar "A Single Line of Code Almost Took Us Down" on the next page.

The database schema will eventually become difficult to manage, as you end up with either tables that have too many concepts embedded in them or a bunch of tables that exist only for the private use of a single app. It's also possible that you may need one app to trigger logic that lives in another app and have no easy way to do so. You will likely need to do a microservices transition.

If you use a shared database, however, you can significantly delay your microservices transition—*if you ever need one*—*and* you can reduce the cost of doing so because you will have already done a lot of work on identifying domain boundaries.

Navigating the evolution of your architecture is difficult. The fact is, your architecture is never done. There is no end state you should aim for and no point at which you stop evolving. Evolution may slow at times, but it won't stop, and if your approach to architecture is to design it and build it, you will fail. Instead, you need principles to guide you and competent technical leadership.

> ### A Single Line of Code Almost Took Us Down
>
> Much of the business logic at Stitch Fix involved updating records in our shared database, and usually several records at once. We made heavy use of database transactions to ensure those operations didn't leave our data in a partially-updated state. One example was updating a shipment record. Any time one was changed, we wrote a database row to a separate events table that tracked all the changes made to that record.
>
> As we grew and scaled, we eventually started using RabbitMQ for messaging. The library that was responsible for updating the shipment was eventually augmented to additionally send a message on RabbitMQ about the change to the shipment. This allowed downstream apps without access to our shared database to know when shipment records changed.
>
> The line of code to send the message was written inside a transaction. It was fine for years. Until one day it wasn't.
>
> We started noticing *massive* slowdowns across all apps and increases in locks inside the database. They would routinely happen in the early morning, then go away on their own. We could not say with any certainty what was happening—locks in the database are rarely the problem, but rather an indicator of some other issue.
>
> We started combing our code for transactions that contained potentially slow-running code. We found the above-mentioned library. We moved the line of code used for sending messages to outside the transaction, distributed the updated library to all apps, and voilà, the problem stopped.
>
> This was pure luck. If we didn't find a solution, it would've been a stop-the-world emergency that could've derailed our team for weeks or even months. Be careful what code you put inside a database transaction.

C
Technical Leadership is Critical

At times in this book I've referenced code reviews, or vague "managing" of changes. Getting a team to work consistently, follow conventions, and also respond to change is difficult. It requires leadership.

Leadership is a deep topic. A leader isn't just in charge, and often great leadership comes from people who don't have any real authority over others.

The most effective leadership I have experienced is where leaders organize everyone around shared values.

C.1 Leadership Is About Shared Values

Top-down leadership, where the person in charge tells everyone below them what to do, is not sustainable. Most programmers don't enjoy being micromanaged, and the leader in this situation will not make universally good decisions. It's simply too hard to manage software from the top, and too unpleasant to be managed this way.

A more effective strategy is to focus everyone on shared values. We discussed some values in the first chapter of this book, such as sustainability and consistency. Your company certainly has values, your team has more values, and if there are sub teams within that team, they have their own values too.

A good leader will first make explicit what the team's values are (not what they should be). Values should be a form of documentation: what sorts of things does everyone believe to be important? When the team agrees on its values, the function of leadership is then to apply those values to situations where a decision needs to be made.

For example, suppose the team is using Sidekiq for background jobs. Suppose an engineer has read about the background job system Que and thinks it would be useful to use. This engineer wants to install it in the app and start using it, but not everyone on the team agrees. How does this get resolved?

A top-down leadership style would be to tell the team what the decision is. A values-based leadership style would be to engage the team with its values and help them apply those values to this decision. Does the team value consistency? If so, this decision does not conform to that value. What if the team also values innovation? Using something new and exciting might conform to that value.

By re-framing the discussion about the team's shared values and how the decision relates to them, the team can arrive at a decision that more or less everyone agrees with... without being told what to do. The great thing about this is that *anyone* on the team can show leadership by using this framing. Anyone can say "we all value consistency, right? So doesn't using Que make our app *less* consistent?".

There is still a reality about leadership and building software to consider, which is that some people on the team are more accountable for the team's output than others.

C.2 Leaders Can be Held Accountable

I've continually stressed that you treat Rails as it is, not how you'd like it to be. I would encourage the same general attitude with your job. You are exchanging your time and labor for money. Your company is paying you money to get a specific result. Just as you have the right to be paid, the company has a right to those results.

Even in the most egalitarian, values-focused, collaborative environment, someone on the team is more accountable for the team's output than the rest of the team members. It's best to be explicit about this so that everyone understands that while the decisions they make affect the team, they have a stronger effect on the people who are held accountable.

The problem arises when the team makes a decision they feel is consistent with their values, but fails to achieve the desired result. It happens. People make mistakes and there is no formula for building software that avoids all mistakes. Mistakes can, however, lead to consequences, and the person who is actually accountable will bear those consequences the most.

As a simple example, suppose the team agrees to use Que in addition to Sidekiq. Suppose that Que is found to have a serious security vulnerability that leads to the exposure of customer data. The team simply missed this in their analysis. The team's manager, however, is the one who could be fired for this mistake.

When you are accountable, you need to be careful. Accountability can lead to a top-down approach that you might think mitigates risk, however a values-based consensus-driven style can lead to mistakes you are held accountable for that you didn't take the opportunity to avoid.

I would highly recommend if you *are* accountable to make that clear to the team. Make it clear that their decisions and output will reflect on you and that because of that, you may need to exercise decision-making authority from time to time. You could use phrases like "veto power" or "51% of the vote" to communicate this concept, but the team must understand that if they make a decision that is, in your judgement, not the right one, you may decide to overrule them.

Of course, you should do this as infrequently as you can, as it removes agency from the team. This makes you a less effective leader in the long run.

To make matters more complicated, accountability isn't always explicit.

C.3 Accountability Can be Implicit

It is often the case that a less experienced member of the team will get stuck on something and turn to a more experienced member for help. Perhaps someone new to the team needs help understanding the domain, or a developer fresh out of a boot camp can't get their development environment working.

On any team there are members who are looked to for answers, help, and guidance, even if they aren't formally blessed as accountable leaders. These team members are nevertheless implicitly accountable. For example, suppose you set up the development environment on macOS that everyone is using. You might be the "go-to" person for the dev environment. If a new engineer decides they want to use Linux, you are now implicitly accountable for their dev environment by virtue of having set up the system everyone else is using.

As the expert on the dev environment, that engineer will come to you for help if they get stuck, even though you were not involved in the decision for them to use Linux. Their actions have created a carrying cost for you. It puts you in a position to either not provide help ("You chose Linux, you live with it") or to put your more urgent tasks on hold to provide help. It's not necessarily fair for this engineer to put you in this position.

I would encourage you to think deeply about each member of the team and what sorts of things would fall to them to do if no one else were available. Each team member contributes in their own unique way, and thus is implicitly accountable for those contributions. Perhaps one team member goes the extra mile with documentation. If you propose a new way of documenting, you are creating additional work regarding something for which they are implicitly accountable.

Be aware of this when navigating the decisions to be made. Defer to others where appropriate, identify values where possible, and be explicit about accountability as much as you can.

Colophon

There's a lot of technology involved in producing this book. But let's start where everyone that makes it to the colophon wants to start: *fonts*.

The cover is set in Helvetica Neue. Titles in the book are set in ITC Avant Garde Gothic with the body text set in Charter. Diagrams use Rufscript and Inconsolata. Inconsolata is also used to set all the code. The epub versions largely ignore these fonts and I'm sorry. Beautifully typeset e-books on e-ink screens are technically possible, but no one cares enough to make it happen.

The book was authored in a modified version of Markdown that executes code samples, runs CLI commands, and takes screenshots as the files are processed. It's managed with a custom toolchain I created that you can read about on my blog[1].

Most diagrams are created using Graphviz or Mermaid, though some were created in Omnigraffle and Numbers. Screenshots were generated by a custom JavaScript command line app that uses Puppeteer.

The cover was created in Pixelmator, based on a photo I took of the House of Eyrabakki[2] in Iceland, which is part of the Byggðasafn Árnesinga, a museum in Eyrabakki. The photo was taken with an Olympus OM-1n 35mm camera, using Ilford Delta 3200 film, developed by me, in my basement, at 2400 ISO using Ilford chemicals. The back cover of the print versions is another shot of the same house from the same roll of film. Both were lightly edited in Adobe Lightroom.

All of this is tied together by Pandoc, which also produces the ePub version. The print and PDF versions are produced via LaTeX. Good ole LaTeX. If you want proper hyphenation and justification, there's not really any other option. I'm sure this book has a lot of overfull hboxes.

I would also be remiss in not pointing out that the entire toolchain is held together by make, which I don't think I could live without when trying to do anything moderately complex. And, of course, all this runs in Docker, because you can't do anything these days without Docker.

---

[1] https://naildrivin5.com/blog/2023/02/03/toolchain-for-building-programming-books.html

[2] The House of Eyrabakki is one of the oldest structures in Iceland, made of wood at a time when houses were made of turf. It was transported to Iceland as a kit, and assembled there. Thus, it's a great analogy for sustainable web development with Ruby on Rails.

Index

.env.development.local, 39
.env.development, 38
.env.test.local, 39
.env.test, 38
.env, 39
.env files, ignoring, 39
ActiveSupport
    CurrentAttributes, 431
ApplicationJob
    for Sidekiq, 337
ENV, 36
Procfile.dev, 334
SECRET_KEY_BASE, 35
after_create, 260
as_json, 393
aside tag, 95
authorize_resource, 372
bin/ci, 50
    parallel execution in CI, 410
bin/dev, 46
bin/rails routes, 74, 77
bin/setup, 40
    customizing for CI, 408
    maintaining, 408
br tag, 97
bundle gem, 419
current_user, 106
    example implementation, 373
div tag, 95
html_safe, 129
load_and_authorize_resource, 374
log, 43
normalizes, 259
perform_async, 337
rails new, 33
rescue_from, 316
set -e, 46

span tag, 95
system
    , 43
to_json, 392
with_clues, 186
12-factor app, 35

accessibility, 94, 141
accountability, 464
Action Cable, 363
Action Mailbox, 363
Action Mailer, 349
    deliveries method, 301
actions
    custom, 84
    patch, 84
Active Job, 329, 335
    trade-offs with sending email, 350
Active Model, 210
    to_key, 210
    alternative to helpers, 134
    unique identifier for, 210
    validations, 258
Active Record, 203
    callbacks, 259
    database logic vs. business logic, 208
    instance methods, 208
    relationships, 205
    scopes, 206, 261
    types of code needed, 204
    validations, 224, 255
        bypassing, 257
        with Active Model, 258
Active Records
    as compared to services, 244
Active Storage, 364
APIs, 377

469

authentication, 381
base controller, 379
code, 378
content types, 387
JSON serialization, 392
routing namespace, 379
testing, 398
versioning, 389
app README, 54
app templates, 420
architecture
consistency, 212
microservices, 455
monolithic, 454
unnecessary decisions, 77, 85
ARIA Roles, 141
assistive devices, 94
authenticated user, 106
authentication
APIs, 381
in-app, 369
multiple mechanisms in one app, 370
token-based, 382
using a third party, 368
authorization, 370
auditing, 371
checking, 372
custom actions, 374
defining, 372
testing, 374
using job title and department, 371
with cancancan, 372
with OmniAuth, 373

background jobs, *see* jobs
bang methods, 297
behavior-revealing code, 242
BEM, 143
Bootstrap, 142
Brakeman, 49
Bulma, 142
Bundler
auto-require, 423
bundler-audit, 49
business logic, 57, 241

does not go in callbacks, 260
example, 295
trade-offs with validations, 258
business outcomes, 427

callbacks
controller, 314
cancanca, 372
carrying cost, 15
churn, 58
clear fix, 98
command pattern, 251
comments
`.gitignore`, 39
`Gemfile`, 38
`bin/` scripts, 42
configuration, 218
database, 230
in migrations, 383
pinned dependencies, 414
regarding missing code, 206
when using `html_safe`, 130
comments,`config/routes.rb`, 81
component, 142
configuration, runtime, 35
consistency, 14
constraints
testing, 237
continues integration
configuration, 406
using `bin/setup`, 408
continuous integration, 50, 405
parallel testing, 411
controllers
APIs, 379
instance variables, 100
multiple instance variables, 104
testing, 318
type conversions, 317
CSS, 139
atomic, 144
custom properties, 147
framework, 142
functional, 144

compared to inline styles, 145
 downsides, 146
 relationship to JavaScript, 173
 object-oriented, 142
 pseudo elements, 145
 semantic, 141
 sheer volume, 139
 specificity, 145
 strategies, 141
 variables, 147
Current Attributes, 431
custom URLs, 79

data
 importance of, 213
database
 constraint usage guidelines, 222
 constraints, 222
 foreign key constraints, 223
 local maintenance, 40
 logical model, 214
  example, 215
 lookup tables, 223
 physical model, 213, 217
 sharing between apps, 456
 types, 220
  booleans, 221
  dates, 221
  enums, 221
  rational numbers, 221
  strings, 221
  timestamps, 219, 221
 uniqueness modeling, 216
database integrity, 217, 255
database migrations
 SQL schema, 218
database normalization, 220
decision aid, 177
dependencies
 automating updates, 414
 carrying cost, 169
 minimizing, 118
 updating, 412
 versioning, 413

dependencies,considerations when choosing, 177
dependency injection, 252
deploying, 405
design system, 140, 279
 in emails, 352
 style guide, 147
developer workflow, 33
development environment
 connect to database, 228
 port, 48
 running app, 46
 running multiple processes from bin/dev, 333
 sending emails, 356
 setup, 40
 tests, 50
Devise, 369
distributed tracing, 430
Docker, 446
domain modeling, 120
dotenv, 36
DRY
 not repeating yourself repetition of, 137
DSL
 internal, 313

ERB, 117, 161
error reporting, 159
example feature, 65, 271
exceptions
 unhandled, 436
extending Rails, 219

factories, 262
 linting, 264
 validations, 309
Factory Bot, 263
Faker, 263
fan-in, 60
fan-out, 60
fixtures, 262
flash message, 95
floats, 96
 clear fix, 98
 clearing, 97

foreign key constraints, 223, 232
Foreman, 333

gemspec, 422
generators, 417
globalid, 336

HAML, 118
helpers, 119
    banning, 119
    generating HTML with, 128
    modular per-controller files, 127
    preventing per-controller files, 126
    rendering inline components with, 124
HTML
    data attributes, 141, 170
    escaping, 129
    escaping with `content_tag`, 129
    semantic, 93, 124, 274
HTTP services, *see* APIs

i2n, *see* i1n
i32n, *see* i2n
idempotency, 342
import maps, 174
indexes
    conditional, 383
    unique, 230, 257
internal DSL, 313
internationalization, 276
internationalization configuration, *see* i32n

JAM Stack, 161, 163
    downsides, 163
JavaScript, 157
    carrying costs, 157
    ecosystem, 160
    framework considerations, 176
    locating markup with, 170
    observability
        lack thereof, 158

    plain, 169
    problems with using multiple frameworks, 178
    runtime environment, 158
    source maps, 159
job backends, 329
jobs, 325
    code, 337
    defer execution, 326
    failure handling, 330
    generator, 338
    idempotent, 342
    mailers, 350
    observability, 331
    parameter serialization, 330, 336
    queuing mechanism, 329
    retrying flaky code, 328
    Sidekiq, 331
    testing strategies, 339
    wrap network calls, 327
JSON serialization, 392
    customizing, 394
    in Rails, 393
    top-level key, 397

Law of Demeter, 101
leadership, 463
logging, 52
    current user ID, 436
    helpful details, 433
    request IDs, 430
    techniques, 429
    use-cases, 429
lograge, 52, 160
    adding request ID, 430
lookup tables, 223

Mailcatcher, 356
mailers, 349
    previewing, 351
    sending in dev, 356
major user flow, 182
    example, 284
metaprogramming
    hacky (as if there is another kind), 121, 269

microservices, 455
Migrations
    applying, 227
    iterative construction, 230
    rolling back, 227
    transactional, 225
monitoring
    business outcomes, 427
    performance, 438
monoliths, 454

namespacing, 89
network calls
    flakiness of, 328
    slowness, 326
new app, 34

observability, 425
OmniAuth, 368
OOCSS, 142
    downsides, 144
OpenStruct, 75, 150
opportunity cost, 15
OWASP Top Ten, 128

partials
    locals as parameters, 108
    strict locals, 109
        default values, 110
perforamnce, 438
port 9999, 48
presenters, 104
    problems, 133
Procfile, 334

rack test, 182
Rails architecture, 19
Railties, 420
    example, 423
    for sharing configuration, 420
rake tasks
    code, 359, 361
    organizing, 358
    purpose, 357
    testing, 360
reality, 253, 256

Redis
    development and test databases, 333
    isolated uses, 333
reference data, 106
regular expressions
    as content assertions, 185
    case-insensitive, 185
resource focused design, 85
rich result objects, 247
routes, 73
    Active Model, 211
    avoiding redirects, 82
    based on `resources`, 74
    custom, 81
    defining with `get`, 76
    development only, 150
    eight automatic, 74
    namespaces, 89
    namespaces for APIs, 379
    nested, 87
    redirecting, 80
    restricting with `except:`, 78
    restricting with `only:`, 77

SASS
    import, 148
    default values, 149
    variables, 149
secrets
    managing, 440
    storing in development, 39
security vulnerabilities, 128
seed data, 273
Selenium, 196
Semver, 389
Server-rendered views, 161
    downsides, 162
service classes, 243
    anti-patterns, 249
    dependent objects, 245
    return values, 247
    testing, 298
service layer, 69, 241, 243
    example, 291
service objects, *see* command pattern

service-oriented architecture, 455
Sidekiq, 331
singleton pattern, 250
Slim, 118
SMACCS, 143
SOLID Principles, 243
spoons
    existence of, 159
SQL
    existential importance of, 220
SQL schema, 218
    setup, 218
stringly-typed, 319
style guide
    for emails, 355
    living, 147
sustainability, 9

Tachyons, 145
Tailwind, 145
TDD
    challenges for system tests, 190
technical leadership, 463
template repositories, 419
testing
    accessing browser console, 201
    APIs, 398
    asserting on markup, 185
    authorization, 374
    callbacks, 262
    confidence checks, 320
    database constraints, 237, 262, 384
    diagnosing failures, 186, 201
    duplicate coverage, 323
    fake test data, 263
    headless Chrome, 196
    helpers, 130
    integration strings, 319
    JavaScript, 178
    jobs, 338, 339
    managing support code, 186
    mocks versus database assertions, 318
    models, 262
    purpose of, 181
    rack test for system tests, 182
    rake tasks, 360
    routing, 323
    Selenium WebDriver, 196
    service class, 298
    system test carrying cost, 186
    system test strategy, 182
    system tests using a browser, 196
    trade-offs with content and data attributes, 195, 286
    using data attributes, 194
    validations, 262
    waiting for DOM elements, 200
text vs varchar, 204
Thor, 417
time zones
    eternal frustration attributed to, 219
    including with timestamps, 219
trust
    third party authentication, 368
Turbo, 166
    progress bar, 166

UNIX Environment
    accessing with `ENV.fetch`, 333
UNIX environment, 35

vanity URLs, 79
versioning policy, 413
View Component, 111
    example, 113
View Components
    alternative to helpers, 136
    example, 280
view concerns, 104, 120

Web services, *see* APIs

web workers, 326
Webpack, 174
Webpacker, 174

Printed in Poland
by Amazon Fulfillment
Poland Sp. z o.o., Wrocław